WITHDRAWN

Distributed Computing and the Mainframe

Distributed Computing and the Mainframe

Leveraging Your Investments

Kurt Ziegler, Jr.

A Wiley-Interscience Publication

John Wiley & Sons, Inc.

New York / Chichester / Brisbane / Toronto / Singapore

Copyright © 1991 by John Wiley & Sons, Inc.

Library of Congress Cataloging in Publication Data:
Ziegler, Kurt, 1947–
    Distributed computing and the mainframe : leveraging your
investments / Kurt Ziegler, Jr.

        p.   cm.
    "A Wiley-Interscience publication."
    Includes bibliographical references.
    ISBN 0-471-51753-4

    1. Electronic data processing—Distributed data processing.
    2. Electronic digital computers.   I. Title.
QA76.9.D5Z54   1991
004'.36—dc20   90-44494
                                                          CIP

Printed in the United States of America

10 9 8 7 6 5 4 3 2 1

Contents

22 DISTRIBUTED OFFICE CAPABILITIES   217

SECTION 4   WHAT EVERY SYSTEMS MANAGER SHOULD
KNOW ABOUT OPERATIONS   237

23 DISTRIBUTED ENVIRONMENT MANAGEMENT   239

24 MANAGING DISTRIBUTED S/390s   251

25 MANAGING MIXED OPERATIONS   261

26 DISTRIBUTED SYSTEMS MANAGEMENT SUMMARY   267

SECTION 5   WHAT EVERY SYSTEMS IMPLEMENTER
SHOULD KNOW ABOUT CONNETIVITY   271

27 S/390 CONNECTIVITY   273

Preface

The information system explosion of the late 1980s and early 1990s is integrating diverse system architectures, solutions, skills, disciplines, and terminology. The information systems organizations' challenge is to make this integration smooth.

WHAT'S NEW?

The 1980s were marked by rapid and fundamental changes in the way many enterprises implement and manage their information processing. These information processing changes were driven by users in response to their immediate business requirements not being addressed by traditional approaches, the need to improve personal productivity, and in response to the pressure on businesses to gain competitive advantage while reducing overhead.

Many of these needs can now be quickly addressed by the user or user departments with stand-alone solutions on personal computers or minicomputer[1] systems. The new responsiveness to needs has been made possible by the lower entry price for systems and tools, improved user interfaces to some fundamental tools (e.g., LOTUS 1-2-3 approach to spread sheets). The result is a significant increase in computer literacy and a plethora of very specific business-oriented solutions designed and frequently developed by industry practitioners who have transferred some of their experience to computer programs.

---

[1]*Minicomputer* is a term used to describe a small, general-purpose system often defined as a rack-mounted system. Other packaging alternatives are also employed.

The benefits and consequences of the increased experimentation and programming by users, while dramatic, have been mixed.

WHAT CHANGED?

The purchase of departmental systems or personal computers and some popular software packages is extremely simple and, relatively speaking, not very intimidating. The system's ability to be used immediately often makes the sale. This could be contrasted to the traditionally longer evaluation and installation periods and the training required for mainframe applications.

THE BENEFITS

On the positive side, many long-standing application requirements, especially those intended to improve end user productivity on existing application systems, have evaporated. These requirements have been addressed using various approaches exploiting personal computer or *mini*computer software and hardware. Many of these solutions are implemented by end users themselves, often providing significant cost reductions and improvements in response to changes in business. Some new implementations are in the order of days and weeks versus months and years.

THE RISKS

On the other hand, while some significant user interface and useability enhancements have been developed, there really haven't been major breakthroughs in systems design, development, and documentation tools. This means that many rapid implementations are being accomplished by the use of some *implicit short cuts* to circumvent the usual application system[2] design, development, and implementation time.[3] Understanding the subtleties of how numbers are calculated, the need for various levels of backup, the consequences of using data across packages that have different assumptions, and the meaning of support and currency are often part of the *discovery cycle,* which frequently doesn't surface until the solution is well entrenched. The resultant rework, retraining, or shift in time spent on nonbusiness issues is sometimes more than was anticipated and can occur at unacceptable levels.

The more obvious problems result from the impact of loss of data and loss of

---

[2]*Application system* is a term intended to encompass not only a specific business application, but also the associated applications that interface with the application, as well as the appropriate utilities, procedures, audit trails, and documentation.

[3]*Implementation time* includes the time from development and installation completion to the time that the user is effectively using the application. For some applications, the implementation time may be greater than the design, development, and install time.

access to a service or from the user's inability to use a new package because of co-existence problems. The less obvious considerations include the less visible aspects of information management, such as: corporate asset management—e.g., theft of data or multiple unsynchronized copies of critical data, or the impact of an outage—and application systems design aspects such as growth flexibility, which when not considered can cause the user to know more and spend more time as the number of options and combinations of products increases.

WHO IS MANAGING THE RISKS?

In short, it is not the hardware technology or the software per se that create exposures to risk; it is the absence of what is sometimes referred to as the *systems view*. The systems view usually takes into consideration what trade-offs can be made and the consequences and contingencies of such decisions. This aspect is usually what contributes to much of the development cycle. It is the expectation of many industry professionals that knowledge-based systems will assist in providing significant improvement in the overall application system design-through-implementation cycle, by providing the prerequisite considerations in the decision process as the application is implemented. Such implementations for general systems are still in the embryonic state.

In the meantime, the skill of the information systems organization or the Chief Information Officer (CIO)[4,5] in influencing the quality of the current solutions, while supporting innovation and responsiveness, will determine the price tag and ongoing effectiveness of the quick solutions as they are integrated into enterprise solutions.

To be effective in influencing the implementations requires that the CIO or information systems organization know the inherent limits of various implementations of solutions. Decision makers must also know which solutions they will be able to integrate should the need arise. Most CIOs and information systems organizations already know which applications will ultimately have to be integrated and those that are relatively stand-alone. Many are learning about the need to understand some very low-level technical details as problems arise in some of the *quick* solutions.

---

[4]The term *Chief Information Officer* (CIO) was first introduced in 1981 by William R. Synnott and William H. Gruber in their book *Information Resource Management: Opportunities and Strategies for the 1980s,* published by John Wiley & Sons, New York, 1981. As commonly used, the title refers to a corporation's chief information strategist. The CIO may be the head of corporate information services (a line executive position) or hold a corporate staff position. In either case, the CIO's responsibilities extend across the corporation's informational needs, far beyond the traditional Management Information Systems (MIS) domain.

[5]John G. Burch, "CIO: Indian or Chief?" *Information Strategy: The Executive's Journal,* Winter 1989, pp. 5–13.

HOW CAN THIS BOOK HELP?

This book offers some pragmatic insights for those at the management level: why and how systems can be interconnected, distributed, integrated, and managed using tried-and-proved management and technical approaches. The discussion focuses on how enterprises are building on lessons managers learned as they developed information systems on their S/370[6] mainframe[7] computers, and how they are using this knowledge—in harmony with the movement to incorporate solutions driven by end-users—in order to address today's needs while positioning for the future.

This book focuses on what does work rather than on what doesn't. The approach is rather straightforward. The assumptions are that open systems and proprietary systems are inevitable, mixed architecture systems are a reality, and that there continues to be a shortage of skilled professionals who are able to anticipate all future problems. Given these assumptions, the thrust of this book is on leveraging what we have learned in mixed hardware and software environments with the intent to apply this knowledge as a basis for new implementations.

The underlying themes are:

- enterprise level information systems leadership can accomplished using mainframe investments
- user and control systems have important roles and require interconnectivity
- interoperability is basic to distributed solutions
- remote systems/network management is fundamental to quality of service

---

[6]On September 5, 1990, IBM announced the ES/9000 line of processors and Enterprise Systems Architecture/390 (ESA/390). This line of processors provides increased commercial and numerically intensive computational power, provides more central and expanded storage for increased transaction processing and data handling, and introduced new transport capabilities via a new connection architecture, Enterprise Connection Architecture (ESCON). At the same time the ES/9000 line preserved the customers' existing S/370 investments by providing a S/370 environment either in native mode or via the Processor Resource/System Manager (PR/SM), which is a standard feature.

The ES/9000 like its S/370 predecessors comes in different sizes and shapes (sometimes referred to as a "foot prints") to meet price and environmental requirements. Unlike its predecessor implementations, this line provides ESA and common channel support across the entire line ranging from air-cooled rack-mounted and frame-mounted models through the large liquid-cooled frames. Collectively these systems are called System/390s (S/390s). Since the S/390 continues to support the S/370 peripherals and software I will use the label S/390 for generic system references throughout this book. The primary exceptions will be when I am referring to the S/370 in the historical sense or further clarification is required with regard to function or support.

[7]*Mainframe* is often used to refer to the large systems. It derives from the system configuration that houses the CPU and sometimes the mainstorage in the mainframe, and which has outboard channels, direct access (e.g., disk drives), and sequential storage devices (e.g., tape drives).

WHO IS THE AUDIENCE?

The book is intended to help information systems executives, their staffs, systems integrators, systems engineers, and marketing representatives by providing a single document that discusses many of the systems aspects and associated products of various distributed solutions. Experience has shown that while specific products or vendors may change, the concepts and approaches discussed in this book are fundamental and evolve very slowly.

An underlying assumption of this book is that not every reader has the same experience base or systems background. An effort has been made to include most of the relevant background items, provide as broad an overview of the issues and solutions as possible, and separate the book into sections and chapters with increasingly more specialized emphasis. Skip the ones that are too detailed or that cover familiar ground.

This book assumes that the reader has been exposed to IBM S/390 systems and the management of information systems organization. The emphasis is on the management aspects of selecting and implementing viable solutions and their technical aspects based on what enterprises are doing today. No attempt is made to assist in business justifications as to why one would distribute or should distribute. There are two assumptions: (1) you have a S/390 or a S/370; and (2) you are interested in or are already implementing distributed solutions. The orientation is from an information systems (IS) organization[8] frame of reference. I am extending the notion of S/390 to entail the *glasshouse*[9] and its extensions.

This book is intended to provide the information systems executive with a framework to assess concepts and technical implementations which address the integration of applications and access using multiple technologies and control styles. The central theme is the interconnection and management of distributed systems. The subject is presented in the context of an enterprise leveraging its S/390 mainframe and networking investments to support both IBM- and non-IBM-based application solutions.

A conscious attempt has been made to use industry jargon (with definitions or explanations) when appropriate. While the jargon is frequently less than precise or sometimes even has very different meanings depending on its context, it is extremely important to be aware of its usage in order to understand the industry trends and directions and to analyze the impact of new developments published in trade publications or presented at technical symposiums.

---

[8]*IS* is an acronym for information systems organization. It refers to an organization that provides information processing services to end users. It is also referred to as the information services organization, the MIS (Management Information Systems) organization, DP organization, or even "glasshouse" organization.

[9]The term *glasshouse* originally referred to the compute room or data center, and was used as a generalized label for central control and mainframe processing. Its origin stems from the glass walls that encased the computer rooms. Most companies were very proud of their computers. In the mid 1970s, most of the glass walls were replaced with brick to minimize security exposures. The label has evolved to refer to the central IS organization and the central computer complex.

In general, the insights and opinions expressed are those of the author and may or may not reflect those of IBM or any vendor whose product is mentioned. The subjects discussed are based on the best information that the author was able to obtain at the time of the writing. The insights are based on input from vendors and information-systems executives as well as industry seminars, industry journals, and books. More recent announcements may alter some of the specific information included, but the concepts discussed should continue to be relevant. Description of products is intentionally presented to convey only the concepts that readers can map to their particular situations. It is not intended as a substitute for vendor-provided information or books on the specific topic. Wherever possible, sources where the reader can obtain further detail are provided.

Kurt Ziegler, Jr.

Acknowledgments

I would like to express my appreciation to my wife, Dianne, for her long hours of data entry, editing, and patience, to IBM and the numerous folks who took the time to provide me with information and feedback, and to the many other vendors, including Intel, Interlink, Joiner Associates Inc., Phaser Systems, Mitek Systems, Forest Computer Inc., and Novell, Inc., for their input and assistance.

TRADEMARK ACKNOWLEDGMENTS

Every effort has been made to supply trademarks about company names, products, and services mentioned in this book. Listed below are the trademarks that I was able to compile.

ADR eMAIL is a registered trademark of Applied Data Research Inc.

ALL-In-One is a trademark of Digital Equipment Corp.

Apollo is a registered trademark of Apollo Computers, Inc.

ASCII is a designation of the American National Standard Code of Information Interchange.

AT&T is a registered trademark of American Telephone & Telegraph Co.

Banyan is a registered trademark of Banyan Systems Inc.

Banyan Mail is a trademark of Banyan Systems Inc.

Burroughs and Sperry are trademarks of Unisys Corp.

CADAM is a registered trademark of CADAM Inc.

CATIA is a registered trademark of Dassault Systems.

CAEDS is a registered trademark of Structural Dynamics Research Corp.

cc:Mail is a trademark of cc:Mail Inc.

DEC is a registered trademark of Digital Equipment Corp.

DECmail is a trademark of Digital Equipment Corp.

DECnet is a trademark of Digital Equipment Corp.

DIF (Data Interchange Format) is a trademark of Lotus Development Corp.

Ethernet is a registered trademark of Xerox Corp.

FASTPATH is a registered trademark of Intel Corp.

FlexLINK, Fullview, Mailbridge, and TapeArchive are trademarks of FlexLINK International

FNP is a trademark of Forest Computer Inc.

Higgins is a registered trademark of Enable Software.

HP is a registered trademark of Hewlett-Packard Corp.

HP Desk is a trademark of Hewlett-Packard Corp.

IDNX (Integrated Digital Network Exchange) is a trademark of Network Equipment Technologies Inc.

IEEE is a designation of the Institute of Electronic and Electrical Engineers.

INed is a registered trademark of Interactive Systems Corp.

INmail and INnet are trademarks of Interactive Systems Corp.

Intel is a registered trademark of Intel Corp.

Interlink is a registered trademark of Interlink Computer Sciences Inc.

Jnet is a registered trademark of Joiner Associates Inc.

Joiner is a trademark of Joiner Associates Inc.

KeyKOS is a trademark of Key Logic.

MCI Mail is a trademark of MCI Communications Corp.

MicroVAX is a trademark of Digital Equipment Corp.

MicroVMS is a trademark of Digital Equipment Corp.

Mitek is a trademark of Mitek Systems Corp.

MS-DOS is a registered trademark of Microsoft Corp.

MULTIBUS is a trademark of Intel Corp.

MUMPS is a trademark of Massachusetts General Hospital.

MUMPS/VM is a trademark of Micronetics Corp.

NetWare is a registered trademark of Novell Inc.

NFS is a trademark of Sun Microsystems Inc.

Novell is a trademark of Novell Inc.

OIS is a trademark of Wang Laboratories Inc.

OpenConnect is a registered trademark of Mitek Systems Corp.

OpenConnect SERVER is a trademark of Mitek Systems Corp.

proNet is a trademark of Proteon Corp.

PSAM, PSAM/NET, PSAM/LAN are trademarks of Phaser Systems.

ROLM is a registered trademark of ROLM Corp.

RPC is a trademark of Sun Microsystems Inc.

SNA Network Server is a trademark of Mitek Systems Corp.

SNS/Link is a trademark of Interlink Computer Sciences Inc.

SNS/LU6.2 is a trademark of Interlink Computer Sciences Inc.

SNS/NETconnect is a trademark of Interlink Computer Sciences Inc.

SNS/SNA Gateway is a trademark of Interlink Computer Sciences Inc.

SNS/SNApath is a trademark of Interlink Computer Sciences Inc.

Soft-Switch is a registered trademark of Soft-Switch Inc.

Sun is a trademark of Sun Microsystems Inc.

The Network Courier is a trademark of Consumers Software Inc.

Telemail is a registered trademark of Telenet Communications Corp.

3COM is a trademark of 3Com Corp.

3+Mail is a trademark of 3Com Corp.

TOPS 10/20 is a trademark of Digital Equipment Corp.

ULTRIX is a trademark of Digital Equipment Corp.

UNIX is a registered trademark of American Telephone and Telegraph Co.

UTS is a trademark of Amdahl Corp.

VAX is a trademark of Digital Equipment Corp.

VAXBI bus is a trademark of Digital Equipment Corp.

VAX/VMS Mail is a trademark of Digital Equipment Corp.

Viewpoint is a trademark of Zentec Inc.

VMS is a trademark of Digital Equipment Corp.

VMSmail is a trademark of Digital Equipment Corp.

VS is a trademark of Wang Laboratories Inc.

Wang is a registered trademark of Wang Laboratories Inc.

Wang MAILWAY is a trademark of Wang Laboratories Inc.

Wang Office is a trademark of Wang Laboratories Inc.

Xerox is a trademark of Xerox Corp.

X-window System is a trademark of Massachusetts Institute of Technology.

TRADEMARKS OF INTERNATIONAL BUSINESS MACHINES CORP.

AIX is a registered trademark

ACF/VTAM

AS/400

DB2 is a trademark for IBM Database 2

DisplayWrite/370

DFSMS

Enterprise Systems Architecture/370 and ESA/370

Enterprise System Architecture/390 and ESA/390

Enterprise System Connection Architecture and ESCON

Enterprise System/9000 and ES/9000

ES/3090

ES/4381

ES/9370

Hiperspace

IBM is a registered trademark

Micro Channel is a registered trademark

MVS/ESA

MVS/SP

MVS/XA

NetView is a registered trademark

OPC/ESA is a registered trademark

Operations Planning and Control/ESA

Operating System/2 and OS/2 is a registered trademark

Operating System/400 and OS/400 are registered trademarks

Personal Computer XT and PC XT

Personal Decision Series and PDS

Personal Systems/2 and PS/2 are registered trademarks

Processor Resource/Systems Manager and PR/SM

PROFS is a registered trademark

RISC System/6000

ROLM is a registered trademark

RT is a registered trademark

SQL/DS is a trademark for IBM Structured Query Language/Data System

Systems Application Architecture and SAA

System/370 and S/370

System/390 and S/390

Virtual Machine/Extended Architecture and VM/XA

VM/ESA

VSE/ESA

VTAM

Distributed Computing and the Mainframe

Chapter *1*

Introduction

If you are an information systems executive or senior systems designer, there are very few days that go by without your being challenged to integrate a new service into your system or are perplexed by the introduction of an alternative approach that you had not considered. You are torn between strategic implications such as on-going costs and your ability to respond to change, and the need to prioritize resources in view of today's business needs to remain competitive and to satisfy your end users' diverse requirements. If you have a mainframe, you probably have to defend your current solutions, the expense, and the merit of continuing the investments associated with centralized controls and mainframe implementations as the apparent costs of distributed solutions continue to become more appealing for a specific department.

This chapter introduces the concepts and ideas associated with implementing distributing computing solutions in an information systems services context. These concepts and ideas are expanded on throughout the book. The information provided should validate or expand your understanding of the considerations and assist your supporting the enterprise's need for timely informational and computational support.

1.1 THE MAINFRAME'S ROLE IN DISTRIBUTED SOLUTIONS

The data processing environment of the late 1980s has forced many senior executives to ask some very tough questions regarding information processing implementations. The use of mainframe computer solutions to address an enterprise's informational needs is continually being challenged. In the 1990s, the implementation considerations will be more diverse and even more critical than in the 1980s because of the momentum and number of organizations implementing unique solutions.

It was predicted that the late 1970s and early 1980s would mark the end of mainframe-based solutions. The introduction of the minicomputer provided a lower entry price for some computing solutions and coincidently allowed the reduction of implementation and ongoing support costs by implementing single-application systems. These two very important considerations had many systems professionals trying to reconcile whether the mini was an economically viable replacement for the more expensive and centrally controlled mainframe.

The "end of the mainframe" prophets focused on technology price-performance. The implementers focused on the ease of implementing affordable application systems on dedicated hardware made possible by the lower hardware price. In many cases these incentives obscured some of the other pertinent management issues such as responsiveness to change, scalability of the solution, the resilience of the solution through reorganizations, and the various budget considerations over time. Other considerations often not included in the initial sizings included security, data backup and recovery, and disaster backup. These costs were often ignored or deferred until the requirement was justified. This approach was in contrast to the central information systems infrastructure procedures which included all of these considerations in the initial sizings and thus presented a larger total bill from the onset.

During the late 1970s, the mini gained acceptance as a less expensive alternative or supplement to mainframe services for less complex[1] and less environmentally taxing[2] systems solutions for business problems. Minis were installed and used by many small companies and small autonomous business units within the enterprise as generalized and specialized systems. The use of minis was especially popular in the engineering, scientific, and manufacturing arenas where specialization and customization of hardware interfaces were key. Specialized systems and minis were installed to extend the mainframe services and capabilities to point of need.

The mini, however, has not really replaced the mainframe as a complete enterprise business solution; it has facilitated the growth of applications of information processing to solve business problems in places that the mainframe by itself did not address, either because of environment, functionality, or price. In fact, in many instances the minis became extensions of the mainframe and are considered part of the **mainframe solution** or **distributed solution.** Three very fundamental considerations drove this evolution:

- the existing application base and data were very closely tied into the mainframe architecture and software

---

[1]*Complex* in this context refers to the large number of uses for the system. For example, a complex systems environment would support a mixture of online transaction processing, which is very response-time sensitive, interactive computing that is very computational intensive, and application development.
[2]*Environmentally taxing* in this context refers to the need for very reliable and fast storage access devices with large capacities which have historically required specialized environments such as dust-free and cooled rooms.

- enterprise critical applications support infrastructure was built around the tools and skills associated with the mainframe
- the mini-solutions systems-management tools rarely extended beyond the basic systems software

In other words, the **mainframe solution** had extended its scope from a pure hardware and software consideration to include the broader systems and network management and administration issues.

During the 1980s, the introduction of newer hardware and software technologies, together with some newer approaches to presenting information to users, had begun to alter the way certain tasks are accomplished for distributed solutions. A very general but pervasive application that demonstrates the changes and complementary nature of distributed computing solutions is word processing. Word processing (text entry and editing) has gone through multiple stages of evolution and names: from private typists, typist pools, text entry workstations, and professionals doing their own typing, to text and graphics reuse. Text reuse can now be accomplished by almost any personal computer user. One can now compose (cut and paste) a formatted document that integrates words, graphics, image, charts, and even voice, and can transmit it to recipients as electronic mail between systems or via facsimile devices without the voice. These strides have been made at some cost, especially storage. Managing the storage of these new *letters*[3] very quickly goes beyond the capacity of the local personal computer, and then almost as rapidly exceeds the parameters of local personal-computer- or mini-based servers, especially if the letters are retained for a long period of time (e.g., one year) and one would like to retrieve the letters quickly.

As a result of the ease with which these solutions can be implemented, trade-press headlines are indicating that midrange systems (powerful superminis), personal computers (micros), and LANs[4] will replace the mainframe for applications, leaving the mainframes as *servers*.[5] But as Yogi Berra's saying goes, "It's not over until it's over." We can now use what was learned from the mini-mainframe experience to extrapolate where this is going. Have the technical considerations regarding the control of applications and data, support, and system-wide support changed? Yes, some of the considerations have, but most of the fundamental control aspects have not. The primary change is that some of the users have decided to manage some applications and associated hardware and software themselves. They have also opted to provide solutions that they can control within their budget. Given these changes and the need to continue to control many of the existing applications using the information systems infrastructure, the viable solution will provide for peaceful

---

[3]*Letters* in this context refers to multimedia letters (electronic mail) and these tend to easily require storage in excess of 50,000 characters per page.

[4]LAN (Local Area Network) in this usage refers to the combination of personal computers, connectivity of these personal computers by such connection technologies as Ethernet and Token Ring, and software control systems that manage the communication and provide sharing services.

[5]*Server* in this context is used to refer to such services as file and data base management for the application systems or application workstations.

coexistence as a prerequisite. The resilience of these new solutions is a function of the mainframe solution (including the infrastructure) to accommodate the newer technologies and the newer technologies to proactively[6] coexist with the mainframe solutions.

1.2   A TYPICAL ENTERPRISE DISTRIBUTED SOLUTION

As a result of the evolution of mainframe, mini, and personal computer implementations, many enterprises (in the enterprise information system context) have system and network configurations that are very similar to the one depicted in Figure 1.1. While this configuration may appear complex, it is probably a gross oversimplification of an average enterprise's configuration.

Some key observations regarding this and similar configurations are:

- They tend to be **application driven**
- Connectivity tends to be **application integration** driven
- Geographically **dispersed organizations** are driving such solutions
- Various mixed systems and vendor **connectivity solutions** are emerging
- **IBM** and **non-IBM** systems **interoperability** are emerging
- **Systems and network management** is typically **assumed**

Systems and network management expectations and capabilities play a very significant role for applications that have enterprise scope or for users who prefer to have someone else do the appropriate planning, problem resolution, software update, data backup, data recovery, connectivity management, and security administration.

From a systems management perspective, it is important to understand how the distributed systems can fit into existing solutions, and that the necessary automated, remote, and unattended operations capabilities should be covered in any solution you invest in.

Figure 1.2 depicts a very high-level view of the types of services and capabilities that are required to effectively implement remote and automated systems and network management. The figure depicts a central S/390 mainframe and a rack-mounted S/390 (e.g., ES/9000). The ES/9000 is a representative example since it demonstrates many of noted services and capabilities. (The noted capabilities will be described in much more depth in subsequent chapters.)

The figure conceptualizes automated operations and remote operations. The objective of these capabilities is to increase the productivity of a centrally located systems operator or administrator while providing quality service to the remote node (system) user. Unattended operations are those capabilities at the distributed node

---

[6]*Proactively* in this context refers to that provision of interfaces that the mainframe solution can access to provide the necessary controls.

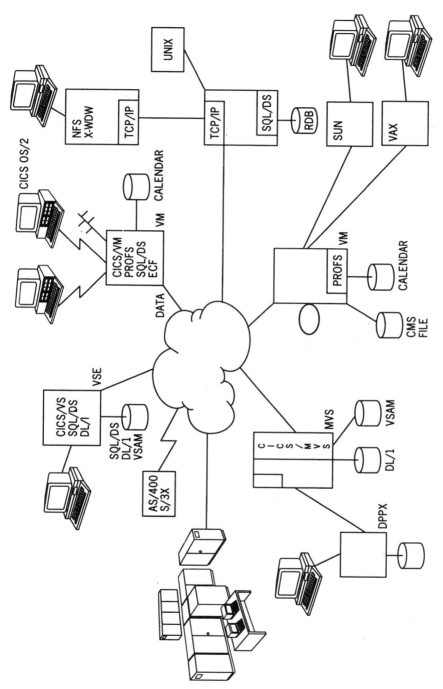

Figure 1.1 A typical distributed solution.

5

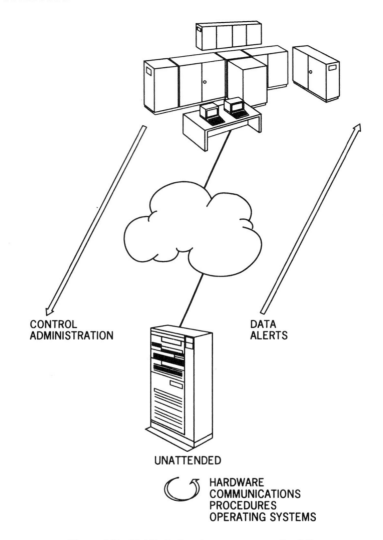

Figure 1.2 *Distributed system management solutions.*

that allow it to operate independently of a host and cause actions or alerts to be shipped to the host only when support is required. An important objective of unattended operations is to minimize the reliance on the host. Remote operations are the capabilities to access data and control the remote node from a central location when the automated responses are not sufficient to resolve the problem or refresh the data at the unattended system.

S/390 mainframe distributed solutions have substantial investments in managing multiple remote systems, control units, and terminals. It therefore becomes an excellent frame of reference for discussing implementations. At the risk of my being suspected of bias, it is also appropriate to note that there are relatively few alternative solutions that provide the appropriate breadth and depth across as broad a range of systems as currently implemented on the S/390. I believe that this is a very objective statement, since the S/390 software is designed with systems management and network management as basic corequisite requirements. As such, the necessary interfaces and functions tend to be included in the various operating systems. The same emphasis is not typical for most of the mini and personal computer solutions, since their focus is usually on function and communication and not on managing multiple systems from a central location. While solutions for the non-S/390 systems are evolving, they will have several years of growth before they achieve a comparable level of sophistication and comprehensiveness.

1.3 HOW TO USE THIS BOOK

This book provides an overview of what has been learned, what is being done, the considerations, and the tools available to implement an effective distributed solution that leverages current S/390 investments. The material is directed at multiple audiences based on their interests and responsibilities, and is sectioned accordingly:

- Distributed Solutions and Mainframe *Evolution*
- What Every *CIO* Should Know about Distributing
- What Every Systems *Architect* Should Know about Distributed
- What Every *Systems Manager* Should Know about Operations
- What Every Implementer Should Know about *Connectivity*

The expectation is that individuals will scan the sections and chapters that meet their immediate interest. The glossary of terms and index can be used to acquire a better understanding of a term's usage and context.

The *Distributed Solutions and Mainframe Evolution* section provides an historical background to various approaches, systems solutions, and their exposures that have given rise to the current focus on distributed systems and applications. It is provided because each reader will have a different background. I would recommend scanning this section, which includes four chapters:

- Chapter 2: Evolution of S/390 mainframes and associated distributed solutions
- Chapter 3: Evolution of minis, personal computers, LANs and *LANs,* touching on computing models being used, e.g., client-server
- Chapter 4: Reasons enterprises are implementing distributed solutions from a technology management, organizational, and interoperability impetus within the S/390 context
- Chapter 5: Snapshot of S/390-based distributed solutions platforms and some conjecture as to what is to follow

The primary message of this section is that the technical hurdles that are being encountered in the newer mixed-environment systems are very fundamental and similar to those already encountered and addressed in earlier implementations; plus, the fundamental considerations are the same. This knowledge can be applied to minimize rediscovery of old problems. The material is covered at a high level and not intended to be a technical tutorial.

The *CIO* section is specifically directed toward understanding the trends and concepts associated with interconnecting systems, leveraging existing IS experiences, investments, and overall project-planning considerations. This section is oriented to the IS executive or staff person responsible for understanding, selecting and managing distributed systems.

The 13 chapters include:

- Chapter 6: Introduction of the theme that distributed solutions are not new, the stages are predictable, and the information executive can influence the outcome
- Chapter 7: Differences between distributed and decentralized
- Chapter 8: User systems role in the information systems infrastructure
- Chapter 9: Focus on some design-point considerations
- Chapter 10: Hardware and software controls required for distributed solutions
- Chapter 11: Pragmatic guidelines about using what is known and available
- Chapter 12: Identification of sponsor(s) and the impact of each
- Chapter 13: Approaches to managing and maintaining a vision
- Chapter 14: Mapping of applications to platforms
- Chapter 15: Support for mixed connectivity and its subtleties
- Chapter 16: Typical enterprise: interoperability and standards
- Chapter 17: Approaches to dealing with multiples
- Chapter 18: Summary of the CIO section

The Systems Architect, Operations Manager, and Implementer sections (Chapters 19–30) are targeted toward the managers and professionals who have a desire to understand approaches being used to interconnect and manage various system implementations. These sections are heavy with *alphabet soup* (acronyms), because, whether we like it or not, vendors and many of the professionals using the components or products tend to discuss these areas with acronyms.

The *Architecture* section (Chapters 19–22) is oriented to the IS technical management and staff who are interested in how their S/390 software interconnects with various IBM and non-IBM operating systems. The focus is on interoperability for transaction processors, data base systems, specialized servers, and non-IBM systems. E-mail connectivity and options are discussed in a mixed architecture and mixed vendor context.

High-level flows are provided to take some of the mystery out of the implementations. The primary messages are: distributed transaction processing is available today; the S/390 is much more open to mixed environments than most people are aware; and there are some very specific interfaces that provide the maximum flexibility. The four chapters include:

- Chapter 19: Various distributed application interfaces
- Chapter 20: Distributed data file and data base implementations
- Chapter 21: Complementary solutions with IBM and non-IBM systems
- Chapter 22: Approaches to supporting electronic mail in mixed environments

The *Operations* section (Chapters 23–26) is directed toward the operational management who are concerned about operating and remotely supporting multiple systems and network components of mixed hardware/software architectures. It describes the considerations and tools available to manage distributed systems. Discussions include the use of the NetView family of products and SNA-addressable and nonaddressable components and LANs. VM, VSE, and DPPX distributed systems management is also discussed.

The primary messages in this section are: the need for software and hardware functions in order to provide unattended and remote management; the wide variety of systems that can be managed by central systems using NetView; and the thrust to minimize the operating system differences (in a S/390 context) in the area of distributed systems management so that the enterprise can focus on the application rather than having to make trade-offs because of the systems management capabilities.

The four chapters include:

- Chapter 23: Facilities available to manage a network and remote systems
- Chapter 24: Distributed systems capabilities of DPPX, VM, and VSE
- Chapter 25: Managing mixed distributed systems
- Chapter 26: Distributed systems management summary

The *Connectivity* section (Chapters 27–30) is directed to the systems implementer who is interested in connecting various software platforms together. The emphasis is on identifying that protocol support of various systems is not sufficient; application-to-application software is required to achieve functions more than terminal emulation. The primary message is that software and hardware placement of the gateway and the supporting software is very relevant to your solution.

The three chapters include:

- Chapter 27: Distributed S/390 physical, SNA, and SNA network connectivity
- Chapter 28: Non-IBM to IBM system connectivity and interoperability options
- Chapter 29: Gateways and application-to-application implementations

A Summary, Appendices including a brief review of the various software platforms and environments (AIX, DPPX, MUMPS, MUSIC, MVS, PICK, VM, VSE), and a Glossary complete the book.

Distributed Solutions and Mainframe Evolution

This section provides a quick look at the evolution of providing data processing services to locations remote from the central processor. The common thread is the central systems services and capabilities and how they fit with distributed solutions and the introduction of new or different technologies.

The section demonstrates that the distributed solution implementations are converging technically as technology and our understanding of the issues improve. This is done by providing a historical background of the technical issues and developments associated with interconnecting or extending systems and a look at where they are leading. A quick scan may be appropriate as a level set prior to reading the CIO section—Section 2—which is based on the observations and insights covered in this section.

Chapter 2

S/390 Distributed Solutions: Background

This chapter provides a brief, high-level overview of IBM S/390 systems in the context of providing service to remote locations. It covers the period beginning with the announcement of the S/360 in 1964 to the mid 1980s. The evolution is discussed in order to provide insights into the drivers, challenges, solutions, and limitations of the various implementations.

2.1 APRIL 7, 1964: A SYSTEM TO GROW ON

The thumbnail history of IBM S/390 based solutions begins with the announcement of the IBM S/360. Hailed as a major step forward from the diverse, special-purpose, incompatible processors of the 1950s and early 1960s, the S/360 was nicely described[1] as follows:

> The International Business Machines Corporation announced a new family of electronic computers named S/360. Within the family were six different models, each implemented by different hardware, but all embodying the same logical design.
>
> System/360's intention is to satisfy the broadest spectrum of users—very small to very large; scientific, commercial, systems, and real-time; single user to large multiprocessor. . . .

The intention was fulfilled; the S/360 Series was a success due to its *architecture* (instruction set, operating systems, and I/O devices) and the systems software

[1]The Staff of Computer Usage Co. *Programming the IBM System/360,* John Wiley & Sons, Inc., 1966.

developed by IBM to enable multiprogramming, telecommunications, transaction processing, and data based applications.

The high price and specialized skills required to operate and program these systems caused the customers to optimize the expense by maximizing the sharing of the resources via centralizing the staff and equipment in the glasshouse.

IBM S/390 HIGHLIGHTS

1964 to 1968

- S/360 announced
- 13 S/360 models

1970

- S/370 succeeded the S/360
- Virtual storage introduced
- 21 S/370 models (include multi processors—symmetric and asymmetric)

1977

- S/370 becomes the generic name
- 7 IBM 303X models (IBM 3031–3033)

1979

- A small data center S/370—the IBM 43XX

1980

- 11 IBM 308X models (IBM 3081–3084)
- 31-bit addressing

1985 through 1989

- IBM 3090
- A departmental (in-rack) S/370—IBM 9370 (8 models)
- Vector processing on the IBM 3090
- Execution and data access across address spaces via Enterprise Systems Architecture (ESA) on IBM 3090 and on IBM 4381-9X models
- Expanded storage for accessing large in-storage data sets using ESA

1990

- IBM Micro Channel Architecture—ES/9371
- S/390—18 ES/9000 models (air cooled and liquid cooled)
- ES/9000 have ESA, expanded storage, and PR/SM
- Enterprise Systems Connection (ESCON) fiber based system for interconnection

The S/360 (and the follow-up S/370) architecture has lived up to its architects' objectives. Its 25-year success record was accomplished through the architects' understanding of the relationship between the program investments, the operating system, the use of microcode to mask the underlying hardware, and the use of microcode to support some of the operating system's unique services.[2] Now the S/390 begins the new era. So, back to the thumbnail chronology.

APRIL 7, 1964: S/360, A SYSTEM ARCHITECTURE TO GROW ON

- Drivers: unique systems, little growth flexibility
- Challenges: providing a broad price range for solutions
- Solutions: single architecture with multiple hardware bases, centralized systems
- Limitations: high price and highly skilled professionals required

---

[2]N. S. Prasad, *IBM Mainframes: Architecture and Design*, McGraw-Hill Book Company, 1989.

2.2   LATE 1960s: REMOTE JOB-ENTRY WORKSTATIONS

By the late 1960s the businesses with S/360 systems at the central location started being pressured to provide the input and output capability to geographically remote locations in order to get the necessary job turnaround time. The time to pick up input and deliver the output was often measurable in days.

Since the cost of geographically placed systems—from the standpoint of hardware prices and employee compensation—was prohibitive, specialized remote input/output hardware evolved to address the turnaround-time requirement. The remote job-entry workstations came in two varieties: specialized printers and card readers that did one task at a time, or *customized low-end general-purpose processors*. The customized general-purpose processors provided the entry of data (via punched cards and tape) and the output of data (via punched cards, printed listings, and tape), and offered such value-added capabilities as storing some of the input and output on disk and interleaving input and output on the line to and from the central system (*the host*).

Operators, often reporting to IS, were assigned to operate remote job-entry workstations. The applications were *batch jobs* and were scheduled to meet critical business schedules. The objectives were clear: reduce turnaround time for data to and from the central computer system. Communication lines were extremely expensive, high-capacity lines were not available in many small, privately serviced areas, and line reliability left much to be desired.

LATE 1960s: REMOTE JOB-ENTRY WORKSTATIONS

- Drivers: input and output turnaround reduction
- Challenges: providing economic quick pickup and delivery
- Solutions: workstations, local operators
- Limitations: costs and reliability of communications, required remote operators

---

2.3   EARLY 1970s: LOCAL DATA CENTERS

By the early 1970s, the S/370—an enhanced implementation based on the S/360 architecture with lower costs, improved price/performance, and increased storage capacity—had been introduced.

As the dependency on timely data became more acute, small satellite data centers began cropping up. This was especially noticeable in the manufacturing industry, which frequently had a large central data center that provided the main programs and systems to geographically dispersed plants.

Data was sent electronically and large amounts of data and systems were shipped via tape, often by overnight services and couriers. A primary driver was the absence of a reliable, high-capacity, low-cost network connection to the central location. The primary criterion was meeting cutoffs. At some locations, the need to be assured that the payroll checks would be available to distribute on time justified a local, small S/360 or S/370 in order to either process the payroll locally or, at a minimum, cut the checks locally.

The significant difference from remote job entry workstations was that the work-stations were essentially *closed* systems in that they did very specific well-defined services. The introduction of *open* operating systems to operate these satellite data centers introduced the seeds of some loss of control from the central organization.

By this time, two generally used IBM operating systems had emerged: OS/360 and DOS. OS/360 provided extensive resource management and control optimization (three different implementations (PCP, MFT, MVT) with various levels of sophistication to address work mix and resource maximization were available). DOS was a more explicitly defined and managed system, more frugal in resource consumption. It did not take on as many of the heuristics that OS/360 did. The DOS system programmer and operator filled in where the dynamics left off.

The "central" data center typically implemented a multitasking OS, while DOS systems were installed at the remote (satellite) data center. Most would have used the same operating system, but the associated hardware and software costs and the need for local skills precluded this option. The DOS system provided a subset of the OS system programming languages and subsystems and represented a smaller expense than OS.

Because the operations of the DOS systems required a small staff of system programmers, operators, and data entry clerks, implementation of local applications on the local systems was initiated despite efforts to limit such efforts by the central organizations. These were the first *distributed open systems,* but only the very large remote locations could afford them.

EARLY 1970s: LOCAL DATA CENTERS

- Drivers: couldn't meet turnaround-time requirements
- Challenges: providing affordable local computing
- Solutions: satellite data centers, subset open operating system, local staff
- Limitations: expensive, local data-center staffs required, degrees of local autonomy

---

2.4 MID 1970s THROUGH EARLY 1980s: POINT OF CAPTURE

In the mid to late 1970s, S/370s were using virtual storage operating systems (DOS/VS, VS1, SVS, and MVS). Additional members of the IBM S/370 family had been introduced: the IBM 3030, 3080, and 4300 series. These systems provided price/performance and capacity enhancements, and featured the 4300, a much more affordable entry priced system. Unlike the earlier and larger S/370s, which require elaborate cooling facilities such as raised floors and chilled water for cooling, the IBM 4300 simply required air cooling.

By this time, the need for on-line systems had taken hold, and was enabled by improved capacity and reduced costs. Terminals were attached to the central processor via a control unit and channel to allow rapid data entry and inquiry response without the operators having to deal with intermediaries and batch cycles and voluminous listings. However, remote data entry via a terminal was still very difficult because of line capacity (response time), reliability, and expense.

Specialized systems that provided the essential data entry, inquiry, and reporting functions local to the user were introduced. They featured local data storage and terminal support. Specialized systems appeared for data entry, point of sale, teller machines, and shop floor control. These systems addressed the need to provide inexpensive, responsive data capture and presentation (response). They also allowed exception access to the host in the online mode and exchanged data electronically via unattended batch mode.

These specialized systems were optimized for unattended operations (no local operator) and for high reliability at a minimum cost. These were typically implemented with *closed* operating systems to *ensure* central control. IBM introduced industry-specific distributed systems designed with the target environment and user in mind: IBM 3790, IBM 3600, IBM 3650, IBM 8100, etc. IBM also introduced the Series/1, which was an *open* minicomputer. This system was used by many companies as the building platform for their distributed data entry, point of capture, and distributed interface and concentrator for non-IBM systems and terminals to IBM host-based applications. The Series/1s were typically implemented as *closed* systems by the information systems organization.

Figure 2.1 and Figure 2.2 depict an insurance data inquiry and data entry and a drugstore point-of-sale application using distributed systems (specialized systems) representative of this period.

MID 1970s THROUGH EARLY 1980s: POINT OF CAPTURE

- Drivers: greater user productivity and need to eliminate batch data entry and output distribution time and cost
- Challenges: providing highly reliable, low response time, low price
- Solutions: distributed specialized "closed" systems, different architectures, different software, unattended operations
- Limitations: central application backlog, unique operating systems and applications required in addition to existing base

At this point in time the optimization of costs required unique hardware architectures and very specialized execution systems. These systems were designed to be *closed* from the end user (only accepting prespecified transactions) and *closed* from any local operations or programming. In fact, the programming was done on the S/370 and only executable code was distributed electronically to the remote system. Similarly, all systems management was done from "central."

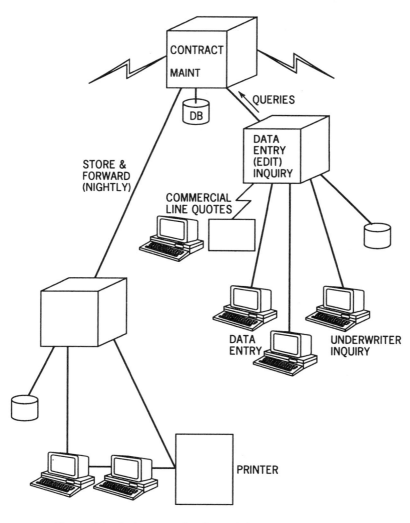

Figure 2.1 *An insurance inquiry and data entry configuration.*

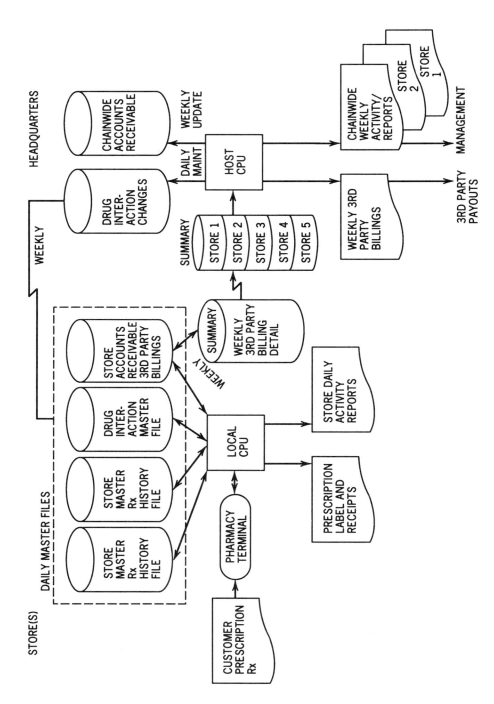

Figure 2.2 A drugstore point-of-sale configuration.

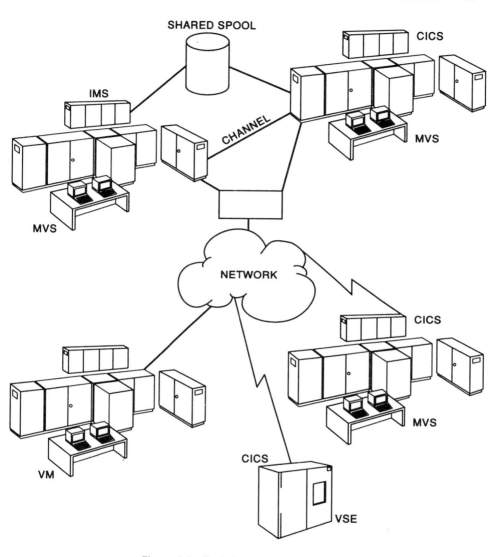

Figure 2.3   *Typical glasshouse of the 1980s.*

2.5   LATE 1970s THROUGH 1980s: MULTIPLE SYSTEMS COUPLING

Independent of the issues associated with getting data to and from remote end users, the central locations were also implementing multiple processors (systems) in the same room in addition to multiple data centers (see Figure 2.3). These are essentially variations of distributed solutions using mainframe systems configuration (both hardware and software) implementations to address capacity, availability, and control requirements. These configurations were driven by single-system capacity limitations (exceeding initial design points in the hardware, operating systems, subsystems, and applications) as well as the need to provide incremental growth options, to isolate certain workloads, and to provide multiple hot backup centers.

To address these requirements, the systems staff implemented a "central" distributed systems complex and learned to operate it efficiently and effectively. They extended the techniques used for a single system to apply to multiple systems. Automated operations, which reduced the need for operator intervention, were installed. Likewise, the operations staff was given the ability to operate the systems from outside of the computer room, providing what is referred to as a *darkroom*[3] operation.

The major transaction processing subsystems (IMS[4] and CICS[5] provided the ability to *exchange data between systems*. In essence, the central data center had implemented both local and remote versions of distributed systems. In this instance the implementations are very similar to the remote specialized implementations with a single, but very important, exception; these systems were not totally unattended (darkroom, but were accessible). After all, the staff was right there if they were needed. The emphasis, however—even in the glasshouse—continues to focus on the systems becoming totally unattended and hardware, communication, and environment control products continue to evolve to meet this objective.

LATE 1970s THROUGH 1980s: MULTIPLE SYSTEMS COUPLING

- Drivers: workload conflicts, complexity, design points
- Challenges: resolve systems and data management conflicts
- Solutions: automated operations, darkroom operations, shared disk storage, system to system
- Limitations: data sharing difficulties across geographically distributed systems for complex transactions (response time and availability)

---

[3]*Darkroom* is the label used for a computer room with the lights out. The consoles are operated from an area physically removed from the computer.

[4]*IMS* refers to IBM's Information Management System, which includes a data communications transaction manager and a data management component that can be accessed via the IMS data communications component or batch jobs. IMS runs exclusively on IBM's high-end operating systems, e.g., MVS. IMS systems can interconnect with other IMS systems and CICS systems. In most cases, the interconnection is at the message level and transactions are switched among the autonomous systems.

[5]*CICS* refers to IBM's Customer Information Control System, which is currently implemented in two variations. It is implemented as a total environment for both data communications and file and data base access on IBM's MVS and IBM's VSE operating systems. It is also implemented as an integrated service in IBM's VM and OS/2 environments. All environments have the ability to access data among participating CICSs, providing full integrity. Transaction routing (somewhat analogous to the IMS message switching) is only available among VSE and MVS implementations.

The 1990s promise to expand and extend this trend with software, hardware, and cost improvements. The software capabilities include switching to backup systems,[6] distributed data base implementations,[7] the enhancements to managing the system complex,[8] new multiple system coupling options such as IBM's Enterprise Systems Connection (ESCON) architecture,[9] and a single processor line that allows the same software to be run across the line make the multiple system coupling much more manageable.

ESCON interconnections will extend the implementation of distributed S/390 systems in distributed environments by reducing the complexity, costs, and physical restrictions associated with earlier interconnection technologies. It will be extensively used for large campuses.

The ES/9000 line provides the I/S executive with more flexibility to install powerful rack-mounted systems and air-cooled mainframes in addition to liquid-cooled mainframes. These can all run the same operating system. This has opened up more opportunity to extend the central complex in more economical chunks than ever before and allows the placement and hardware decisions without forcing software trade-offs.

Given the new capabilities, the implementations of 1990s appear to focused on addressing the lessons of the past two decades and removing many of the challenges.

---

[6]IBM's Extended Recovery Facility (XRF) provides automatic switch over to alternate systems using IMS and CICS (both MVS and VSE) should a failure occur.

[7]Data Base 2 (DB2) and SQL/DS provide distributed relational data base capabilities with the ability to assure multiple data base updates (called *two phase commit*) among MVS and VM systems.

[8]System complex is also referred to as *sysplex* (SYStem comPLEX) and is associated with management mechanisms to set common time across systems and monitoring subsystems within the sysplex in order to switch to a hot standby if a problem is encountered.

[9]IBM's Enterprise Systems Connection (ESCON) architecture enables enterprises to distribute their systems and peripherals to distances up to 5.6 miles (9 km) supporting a ten million byte bandwidth. The ESCON optical fiber based connection system consists of ESCON channels (very thin fiber jumpers), ESCON Directors to provide additional distance and configuration flexibility, fiber optic trunk cables (half-inch in diameter) which have 72 channel links that span between ESCON Directors, and ESCON Converters to accommodate a connection for controllers that have interfaces for the IBM parallel channels. For systems management an ESCON Analyzer provides a mechanism to diagnose problems and coordinate operator consoles. An ESCON Monitor provides a mechanism to watch remote unattended areas for environmental and systems conditions such as power loss, water leaks, temperature, smoke, fire, etc.

Chapter *3*

Departmental Solutions: Background

This chapter discusses the evolution of departmental and user systems. The discussion includes minis, LANs, PCs, and the computing models used in today's *LANs*.

3.1 MINIs

While the glasshouse organizations focused on handling the demands for data and information processing in an orderly and cost-justifiable manner, other approaches to solving immediate business problems with readily available technology emerged. The four major forces that accelerated the focus on requirements and approaches to implementing distributed systems were:

- Increased attractiveness (*price, function, skill* requirements) of minicomputers in the mid to late 1970s
- Introduction of the personal computer in the early 1980s
- Introduction of inexpensive, easy to install and operate, and high bandwidth LANs
- Implementation of numerous local area networks (*LANs*[1]) to share resources and data.

Solutions included systems such as IBM S/3, S/36, and S/38, as well as non-IBM minicomputers.

---

[1]*LAN* (italicized) is a label currently being used generically to refer to the combination of personal computers and/or minicomputers and services connected by Local Area Network (not italicized) technology.

DISTRIBUTED IS GREAT!

Figure 3.1   1977: "Distributed is great!"

Common denominators among such systems are ease of entry (price and ease of installation), number of business solutions available,[2] and the ability of non-data-processing-trained professionals to operate the solutions. These systems were installed to address specific business problems with little consideration for host application or data access affinity. These solutions met the immediate objectives; now many of these system owners are seeking help in accessing data at the host (in other than terminal access mode) or trying to access data in another department with an entirely different system implementation. This, as you recall, was the same scenario that pre-S/360 system implementations went through.

The minicomputer distributed (frequently connected decentralized) solutions implemented outside of the glasshouse went through the same iterations, although much faster. For example, as noted in trade journal headlines in 1977, the minicomputer and the soon-to-be-available micro were predicted to be capable of addressing business problems quickly, with the key themes being a focus on building blocks, networking, cost containment, and skill reduction (Figure 3.1).

---

[2]Many business solutions surfaced because less investment is required for application development in terms of development hardware and software and there is a greater availability of skills for the less complex environments. Educating the developers is also easier when dedicated test systems are affordable.

WAIT A SEC!

Figure 3.2 1980: "More than hardware price improvements required."

By 1980 some of the euphoria had been replaced with the realization that while the equipment was less expensive and the technology economics had allowed for some simplification in systems complexity, many of the central IS problems had not been reduced. In fact, the choices were greater than ever. As noted in the news clippings, the key focus items became selection, absence of standards, skills, application software, and solution integration (Figure 3.2).

MINIs

- Low entry price
- Relative simplicity
- Autonomy
- Availability of solutions (packages and turnkey)
- No general system implementation standards

3.2 LANs

Local area networks (LANs) have evolved to address the in-premise attachment of terminals and computers in a cost-efficient manner. Current LAN technologies are typically described in terms of the transport protocols and can be built on multiple connectivity bases such as twisted pair wires (shielded and unshielded), coax cables, fiberoptic lines, etc.

Currently, Ethernet[3] and IBM Token Ring[4] are the dominant LAN technologies. Other LANs include ARCNET,[5] Starlan,[6] etc. Each LAN implementation addresses some aspect of cost per user, performance, ease of installation, and interconnectivity among similar and dissimilar computer systems as well as other LANs, WANs,[7] and hosts.

A primary difference between Ethernet and Token Ring concerns the rules of who is served. In the Ethernet implementation, a collision (or contention) approach is used for requesting transport service, while Token Ring allocates service (logical polling). Figure 3.3 depicts a typical early 1980 manufacturing Ethernet LAN configuration. Figure 3.4 depicts IBM Token Ring attachments.

LANs

- High-bandwidth and efficient in-building connection wiring
- Extensively used in manufacturing environments (initially)
- Emerging in commercial environments
- Mainframes, minis, PCs, workstations, and terminals share media
- Ethernet and IBM Token Ring are most common
- Pervasively used in departmental solutions

---

[3]*Ethernet* (IEEE 802.3 standard) was pioneered by Xerox and DEC more than ten years ago. It operates over a coaxial and fiberoptic cable or twisted pair wire, has a 10 Mbits/sec bandwidth, uses a CSMA/CD access (Carrier-Sense Multiple-Access with Collison Detection). It has a strong established base in manufacturing and has expanded into commercial environments. There are three versions: standard Ethernet, ThinNet, and twisted pair Ethernet. Standard and ThinNet use a coax with a bus topology. Twisted pair Ethernet uses a hierarchical star topology with wiring concentrator hubs.

[4]*IBM Token Ring* (compatible with IEEE 802.2 and 802.5 standards) is a LAN technology used with the IBM cabling system. It is the fastest growing installed network base. It provides high throughput, up to 16 Mbits/sec using a token passing access method, and is highly fault tolerant. It uses token passing via a physical star, logical ring topology.

[5]*ARCNET* was developed by Datapoint Corporation. It provides a 2.5 Mbit/second token passing network using a distributed star topology over coaxial cable.

[6]*Starlan* was developed by AT&T. It supports a 1 Mbit/second distributed star topology with CSMA/CD access. It operates over two unshielded twisted pairs and can be configured using a hub, daisy chain, or both.

[7]*WAN* refers to Wide Area Network. Local Area Network technologies are limited by physical distance. In order to connect to another remote LAN or host, a WAN is used. WANs include the national networking and telecommunication technologies.

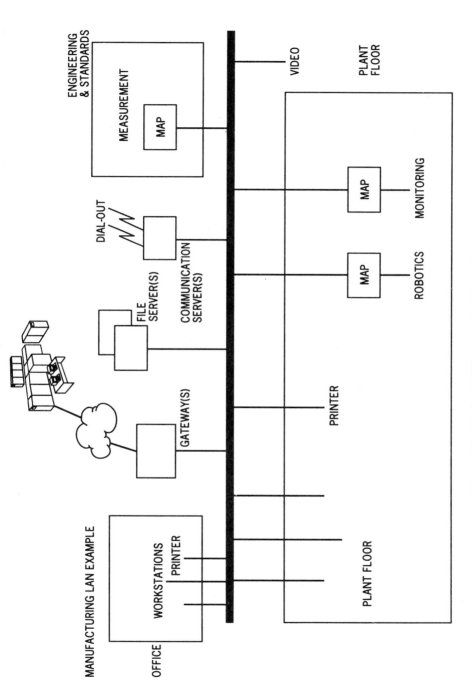

Figure 3.3 *A typical LAN in a manufacturing environment.*

29

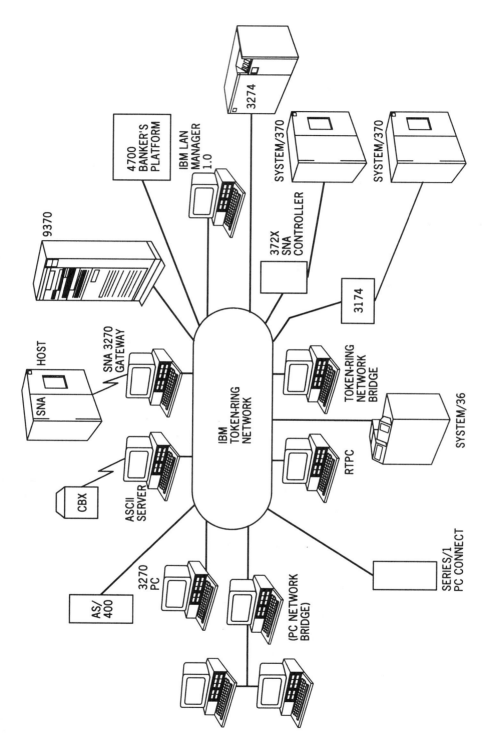

Figure 3.4 An IBM Token Ring LAN with attachments.

30

3.3 PERSONAL COMPUTERS

Probably the biggest impact on the pace of the implementation of business solutions and proliferation of solutions and interfaces was the introduction of an open personal computer. The IBM Personal Computer was introduced with a very simple to use yet extremely flexible hardware and software base.

The price, standard open hardware interface, easy-to-use operating system interface, and simple tools combined with relatively powerful execution capability and direct access storage capacity allowed the implementations to be driven by peoples' imaginations and to use their specific knowledge of their application rather than being dependent on systems resource oriented specialists and experienced programmers. This provided a lot of practical experimentation with interfaces, ease of use, new external interfaces such as facsimile, voice, scanners, etc. These solutions could be implemented in a truly autonomous manner unencumbered by the underlying disciplines that drove the glasshouse, such as security, sharing rules, data backup, administration, data integrity, resource optimization, billings, etc. These encumbrances (corequisites) are associated with shared systems, large number of users, and sharing among users, not with a single user system (or so the implementers initially thought).

The majority of personal computers (generically PCs) essentially operate in a single-user and single-task environment. Over time PCs and operating systems will be replaced by more sophisticated operating systems such as OS/2 Extended Edition and more powerful personal computers (or workstations).

As the number of systems and applications increase and the users begin to interconnect their PCs using LANs to exchange data, the overall environment becomes more sophisticated, and the management of software currency and software integration becomes extremely important and extremely bothersome. A logical next step for these users is to share the operating environment and user applications from some master, a master that is supported by someone who is skilled enough to set up and maintain the required level of currency. In short, a level of *control* is imple-

---

PERSONAL COMPUTER

- Low price
- Easy to understand
- Plethora of tools
- Open platform
- Users' desire to access and share resources and data
- Evolving into more sophisticated environment
- Users have an increasing interest in sharing software libraries

mented. Similarly, certain data controls need to be implemented for data should never be exportable from the PC (for legal, privacy, or asset protection reasons). File servers and diskless PCs are gaining in popularity as methods of addressing these requirements.

3.4 LANs

LANs (italicized) are an extension of the PC and LAN technologies. However, their significance goes far beyond the LAN technology. The *LAN* is really a *"build and configure it yourself operating system"* that has exploited:

- Low entry price
- Erector-set flexibility of personal computers
- High bandwidths of LAN technologies
- Ease of installation of personal computer hardware
- Ease of installation of personal computer software
- Straightforward operation of personal computer solutions
- Dedicated system and application (server) simplicity

These attributes, together with some software, have allowed users to create *LANs* by placing specialized functions that can be shared among users on workstations on dedicated personal computers to provide file servers, print servers, data base servers, communication servers, gateways, and application servers to augment their workstation services and capacity.

There are multiple computing models that can be used for implementing *LANs*. One of the primary differentiators is the distribution of control which typically reflects in the degree of transparency to existing applications (see Figure 3.5), but the *client-server* computing model has prompted much grassroots popularity because it is inherently simple and flexible. The client-server model also provided an opportunity to introduce specialized operating systems[8] or subsystems[9] without impacting the existing personal computer software base in the user's computer.

This was accomplished by placing the new operating systems into dedicated systems referred to as servers and providing a transparent client component into each of the participating users' computers.[10] The server can be likened to transac-

---

[8]*Specialized operating system* refers to an operating system that has been designed (and optimized) to handle a specific workload. Examples include IBM's TPF, which is optimized to process messages, IBM DPPX, which has been optimized to provide distributed transaction processing services in unattended environments, and Novell's Netware, which has been optimized to handle specific I/O services, e.g., file requests for a variety of client environments.

[9]*Subsystem* is a term used to refer to a package of system services that essentially extend the operating system. For example, CICS is a subsystem that provides a transaction operating system environment for applications on MVS on VSE.

[10]There are *client-server* implementations that allow both the client and server components and the user's application to co-reside in a single personal computer, but this implementation is not very popular because it introduces more complexity and less flexibility than does placing the server function on a separate system (personal computer).

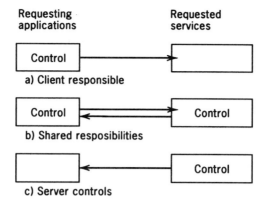

Figure 3.5   *Control variations.*

tion processor system which handles a finite set of requests generated by an application which resides outside of that system.

As illustrated in Figure 3.6, the user computer (currently most often a personal computer) has some software (client software) that interfaces with the services of the server. The more dominant client-server implementations introduce the client software transparently to the user's existing application interfaces.

For example, the client software might intercept requests for disk I/O. This would allow the user to access disk capacity beyond that of the user system with total transparency. The data request times are frequently equal to or even faster than his or her own system's disk access if the server uses memory-caching techniques to eliminate mechanical random access times or faster more expensive direct access storage devices. These techniques overcome the impact of delays introduced by using a *pipe* (system interconnection) that is slower than an internal bus to storage.

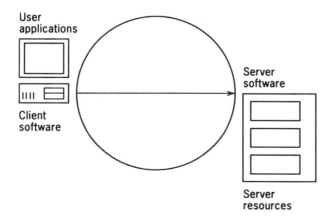

Figure 3.6   *Client-server concept.*

In such implementations the server truly only serves, the control is retained within the user's system and its software, and the server acts as a peripheral. When control is retained at each user system, the server can support multiple different operating systems providing that client software exists for each user system environment. The essence of LAN client-server computing today is:

- Absence of an overall control program
- Retention of ownership (control) responsibilities at client systems
- Connection of computing components (slower than memory pipes)
- Using system memory to compensate for slower pipes
- Mixed operating systems support for clients
- Specialized servers

Server implementations are not new. For example, what is now IBM's VM operating system essentially introduced this concept in the late 1960s. Servers have been implemented to support PCs from both VM and MVS via an implementation referred to as Enhanced Connectivity Facilities (ECF).[11] What is new are the assumptions associated with the responsibilities (control) of clients (versus servers) and the applicability of this assumption in the commercial environment.

How will client-server solutions evolve? They appear to be evolving in two directions: they are taking on more application function and evolving into more integrated (centralized and shared responsibility model) solutions as reflected in Figure 3.5. The increase in function available in the server will allow user code in the server and this will be provided as normal vendor product growth.

The evolution to more integrated relationships between the client and server will be to reduce the delays introduced by not having access across the memory bus. This requirement is driven by placement (especially as the *LANs* begin to communicate with one another). The integrated solutions exchange less data than simple client-server implementations by having application logic on both the clients and server as well as using interfaces visible to the application. (This is expanded on in Chapter 9.)

The more integrated implementations look like the traditional systems so we can postulate that the capacity of the servers[12] will continue to increase, several new subsystems will evolve, and the need for standards and interoperability capabilities will become even more important.

In summary, *LAN* evolution is essentially a revisiting of the concepts of centralized and earlier distributed computing evolution. The ease of entry has allowed more rapid and frequent experimentation of implementations. The endgame, however, is rather deterministic and most of us who have been active in IS for more than five years have lived through at least one such cycle.

---

[11]*ECF* is discussed in more detail in Chapter 21 on Complementary Services.
[12]Server capacity demand is currently being addressed via various approaches, including demand for increasingly more capable personal computer based systems, superminis, and specialized server hardware.

LANs

- Driven as extension of personal computers
- Grassroots driven
- Client-server model most prevalent
- Servers modelled after transaction processors
- Separate service responsibilities
- Connection capacity sensitive
- Facilitates resource, data, and function sharing
- Driving need for interoperability and standards

**OUTSIDE THE "GLASSHOUSE": DEPARTMENTAL
SYSTEMS AND** *LANs*

- Drivers: responsive and flexible business solutions
- Challenges: responsive, affordable, and manageable services
- Solutions: turnkey minisystems, personal computer, LANs, computer-literate end users, package solutions, user staff
- Limitations: access to host data, application and system integration, user staff skills, systems management

Chapter *4*

The S/390 Distributed Solutions Drivers

This chapter discusses why companies are looking at distributed solutions with S/390-based systems. The reasons were compiled from input from IS executives during a world-wide survey that I conducted between August 1988 and January 1989. The resultant analysis identified that the most prevalent solutions are driven by three forces. These forces appear to provide a basis for projecting the S/390 applications of the 1990s.

4.1   THREE DRIVERS TO DISTRIBUTED S/390s

Technology management, organizational demands, and *interoperability* appear to be the most descriptive categories to discuss the drivers. Figure 4.1 depicts a *pragmatic view* of the three *primary reasons* why companies are *installing S/390 distributed or remote solutions.*

4.2   TECHNOLOGY MANAGEMENT

The technology management thrust is usually *initiated by* the *IS organization* to address end user service requirements, improve operational productivity, or reduce data processing expenses by distributing services or applications. These solutions are typically developed without the involvement of the end users. The end users usually become aware of the technology management solution as their procedures change and their service improves (see Figure 4.2).

Recently, a new informal IS organization has emerged to operate and manage

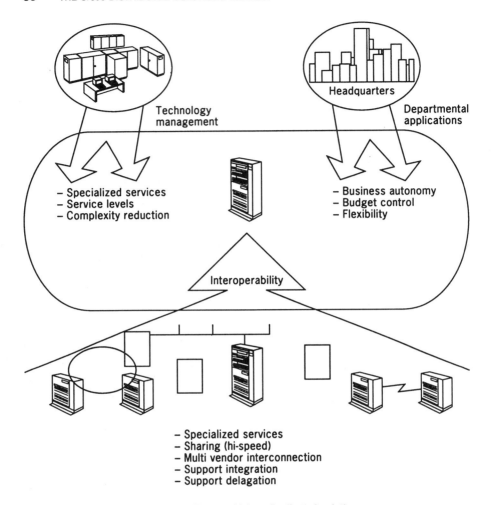

Figure 4.1 Forces driving distributed solutions.

departmentally controlled systems and LANs. These informal IS organizations may be comprised of a single individual or the responsibilities may be shared among multiple end users. Conceptually, these folks constitute an IS organization. (We'll discuss this in more detail later.) This organization also drives technology management solutions such as servers.

Characteristic technology management solutions include:

• Specialized services
• Service level improvements
• Complexity reductions

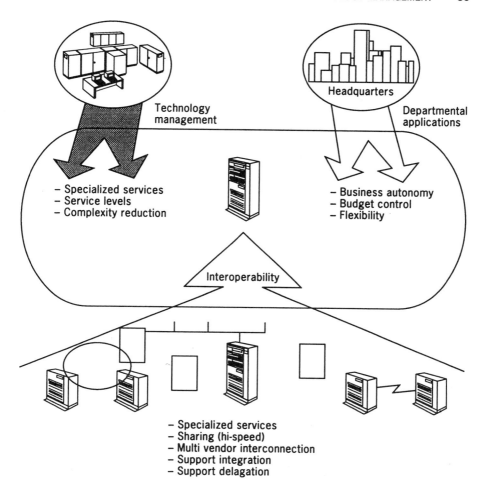

Figure 4.2 Technology management reasons for distributing.

4.2.1 Specialized Services

Specialized Services include such solutions as *remote printer,* remote *gateway* support and *remote tape* support. These are implemented to improve the operability of peripherals and communications equipment at a remote location—either geographically or just removed from an operator.

The introduction of a low entry priced systems, such as the *ES/9000* or *Micro Channel 370,* has made the S/390 a *viable* technology management solution candidate which scales.[1] These can be viewed as a full function intelligent remote control

---

[1]*Scales* in this context means that the same procedures, applications, and software can be applied across the price and performance spectrum.

unit and treated as a closed system. Such systems have network attachment flexibility, and a remote service capability that can use standard software, integrated adapters, operational intelligence, and spool files. This takes advantage of existing procedures and operations expertise, which reducing the need for operational staff to travel to locations outside the computer room.

TECHNOLOGY MANAGEMENT: SPECIALIZED SERVICES

- I/S initiated
- Intelligent remote control unit
- Remote print, tape, network gateway
- High host affinity

4.2.2 Service Level Improvements

The decision to place a system local to a user may be driven by the need for good response time, less change, more responsiveness, etc. Often, hard-to-achieve response objectives can be addressed by moving the computing and/or data closer to the end user. While communications technology continues to provide higher and more reliable bandwidths, there are many instances that cannot be addressed by such communication technologies. For example, many outlying locations and private phone companies do not provide T1-type services yet, while others have a significant backlog. Depending on the bandwidth requirements, there may also be some line cost savings.

Similarly, end users today are using more cooperative processing. The movement of files back and forth is a typical requirement. In many cases even the bandwidth of a T1 cannot keep up with the need for expanded data rate. Moving a system on the premises can address the response time and bandwidth requirements by bringing the data closer to the end user without introducing a new application. Once the data is local, LAN technologies such as Token Ring and Ethernet can provide substantially higher bandwidths than can T1s.

From another perspective, user departments frequently have unique software requirements. The uniqueness often manifests itself in a new application that requires the most current operating system with current service level. Other applications often cannot be moved to the most current operating system without some additional upgrading and testing efforts. The IS organization can respond to one group's business needs without impacting the general user population with a distributed system managed by the central location. This solution protects and builds on existing investments and utilizes unattended and distributed systems management enhancements to contain the u. ˙que systems.

**TECHNOLOGY MANAGEMENT: SERVICE LEVEL
IMPROVEMENTS**

- I/S initiated
- I/S data closer to user for response time
- Unique software requirements isolated
- More response to special requirements

4.2.3 Complexity Reductions

Separating a group of users may solve the need to *reduce* the *interdependencies* on unrelated applications just as in the previous scenario. For this discussion's purposes, the distribution provides a degree of isolation and flexibility. This isolation is frequently done today to separate the application developers from the production environment. IS typically provides separate development and test systems in order to avoid affecting production environments.

Today the separation (distribution) may take the form of a separate system within the glasshouse or a separate system running as a "guest" on VM. With reduced cost and environmental requirements, enhanced remote systems management tools, and remote access to dependent data and services, this same level of separation may be economically applied to applications. This gives the IS organization the option of distributing some key line of business applications entirely for the purpose of reducing the complexity associated with change management and introducing additional workload and applications.

For example, a division needs substantial new function *now*. This new function requires a new release of software. Every time the information systems group makes such a change, they must spend hundreds of hours verifying or making the necessary changes to all the other divisions' applications and they must run test cases. By isolating the leading-edge division, the focus can be narrowed to address the unique requirements while staging the other systems at a different pace. This reduces conversion and testing resources while improving responsiveness.

Independent of whether the systems are geographically dispersed or located within the same system computer center, the distribution may afford some substantial reductions of complexity. The economics of using an air-cooled system, or an ES/9000 with PR/SM or VM as a hypervisor are frequently considered.

Each choice affords a different incremental cost option. The Micro Channel 370 and rack model ES/9000s accommodate local or remote distribution at a relatively low price. Frame models are also viable for physical distribution. However, from an environmental standpoint, they do require a small glasshouse.

The ES/9000 also has the flexibility to use VM as a hypervisor for a guest system to provide a logically distributed solution using the existing system. Similarly, the ES/9000 can use the PR/SM capability, which essentially provides the VM guest environment without revealing VM interfaces. PR/SM provides *Logical Partitions*. The key difference between the PR/SM using Logical Partitions and the VM solutions are the sharing of physical resources. PR/SM provides an isolated slice of the system and requires dedicated resources (e.g., channels). VM isolates logical resources while sharing the physical resources. PR/SM is implemented in the microcode, and VM is a software hypervisor.

TECHNOLOGY MANAGEMENT: COMPLEXITY REDUCTIONS

- Affordable separation
- Access to dependent services and data
- Physically local or remote distribution
- Separated on some or different system
- Small incremental growth options

4.2.4 Technology Management Summary

There are many reasons why IS is looking at distributed solutions to address people productivity and response time problems. These solutions are initiated by IS to address their service level, budget, and responsiveness needs. Lower priced and less environmentally demanding S/390 options, new remote systems management capabilities, and new intersystem capabilities make specialized services, service level improvements, and complexity reductions possible by using existing IS skills and without retooling. Last, and definitely not least, is that S/390 currently has the most comprehensive systems management tools available.

TECHNOLOGY MANAGEMENT

- I/S initiated
- Host extension
- Utilize existing skills
- Responsiveness improvements
- Workload segregation
- S/390 most comprehensive systems management

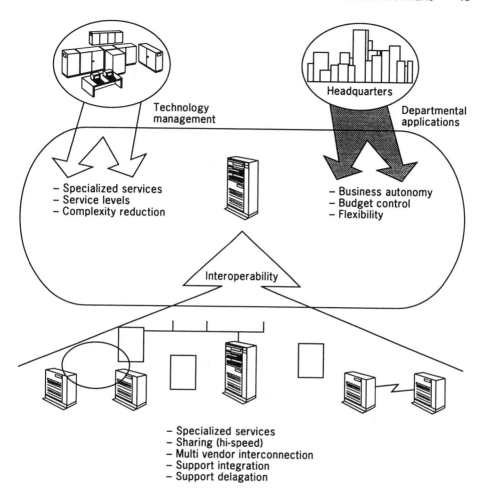

Figure 4.3 *Organizational reasons to distribute.*

4.3 ORGANIZATIONAL DRIVERS

Organizational pressures to distribute are driven by a corporation, a division, an end user department, or a mission-critical project to address budget control, project dynamics and business autonomy (see Figure 4.3).

4.3.1 Budget Control

Moving or building support on a dedicated but connected system provides the capability to control the expenses associated with data processing. Many organizations hold their department management accountable for their budgets, including each department's consumption of data processing resources. Many of these same organizations run their IS as a *cost center*.

The departmental manager's major concern with cost center chargebacks is that the manager's department is *taxed* for services that it does not necessarily need and the chargeback rate usually varies, depending on the overall system usage pattern. The department manager therefore *cannot* have *control* of the *department's budget*. Also, anytime the manager would like unique software or services, he or she must go through a very comprehensive *justification process* because of the overall implications. This justification process often requires that the requesting department go out and *sell* or rationalize to all the other departments why the additional function or capacity is important. The objective here is to gain approval for a rate increase for all or to gain agreement to reprioritize this requirement over the contending efforts. None of these activities relate to the business problem that initiated the activity.

Given how affordable midrange systems (e.g., AS/400 and ES/9000) are, many departments have established their own departmental systems which provide services that are mission-critical and affect their measurements. These departmental users still need to access the central services that are beyond their budgets or expertise. The user departments are still very interested in delegating the information system's disciplines, rigor, and skills, but only as a fixed charge.

ORGANIZATIONAL DRIVERS: BUDGET CONTROL

- User department initiated
- Cost center charge-out causes fluctuations in expenses
- Cost center justifications not responsive to single department
- Distributed offers fixed expenses
- Distributed offers crisp cost benefits analysis
- Host data and transaction access still required
- Would prefer to delegate systems management

4.3.2 Project Dynamics

Frequently, providing a dedicated but connected system provides for responsiveness *outside the normal planning* cycle or control rigors. Distributed autonomous systems afford a new organization (or an organization that anticipates substantial changes to its plan) the flexibility to use *centrally developed applications* and to contract *systems management*.

These organizations are compelled to work outside the normal information systems and corporate processes because of the substantial planning lead time and rigor demanded by these processes (often measured in years). As an alternative, they choose to have their own departmental system(s), to retain the necessary flexibility to respond to the dynamics of their projects. Again, these organizations would *prefer* to have access to the *centrally provided services* that offer more capabilities and cost more than what the department can afford to own exclusively. The departmental groups are typically interested in buying support at a fixed rate they control. These implementations are often called *project systems*.

ORGANIZATIONAL DRIVERS: PROJECT DYNAMICS

- Organization initiated with corporate/division support
- Special projects and task forces need maximum flexibility
- Existing processes and rigors often stifle quick starts
- Existing processes and systems base may impede flexibility
- New organizations don't want to become a mini-I/S
- Are willing to buy systems management and support

4.3.3 Business Autonomy

Sometimes the primary impetus to provide dedicated but connected systems is to be flexible for *organizational changes* and spinoffs. Distributed S/390s are frequently considered by companies that would like to posture themselves to accommodate reorganizations or major restructuring (spinoffs, etc.). These companies have noted that the dependency on data processing implementation can have a significant impact on their flexibility. This allows the enterprise to consolidate or separate using the same architecture and applications.

It has been discovered, usually during mergers and spinoffs, that many centralized applications have been optimized to benefit from being in the same system as other data and services (usually for performance and data access response time). Splitting these applications often results in a major conversion effort and/or redundant expense incurred when a corporation reorganizes or spins off a division.

On the other hand, applications that have been designed with the possibility of distribution in mind have been relatively simple to split out. The design trade-off was one of performance and response time optimization versus flexibility to the old organization. As a related aside, this "system optimized" design point surfaces not only during organizational changes, but also—usually very painfully—when a system must be split because of capacity constraints. Many enterprises have been struggling to overcome this exposure since the early 1970s. In many cases the only tactical solution is to seek an even larger system independent of the large incremental costs. The incremental costs have traditionally been less than converting the existing application.

As indicated earlier with regard to centralized computing and the client-server computing model, there are some performance- and overhead-related tradeoffs when the ability to distribute is built into applications. The *balance of organizational flexibility versus centrally managed economies* is often tipped in favor of flexibility when the corporate offices declare that they are willing to make that trade-off. IS addresses the operational aspects with the central support organization providing services on a distributed basis, charging out along organizational lines. The S/390 and its product lines (both hardware and software) provide the basis and granularity that *supply* the organizational flexibility while allowing the *optimization* of the *central support resources.*

ORGANIZATIONAL DRIVERS: BUSINESS AUTONOMY

- Corporation or division initiated
- Systems designed with central in mind are hard to distribute (a centralized application can hinder organizational splits)
- Systems designed for distributed provide the greatest flexibility (S/390 investments can be protected and built upon)

ORGANIZATIONAL DRIVERS

- Department, division, or corporation initiated
- Autonomy and flexibility driven
- Budget control
- Project systems
- Re-organizational flexibility

4.4 INTEROPERABILITY

Interoperability represents a class of *special purpose solutions* currently emerging that take advantage of the power, function, capacity, manageability and interconnectivity of various user and departmental systems (see Figure 4.4). In many cases the resultant application uses services provided by the traditional central processors and distributed processors across different systems and architectures (multi-vendor).

While interoperability solutions have been evolving for many years, the recent rapid growth of end user and department solutions has driven the general introduc-

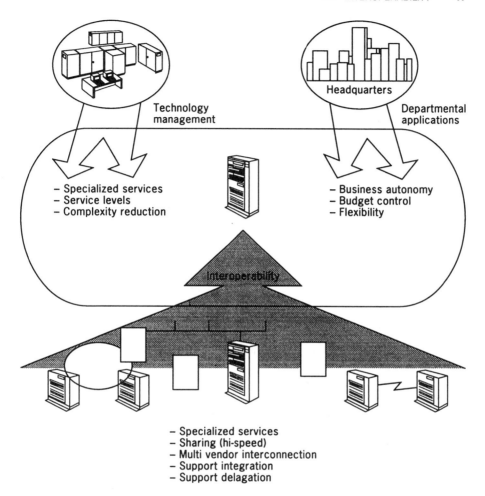

Figure 4.4 *Interoperability drivers to embrace distributed.*

tion of interoperability among personal computers, departmental systems, LANs, and hosts. As the owners' solution sophistication increases, so does the need for data beyond their control, for computing capability beyond their resources, and their desire to integrate these resources beyond terminal access.

Additionally, as these users mature in their understanding of the significance of the corporate assets that they now manage and own, and the responsibilities that go with those assets with regard to management of the data, integrity, availability, response time, security, and connectivity, they look to services that can address these requirements.

These departmental groups are now looking for solutions that augment their departmental systems, *LANs,* and personal computer solutions with the services provided by the more traditional information services.

A viable solution would be for the departmental groups to contract service from their information systems house, if it is service-oriented. These departments do not want to give up any of their freedom and flexibility when they engage the information systems organization. The major current focus is on interconnectivity for terminals, data access, file transfer, and the more sophisticated and capable servers that are being driven by the end users.

Interoperability includes these services:

- Specialized services
- Sharing resources
- Support integration
- Support delegation

4.4.1 Specialized Services

End user departments with personal computer applications often install a midrange system to improve the quality of their capabilities while minimizing the costs. Typical solutions include *print servers, tape server, remote tape, file servers and network gateways*. The solutions are driven by the need for high-priced resources that are not affordable if replicated by each user or departmental system. The distributed system(s) affords the ability to provide very reliable and full-function resources to the currently independent users.

In the context described for specialized services, only the physical resources are shared. For example, disk capacity (files), print capability, tape capacity, and line capacity are being shared in order to afford a high-priced resource. Each apportioned capacity is used only by the designated owner. There is no concurrent sharing of the allocated resource, making this a straightforward environment to manage. It can be initiated by a system administrator.

A key difference between sharing physical resources on a locally distributed system such as an ES/9000 and sharing the same resources via a remote central ES/9000 is the availability and affordability of bandwidth to meet the response time to which these users have grown accustomed with their PCs.

INTEROPERABILITY: SPECIALIZED SERVICES

- Department initiated
- Extension of personal computers
- Physical resource sharing
- Expense sharing
- Print, tape, files (space), network servers
- Response time expenses drive local versus host-provided

4.4.2 Sharing Resources

Resource sharing is a logical extension of the specialized services solutions. In this context, the resource to be shared is accessed concurrently rather than serially. The most commonly *concurrently shared resources* are files and data bases. These differ from physically shared resources that are essentially accessed serially (for example, one user gets a file and then returns it before the next user can access it.). Two systems management aspects of sharing data immediately surface when concurrent access is desired: *ownership and update* flexibility.

The solution to sharing data requires the designation of a shared file or data base owner. This designated owner establishes the data definitions, currency rules, update rules, access authority, and data integrity. Sophisticated data systems and systems management software are typically required to meet the accessibility, data integrity, and performance needs of this type of service as the usage increases among multiple users. As a result, most current distributed shared systems emerge as complementary solutions providing shared data access rather than access with shared update capabilities. Other approaches delegate the responsibilities for data integrity to the client software or applications or limit the sharing interface to applications that only update a single record per transaction.

For now, let it suffice that S/390 systems software has traditionally focused on the management for controlled data integrity via central mechanisms, with recently introduced implementations that allow the delegation of some of the responsibilities to the clients (e.g., TCP/IP Network File System—NFS).

IBM's System Application Architecture (SAA) also spends much of the interface definition efforts on distribution. SAA implementations have approached the development of distributed applications in a staged manner, initially by introducing consistent interfaces, then focusing on communications support to move data around a network and access data on interconnected SAA systems. Next will be the ability to reconfigure processing locations.

As of this writing, SAA has added the Communication Interface to the Common Programming Interface (CPI) list and distributed data (file access via Distributed Data Management—DDM) capability. The ability to access data across relational data bases such as DB2 and SQL/DS systems has been discussed[2] and is expected in the early 1990s using IBM SAA code.

From a distributed processing implementation standpoint, distributed dialog and presentation services provide the ability to distribute some of the standard interactions of a session on a workstation while accessing the data from the host. This reduces the transmission of redundant data and unnecessary interactions with the host. Similarly, distributed program-to-program interfaces provide the ability to access application services from distributed locations.[3]

---

[2]*Writing Applications: A Design Guide. Systems Application Architecture,* July 1988, IBM Order Number SC26-4362-1, published by IBM, pp. 27–32.
[3]"SAA distributed processing," *IBM Systems Journal,* 1988, vol. 27, no. 3, by A. L. Scherr, pp. 370–389.

INTEROPERABILITY: SHARING (DATA) RESOURCES

- Driven by users for common data access with update
- Owners of data must be designated
- Data integrity can be controlled or delegated
- S/390 affords variety of control options
- S/390 provides most sophisticated shared data management controls
- SAA provides blueprint for protected interoperability interfaces

---

4.4.3 Support Integration

As the sophistication of departmental users increases, so does their need to *access data currently* available on the central computers and other departmental systems. Currently, there is a concerted effort to implement solutions that provide controlled access-to-host resident data. These implementations initially begin by supporting connectivity requirements: physical connectivity, communications software connectivity, and application connectivity.

Most organizations are beginning to interconnect various departmental systems with a central site using passthrough capability and basic file transfers. Numerous software gateways for mixed vendor and mixed systems are currently being used and more are surfacing daily. Several will be discussed in later chapters.

The next step for many organizations will be to address interapplication communications, security, data access rules, and intersystem operability. This will have many departmental initiated systems looking to the IS organization or outside organizations to provide this integration expertise. IS is a good candidate since the IS organization owns the host application and has some of the expertise required to support the various operating systems, support products, and controls.

INTEROPERABILITY: SYSTEMS INTEGRATION

- Mixed software, hardware, vendor solutions
- Phases of information systems evolution tracking
- Next phases are predictable
- Need for shared data and shared responsibility growing
- I/S can provide support and facilitate
- Department must retain flexibility to succeed

4.4.4 Support Delegation

As the departmental solutions increase in sophistication (in terms of relationships with other systems and products installed), the users begin to recognize that skills are needed to administer shared resources. Sharing data can be extremely complex. Accessing data from the central computers and interconnecting systems with security and associated service levels require skills and relationships outside the department's mission.

Many departmental systems owners are looking for help to delegate the planning, operations, and systems administration for the basic system functions. The departmental owners want to retain application and budget controls. S/390-based distributed support tools can assist the systems management while not imposing unnecessary rigidity, although granting this autonomy may require a fundamental change to the *modes operandi:* and management measurement systems in some IS organizations.

Many enterprises have already taken the first step by having a group that addresses *LAN* support from a departmental system organization reporting to IS. This organization is typically staffed with non-IS people who have grown up with the PC, mini, or midrange system and the evolution of *LANs*. Their role is to facilitate the required responsiveness while introducing some of the necessary rigors. The evolution of these organizations inside the IS infrastructure is just beginning to occur.

INTEROPERABILITY: SUPPORT DELEGATION

- Departmental solutions increasing in complexity
- Departments don't want mini I/S organization
- Looking for support help
- Don't want to give up flexibility
- I/S can help

4.4.5 Interoperability Summary

As we can see, the need to access resources, data, and services and to delegate some systems management responsibilities is being driven by end users as much as the glasshouse was. Both the user and glasshouse organizations would like to access the distributed services transparently, to gain optimum response time using minimal systems management resources as inexpensively as possible.

Additionally, the current direction being followed by the departmental solutions is similar to the path previously experienced by IS organizations. The fundamental tools that were used to address the requirements of IS are applicable to the departmental requirements. However, a fundamental change to the introduction of controls is required. The tools and services that the IS organization used to address its requirements have been tailored to an authoritarian control point.

The tools themselves have, in fact, evolved to support this approach. However, there is nothing fundamental to these tools that will not accommodate a level of shared authority that will allow the departments to retain their solution flexibility while delegating the support to IS. IS, on the other hand, has the unique opportunity to subcontract support on a competitive rather than cost-recovery basis. IS can bid support at a flat-rate and the department will provide the cost-benefits justification for only the services it needs.

INTEROPERABILITY

- Evolutionary
- Data or compute power driven
- Cost sharing driven
- Connectivity already exists
- Systems management weakest link
- I/S can become an important player in the solution

4.5   S/390 DISTRIBUTED SOLUTIONS DRIVERS SUMMARY

Companies are currently using or planning to use distributed solutions to address immediate business needs. The solutions address pressing business issues such as responding to needs, reducing cost, providing flexibility, or providing access to critical information.

These drivers have stressed some of the traditional ways systems and their users have implemented their own systems. In many instances this has been viewed by the IS organization as the giving up or losing control. It also appears that if these changes are understood and some approaches to control are changed by the IS infrastructure, it can place IS in a far more influential position and become part of the users' solutions. The first significant visible steps include the incorporation of *LAN* and departmental support organizations into the IS infrastructure.

Chapter 5

S/390 Solutions' Status and Directions

The resilience and flexibility of the S/390 architecture base was demonstrated by S/370's hardware and associated software platforms evolution with the various drivers to distributed solutions. A key theme has been to leverage and preserve an enterprise's current application and skills investment while utilizing their systems' management experience base. A rack-mounted S/370, the ES/9370, and subsequently the Micro Channel–based S/370, 9371, were the vehicles for increased focus on placing S/370s closer to the user.

The ES/9370 was essentially a super-minisystem targeted at small companies or departments that want to use a specific S/370-based application(s), and for use by larger companies for extending their computing—such as interoperability concentrators or host service extensions—closer to the user and technology management.

These new systems required some very fundamental hardware packaging changes to deal with the different environmental and staffing expectations in terms of size, air-conditioning requirements, noise, power, operational interfaces, and remote access and control. It also required operational enhancements and flexibility to provide connectivity, remote systems management, unattended operations, and additional distributed function capabilities. All were incorporated in the ES/9000 rack models.

The S/370-based software environments were also expanded to allow convergence to the S/370 architectural base from both IBM non-S/370 hardware-based platforms and non-IBM software platforms. The ES/9370 supports five IBM-developed operating systems—VM, VSE, DPPX, MVS, and TPF—one of which was ported from a non-S/370 hardware base (DPPX). Additionally, the ES/9370 supports four operating environments not developed by IBM—MUMPS, PICK, MU-

---

ES/9370

- Super-minicomputer with S/370 instruction set
- IBM-developed S/370 operating systems: VM, VSE, MVS, TPF, AIX
- DPPX ported from IBM 8100 System
- MUMPS and PICK environments ported from OEM systems
- MUSIC and KeyKOS specialized environments
- S/370 architecture provides a very broad base
- Several models use the IBM Micro Channel Architecture
- Model 14 provides a S/370 and PS/2 hybrid

SIC, and KeyKOS—two of which were ports from non-IBM systems. (See Software Platforms in Appendices.)

Figure 5.1 depicts the Enterprise Systems processors; note the reduction in size of the central electronic complex (CEC) which provides the computing capacity. The ES/9000 liquid-cooled configuration, the ES/9000 air-cooled frame, the ES/9000 rack-mounted drawer models, and the Micro Channel 370 processor card reflect the scalability of the architecture. This constitutes different S/370 lines from cost, environmental, and capacity standpoint, which adhere to the architectural constructs for software. The compute and peripheral capabilities span over two orders of magnitude. The ES/9000 rack-mounted models succeed the 9370.

Few have risked a prediction as to where the high end will stop. There is a lot of discussion about how the S/390 fits in the very low end and midrange (these are as much price statements as capacity), especially in light of the availability of apparent alternative solutions based on the PC (PS/2) and the AS/400. I am now stepping

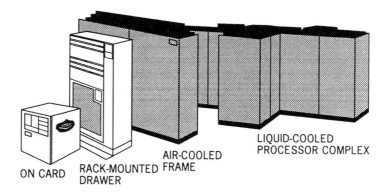

ON CARD   RACK-MOUNTED   AIR-COOLED   LIQUID-COOLED
           DRAWER   FRAME   PROCESSOR COMPLEX

Figure 5.1 Enterprise Systems processors (September 1990).

into a world of fortune tellers and prophets; being neither, I will rely on history, recognizing that both IS and users are driving the solutions more than are venders' plans and technology.

The user selection criterion is rather straightforward: solve a problem, based on what they know, at a price they can afford.

The IS selection criterion is more complicated because it considers the longer range and bigger picture issues in addition to the more straightforward solution. As a result IS tends to be more of an advocate of the S/390 family, since it offers the distributed solution and the necessary corequisite elements: tested capability; synergy with existing systems; price performance; reliability, availability, and serviceability (RAS); growth flexibility; and systems management mechanisms. The solutions have been tested and the staffs are in most cases already trained.

There have been several efforts to provide a very low-end S/370 (e.g., a desktop S/370), with mixed results. From what we have seen, the hardware technology does not appear to be the primary inhibitor to using the S/370 across the entire spectrum of user profiles. The corequisite implicit need for S/370 programming skills by a large user population and the need for a myriad of software components are probably the primary reasons that the desktop S/370 notion hasn't become a reality. For example, one such implementation was a PC (AT/370 Personal Computer) that provided a subset of VM/370 (VM/PC). It is used for very specific applications and some programmers really like it for program development.[1,2]

In early 1988, a variation on the theme surfaced as a special-request system from IBM, the IBM 7437,[3] was introduced. The IBM 7437 is a coprocessor approach that uses a PS/2 and attaches a S/370 coprocessor to provide a single-user multitasking environment. It is supported by VM/SP and optionally supports an IBM 5080 high-resolution graphic attachment, making a very attractive engineering workstation.

It supports peer-to-peer communications with other 7437s over Token Ring LANs, multiple concurrent VM sessions, as well as concurrent execution of DOS and VM sessions. This approach takes advantage of the PS/2 technologies and the S/370 software investments and programming tools. It also doesn't impose a functional subset upon the user. This implementation provided a personal S/370. The software is down-loaded from a S/370 host.

In early 1990, IBM introduced three new models of the ES/9370 family, the models 10, 12, and 14. These models leverage the price and performance characteristics of the PS/2 and the IBM Micro Channel architecture. This provides both a very low system price entry point for multi-user full function S/370-based solutions and it opens the S/370 up to new and innovative applications which merge device flexibility with traditional S/370 platforms.

I am highlighting these models since they represent two very different implementations using S/370 and PS/2 technologies. The first implementation (models 10

---

[1]Brad Schultz, "VM: The Crossroads of Operating Systems". *Datamation,* July 5, 1988, pp. 79–84.
[2]G. R. McClain, *VM and Departmental Computing,* McGraw-Hill, 1988, p. 26.
[3]*The IBM 7437 VM/SP Technical Workstation,* IBM Order Number GA23-0368.

and 12) is the utilization of PS/2 technology and investments by IBM to provide a lower priced S/370. Figure 5.2 portrays the models 10 and 12 as a S/370 CPU with one or two 80386 microprocessors, which essentially make selected IBM Micro Channel architecture devices to appear as S/370 devices to the S/370 software.

The second implementation, which almost looks identical from a hardware-base standpoint, introduces a hybrid implementation that customers and vendors can integrate to address very specific business needs using both S/370 investments and PS/2 investments and flexibility. It is referred to as the "biprocessor."

At this writing, software for communicating between the PS/2 and S/370 across the Data Exchange Adapter using a very low-level interface (from DOS and OS/2) and an APPC Common Programming Interface from OS/2 to VM/SP is available. Because of the open nature of the systems, and since software involved additional operating systems, interfaces are expected to surface from software vendors and integrators.

MICRO CHANNEL 370 (370 MODELS)

- Use a S/370 processor and a 80386 microprocessor(s) to attach selected Micro Channel compatible input and output devices
- IBM software platforms include DPPX/370, VM/SP, and VSE/SP
- Remote power on and off
- Battery backup

MICRO CHANNEL 370 (BIPROCESSOR MODELS)

- Use a S/370 processor and a 80386 microprocessor(s) to attach selected Micro Channel compatible input and output devices
- Two separate systems within the same enclosure
    A S/370 using an 80386 microprocessor for I/O
    A PS/2 Model 80 equivalent system
- An optional Data Exchange Adapter is provided for communication between the S/370 and the PS/2 side
- Each side operates independently of the other
- IBM S/370 software platforms include DPPX/370, VM/SP, and VSE/SP
- IBM PS/2 supported platforms include DOS and OS/2
- Remote power on and off
- Battery backup

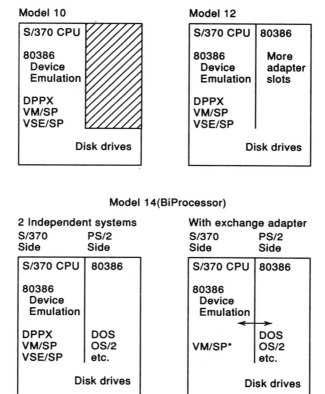

Figure 5.2 *IBM Micro Channel 370.*

It is too soon to tell how pervasive this S/370 and PS/2 hybrid will be, and which operating systems will be used, but the use of coprocessors shows a lot of promise in merging old system management rigors and investments with some newer end-user-oriented interfaces and facilities. Mixing technologies and platforms within the same box sounds appealing, as does the concept of an open S/370 that would allow one to plug in PC cards and drivers to support many of the exotic devices currently only available with PCs. Only time will tell if the hybrid requirement is addressed by a box packaging or with multiple boxes lashed together on a LAN, or connected to a MAN,[4] or connected via a WAN, or a combination of all of these.

[4]*MAN* refers to a *m*etropolitan *a*rea *n*etwork which extends the concepts of LANs out of buildings to substantially larger distances than *LANs* today. It differs from WANs (wide area networks), which refer to telecommunications connections for distances of many miles. The 802.6 MAN standard will accommodate data, digital voice, and compressed video and is designed to serve as a LAN/WAN gateway. Data rates between 45 to 600 Mbps are expected.

Both the S/370 only capable models and the BiProcessor system are being explored by many enterprises to provide a distributed system base that leverages their S/370 skills and investments, or simply to address a very specific application. Applications that have surfaced to date include implementations which replace and converge IBM S/1 investments, *LAN* systems management services, print servers, and interoperability gateways, as well as dedicated project or departmental systems for specific application or application or system development.

History tells us that all of the alternatives cited will surface. The volumes of low end system implementations, however, will be driven by IS or vendors with packaged solutions rather than by end users, primarily because most end users are not familiar with these systems beyond a terminal interface for the applications they currently use. Therefore, frontending of the S/390 facilities and services with the more pervasive personal computer interfaces and services is inevitable. IBMs SAA distributed model provides one such model. The placement of some of the S/390 capabilities is the question.

The discussions regarding low end S/370s and midrange S/390s in light of the applicability of the IBM AS/400 is equally a time-will-tell scenario. Again, the discussion is really not so much one of technology, since many of the hardware components on the rack-mounted ES/9000 models and the AS/400 are the same. In fact, the racks are almost identical. The difference has to do with the application to which these systems will be put; that will determine how they evolve.

The AS/400 is an application system, as its acronym implies. The AS/400's system base was designed with business applications in mind, relatively straightforward interfaces, and a very well integrated operating environment. It has integrated function, integrated relational data base, single level store, and is object oriented, with a very high-level machine interface. It is the successor to the S/3X, and most of their programs can be directly migrated. The strength of the AS/400 is the closed[5] nature of the system.

The S/390 on the other hand is an open[6] system, by design. As a result, many software implementations with varying design points can use the same architectural base and various software platforms and tools. Both systems are being pulled into each other's natural marketplace. The S/390 via such operating environments as MUMPS and PICK has demonstrated that it can be just as closed and easy to use as the AS/400. Similarly, the AS/400 environment is expanding to include SAA and OSI interfaces and LANs.

In general, a very important part of postulating where your systems platforms will go is determining who likes the system and how many of these supporters there are within your enterprise and industry. Additionally, how flexible are these supporters after they have become comfortable with a specific interface. Again, history has shown that those of us who are used to solving our business problems with tailored solutions will continue to pursue tailored solutions.

[5]*Closed* in this context means that the number of parameters, choices, interfaces, and components exposed to the programmer or user is controlled.
[6]*Open* in this context means that the S/390 exposes multiple levels of software interfaces from the very detailed exits in the operating system to the very high level of application interfaces.

Some will let others tailor the solutions and adjust the problems to the solutions available. This approach is usually appealing to those with small problems and have the primary attributes of quick installation and benefits. For more company-unique problems and systems that are woven into the business, open systems tend to address these requirements; however, these implementations tend to require longer lead times to design and integrate.

New applications on closed systems install quickly (usually in six-month time frames) gated by the cut-over logistics, and new application systems installed on open systems tend to have a cut-over cycle that approaches two years (obviously depending on scope). The difference is driven by the number of options that are addressed. In most cases, the open system will respond to change with more flexibility, assuming the analysis, design, and programming skill is available. Both systems address specific environments. The hardware is frequently not as important as the software platform that the application uses. Technically, however, the hardware does play a very important part in terms of support, reliability, availability, and life. Many S/370s continue to be used long after the normal five-year depreciation.

The S/390 is the open multi-user hardware system platform of both open and closed software platforms and continues to provide flexibility and support for those who have to tailor their solutions to their environment. Over time (many years), standards and architectural interfaces will converge a large portion of the platform interfaces, but the open requirements will not disappear. So where is the midrange S/390 going? From a hardware standpoint, the rack- and frame-mounted air-cooled systems have the same architectural functions as the liquid-cooled processors. From a software platform standpoint, more systems appear to be porting to S/390. How will S/390 be applied in a distributed environment? That's the substance of the rest of this book.

Section 2

What Every CIO Should Know about Distributing

This section is directed toward the information systems executive responsible for setting corporate and divisional systems directions, as well as the information systems management team responsible for implementing distributed solutions. The primary themes are that the evolution of technology is predictable and existing information systems experience, skills, and investments can be leveraged to provide near-in and long-range solutions.

The guidelines presented should assist the information executive in reviewing what has been done to date, in assessing the current state of the art, and in projecting durable solutions based on first-hand experiences.

The orientation is from a *S/390 information services (IS)* organization *frame of reference*. The *S/390* concepts are portrayed as consistent with the infracture of the glasshouse and its extensions. Using this frame of reference provides the information systems executive with insights that can be useful when selecting responsive and durable solutions.

Chapter 6

Distributed Solutions: Introduction

6.1 DISTRIBUTED: NOT NEW

Distributing computer power to solve business problems is *not new*. In fact, many large businesses have been using degrees of distributed computing for more than 20 years.

The *primary* business and technical *reason for distributing* is to provide *data* (and/or computation) *where* the ultimate *user needs it,* whether that user is a person or a machine. The objective is to provide this data as *rapidly, reliably,* and *inexpensively* as possible.

DISTRIBUTED SOLUTIONS

- Evolving
- Address responsiveness and flexibility
- Provide timely data
- Provide compute power where and when needed
- Address physical-distance-related delays
- Respond to organizational changes
- Protect existing investments
- Introduce interrelated systems
- Isolate user specifics from *the system*
- Require standards to grow

TABLE 6.1 Implementation Guidelines

- Distributed and decentralized implementations differ.
- User, departmental, and I/S owned systems can be strategic.
- Understand your implicit design points.
- Unattended and remote operations must be designed into the solution and are very difficult to add later.
- Use what you know and have; push from there.
- Sponsorship and implementation approach make the difference.
- A vision and comprehensive project plan are required.
- The application and five factors determine the platform(s).
- Connectivity provides far less function and requires far more expertise than expected.
- Interoperability and multiple standards are in the cards.
- Multiples require a fundamental change in detail and/or customizing.

From an executive viewpoint, the business challenges that various implementations address have essentially *remained the same*. While this assertion may appear significantly oversimplified, it is true. Organizations that recognize this are much quicker to successfully respond to change, since they understand which parameters will change, along with the consequences.

6.2 WHAT WORKS

The subsequent chapters of this section are structured around some basic guidelines (see Table 6.1) that were compiled from first-hand experience, project and installation reviews, and discussions with IS executives who have and/or are installing distributed systems. These guidelines are provided to help you *learn and benefit from the experience* gained by current distributed systems implementers.

These *guidelines* are often independent of specific hardware and software or vendor. The lessons learned come from companies using IBM solutions or a mix of IBM and other vendor solutions. The essence of the challenges is the placement of control(s) and services, the physical remoteness of resources, and dealing with multiples (installations) with minimal resources and expense.

Chapter *7*

Distributed and Decentralized Implementations Differ

7.1 TECHNOLOGY IS ORGANIZATIONALLY NEUTRAL

The ongoing and ever-increasing demand for responsiveness to business changes, organizational changes (decentralization and centralization), and the changing size of organizations,[1] combined with the affordability of personal computers and mini-systems and the resultant computer literacy, have merely increased the needs for both loosely and tightly integrated distributed implementations to address the challenge of providing a comprehensive solution. However, it is very important to separate distributed implementations from organizational decentralization, as Bruns and McFarland[2] point out:

> Technology is organizationally neutral. It does not favor centralization over decentralization. It simply offers top managers choices they have not had before.

In other words, management must decide what needs to be controlled, to what degree, and by whom, based on the business's needs. It is important to recognize that while the terms distributed and decentralized are frequently interchanged, they mean different things but are not mutually exclusive.

The terms centralized and decentralized apply to organizational control. Centralized is used when a single person (or organization) determines and controls.

---

[1]*Downsizing* is currently the term used for organizational size reductions as many organizations consolidate, reduce staff management, and put more responsibility in the hands of the line management.
[2]William J. Bruns, Jr., and F. Warren McFarland, "Information Technology Puts Power in Control Systems," *Harvard Business Review*, September–October 1987, No. 5, pp. 89–94.

VARIETIES OF DISTRIBUTION
CONTROLS

CENTRAL ◄ — — — — — — — — — — ► LOCAL

SUPPORT SKILLS
SOFTWARE SKILLS
ADMINISTRATION
DATA DEPENDENCIES
HARDWARE CONFIGURATION
BUDGET
SERVICE LEVEL RESPONSIBILITY
DATA ASSET RESPONSIBILITY

Figure 7.1 *Degrees of central and distributed control.*

Decentralized is applicable when organizations control themselves. Central and distributed refer to system configurations and the placement of different aspects of a service.

For example, the label "central system" is used to refer to one computer being used, i.e., shared by various organizations. This computer can support applications that have been developed by different, unrelated organizations sharing some physical resources. A time-sharing service is a good example; it is a central configuration supporting a decentralized management style since it is used by various customers.

On the other end of the spectrum, multiple physically distributed systems can be centrally managed both from an organizational and resource standpoint. This book focuses on the physical (configuration) aspects (central and distributed) of dealing with interconnections of business applications and the ramifications of the using and providing organizations' approach to control.

It is important to recognize that there are degrees of distribution and centralization with regard to system ownership, management, and support. Consider a sample spectrum depicted in Figure 7.1. I have used the label "local" to refer to distributed from the central organization's control. The point being made is that the various activities and responsibilities can either be centralized or decentralized in any combination, while the configuration can be either "central" or "distributed."

In other words, conversations regarding control approaches need to move beyond simple labels such as centralized and distributed when discussing implementations. This is especially true when dealing with companies that provide interenterprise services, such as insurance companies to agencies and banks to member banks, etc. In these situations, the control approach may depend on the degree of support the outside company wants or is willing to delegate to the service provider.

7.2 PICK YOUR RUT CAREFULLY!

While the degree of control can readily shift with business needs, the same is not necessarily true for systems. A mistake made when selecting a *distributed* or *centralized system model* or *architecture* can become a serious inhibitor to the company's ability to respond to business and organizational needs in a timely manner. For example, a totally centralized system model and implementation can become a bottleneck due to the serialization of priorities and controls; remember, the support and development structure is a significant portion of the system.

This serialization often results in lack of responsiveness and can significantly *retard* the company's *ability to grow*. In some cases it may be the primary contributor to loss of a company's *market share*. Similarly, a totally autonomous distributed model may provide the immediate responsiveness to meet each organization's requirements today, but the implementation may have an inherent break point in the management controls flexibility or scalability.

These problems are very real, as witnessed by national media coverage about companies that fail to achieve their business objectives (or worse) because of an inability to process orders. This even happened to several major high-technology companies in the computer industry!

The system-model selection dilemma between the two approaches frustrates many implementors.

The use of a centralized system model has traditionally provided the most control. However, the management of this model (aside from any hardware or software) and its surrounding bureaucracy can thwart responsiveness, as the company's dependency on information processing grows—especially if the support organization doesn't respond to the changes. Similarly, if the underlying application-system design approach assumes the centralized model, it can be very difficult to distribute later.

The use of a standalone distributed systems model (e.g., departmental systems) provides the much desired autonomy and the ability to throw out old systems and replace them with fresh, new, off-the-shelf[3] applications. Each system owner becomes the control point. These systems are not typically designed to be integrated into a corporate model. In fact, the very reason for their simplicity is the reduction of all the considerations that an enterprise-based system has to consider to accommodate integration. Integrating or managing these systems from central in an economical manner may prove to be very difficult.

DISTRIBUTED SYSTEMS OR CENTRALIZED SYSTEMS?

- Both have pros and cons
- Both have distinct design considerations
- Distributed systems can be managed centrally
- Centralized systems can support decentralized organizations
- Distributed does not equal decentralized
- Distributed systems can be easily centralized
- Systems designed to be centralized are difficult to distribute

---

[3]*Off-the-shelf applications* is a term used to describe functionally complete applications that can be purchased. In the PC environment, many off-the-shelf applications such as spreadsheets, word processors, and desk top publishers—are really tools.

Chapter *8*

User, Department, and IS-owned Systems Can Be Strategic

The design and ownership of systems[1] by individual users and departments are becoming very important aspects of the enterprise's information strategy. This is happening by natural evolution or by plan, as users, departments, and IS management recognize they can't and perhaps shouldn't do it all. However, there are some significant short- and longer-range exposures that must be considered as these mixed-owner systems are selected, grow, and interface with the enterprise's information system.

This evolution appears to follow a specific pattern that can be anticipated by the information systems strategist. The most resilient enterprise solutions will involve delegation of some control by all involved. The challenge is to recognize which controls can and should be delegated and under what circumstances.

In order to discuss these system ownership considerations, I will focus on the applications rather than the hardware or even the operating systems. Applications can be separated into the categories of control systems and user systems. Each plays a significant role in the enterprise's information strategy, either by plan or by accident. Many of the growing pains can be reduced if the information systems management recognizes which applications are user systems and which are control systems, and where they overlap. Consider Figure 8.1.

---

[1]*System* in this usage implies the systematizing of steps and functions to provide a complete application. For example, a spreadsheet tool is not a system unless it is surrounded by a process with some well-defined inputs and outputs and appropriate controls.

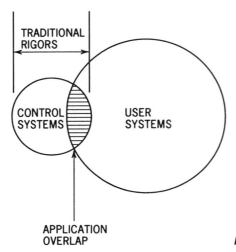

Figure 8.1 *User and control system overlaps.*

8.1 CONTROL SYSTEMS

Control systems are those application systems that are fundamental to running the business. These application systems are known by a variety of names ranging from *production systems* to *boiler room* or *backroom* operations to more current terms such as *mission-critical* applications. Sometimes they are simply referred to as online transaction processing systems or batch systems. Without these systems the business doesn't function.

In many cases, these systems operate so smoothly that they are taken for granted and we expect them to be there just as we expect the room to brighten when we flick the light switch on in our office. These applications very accurately keep track of inventory, checking accounts, money, policies, etc. They have extremely rigorous controls built into them to ensure accuracy, dependability, and the ability to audit. These applications are the result of years of testing and analysis.

The system platforms and the support structure have become implicit corequisites of these applications. Similarly, the other applications rely on the data (with implicit attributes), as do the users who know what the data means and how it can be used. These applications are designed around very well-entrenched interfaces to operating system services and user interfaces.[2] Unless these applications were designed for portability it is very difficult to open them up and alter the fundamental user- and operating-services interfaces.

A significant portion of the currently installed IBM S/390 application systems fall into the control systems category. It is estimated that there are around 100 billion lines of third-generation language code associated with these systems

---

[2]Many S/390 applications user interfaces have been designed for the IBM 3270 display interfaces, and application programs tend to align with the operation of specific interfaces.

(mostly on-line transaction processing applications). Estimated worth? $2 trillion. These implementations will be with us for many years to come.

8.2 USER SYSTEMS

User systems are characterized as applications that can be self-contained and do not or *will not* require the rigors and controls imposed on control systems. This is possible for use support systems which do not interface with host control systems as well as for user mission-critical applications that can be managed locally. The ability of the user organization to support these systems is really independent of the hardware on which the system is installed, although the hardware and operating system can dictate its viability (or survival) as a user or control system. Using today's technology, many individuals and departments have implemented applications on there own hardware and some have built networks of applications that appear to fall into the user system category, if by no other criteria than ownership and control.

Terms like *user application, departmental systems,* or *front-end applications* are often used to describe these applications. This type of implementation becomes popular as the technology and affordability makes the option available to the department or the average person. These user systems are where the sizzle and glamour are, not only because of the technologies being used, but also since such systems are involved with very specific aspects of the business and tend to have a quick implementation cycle.

Key areas of focus are ease of use, exciting interfaces, user customization, and user control. These systems are characterized as timely, easy-to-install, pragmatic solutions to business problems—especially the end users' business problems.

User systems include the spectrum of applications built upon simple spreadsheets to complete business systems packages that cover order entry, inventory, through billing applications. Many individuals and departments that have installed systems designed as user systems to be control systems. As their sophistication with applications increase, they become aware of the manually intensive administrative controls required to deal with increased users, data backup and recovery, and adding additional functions, facilities that are usually fundamental to control systems.

For example, relational data base systems (products) are readily available for users to implement their applications. Data backup and recovery facilities vary in both capability and complexity. Probably the easiest approach is to have a backup copy and to fall back on it when a data problem occurs. The recovery step is to re-enter the work since the last backup, assuming there is a log or the input is recreatable. Sometimes it takes such an incident to discover that the capability to log exists but was not enabled.

Other approaches include patching the area that has the damage and having an application utility fix it and then manually note and flag an audit trail. More rudimentary "fixes" include a manual override, literally ignoring the problem. Probably the most comprehensive approach is to have a combination of backup copies, a log of all changes since the backup and fix utilities. Picking a system that doesn't log changes and doesn't have a forward-apply capability substantially increases the frequency that a backup is done. This increases the need to provide a backup management system with lots of interventions. Understanding which types of data problems can occur is also part of the solution selection process.

Considerations include questions such as: will the majority of failures occur because of storage media failures or because of data errors resulting from program or systems problems. Again there trade-offs as a consequence of the choice. Having a system (software or hardware) that creates duplicate copies of the data reduces the exposure to media-related problems surfacing in the application, but it does nothing for program-related problems.

Similarly, if multiple problems occur, the solutions get even more confusing. The thing to keep in mind is that these complexities typically occur as the volume of activity and the number of users increases. Well-designed user systems have reduced the complexity by establishing design points that match the skill and time that the user is willing to invest. There are thresholds where these design points are exceeded and dissatisfaction and exposures occur.

The simple question that I would ask to distinguish whether a particular application system can evolve into a control system is, can it scale? That is, can the application grow with volume? Are the necessary interfaces available? Can this application and operation be managed by someone other than the user? This obviously requires some experience with the relevant considerations.

8.3   NEW SYSTEMS OR INTERRELATED SYSTEMS

Many existing control systems are typically not as easy to upgrade to a newer technology as quickly as desired if more than installing faster or larger systems is involved. The group that starts from scratch very typically has the "spiffier" or more eye-catching exploitation of the newer technologies. This is a reality that has many information systems executives losing a lot of sleep. The media hype suggesting that "the company using the newest technology wins," use such powerful terms as "strategic weapons" for applications that employ the latest widget. The stories, often implying that those companies not using the newest technology will be less successful, has even the more-confident decisionmakers doubting their solutions. The less-confident are often left in an evaluation loop.

The fact of the matter is that today's newest is tomorrow's old! However, "old technology" will probably provide a viable solution for many years. This is especially true if the application is complex.

I remember my first initiation to this sobering realization. My first assignment with IBM was to work on the Federal Aviation Administration (FAA) Air Traffic Control system in 1970. This system, which used four modified IBM S/360 Model 65s lashed together using four IBM S/360 Model 50s as channels, was especially designed and customized to handle very critical flight tracking. It had special instructions to deal with tracking and was designed for fault tolerance. By the time I was involved, hundreds of worker-years worth of effort had been expended in designing the hardware and software for this very critical application. There had literally been hundreds of new hardware and software techniques applied. The first fully configured system shipped late 1970.

In mid 1971 I read an article in a popular trade journal that challenged the FAA's judgment in selecting the S/360 base since the S/370 had recently been announced! I recently read that this customized S/360 system is still operating at some control centers 25 years later!

The point is rather basic; if the proper design work and solid base are provided, a quality, durable solution is achievable. Perhaps equally important is the recognition that a system is substantially more than a single hardware or software component.

8.3.1 Using Newer Technologies Can Be Tough

Companies embracing the exploitation of newer technologies have traditionally been faced with a rather limited set of alternatives and pressures. The spectrum extended from encouraging their hardware and software vendor(s) to provide new technology while preserving existing environments and interfaces for designing and implementing a replacement system.

The preserving of environment approach has worked for many companies, but because of the design of their application they are faced with having to change applications to exploit the new technology. Sometimes the application changes are more expensive than just the use of brute force via a more powerful hardware system. There are still many emulated systems running on newer equipment.

Designing and building a replacement application is even more difficult because the company typically has to take on more work than the maintenance of the old and the development of the new. The existing system must be maintained to meet the requirements until the new system is cut over. The new system must be updated to stay current with the old system. A conversion is required. Options include freezing the old system. The viability of this option is usually a function of the size and timing of the new system. In either case, critical resources are diverted from other projects or less-important user requirements are postponed due to priorities.

Most large companies do not have the option to start from scratch or extensively redesign their existing inventory of control systems. Writing new applications, despite substantial improvements in programming technologies, is still very expensive and takes a long time. This is especially true for durable solutions. In many cases, the existing applications are the only knowledge base of company policies and exception conditions for particular types of transactions; the analysts having long ago gone on to other positions or retired. Redesigning existing applications is equally difficult, since many of the existing applications are too brittle. Some, in fact, are over 20 years old.

8.3.2 Spreading Out the Workload

The recent viability of users and departments addressing some of the immediate information processing needs together with some organizational responsibility shifts downward have reintroduced[3] the viability of introducing new technologies and systems more rapidly than before. These end user solutions tend to exploit the touch and feel of the personal computer and other character and bit-oriented work stations, and have reduced the definition of the application to be the usage of some canned packages[4] of user oriented software tools.

This shift of responsibility has also reintroduced the same exposures. Critics of user system solutions point out that they are much more narrowly focused and generally not built with the rigor required to build control systems. The critics go on to add that user systems are frequently exposed in security and asset protection (data backup) disciplines. The latter two items are probably as much of an administrative rigor[5] statement as they are a hardware and software application concern. The same critics assert that the approaches being used to implement user systems have left out of the development and implementation cycle those items that give rise to the perception of excessive cost and unresponsiveness of traditional systems: the analysis, design, documentation, testing, integration, implementation, education, administration, and control aspects.

Allowing professionals unskilled in information systems to select and implement comprehensive and durable solutions may be very risky for an enterprise. To many, the activities of unskilled professionals is viewed as a ticking time bomb. To others, it is a risk they are willing to take based on the immediate benefits and the position of the competition. Unfortunately, this choice between IS-developed or user-developed solutions may be de facto if the enterprise's information strategists and implementors aren't responsive to the daily business requirements. I have noted that there are more user systems than control systems. Whether we like it or not, user systems will set the pace unless the enterprise information systems organization provides better and equally responsive solutions to the same problem.

8.3.3 Your, Mine, and Our Systems

Several companies have addressed this dilemma and kept, gained, or regained informational control by embracing both the user systems and control systems approach. This included keeping the appropriate systems apart and focusing on those areas where they overlap and those applications that need control.[6]

In other words, viable solutions are coming from an approach that marries the existing investments, rigors, and application cultures with newer technologies and

[3]I say reintroduced because in the early 1970s many insurance companies had line-of-business computer centers, each addressing their specific line of business with their own staffs. Many of these separate systems became integrated with the introduction of centralized data based systems.

[4]*Canned packages* is an expression used to describe a packaged solution that is ready to use as a complete solution, versus a set of components that the user has to integrate.

[5]In many cases the implementers of user systems have not understood the need to secure their programs and data and regularly backup their data until a problem is encountered. I/S organizations typically provide these types of services as part of their service.

[6]There is no reason that a user or department should not own and drive a control system, but they must be made aware of and accept the responsibilities that go with that system.

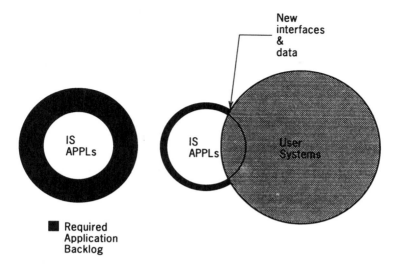

Figure 8.2 *Traditional application ownership versus incorporating user systems.*

people interfaces (see Figure 8.2). Hence, these systems are sometimes referred to as front-end applications since they are literally in front of the control system. Others use the terms cooperative processing, interoperability, and interconnectivity. I tend to use the term *distributed* or *distributed computing* to describe the broad spectrum of providing degrees of local autonomy for computing.

A marriage of user systems and control systems requires management insight and flexibility to *control that which needs to be controlled by central* and to *support* operations and applications *that don't need control.* This has been recognized by many information technologists,[7,8] but only the most progressive companies appear to have built upon such knowledge. Some advocates of loosening the controls have gone so far as to suggest that CIO candidates should be chosen from among the executives with telecommunications backgrounds, since they have the experience at interconnecting:

> most effective way to oversee a company's computer resources is to relinquish control of them and instead focus on the networks that connect them.[9]

Others are even suggesting that the CIO is really a network manager who facilitates interoperability.[10] This is a far cry from the CIO's traditional primary focus on control of the data and its use.

---

[7]Clinton Wilder, "Gaining Control by Dispersing It," *Computerworld,* May 1989, pp. 80–81.
[8]"Dropping Walls and Building New Identities," *Computerworld,* January 23, 1989, pp. 65–68.
[9]Byron Belitos, "Telecomm & I/S Worlds Converge," *Computer Decisions,* March 1989, pp. 61–64.
[10]John J. Donovan, "Beyond Chief Information Officer to Network Manager," *Harvard Business Review,* September–October 1988, pp. 134–140.

Those organizations that have loosened the control exploit their existing control system investments while opening up those applications that don't require the central administrative rigors and controls (see Figure 8.2). Those who use this approach recognize that there are more of them (departments and users willing to solve business problems using computers) than there are of IS (the formal IS organization applications-development folks).

In short, by sanctioning and supporting user efforts, more people are put on the job of using technology in parallel to solve a variety of business problems but not competing for IS resource or IS budget. A key element in making the interrelationship between users and IS work effectively is the program and data interface that drives the requirements for interconnection and interoperability standards and guidelines.

8.3.3.1 Give Some. For some enterprises this means giving up some central applications to newer departmental solutions. IS organizations in some companies have recommended that their branches install IBM AS/400s with some industry-specific applications to address their local needs and then focus on enabling the network to allow the user to pass through to the S/390 host-based applications. Others are exploring using *LANs* and customized personal computer solutions.

For other enterprises it means officially recognizing some of the renegade systems as legitimate strategic applications and providing education, consultation, and support.

Some of the user systems being implemented are beginning to take on the implementation duration of the traditional control systems. A survey* of twenty-nine applications that were built with personal computer components and software indicated that the development period ranged from 60 hours to six years. More than three of these applications had a two-year or greater development duration. The applications covered a broad spectrum of data based oriented applications ranging from specific applications, such as corporate travel reporting to dental office management, and full range accounting systems.

*"Case Studies," *Data Base Advisor,* September 1989, pp. 65–147.

8.3.3.2 Take Some. In some cases the marriage means that IS must become more involved with some user system applications in order to assure that the control aspects are understood and the interconnections are anticipated. An initial step taken by some enterprises has been to apply some new lines on the organization chart. They have the user department folks who support the user systems at a specific location report to the IS organization via either solid or dotted lines.[11] This, while not addressing a technical problem, is the first and probably least disruptive or

---

[11]*Solid line* reporting refers to direct reporting in terms of mission and personal, while *dotted line* refers to mission reporting and personnel reporting is with a different organization.

controversial step to affecting the marriage between the user systems and control systems.

What is probably even more interesting is that in most cases the departments are emotionally ready to make this organizational change. Given the mission of being accountable for information services locally, these organizations tend to focus on service level (availability) and data control (both software and business data). You will recognize these issues by the discussions regarding outage and recovery, software distribution data backup, server-based libraries,[12] and diskless workstations.[13]

8.4 USER SYSTEM OWNERS NEED AND WANT I/S HELP

There appear to be four primary reasons that user systems owners are looking for help: corporate data access, administrative, product evaluation, and most recently communications expenses.

In most of these cases the momentum is economical; the cost of skills or resources and risk exposure has the owners looking for help, but not necessarily interested in giving up application control.

8.4.1 Corporate Data Access

As user systems evolve, their owner's sophistication in understanding the capabilities of electronic information increases. They begin to focus more on productivity and look for alternatives to re-entering data manually into their systems when it could be directly input from some IS-managed data and applications. The next step for these organizations in their evolution to interrelated systems is to address interapplication communications, security, data access rules, and intersystem operability.

This evolution tracks very closely to the three stages of end user distributed[14] growth that I noticed in 1979 (see Figure 8.3), which was extrapolated from initial observations of minisystems evolution and with Richard Nolan's six stages of EDP growth (central).[15]

8.4.1.1 Interfacing versus Integration. It appears that many enterprises with autonomous distributed solutions are in or at the end third User Solution Stage, interfacing, which aligns with Nolan's Data Processing Stage IV, integration. The primary difference between the two is the degree of control required.

---

[12]*Server-based libraries* refers to an approach that has all workstation users share a common program library for the common applications. This could include a copy of the underlying operating system(s).
[13]*Diskless workstations* refers to PCs that essentially don't have any disks. There are several approaches. Some workstations just don't have any removable media, while other implementations use servers for all data storage.
[14]Kurt Ziegler, "Languages in a Distributed Environment," *GUIDE 48*, 1979, pp. 40–51.
[15]Richard L. Nolan, "Restructuring the Data Processing Organization for Data Resource Management," proceedings of *IFIP '77*, August 1977, pp. 261–265.

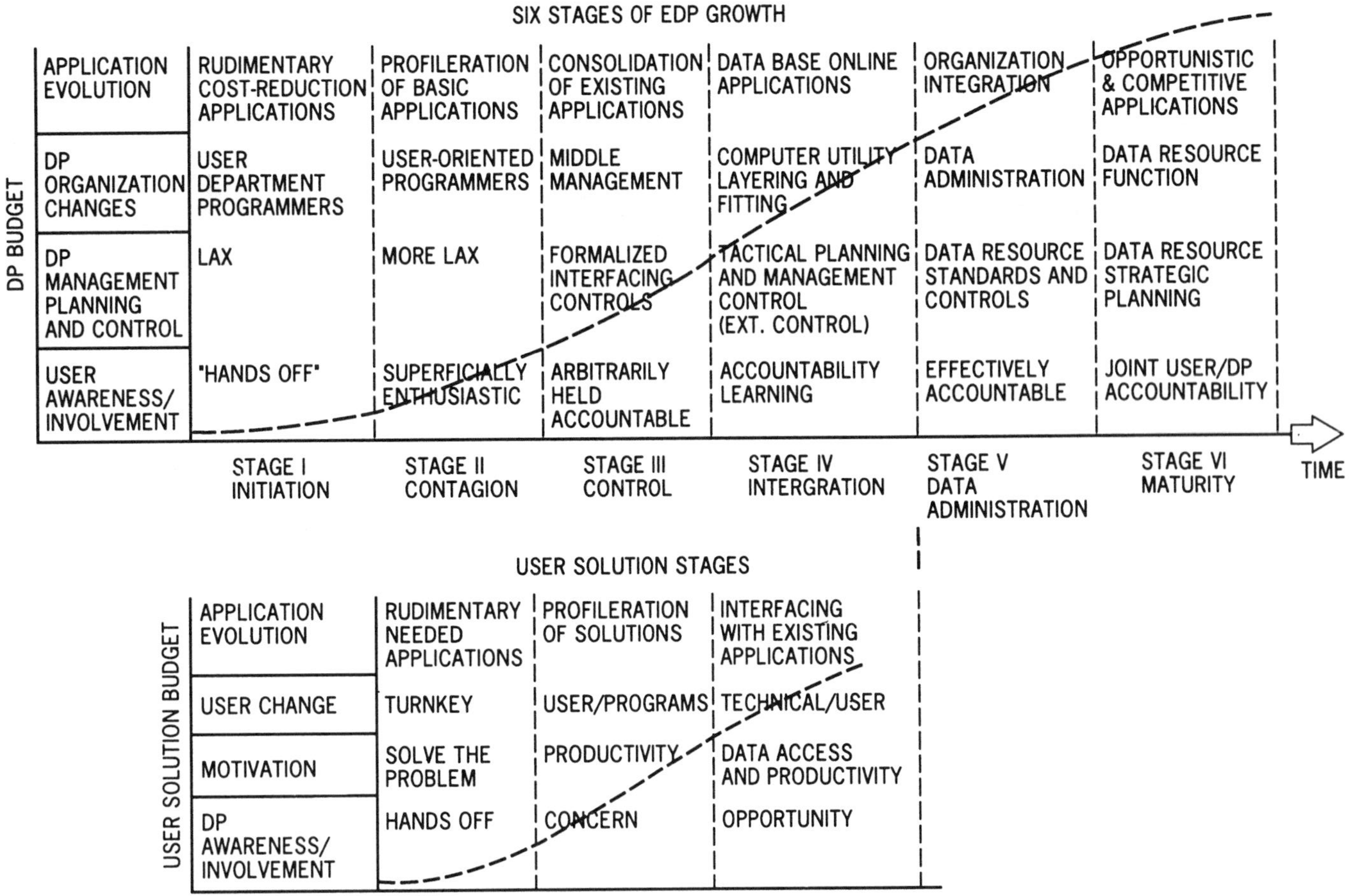

SIX STAGES OF EDP GROWTH

DP BUDGET	STAGE I INITIATION	STAGE II CONTAGION	STAGE III CONTROL	STAGE IV INTERGRATION	STAGE V DATA ADMINISTRATION	STAGE VI MATURITY
APPLICATION EVOLUTION	RUDIMENTARY COST-REDUCTION APPLICATIONS	PROFILERATION OF BASIC APPLICATIONS	CONSOLIDATION OF EXISTING APPLICATIONS	DATA BASE ONLINE APPLICATIONS	ORGANIZATION INTEGRATION	OPPORTUNISTIC & COMPETITIVE APPLICATIONS
DP ORGANIZATION CHANGES	USER DEPARTMENT PROGRAMMERS	USER-ORIENTED PROGRAMMERS	MIDDLE MANAGEMENT	COMPUTER UTILITY LAYERING AND FITTING	DATA ADMINISTRATION	DATA RESOURCE FUNCTION
DP MANAGEMENT PLANNING AND CONTROL	LAX	MORE LAX	FORMALIZED INTERFACING CONTROLS	TACTICAL PLANNING AND MANAGEMENT CONTROL (EXT. CONTROL)	DATA RESOURCE STANDARDS AND CONTROLS	DATA RESOURCE STRATEGIC PLANNING
USER AWARENESS/INVOLVEMENT	"HANDS OFF"	SUPERFICIALLY ENTHUSIASTIC	ARBITRARILY HELD ACCOUNTABLE	ACCOUNTABILITY LEARNING	EFFECTIVELY ACCOUNTABLE	JOINT USER/DP ACCOUNTABILITY

USER SOLUTION STAGES

USER SOLUTION BUDGET			
APPLICATION EVOLUTION	RUDIMENTARY NEEDED APPLICATIONS	PROFILERATION OF SOLUTIONS	INTERFACING WITH EXISTING APPLICATIONS
USER CHANGE	TURNKEY	USER/PROGRAMS	TECHNICAL/USER
MOTIVATION	SOLVE THE PROBLEM	PRODUCTIVITY	DATA ACCESS AND PRODUCTIVITY
DP AWARENESS/INVOLVEMENT	HANDS OFF	CONCERN	OPPORTUNITY

TIME

Figure 8.3 Stages of distributed systems growth.

Integration requires substantially more control than does interfacing. However, since the bulk of the corporate data is managed by IS and resides on hosts, interfacing with any degree of sophistication—other than mapping to terminal screens—requires IS permission and expertise if data integrity is to be assured. Ergo, the next User Solution Stage will be a combination of the data administration and data resource function with joint accountability (a combination of Nolan's Stage V and VI). For some enterprises the user-owned systems have grown into control systems, and as a result they are having to be integrated into the existing control system.

This integration is a very touchy effort unless the control responsibilities have been clearly identified, articulated, and agreed to. Integration requires a single controlling party to assure application and data integrity is achieved, while interfacing requires only data integrity control and is usually provided via a documented format that are used selectively rather than anyone being placed in control to assure compliance. This distinction is often missed until well into a project implementation, causing confusion to the user.

For simplicity, I characterize the difference between the two as data access (interface) versus data management (integrated). User systems prefer data access over data management implementations because data management implies more integration. Client-server implementations frequently address the interface requirements until more control is required.

8.4.1.2 *Data Access and Data Management Differ.* Most user- and control-systems users would like to have a data interface that allows a query or data request to access data independently of where they are. Not only do these individuals want to *access* this data, they would like this access to be totally *transparent* to the requestor. In other words, the requestor wishes to be unaware of the data's location and that the data is distributed. Much of the current user system focus is on relational databases, since these data systems have an open interface and they appear to be easier to distribute. They have the potential to provide dynamic optimization of queries rather than more unneeded data back and forth.

Various products, both provided by IBM and other vendors, provide degrees of access to distributed data. However, these products currently all fall short of providing this access and update transparently without restrictions. Most vendors offer distributed queries with limited update capability. While there is much disagreement as to what constitutes a distributed data base, transparency appears to be the one theme the products all have in common.[16,17,18] The primary transparent access challenges are associated with:

- *Data Location Transparency:* The ability to access data without knowing where the data resides or the system (operating system) upon which it resides

[16]John Mahnke, "Distributed Database Technology to Drive DBMS Mart Upward," *MIS Week*, February 27, 1989, p. 36.
[17]Robert Holbrook, "Distributed RDBMSs Put Opportunities Online," *Business Software Review*, June 1988, pp. 46–53.
[18]Jean S. Bozman, "Distributed DBMS Means Cost, Trouble," *Computerworld*, February 13, 1989, pp. 25, 33.

- *Response Time:* The level of transparency in terms of response time, which typically is affected by the location(s) involved and the bandwidth of the network path
- *Multiple Location Data Update:* The ability to reflect current data at multiple locations while retaining data integrity for work in progress along with reasonable response time for other users of the data
- *Administration:* The ability to administer access rules and security while retaining referential integrity at all affected locations

For the most part, these attributes align themselves more closely with the management and control trade-offs implemented with a control system than with a user system.

At the time of this writing there are no commercially distributed data base management systems that I am aware of that generally addresses all of the above-mentioned items. Although there are several systems that appear to address many of the checklisted items, they are still very fragile as the application usage increases. General solutions will be forthcoming over the next five years. The most prevalent distributed relational data base implementations today work best when read only extracts of a central data base which are updated from central on specified cycles. These are managed (or administered) via copy management[19] techniques.

Independent of the application software interface, other challenges still in their infancy include the provision of *data base design tools* that address response time, data integrity, data synchronization, resource consumption, and data placement. Most of the tools in this area are in the form of guidelines, checklists, and methodologies.

For the most part, real-time, update-oriented operational business data base transactions are still accomplished via a transaction manager (control system), which manages the entire transaction. Probably the most functionally comprehensive and used transaction manager capable of managed distributed data access in the S/390 family is IBM's Customer Information Control System (CICS). It aligns very nicely with the list of requirements associated with distributed data bases for CICS-managed data bases such as IBM's DL/I, and provides a Virtual Storage Access Method (VSAM)-based file system. There are literally hundreds of such distributed implementations today.[20]

8.4.2 Administration

As the need for data has increased, it has caused user system owners to work more closely with IS and to increase their understanding of control systems and user systems. The user systems owners are also beginning to appreciate the amount of time and on-demand skill that is required to provide the service they expect and to protect the assets for which they are accountable.

---

[19]*Copy management* is a catchall term to refer to the approach and administration associated with preparation of multiple copies of data segmented and synchronized to support multiple distributed users.
[20]Elisabeth Horwitt, "Bank Builds Own Distributed Data Base," *Computerworld*, April 20, 1987.

ADMINISTRATION OF ASSETS/RESOURCES

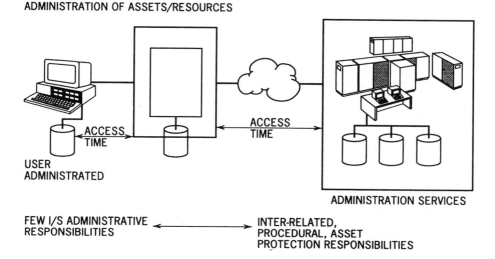

USER
ADMINISTRATED

ADMINISTRATION SERVICES

FEW I/S ADMINISTRATIVE ⟷ INTER-RELATED,
RESPONSIBILITIES PROCEDURAL, ASSET
PROTECTION RESPONSIBILITIES

Figure 8.4 *Administration.*

These owners are now looking for ways to support these needs from remote locations and purchase expertise on demand. The original idea was to improve the productiveness and responsiveness of the worker. This administrative time is becoming very apparent as the sophistication of the personal computer or departmental system increases. As the administrative time[21] consumed and risk of loss or corruption of data increases, some user system owners are gravitating back to IS help in the hopes of delegating certain administrative tasks (see Figure 8.4).

One such administration aspect that has recently surfaced has to do with locating objects.[22] For example, how does one find a specific engineering drawing? Who has it checked out? Is it being updated? If one provides this type of service at a LAN level, who provides the next level in the hierarchy? The same is applicable for documents, letters, etc. As user systems' inventory of objects increases, in terms of the objects currently accessed as well as those aged and archived, the user system solutions tend to stretch and break under the sheer volume and exceptions. Again, this requires some delegation to a control system that supports the user systems.

8.4.3 Product Evaluation

Probably one of the biggest challenges that is faced by the owner of user systems is selection of a basic platform.

After the initial selection of the hardware base, e.g., PC, AT, PS/2s, MAC, etc., comes the selection of the operating system—DOS or OS/2 for PS/2s, VM or VSE

---

[21]Time spent on care and feeding of the personal computer or departmental system, and not spent on business transactions.

[22]*Object* is a term being used to identify a labelled entity such as a program, file, document, or even information about another object.

for S/390s, etc. (Sometimes a platform such as the AS/400 is the most straightforward choice because it provides a single hardware and software platform.) Part of the evaluation must consider the expected equipment life and its ability to grow with needs.

The selection of platforms includes assessing the communications capabilities that the platform supports—communication with existing devices and systems, as well as its openness to additions. The focus is usually on which individual personal workstations will communicate with one another, communicate to the host, and share resources.

The next step includes evaluating the myriad of tools that enhance the operation, the capacity, the performance, the data backup, and the data compaction. This choice process is initially rather simple since the specific application tends to pinpoint the minimum hardware and software requirements. As users' sophistication and demands increase, they typically want to add applications and tools. This is where the fun really begins and the user or department begins the trade-off process of deciding what can coreside, what else is needed, which vendors' solution is most appropriate, and whether to choose an open, closed, or proprietary system. All this is often confusing and can be overwhelming to the untrained selector.

While the platform, communication, and tool selection process may be complex, the choice may not be nearly as risky as that for the application itself. The assessment of features may be trivial when compared to the analysis of underlying techniques used to provide the simple and easy-to-use solution at low cost. (We'll look at some of these considerations shortly as part of the design point discussion in Chapter 9.)

In short, this selection process can easily require outside help and experience.

8.4.4 Communication Expenses

Attention has also recently moved to the communication costs associated with the recent increase in the electronic exchange of data, programs, and mail among distributed users. While in many cases existing lines and networks are already present at the locations for terminal access, the new user systems grew up around, rather than using, these resources. The increase in number of user-leased lines and long distance dial-up expense has many companies reexamining how the user systems may use the existing lines on a shared basis.

A company I visited recently had just discovered that it had no fewer than six dedicated leased lines almost paralleling each other between New York and Los Angeles when it was pointed out that an existing backbone network tail circuit[23] (a seventh circuit) was available and very lightly used. This was very disconcerting even though the response time was excellent, because the costs were excessive even with the new fractional T1 tariffs. Even more disconcerting was that this was to become only the tip of the iceberg in terms of redundant lines. They followed up by

---

[23]*Tail circuit* refers to the point-to-point line between the backbone network and the local resource entry point.

evaluating line consolidation options using SNA gateways but couldn't get the necessary support software without upgrading multiple systems.

USER, DEPARTMENTAL, AND I/S SYSTEMS REQUIRED

- Reduced I/S application backlog
- Address bounded problems
- Interfaces must be understood
- Can coexist, can interface, can sometimes replace
- I/S skills required with application sophistication
- User systems are following a predictable path

Chapter 9

Understand Your Implicit Design Points

9.1 WHO IS WATCHING YOUR DESIGN POINTS?

Most executives recognize that the system is a key cog in the enterprise's ability to deliver product and grow. The system encompasses the hardware, software, connections, procedures, administration and composite usage attributes. Many companies have appointed a *chief information systems strategist* to focus on identifying exposed areas and addressing them while facilitating the tools and technologies to respond to current business needs.

The chief information systems strategist's challenge is to select a *durable solution*. Durable means that the solution will remain competitive and flexible long enough to recover the equipment and application investments. The plans must also allow sufficient resource and budget to pursue strategic requirements as well as to respond to late-breaking demands.

The strategist has to accomplish this in light of rapid business and organizational changes and must have the flexibility to change direction while recognizing the substantial investments already expended for training, applications, and hardware. He or she must also be willing to be open to the ongoing introduction of newer technologies, which promise more economical solutions. He or she also has to determine whether the newer technologies can address the total problem by themselves or if they are best suited for a specific portion of the problem.

The high-level test criteria include: control approach, location(s) of solution placement, benefits, costs, the cost of displacing the existing solution, and the cost of maintaining the old and new solutions. In many cases, the size of the existing application investment and the cost of changing it may determine the technical implementation options. Sometimes it is possible to replace a major system with a new solution before it has paid for itself, but such decisions tend to be very painful and usually come from a new management team unless a very major change has occurred to rationalize differing from the previous decision.

This chapter discusses some of the key technical considerations that I have encountered specifically when analyzing designs where distributed solutions would fit or are being considered. The three areas focused on are weak link analysis, work and data placement considerations, and platform product considerations. In most cases, it is important to understand your design points (or breakpoints) so that you can consciously make a risk assessment and decision based on the trade-offs.

9.2 WHERE ARE THE EXPOSURES?

For most designs, system breakpoints can be identified and the exposures minimized by identifying those that would put your business at risk and by testing the designs of your application and computing system platforms against your expectations. Recent American industries' focus on quality and the applications of techniques used for quality analysis and correction such as "Ishikawa charts"[1] apply here.

The first step is to identify the business-critical applications and document the business assumptions. Traditional information systems analysis and design techniques can then be applied to identify the sensitive areas in your application systems. The insights that answering such high-level questions can produce are sometimes very surprising.

- What data do you need to operate (to process orders, ship, bill, etc.)?
- What data is critical for decisions?
- What sensitivity do your systems have to business volumes doubling? Tripling?
- How long can an application be unavailable to some portion of the business?
- How long would it take to alter the application system to address any of the stress points identified?
- What triggering mechanisms are in place to identify the needs for change?

The answers that are often articulated concern business volumes, organization, product shifts, skills, and technologies. Fundamental to these are basic assumptions about the availability of application systems, access to data, the timeliness (currency) of the data, and the security of the data. A good test is to change some of the assumptions and use sensitivity analysis.

Sensitivity analysis is a label used to describe an approach that alters assumptions and highlights the impact of the change. If the change could substantially impact the business, a sensitive area has been found. Obviously, these sensitive areas must be assessed for risk and kept secret until resolved since, in the wrong hands, this information could be very damaging.

---

[1]A diagramming technique named after Dr. Kaoru Ishikawa considered to be the father of Quality Control Circles. The chart is also referred to as a fishbone chart used to analyze cause and effect.

Many of these sensitive areas can be mapped to your application system's design points. Design points (perhaps sometimes more appropriately referred to as breaking points or bottlenecks) are often hidden from analysts unless the work flows, the system connectivity, and the implicit support structure are understood. It certainly helps to have an understanding of the fundamental system components that extend beyond the technical. The user paradigms[2] may be as important as any of the technical aspects. Consider the scenario in the "A conflict in paradigms?" example.

A CONFLICT IN PARADIGMS?

A project to implement a major accounts-payable system had been discussed for several years. The date for cutover was driven by the existing system's inability to cope with the volumes. The volume design point would be reached within 12 months. The financial vice president in charge commissioned the work.

A specialty team was selected. The user team was led by a very aggressive and competent manager from that community. Original sizings of this project by previous teams were in the two-to-three-year durations to cut-over. None of the existing implementation was salvageable. The original developers had retired and it was discovered that the input to the existing system would disappear because—with a planned cutover to a corporatewide general ledger system—the feeder system would no longer have access to the data structures.

An extremely aggressive six-month plan using fourth-generation application generating technologies and relational data bases was proposed by the team. Information systems consultants and experts were brought in and trained the analyst and programmers. The idea was to build the kernel and other system interfaces and provide query and report-oriented capabilities on a step-by-step basis so that there was always something to deliver or cutover to should the cutover date be brought in sooner. Together with user and development focus, the system was implemented and delivered for acceptance within six months.

The individual users, however, were not prepared, even though they had been seeing reports, exercising queries, reviewing the results, and had been intimately involved in making sure they had what they needed. They were unaccustomed to the quick turnaround on requirements (often measured in minutes) and uncomfortable with the system because it hadn't gone through the normal formal requirements, documentation, negotiation, and time. Another six months passed—without any substantial technical additions to the work—before the application system was formally accepted by the user organization. In short, the users' paradigm did not accept the more aggressive implementation cycle and absence of traditional checkpoints and milestones.

---

[2]*Paradigms* in this context refers to "a set of rules and regulations that (1) defines boundaries and (2) tells you what to do to be successful within those boundaries," as outlined in Joel A. Barker's book *Discovering The Future,* published by ILI Press in 1988.

In this scenario, the focus was on the technical issues and mechanical aspects of the problem. A consideration that had not been considered was the user community paradigm for cut-over. This community was much slower to accept change (shift their paradigm) than the developers were able to predict, despite all the right user-participation and instruction. The paradigm shouldn't really have been a surprise since the track record of previous implementations gave grounds for predicting it. The good news was that the time spent on the implementation cycle had been substantially reduced since previous implementations. But the safety factor had been underestimated by six months.

For the most part, the areas exposed to risk make themselves known several times before they stop the business, but someone has to be watching—someone who does not view the problems as a fluke. Consider the "A Freak Occurrence" scenario.

A FREAK OCCURRENCE

In May of 1988 a fire closed down a major phone switching station in Chicago. Although partial bypass services were implemented in days, the complete central office restoration took almost six weeks.

This particular outage stressed many I/S disaster recovery procedures, since most of the computer installations had focused on the contingency of losing a data center and had hot and cold backup sites established. This situation, however, was different; the systems were all intact, but the central sites were effectively without communications to their branch offices, plants, and warehouses.

Even the local disaster backup sites could not accommodate the demand for their facilities and many of them relied on the normal telecommunications for at least part of their bandwidth.

Even with emergency microwave equipment and moving some of the processing having been moved to other cities, the business application outage for some was measured in days.

Based on this experience, some I/S executives immediately initiated plans to distribute some of the processing; others reviewed and updated their backup plans; some are still analyzing the options. And for others it was . . . just a freak accident!

This was a chance to see what happens when all the eggs are in one basket. The point is that the importance of the data processing to the bottom line of the business had crept up and challenged the previous disaster plan design points, which assumed a lesser impact. I'm assuming this, since I noted a lot of surprised IS executives. I talked to one CEO who was in the process of helping his organization focus on that problem.

Analysis of the options and contingencies might have revealed that there were too many possibilities to consider. Alternative approaches might have assumed worst-case failures and provided options that were insensitive to such possible disasters. One such solution might be to distribute the operational portion of the business as a normal business practice. That was one CEO's view. The IS executive for that company, however, was not convinced this was the right answer. A lot more budget, technical, and management considerations had to be investigated. (Perhaps another paradigm had been encountered.)

Distributing systems introduces two fundamental changes: remoteness from control (or comfort level) and multiples. Given the appropriate control point and design focus, distributed solutions can provide built-in protection. Control systems by their very nature tend to be more predictable as to design points and their ability to scale, and typically come with a relatively exhaustive repertoire of tools and service to deal with performance prediction, recovery, and remote servicing. However, the selection of the appropriate control system platform becomes extremely important if one wants to distribute.

User systems tend to be self-healing in that each owner manages his own problems the best he or she can. User systems run into problems when the problem results from an inability to scale or obsolescence. In this case, user system owners may encounter an expense that their budgets can't afford.

In short, a design point should consider the strengths and weaknesses of both approaches and use the appropriate model where it fits your business need. No single answer has emerged yet.

9.3   WHERE SHOULD THE WORK BE?

If we ignore control and organizational reasons for distributing, a primary reason for distributing computing capabilities, data, and input/output devices is to allow the user to be more responsive and productive at a cost-effective price. If one steps back to look at what is being installed, this objective appears to be being met. It can also be noted that certain types of capabilities and services tend to gravitate to locations very close to the ultimate user, while other capabilities and services are destined for local or remote centralization.

For example, serially accessible devices such as laser printers, scanners, and plotters placed at users' workstations are viewed as significantly improving their responsiveness and productivity in support of work that requires them to be near their desks (see Figure 9.1). High-priced peripherals will continue to remain in local shared points within a building, or in an office area, or in remotely shared locations with administrative support as long as the value of having them dedicated remains substantially below the cost of having them local and/or dedicated. The trend, however, is toward very well-outfitted user workstations.

Similarly, data close to the worker potentially improves response time and availability as long as there is a certain level of independence of the data from data at other locations (see Figure 9.2). The more interdependence with data stored in other

SERIALLY USED RESOURCES

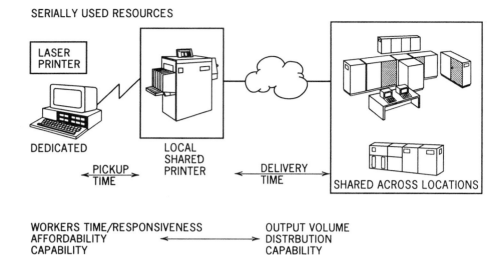

WORKERS TIME/RESPONSIVENESS OUTPUT VOLUME
AFFORDABILITY ←——————————→ DISTRBUTION
CAPABILITY CAPABILITY
  MULTIPLE COPIES

Figure 9.1 *Serial accessible resources.*

workstations and locations, the greater the overhead and visibility[3] of data management issues to the user in terms of temporary denied access, longer response times, and different answers depending on the snapshot of time being used.

Sending and caching batches of data locally reduces the elapsed time somewhat, but requires scheduling to send and more coordination for update situations. In some cases, users of user systems are giving up their personal copy of data and sharing it on a *LAN* server. As a further extension, some users are migrating data back to superminis and hosts in order to address data sharing that extends outside of their *LAN*.

There are, however, some subtle design point changes that can be anticipated but often are counterintuitive. For example, one of the conceptually easier approaches to quantify, which can be cited to justify the distribution of computing outward, is line-cost savings. The rationale is that since more of the data and programs are local to the user, lower line speeds should accommodate the workload.

This approach is a lot more tangible than quantifying and arguing for the potential impact reduction and complexity reduction. Unfortunately, the line-cost savings rarely surface initially as central applications are distributed. In fact, frequently more bandwidth than before is required even to provide comparable solutions to terminals attached directly to the central application. Consider the "Where's the savings?" scenario.

---

[3]The overheads associated with distributed data show themselves to the end user in terms of longer response time to certain data queries, the need to be sensitive to the currency of certain data, and sometimes the need to know where certain data is stored.

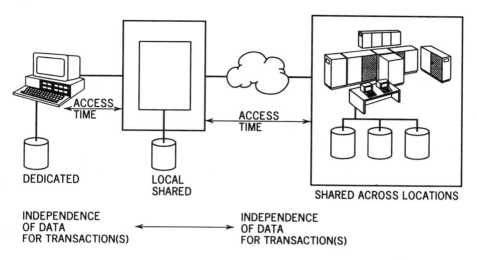

DEDICATED

**LOCAL
SHARED**

SHARED ACROSS LOCATIONS

INDEPENDENCE
OF DATA
FOR TRANSACTION(S)

INDEPENDENCE
OF DATA
FOR TRANSACTION(S)

Figure 9.2   *Dedicated data.*

WHERE'S THE SAVINGS?

A large company with multiple geographically dispersed branch offices has noted that user systems are emerging at the branches. Multiple PCs are emerging per LAN as print servers, additionally, despite the central control, private messaging systems among the LAN users have emerged.

An executive decision commits the company to a distributed solution in which midrange processors are located in each branch to act as local shared printer servers, provide a local application platform, and act as a communications concentrator.

   The rollout begins and midrange processors are inserted between the users' terminals and workstations and the host. The users begin to complain about substantial increases in response time and operations is overwhelmed by network management workload and tools.

   An investigation team is called in. It is demonstrated that the communications lines have become bottlenecks. A proposal to increase the bandwidth is brought forward but rejected, since the ability to retain the 9,600-bps lines was part of the justification and an increase would mean a substantial rise in monthly expenses. The team is instructed to go back to fix the system.

   Weeks transpire and users' and operations' dissatisfaction increases. An out-side team is called in and studies the operating system path lengths and the network subsystem flows. They find that the midrange system is not a good concentrator and propose a communications concentrator to be colocated with each distributed system. This proposal is received with even more displeasure than the increased bandwidth proposal.

A third team is brought in and asks some high-level questions. Why wouldn't injecting a system between the host application and the terminal degrade performance? Why wouldn't the introduction of an additional system with terminals attached to it imply more operations workload? What were the distributed systems doing other than providing a passthrough?

A recommendation is brought forward to increase the bandwidth, redesign the network, and focus on moving some of the applications to the distributed locations.

This is a very common scenario. Several issues in this scenario were not addressed prior to the rollout. Probably the most important item not focused on was the line bandwidth. Line bandwidth is rarely reduced when distributing central applications to distributed systems. In fact, it usually increases as the amount of host-originated data increases at the distributed system. Additionally, until a significant portion of the host-based transactions is distributed, the additional systems overhead of the system usually requires a boost in bandwidth to compensate for the difference. What happened in this scenario was that there was confusion about the difference between a vision implementation and a rollout plan.

The vision that less transaction-related data would flow from the branch offices was sound, but in the interim there were very few transactions distributed. Similarly, as the capability of the distributed system is understood, additional applications that demand higher bandwidth typically emerge. It is doubtful that this distribution of a control system without introducing some of the attributes of a user system would reduce the line bandwidth. On the other hand, line-cost savings and improved service levels can be accomplished by reexamining the network to work with intelligent end points (systems) rather than terminals.

9.4 ANY MAGIC?

9.4.1 What Is the Price of Easy-to-Use?

Part of the appeal that exploded the volumes of user systems stems from the notion that they are easy to use: easy to use as a user, since they employ newer technologies of presentation; easy to use as an administrator, since they are designed to minimize the need for administration; easy to use as an implementer in that they tend to be rather straightforward with a minimum of parameters to consider. Plus, these user systems can be implemented at relatively low cost if considered one at a time.

In many cases the simplification, expense reduction, and development-cycle reduction is achieved by design simplification, minimizing the number variables that the user selects, delegating system management responsibilities to the user consumer, and providing minimal documentation. On the surface these processes address both the user's and the vendor's objectives.

For example, a quick implementation can be accomplished by reducing the number of choices that the implementer (or user) has to make. To accomplish this, product designers and implementers make specific choices as to how error conditions, rounding, and data conversions are to be handled. These trade-offs and techniques should be understood by the user if the results are critical. These are even more critical if they interface with a control system.

Similarly, very straightforward programming techniques that assume very specific usages are frequently employed. These design points[4] sometimes surface as major problems as the users' usage of the tool exceeds the design point, or when the hardware is upgraded. For example, problems might arise when a design point limitation is reached and the program has not been designed to recognize the condition. This problem sometimes manifests itself as two different modules writing to the same place in storage, neither realizing the other is using the space. The results are unpredictable without necessarily indicating a problem to the user.

Many recent user systems products implicitly assume that the underlying hardware reliability, problem recognition, and backup procedures are the users' responsibility. For example, a simple undetected media error—possibly because the hardware isn't using very sophisticated checking and correction techniques—can cause immeasurable damage to business decisions and ripple the result of the problem into corporate data bases. This is not paranoia; it can and does happen, so the exposure needs to be understood. Many products and utilities also tend to bound their scope for a target environment, which in many cases is very different from the environment that your system requires to address your application needs. Each user may be the production test for a unique environment. How are your user systems applications evaluated and tested?

Perhaps an even more frightening revelation about the easy-to-use systems is that there is no magic to grow them. The responsiveness that came with the initial implementations is often short-lived as the user base increases and has more diverse needs. The life cycle of these products tends to be very similar to most application systems as they evolve into an integrated environment and increase in size supporting earlier implementations. Some of the software delivery delays across the industry in this arena seems to point to this as a substantial piece of the problem.

9.4.2 Is a *LAN* an Operating System or a Configuration?

As mentioned earlier, *LANs* are the current revisiting of the concepts of some of the distributed implementations. Most information systems executives have experienced most of the aspects of the evolution.

To understand current implementations of *LANs* and to see where they are going,

---

[4]*Design point* in this context is the size of the document being handled, the minimum amount of disk storage available for temporary files, the time expected to read or write data to a disk, the coexistence with other shells, etc.

we can look at the models and paths that their earlier implementations took. To set the stage, let us assume that there are two computing models: central and distributed. The most distinguishing variables associated with these models are control and physical placement of the equipment. In its simplest form the central computing model assumes that all the software runs within the same physical frame. Similarly, the distributed model assumes that the application programs are running on separate systems (both hardware and software).

9.4.2.1 Central Model.
Historically, the central model evolved from the economics of computer costs and the desire to maximize resource utilization and minimize response time (or turnaround time for batch environments). With the goal of accomplishing this end, certain hardware and program design considerations were assumed by the implementors. For example:

- Maximize transmission bandwidth by blocking data
- Minimize interruptions to the central processor
- Operating system controls all system resources

Given these assumptions, the fundamental design approach is based on control. Much of this control focuses on ways to minimize wait time in the system by using mainstorage data as much as possible since I/O waits waste precious system resource and to minimize instruction pathlength.

Specialized systems are optimized for specific workload characteristics. Trade-offs are made in order to maximize system utilization if operations is mixing

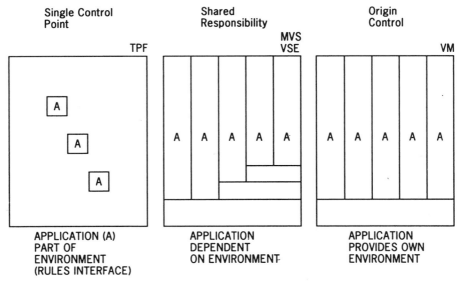

Figure 9.3 *Central model variations.*

workload types such as online transactions and batch workload. Most current *LAN* server implementations are optimized as specialized systems with predictable workload designs.

For illustrative purposes as depicted in Figure 9.3, let us assume that there are three control models: single control point, shared responsibility, and origin control point.

The single control point implementation provides a see-all control-all service, thus giving maximum control of all aspects of the application. For example, operating systems such as IBM's TPF control the transactions from entry into the system until they are complete. The word "control" can be associated with this model.

The shared responsibility implementation requires that the components that it calls upon or participate with have peer functionality and assumes the control responsibilities passed to it by the calling component until it returns control. For example, an operating system such as MVS operates with multiple subsystems, e.g., CICS, VTAM, etc., upon which the application depend in order to operate. The word interdependence can be associated with this model.

SINGLE CONTROL POINT MODEL

The single control point environment is targeted to very tight control and high performance. The key to the performance is the predictability of the transaction (or message). These systems run the transactions inside the operating system and these transactions tend to be sensitive to the physical aspects and capabilities of the hardware. These systems environments tend to be very restrictive in terms of application flexibility. The workload is optimized to use in-storage data whenever possible and the objective is to minimize any wait time. Several S/370 transaction processors are optimized to these criteria (e.g., IBM's Transaction Processing Facility, which processes complex transactions at message rates exceeding 1,600 each second).

The origin control point assumes that the components requested provide a very specific service, and control responsibility always remains with the requesting component. For example, in the VM environment an application may request a server such as SQL/DS to provide some data. The only interface between the two components is at the interface, and SQL/DS does not influence the application and visa versa. Each is essentially standalone. The word "independence" can be associated with this model.

As has been pointed out, each of these three models is implemented on a single S/390; it could be an S/390 multiprocessor.

The difference among the three models is the degrees of freedom from the operating system that the application has. The single control point environment applications in Figure 9.3 (on the left) have the least freedom, while origin control point environment applications (on the right) have the most freedom. The primary differences among the three model implementations are performance and who provides the function. In the single control point environment, the tight control provides very high-performance transactions. The shared responsibility environment handles mixed environments and arbitrates service levels. The origin control point environment is best suited for interactive applications or special applications optimized for some design point. Any of the three environments can be used to solve any of the application requirements, however, each is optimized for its specialty and deviations require special disablers or additional sophisticated functions.

SHARED RESPONSIBILITY MODEL

The shared responsibility environment is tuned for less predictable workload. Interactive computing, batch, and transaction processing workloads may coexist on the same physical system due to economics or the need to share the data. These implementations assume:

- The hardware and operating system ensure application interface integrity
- Common services within the system will provide the support services

Additional pathlength and control-oriented overheads are opted in order to gain more general program services, security, etc. This is best suited for a mixed environment. The system controls the applications for any use of shared resource. The most dominant environment for processing mixtures of transaction, batch, and interactive is an operating system such as MVS. It provides the services in a managed but layered manner. Each layer provides increasingly more sophisticated services and control built upon the layers underneath.

ORIGIN CONTROL POINT

The origin control point variation of freedom favors delegating the application controls to the applications. The operating system basically provides rudimentary physical resource management and interaddress space communications. The services are viewed as just another application by the operating system. Therefore, an application would request a service via a message. One could think of the service as a server. This approach provides a high degree of isolation among users with the fundamental arbitration being done on CPU time allocated. VM is implemented using this approach. VM is designed around this structure.

CENTRAL MODEL

- Assumes one operating system and one physical system
- Variations based on degrees of application freedom
- These variations exist in S/370 implementations
- Biggest commercial investment is in limited freedom implementations

9.4.2.2   Distributed Model. The distributed model accommodates the execution of an application across multiple platforms and supports bringing the computing closer to the user on demand. The primary issue here is the time for the program flow to traverse among the systems from end user workstation to the system(s) where the user's data and computation resources reside.

The distributed model variations are essentially logical extensions of the central model (see Figure 9.4). The key issues are the location of the operating system(s) and the introduction of a pipe connection rather than a direct main storage access.

The distributed single control point model is the easiest to implement. It can be characterized as peer systems with similar or dissimilar platforms interconnected via a communication interface. The application flows among the systems and control passes from system to system with the application. One could easily lash multiple

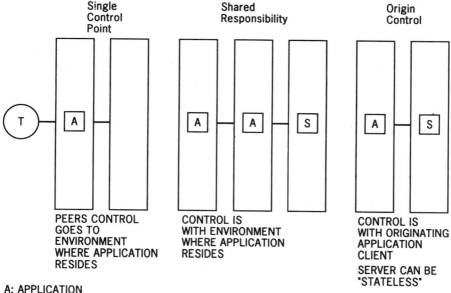

A: APPLICATION
S: SERVER

Figure 9.4   Distributed model variations.

single control point central systems environments together and provide a distributed solution.

Use of multiple IBM TPF systems or IMS systems would accomplish this level of control. This approach is frequently used for credit card, check cashing, and reservations switching applications. In this arrangement, control of the environment is passed to each operational environment; at any instant in time, only one system has responsibility for the entire message, or transaction, or batch job. In other words the distributed single control point model is a peer-to-peer system relationship that passes control to the environment where the application resides.

The distributed shared responsibility model can be used to reduce response time by bringing the compute power and data to the user by segmenting the application and reducing the network traversals to complete an execution. Control is shared among the various systems components and elaborate protocols and rules are put into place to assure the health and integrity of service in the path.

Both single control point and shared responsibility environment applications typically entrust their destinies to the underlying systems. As depicted in Figure 9.5, the flow from terminal to data may be across multiple systems which provide either specialty services or application functions. Even the application itself can be distributed. In this implementation the application environment and platform services work together to support the application. The application is essentially dependent on and managed (controlled) by the environment.

The distributed origin control point model gives the application control and has the environment providing linkage among the participating platforms. Unlike the single control point and shared responsibility model implementation, the origin control point implementation puts the control burden on the application, not the platforms.

In this implementation there is no need for a single sophisticated operating system, since the only common service required is the provision of connection services. This applies equally if the connection media is managed within a single system or connecting systems by VM or managed by LAN support of LAN/WAN service. One can provide simple high-performance services without instituting a global resource management control. Many of the currently popular client-server implementations fit into the distributed origin control point model.

DISTRIBUTED MODEL

- Can be mapped to central model variations
- Application control versus system control
- Primary technical difference is pipe speed
- Client-server model currently popular
- Client-server assumes client application responsible
- Client-server has minimum intersystem control overheads

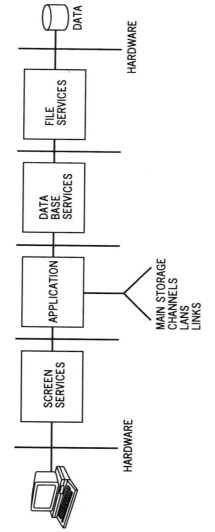

Figure 9.5 A shared responsibility implementation.

99

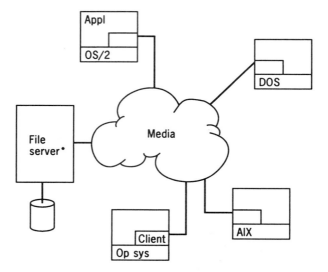

* Proprietary operating system
  or
* Proprietary environment
  or
* Function on various operating systems

Figure 9.6   *Client-server example.*

9.4.2.3   Client-Server. In client-server implementations the client is essentially an application component and the server is essentially the application environment and service for a particular distributed execution. The client (the application)—not the server (the underlying services or environment)—is responsible for the well-being of the transaction. As depicted in Figure 9.6, multiple operating environments can be used to access a server.

This shift from the single control point and shared responsibility implementations to the origin control point implement can substantially reduce the sophistication of the environment. By separating the client and server, it allows the server to process well-defined and predictable messages. In other words, the server fits the central single control point variation. (Think of a server as a transaction processor!) In some cases the servers are essentially highly optimized transaction processing systems, like IBM's TPF, which runs as a dedicated environment on the S/390. Others may be likened to a subset of IBM's CICS, which runs as a subsystem on several IBM operating systems.

The client-server model initially introduces a reversal of control assumptions. Systems issues such as response time and control are delegated to the each client. In this implementation, the server has separated itself from the performance and controls aspects of the application and allowed users to manage their client environments. Therefore, clients can run on any operating system and deal with as many servers as desired without the server handling anything more than the messages (transactions).

The trade-off is one of distributing more control to the distributed systems (or workstations) by delegating coordination control to the application point of origin (client) versus a more sophisticated operating system platform which controls the application. The benefit is more flexibility to introduce new services and hardware and a less complex server environment operating system management. This approach also facilitates giving up (or delegating) some operational environment responsibilities to user organizations. As always, these benefits require some design point considerations.

Changing from one model to another model does not alter the need for the controls provided by the environment in the other models. Using an origin control point simply changes the entry point. The other models have traditionally been implemented in such a way that they introduce the sophisticated interfaces for most applications. The origin control point model provides a less sophisticated interface and allows the application to select its level of sophistication. Obviously, the services provided by the server must increase as the sophistication demanded by the applications increases. As this happens, the client-server implementation begins to take on the attributes of the shared responsibility and single control point implementations and the interface considerations that go with them.

There are also some fundamental assumptions associated with client-server implementations that must be understood. For example, as the sophistication of the application increases in terms of need for access to various locations of data in update mode, a desire to assure an acceptable response time, the desire to integrate several application components together, etc., the need for skills, controls, procedures, and computing resource at the workstation or distributed system increases.

Most current tuning options provided by a client-server implementation are faster systems and faster pipes. Because fast pipes are a significant ingredient in most commercially viable client-server implementations, and these fast pipes are currently limited to LAN and channel attach implementations, client-servers are most popular on LANs.

9.4.2.4 So What?

> The client-server implementation is most effective in situations where changing control assumptions is appropriate and where there is always sufficient capacity not to need a resource manager to arbitrate service. Contrast this with the more traditional system-control-oriented implementations which use a session orientation where the user program is in session with a subsystem that can detect problems, cancel the user program, do backouts and resynchronize.

It is important to recognize that placement, not control, is the primary difference between the central and distributed models. The fundamental difference from an interface standpoint is that rather than branching to a system service, the requests for services are essentially messages and the server is only responsible for the integrity and security of the services it provides. The message-oriented interface could also mean longer response times due to longer instruction path lengths associated with request transfers—but provides service placement flexibility.

This means that system management substitutes must be provided to address the placement ramifications. Additionally, the degree to which the specific operating system and hardware configuration implementation is optimized to this placement determines whether the operating system and its subsystems could easily provide a central and/or distributed base.

The implications of placement are important because if one steps back from the specific configurations, it is relatively easy to recognize that *LANs* are *not* typically placement driven. They are local, not remote! *LANs* are only remote from other LANs and systems. Therefore, a *LAN* is essentially a distributed system with some unique configuration aspects when viewed from an enterprise standpoint.

One can conclude that the essence of *LANs* is the granularity of growth and the apparent application degrees of freedom from operating systems and specific hardware bases. One could extrapolate further to suggest that if one could house the various hardware and software bases within a single open-ended frame, the *LAN* would fall into the central computing model category.

In short, *LANs* are the embodiment of a new hardware model comprised of coprocessors upon which various specially optimized operating systems will run. The subsystem and operating systems interfaces determine this configuration's viability as a central or distributed model participant. The primary differences between the central and distributed models are performance and where the function is provided.

Thus far, we have explored central and distributed computing models and conceptualized that *LANs* could be implemented to fit a central computing model.

The second analysis is to see where client-server fits. Just as central and distributed is separated by placement, the essence of the client-server model is control *not* placement. Client-server initially falls into the origin control point category. This allows the server to be very specialized and compact since it has very finite and specialized responsibilities. The client is responsible for its own integrity. (In fact, some servers are entirely stateless; they have no session notion at all and handle each request as unique.

As client-server implementations grow, driven by application growth, the specific client-server implementation may take on more attributes of the shared responsibility and possibly the control point models with the associated complexities. The key question as this evolves is whether or not this evolution can occur without changing the existing interfaces.

So is a *LAN* an operating system or configuration? A *LAN* appears to be an environment that uses LAN technologies and protocols for communications and uses several different control approaches which, in composite on a configuration-specific basis, can be loosely referred to as an operating system. For example, those configurations using only the client-server implementation have opted to use interface rules and distributed control as the embodiment of their operating system.

WHAT THE MODELS TELL US

- Central and distributed differentiated by placement
- *LANs* are not placement driven
- Client-server is a control option
- A *LAN* is a combination of configuration and controls
- *LANs* can use multiple operating systems within the configuration
- As control requirements evolve, the implementations assume different models

---

9.4.2.5 *Model Design Points.*
The key to evaluating the robustness of the implementation is to map it to the model, apply the salient attributes and considerations, and volume test to identify the fit.

The central model's effectiveness breaks when the resources and production cycles grow so large that they require an increasingly disproportionate amount of resources and skills to provide the same level of service. This phenomenon is not necessarily a function of the model, but rather an implementation-specific characteristic. Most current central implementations have these inherent exposures.

The distributed model's effectiveness breaks when the pipes between the participating components aren't fast enough or don't have sufficient capacity. This is especially true if overall transaction response time or elapsed time consistency is important. For the origin control point model, especially the client-server implementation, the flexibility dwindles if the server doesn't accommodate multiple client interfaces or if the client interfaces can't accommodate different servers.

9.4.2.6 *The Pipe Capacity Will Cause Changes!*
The introduction of LAN technologies with very big pipes was a primary catalyst to the broad implementation of client-server-based *LANs*. The exposure is that the pipe cannot keep up with the need for faster pipes. Currently, the capacity of the pipe and the effective response times are being kept in check if small blocks of data are being transmitted and large buffers[5] are retained.

As the characteristics of the applications change to processing image data and more sophisticated presentation of data, the solutions will demand bigger pipes and/or server-manager control mechanisms, as well as changes in how the data is

---

[5]Large buffers or mainstorage files are frequently used to offset the transmission elapsed time by saving the physical access time to the storage media and the wait times associated with serving the data requests.

TABLE 9.1   Maximum Bandwidth of WANs, LANs, and S/390 Parallel Channel Data Rates without Considering Protocol Overheads

Service	Bandwidth (in bits/sec)	Bandwidth (in bytes/sec)
Dial-up	1200 bps– 9.6 Kbps	150 Bps–1.2 KB
Leased		
analog	4800 bps–19.2 Kbps	600 Bps–2.4 KB
digital	2400 bps–56.0 Kbps	300 Bps–7.0 KB
T1	1.5 Mps	193.0 KB
Ethernet	10 Mbps	1.3 MB
Token Ring	4 Mbps–16 Mbps	500 KB–2.0 MB
S/390 Parallel Channel		4.5 MB
T3	45 Mbps	5.6 MB
IBM ESCON		10.0 MB
FDDI	100 Mbps	12.5 MB
IBM High Performance Parallel Interface		100.0 MB

stored and accessed. To date, there is a significant demand for affordable pipe capacity and there is an even more significant pent-up demand for bigger pipes. FDDI[6] promises to be the next pipe for large campuses and small metropolitan areas.

Consider the comparison on bandwidth capacities for the various connection media in Table 9.1.

Figure 9.7 depicts a smoothed representation of the impact of pipe utilization[7] on response time. The "Containing a Scarce Resource" scenario portrays a client-server evolution, applying the utilization to response time characteristics for data server implementations.

CONTAINING A SCARCE RESOURCE—THE PIPE

Initially, the I/O requests/responses are shipped to/from the physically distributed server. There is a minimum of instructions on the client system and the server is optimized to minimize the physical I/O time. If we assume no physical I/Os to storage at all, the primary bottleneck will be the pipe as the traffic patterns and size of records congest the pipe. Supporting disk I/O is the easiest

---

[6]*FDDI* refers to Fiber Distributed Data Interface, a proposed 100-Mbps token-passing ring network ANSI standard.

[7]Utilization in this representation is in the number of requests per second. This relationship assumes a fairly uniform request rate and constant response transmission size pairs.

and most transparent to the application, but tends to have the most traffic to the data server.

The next step to overcome the existing pipe capacity constraints is to send file requests. More logic and storage on both sides are required, but the traffic across the pipe is reduced since there are fewer requests because of file system logic. Supporting file requests requires an application interface hook or change, takes a little more overhead in the client, but extends the existing capacity of the pipe.

Distributing data base requests takes more logic and storage at each of the systems and typically moves the bottleneck to cycles rather than the pipe. The more application logic that gets transferred into the client and server the less the pipe capacity impacts the response time. Supporting data base requests usually intimately involves the application. It adds CPU workload on both the client and server, but can significantly reduce the traffic on the pipe.

How will client-server solutions really evolve? I will postulate that the evolution will proceed in two directions: they'll take on more application function and evolve into more integrated solutions. The increase in function will help overcome the physical and cost limits associated with the pipes. This will probably be accelerated as the *LANs* increase their communications with one another.

Some of the more advanced client-server data base implementations have already introduced application logic embedded in the data base engine. As the demand to transparently access geographically distributed data increases, more implementa-

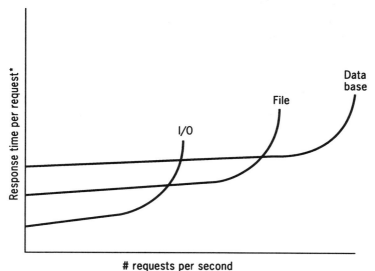

Figure 9.7 Comparison of various level of requests across pipe.

tions of this type will emerge. With them will come the need for more control[8] and function level support. Additionally, there appears to be gravitation to more control and control-oriented services. These have surfaced as new pseudoservers, or agents, which provide queue management, locking services, a traffic pacer, directory telephone book services, etc. In short, a higher-level operating system that can function on a single or multiple system and/or workstation is evolving.

The primary differences between the distributed and central implementations are those associated with placement, specifically mainstorage access versus pipes and implementation of systems management versus component management. Many system management aspects have yet to be defined and implemented in a systems context in this evolution cycle to integration.

If what we've learned from crystal ball gazing is even close to reality, we already know where the technical and business challenges will be. We have seen all of these implementations and evolution before at various levels of sophistication across the S/370 line. We already know what these solutions look like and what the exposures are—so we can postulate the end game.

IMPLICIT DESIGN POINTS

- Identify critical applications and assumptions
- Assess ability to respond to change
- Distribute to meet objectives
- Ease of use does not equal ease of change
- Central and distributed models and issues are similar
- *LANs* and central systems have a lot in common
- *Client-server* following a course to integration
- You know more than you think

---

[8]The need for control tends to increase as the reliability decreases. In other words, mainstorage communications requires much less logic and control than a phone line with all of its associated components.

Chapter 10

Unattended and Remote Operations Must Be Designed into the Solution and Are Very Difficult to Add Later

A comprehensive systems management approach is required to effectively introduce and economically operate distributed systems that have a strong dependence on or relationship with a host system. IBM offers a very comprehensive set of distributed systems and network management tools. In fact, there is a very consistent convergence of tools and services for nodes, networks, and systems management. This is seen by the ongoing growth of NetView and other systems management tools.

This chapter focuses on those capabilities that are fundamental for remote and unattended operations. The specifics focus on S/390 implementations. An underlying assumption of the following discussion is that the current *data centers and network operations* have well-*established* system management *disciplines* at various states of automation.

Figure 10.1 highlights the relationships that distributed systems have with existing centralized systems. More specifically, this chart focuses on existing systems and operational management disciplines, development approach, and remote (distributed) node management. The key message is that *distributed* can and should be viewed as a natural extension of existing processes. The technical solutions will, in fact, assist existing data centers with multiple systems.

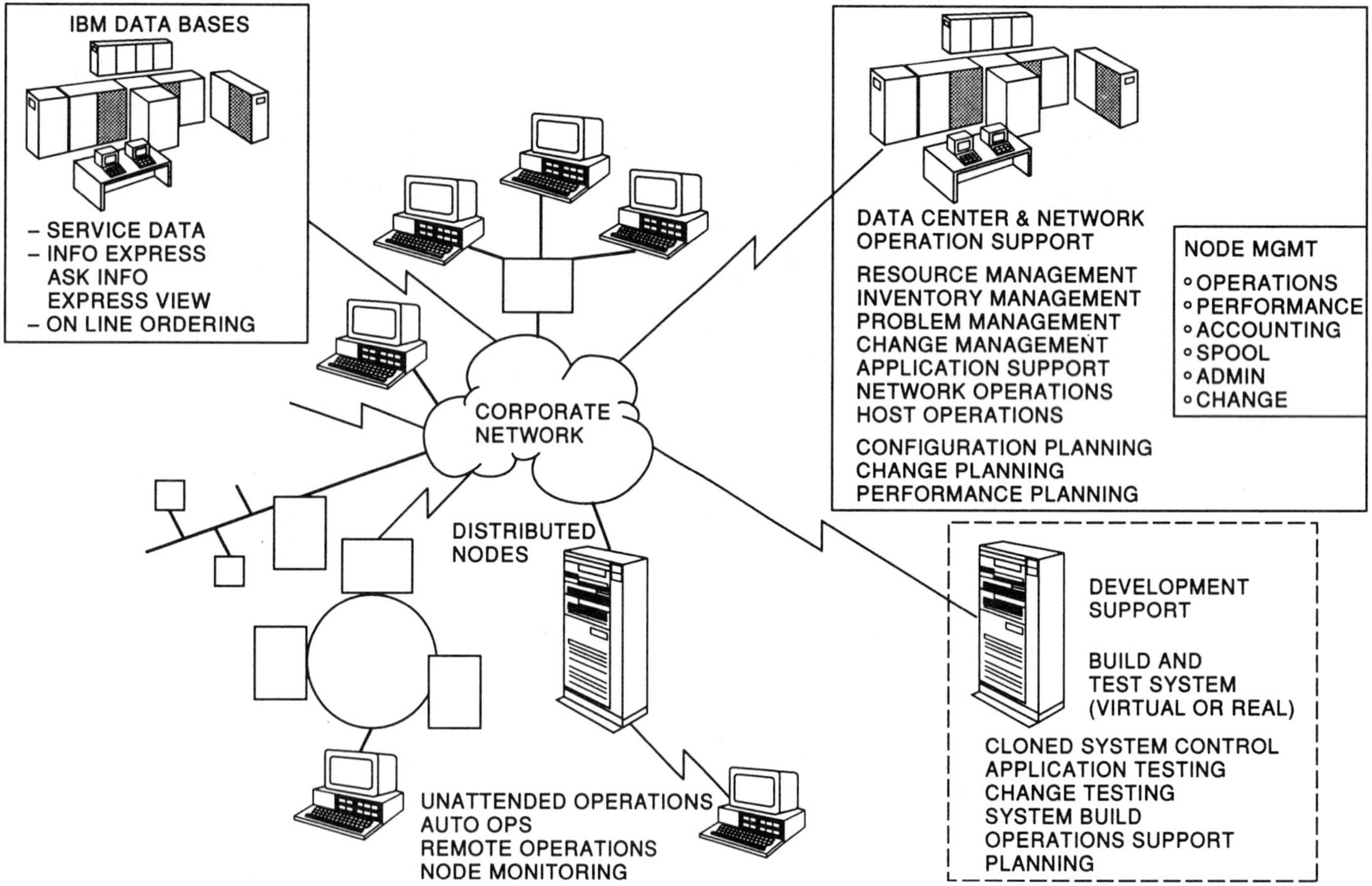

Figure 10.1 Distributed systems management.

NODE MGMT
- OPERATIONS
- PERFORMANCE
- ACCOUNTING
- SPOOL
- ADMIN
- CHANGE

DATA CENTER & NETWORK
OPERATION SUPPORT

RESOURCE MANAGEMENT
INVENTORY MANAGEMENT
PROBLEM MANAGEMENT
CHANGE MANAGEMENT
APPLICATION SUPPORT
NETWORK OPERATIONS
HOST OPERATIONS

CONFIGURATION PLANNING
CHANGE PLANNING
PERFORMANCE PLANNING

DEVELOPMENT
SUPPORT

BUILD AND
TEST SYSTEM
(VIRTUAL OR REAL)

CLONED SYSTEM CONTROL
APPLICATION TESTING
CHANGE TESTING
SYSTEM BUILD
OPERATIONS SUPPORT
PLANNING

CORPORATE
NETWORK

DISTRIBUTED
NODES

UNATTENDED OPERATIONS
AUTO OPS
REMOTE OPERATIONS
NODE MONITORING

IBM DATA BASES

– SERVICE DATA
– INFO EXPRESS
  ASK INFO
  EXPRESS VIEW
– ON LINE ORDERING

The rest of this chapter and the subsequent section focuses on key distributed systems management considerations, requirements, and IBM solutions.

10.1 IMPACT ON EXISTING PROCEDURES

Introduction of the distributed node into the existing systems management disciplines and operational environment should be nondisruptive and existing procedures should be used to improve productivity to allow node additions without requiring additional systems or operational support.

10.2 IMPACT ON OPERATIONS (AVAILABILITY MANAGEMENT)

Distributed node operations for the most part are not very different from operations at a local data center, with the exception that the operator skills are typically not close enough if physical presence is required.

The requirements associated with operating a data center and operating a remote system are very similar. For example, consider this scenario:

2:00 a.m. Sunday a system crashes.

2:01 a.m. A phone call is made to the on-duty application or systems programmer. He or she is at home, a 30 minute drive from the center.

2:03 a.m. The programmer calls into the system or a surrogate in order to get the application operational and begins problem determination.

2:18 a.m. The application resumes with a circumvention.

This is essentially no different from addressing a distributed node.

The operations of a remote system require three fundamental elements to address the potential exposures introduced by remoteness: unattended operations, remote access, and remote change.

10.3 UNATTENDED OPERATIONS

Unattended operations is a subset of automated operations. *Unattended* operations has a goal to require *no manual intervention*. Automated operations, as the superset, focuses on operations productivity, which implies *no manual intervention*. Automated operations includes tables of fixed responses to dynamic responses generated by artificial intelligence components for actions that can be accomplished electronically. For those actions that require manual action, electronic calls can be made to people or other systems.

The primary reason that distributed systems push the state-of-the-art more toward the automated operations arena is that the remote locations rarely have local skills, while central locations still tend to have operators or technical skill available for those tough situations that have not been automated. However, it is extremely desirable to run all systems, both central and distributed, unattended.

While no manual intervention is the goal, most solutions still require the ability to *alert* a more comprehensive procedure or a skilled person to those situations that require judgment or fixes. Some alert systems have been set up to directly contact the service organization that does the diagnosis electronically, and either electronically resolves the problem or dispatches a customer engineer with the appropriate parts. Such alert systems are just beginning to emerge and many control considerations having to do with security and service-level decisions requiring resolution on a location and systems basis have yet to be resolved. In most situations, however, the technology exists today.

In reference to the previous system-crash scenario, either an operator or an unattended operations system could have awakened the programmer at home or an operator at central.

Unattended operations reduce the need for operator intervention by filtering messages, responding to messages with preprogrammed actions, logging necessary information, forwarding information or messages to more sophisticated services at central, and initiating alerts. In the purest sense, unattended operations must be designed into the hardware and operating system in order to be totally effective.

10.4 REMOTE ACCESS AND CHANGE

Remote access is required to allow *operational, administrative,* and *programming access* to the remote system without having anyone near the system. This remote access should be available from the necessary systems operations and control subsystems from the designated control and support sites. (The control sites may be different, depending on the application and subsystem.)

There are really multiple discrete systems associated with any remote system. There is the hardware, such as the CPU itself, the operating system, the application system and subsystem, the communications subsystem, and the communication hardware. All of these components must either be accessed or bypassed in order to have a system that is capable of being fully controlled from a remote location or system.

The most rudimentary capabilities required are the ability to operate the hardware in an operational and diagnostic mode from a remote location and the ability to bring up the operating system or alternate operating system from a remote location. I'll characterize the access to these two targets, the hardware and the operating system, as ports (conceptualized in Figure 10.2). I'll defer the communication and network management discussion to Chapter 23 in the "What Every Systems Manager Should Know about Operations" section.

The two remote system access ports available for remotely managed IBM systems have various implementations based on the software and hardware platform.

The most commonly implemented and frequently used port for operating the

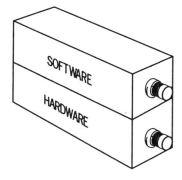

Figure 10.2   *Two remote access ports.*

systems remotely is a logical port access via normal communication sessions with the operating system via standard interfaces or subsystems and the communications software.

The second port, the hardware and system port, has various implementations and is used to access the physical system console to operate the system during exception conditions for such services as power off, power on, hardware problem determination, or if the network software should become inoperative.

The primary reason that there is a hardware port and a software port is that a very basic access port is required to access the system hardware and the system console independent of the software. This port should bypass the sophisticated communications software required for normal communications and network management.

In fact, the communication software or the normal communication network may be the source of the problem being diagnosed. Additionally, the very sophisticated functions sometimes have synchronization problems. For a distributed system, this hardware port should allow an operator to power up, bring up, and perform diagnostic functions.

There are essentially three remote management capabilities that use the hardware ports currently available from IBM: remote service, remote hardware status and operations, and remote systems console.

Remote service capabilities are available to all S/390s. This capability provides for authorized access for remote problem diagnosis and microcode transfer via a dialup port on the service processor. (This is sometimes referred to as a remote service facility).

The remote hardware status and operations capability has various implementations. Rack-mounted models (see Figure 10.3) provide a service processor with a dialin port allowing for both active and passive operations, hardware-related operations such as remote system power control, remote microcode load, manual operations, configuration customization, and status checking and problem analysis. (This is sometimes referred to as a remote operator facility and some functions work from NetView).

The port for frame models is provided via an implementation of a PS/2 and IBM Target System Control Facilities (TSCF) consisting of host and PS/2 software.

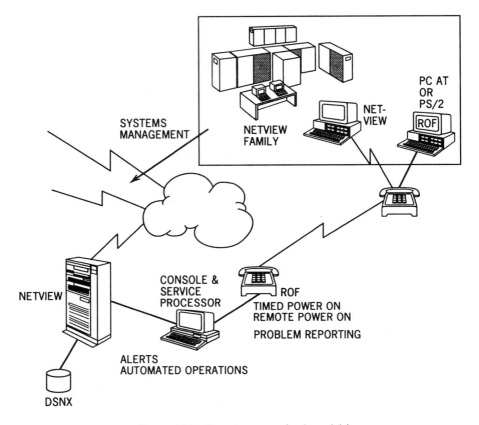

Figure 10.3 *Remote access (rack models).*

TSCF provides visibility to selected hardware status and configurations as well as providing notification of CPU status changes. This implementation cannot power on/power off.[1]

The remote systems console operations capabilities using (TSCF) allow remote access to the system console for operating system initiation and systems level operations such as remote Initial Machine Load (warmstart-power on reset), Initial Program Load (IPL), time-of-day clock setting, and systems initialization of the operating system and subsystem for MVS, VM, VSE, and TPF.

Remote access implementations to the hardware ports from the support location also differ. The ES/9370 hardware port is only accessible from an IBM PC/AT or PS/2, as indicated in Figure 10.3. ES/9000 racks require a PS/2 and/or NetView. TSCF is implemented with a PS/2 and 3270 emulation cards.

TSCF consists of a NetView command processor and multiple NetView tasks,

---

[1] "Target System Control Facility," *General Information Manual,* IBM order number GC28-1063.

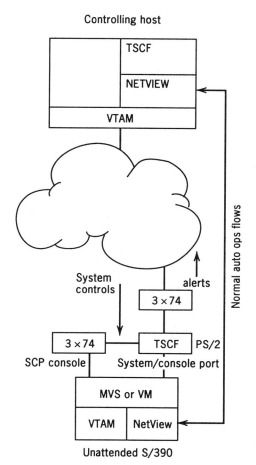

Controlling host

Unattended S/390

Figure 10.4   *Target System Control Facility (ES/9000 frames).*

which communicate with specific target systems. The TSCF/PS/2 is essentially a relay service and monitoring service with a backup port in case the primary port or line become unavailable. Similarly, two TSCF/PS/2s may be resident beside the remote system and TSCF will switch if one should become unavailable. (See Figure 10.4.)

The software ports across the S/390 are essentially the same in that they interface with NetView and VTAM and then interface to each operating specific implementation.

Remote change is required to *load* and *update data, software, procedures,* and *microcode* at the remote processor. Just as in the remote access case, two ports—software and hardware—are provided. One is to address the software changes and the second is to address the microcode changes. In this regard the software flows are the same across the S/390 and require the appropriate software port. The software distribution functions and flows will be discussed in later chapters. The microcode

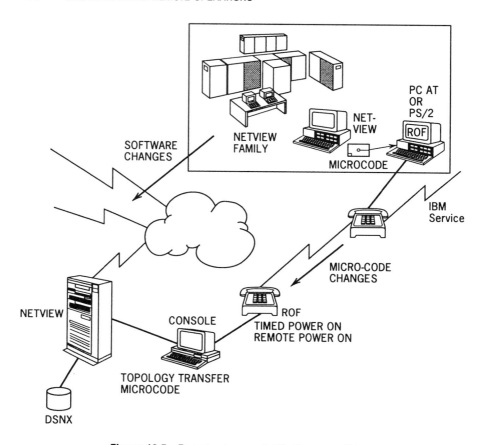

Figure 10.5 Remote change distribution capabilities.

is shipped via diskettes or shipped electronically via the service processor (hardware port) as conceptualized in Figure 10.5.

10.5 NODE MANAGEMENT CAPABILITIES

In general, the unattended operations, remote access, and remote change capabilities need to be systemized with IBM components and the enterprises' unique processes. These systems management capabilities can be conceptualized as depicted in Figure 10.6. They also need to provide a solid base for the information systems organization to augment with their enterprise and organizational unique controls and processes.

These services are placed at the appropriate control points or distributed. The arrows indicate the source of the action or flow and its direction. These will be discussed in more detail later.

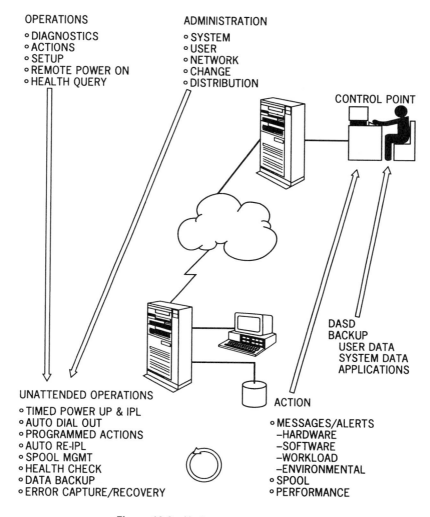

OPERATIONS
- ∘ DIAGNOSTICS
- ∘ ACTIONS
- ∘ SETUP
- ∘ REMOTE POWER ON
- ∘ HEALTH QUERY

ADMINISTRATION
- ∘ SYSTEM
- ∘ USER
- ∘ NETWORK
- ∘ CHANGE
- ∘ DISTRIBUTION

CONTROL POINT

DASD
BACKUP
  USER DATA
  SYSTEM DATA
  APPLICATIONS

UNATTENDED OPERATIONS
- ∘ TIMED POWER UP & IPL
- ∘ AUTO DIAL OUT
- ∘ PROGRAMMED ACTIONS
- ∘ AUTO RE-IPL
- ∘ SPOOL MGMT
- ∘ HEALTH CHECK
- ∘ DATA BACKUP
- ∘ ERROR CAPTURE/RECOVERY

ACTION
- ∘ MESSAGES/ALERTS
- –HARDWARE
- –SOFTWARE
- –WORKLOAD
- –ENVIRONMENTAL
- ∘ SPOOL
- ∘ PERFORMANCE

Figure 10.6 *Node management checklist.*

In general, the *central site* needs the ability to *initiate* the standard multisite operational functions, such as:

System Startup: Power up, IML, IPL, select any relevant startup parameters, systems software changes, startup subsystems, and applications for groups of systems.

Administrative: Download any software changes, add and delete user identifications, administrate security, administrate storage, etc.

Monitor: Check on the health of subsystems, servers, and applications, and take corrective actions.

The *remote system* needs the ability to:

System Startup: Automatically power up (timed), IPL, select appropriate system copy, select any relevant startup parameters, systems software changes, startup subsystems and applications, establish any host links.

Operations: Process normal operational messages, filter and log relevant messages, forward important messages and alerts, achieve important data, forward relevant performance and capacity data via program logic.

Monitor: Check on the health of subsystems, servers, and applications, and take corrective actions.

Error Recovery: Capture relevant error data, IPL itself in error situations, handle runaway program situations, handle spool capacity situations, provide alternate systems packs, backout, and recovery.

An important element in planning for such distribution is the establishment of a *control philosophy* concerning the roles played by the central and remote system. While it is desirable that each system should be able to detect and handle software, hardware, and environmental situations, there is a need to establish a leader and follower relationship.

Traditional designs tend to be central-control oriented and require that the central systems be aware of all that is happening throughout the managed network and distributed system. This approach becomes exposed as the number of system components and probe points being tracked increase. This exposure is not exclusive to a distributed system, it occurs as the number of elements being controlled increase and are processed at a single point. In response to this increase in system components, some implementers of large networks and distributed systems *delegate* the data and *initial recovery responsibility* to the distributed systems for isolated problems. This is not unlike the system of the human body, which automatically attempts to withdraw your hand from fire as it communicates pain to your brain.

The following scenarios describe some different approaches. Scenario 1 is a traditional central approach (this is natural since it is most appropriate on a single processor) implementation, which assumes that all failures should require central awareness or involvement. Since detection may come from either the node or central, the implementation must provide established rules about which support location does what. This prevents unattended operations and host-initiated actions from interfering with one another. It can also increase the complexity of the solution.

Scenario 1

- Node software application terminates
- Node unattended operations begins recovery
- Host remote operations logic detects the application outage
- Host logic requires some status from the node in order not to take action

- Node remote logic provides status to the host—*working on it* message
- If the node fails to respond after a time frame, the host initiates action

A frequently used alternative implementation (scenario 2) reduces the sophistication and amount of automated control, so only the node or the host has the authority to initiate action.

Scenario 2

- Unattended node (not connected to the host) detects a failure
- Recovery begins
- Recovery fails
- System administrator or user calls the hotline and central takes over
- Central establishes a connection to the remote operator console
- Status of the node is checked
- Recovery attempts are overridden and central begins

There are many variants to the above scenarios, but the point is that simple solutions may be the most expedient and the most practical for your enterprise. The decision regarding the approach and its degree of sophistication is with the implementer, not the vendor. The *implementer,* not the vendor, *determines* the required business and operational *needs.* These are decided by such parameters as the service level objectives, skills, and people available, and cost. Because of the need for this decision flexibility, the *vendor* must typically provide a *comprehensive set of tools* and scenarios to assist the implementer. The S/390 systems management hardware and related software, plus the ongoing systems and network management enhancements, provide a very solid base for the various implementations.

10.6 IMPACT ON EXISTING APPLICATION DEVELOPMENT

Application and systems development is often done on a separate system. The introduction of *distributed nodes* can be a *natural extension* to this environment. If the distributed nodes run on a different operating system, the development and support organization may use *VM* as a hypervisor, and the development tools do not require a physical representative node.

Physical development systems may be required if non-S/390-based hardware is used. This is also true if the application or system is dependent or sensitive to specific hardware that cannot connect to the existing development system (e.g., a fixed block architecture drive or a special adapter). While developing code on one system and executing the code on another is technically feasible, it requires a very comprehensive workbench.[2] For the most part, however, the confidence in testing without the target environment diminishes after the unit test.

---

[2]Workbench is a term being used to describe a set of tools available to the programmer to accomplish his or her tasks associated with developing and testing code.

UNATTENDED AND REMOTE OPERATIONS

- Extension of central
- Hardware and software access ports required
- Remote change capabilities required
- Multiple systems demand automation and tools
- System ports must be designed in
- Existing central oriented processes may require changes in detail

Chapter *11*

Use What You Know and Have; Push from There

11.1 LEVERAGE EXISTING SKILLS, TOOLS, EXPERIENCE, AND INVESTMENTS

One cannot read a trade journal today without finding an article on systems interoperability, whether it is an article regarding systems interconnection or access of data on a remote system. This interest in interoperability is increasing across the industry and solutions are emerging to the benefit of the customer. Since this is the case, it is becoming increasingly obvious that networking implementations based on SNA are among those most converged to solutions. Also, *NetView* and its associated family of network and systems management products are becoming a solid basis for distributed IBM and OEM systems connected to IBM-based networks and systems.

Similarly, the introduction of *SAA* has demonstrated IBM's commitment to crosssystem portability of code and the standardization of application interfaces to system and network services (e.g., *APPC CPI-C* for LU6.2 protocol sessions). While much of the crosssystem interconnectivity for applications has yet to be shipped, a solid base is available today so applications can be ready for future enhancements.

11.2 AVOID GENERALIZED ECONOMY STATEMENTS ABOUT SOLUTIONS

Frequently we hear statements about economies of scale and gross technology statements regarding the economics of distributed or the price of personal computer

119

technologies versus the price of midrange processors versus the price of the highend processors. These statements can be very misleading if taken out of context, and at the same time they can cause one to reassess the current solutions and make some substantial improvements.

From a very precise definition, one can make very sweeping generalizations regarding the price per instruction, the price per byte of storage, etc. Unfortunately, these comparisons are often extrapolated and generalized for the price of systems. Everyone would love to have a definitive rule of thumb to help make a system approach decision. However, as of this writing, there is no agreed-to definition of what the bounds of a system are to help develop a simple formula.

For example, there is discussion of applying Grosch's law to specific categories of workload and operational attributes. One powerful microcomputer is preferable to two less powerful micros. Additionally, organizations tend to use mixes of both small and large computers based on their evaluation of the overall costs for the specific work[1] (e.g., user systems versus control systems).

When discussing the systems economics, many considerations are often overlooked. Some of these issues are reliability, software, line and staff organizations, communication lines, communication processors, and the availability of application software to serve the intended purpose. The primary message voiced by experienced distributed implementers is to assess the economics for your solution on a specific, not general, basis within your organization's normal process and reconcile any substantial expense differences with user- or IS-quantified benefits or savings.

GENERALIZED ECONOMIC BENEFITS ARE DIFFICULT: TOO MANY VARIABLES

- Economics depended on specific work
- Some solutions justified emotionally
- Relevant factors include productivity, flexibility, etc.
- Only you can determine relevant criteria

11.3 DON'T STRETCH THE STATE-OF-THE-ART

Oftentimes the implementers of distributed systems focus on announced function and fill in the gaps with assumptions on how the announced function and capability are to fit into their existing operational environment. Frequently, they discover that some prerequisite or corequisite does not work the way they had expected, causing a substantial impact on schedules and credibility. Those implementers who have been stung by discovery or who have wished to avoid this exposure have taken one of two

---

[1]P. Ein-Dor, "Grosch's Law Revisited: CPU Power and the Cost of Computation," Communication of the ACM, Feb. 1985, pp. 142–151.

approaches to deal with this exposure on following projects. The first approach attempts to gain a more *detailed insight* into what was announced in the hopes of resolving all potential problems.

The second approach reviews the announcement material for philosophical changes and technological breakthroughs. Implementers then build their plans on available knowledge, tools, and function, which includes an introduction plan for the new functions.

Of the two approaches, the *second* is *most effective* because it is based on *first-hand knowledge* and *experience,* while the first approach is always prone to surprises. This is because the effectiveness of the first approach is dependent on detailed knowledge that is often beyond the information available or understood.

Successful distributed implementations stem from a *solid comfort level* by the operational, software, and support staffs. The most effective vehicle for introduction is based on what these individuals and their organization currently understand.

Successful distributed implementations that *grow with the technology* are continually tested against new announcements regarding changes in direction or convergence of directions.

Successful distributed solutions have recognized the difference between product availability date and cutover into rolled-out production dates. These successful solutions have been managed to handle the expectations accordingly. The plans are aligned with the business dates required using the capabilities that are understood and *merging in new function* as appropriate.

DON'T STRETCH THE STATE-OF-THE-ART

- State-of-the-art = new to you
- Two approaches: learn everything or bridge from existing
- Manage your organization's expectations

11.4 LET YOUR INSTALL SCHEDULE DRIVE YOUR TECHNOLOGY NEEDS

Most successful installations begin with a well-understood statement of the problem being addressed by distribution. This statement also crisply relates to the tactical or strategic nature of the solution. Often, distributed implementations have had major false starts and disappointments because the pilot implementations ran into major technology limitations.

These limitations are usually associated with price performance, distributed functions, and systems management controls. After revisiting these pilots and examining the show-stopper problems, it becomes very obvious that the *show stoppers* were *predictable* before the technical efforts were begun. Also, they *could have been managed around* while implementers were still validating the feasibility of the technical solutions or implementing tactical solutions. Instead, many of the initial projects ran into what some technologists refer to as analysis paralysis[2] or terminal perfects.

In retrospect, many of the price performance concerns (usually a price/performance concern rather than capacity) would have been solved when the production rollout got into full swing if a price performance chart had been drawn and intersected with the volume production rollouts. Similarly, if the production absorption of major new function were tracked, the distributed issues with such functions could have been tested in an evolutionary rather than revolutionary manner. The same observations are true for systems management.

There really is no meaningful way to postulate problems and requirements for *managing hundreds of distributed systems from a central control* mapping to how central processors are currently managed. One cannot extrapolate the management approaches used for managing large ES/9000s down to many smaller systems.

It is very easy to state that there are very few operating systems, subsystems, and applications commercially available today that lend themselves to being managed as tightly as central complexes are managed today. *DPPX* is probably the *closest solution* to that management approach, and it was explicitly designed for this very purpose. In fact, many of the efforts to manage departmental systems have resulted in end user departments looking for solutions without the involvement of the information systems organization's involvement, because the rigor was perceived as too inflexible to the business needs of that department.

Starting with a few distributed systems supported by end user departments may provide substantially more significant and successful pilots than would a large-scale project. This approach allows for more openness for implementers to learn some unexpected differences and provides a level of flexibility that was unavailable in the central complex. This increase in flexibility may arise because the extensive sharing required for a multiple-department environment does not take place on each specific departmental system.

LET YOUR INSTALL SCHEDULE DRIVE YOUR TECHNOLOGY NEEDS

- Validate concepts
- Solve immediate problems
- Volumes require approach changes
- When do you really need it all?

---

[2]*Analysis paralysis* and *terminal perfects* are descriptive labels for many work efforts that continue to find problems rather than solutions because of an absence of a crisp problem statement and an unclear understanding of the possible trade-offs. The result is lack of progress and additional requirement statements.

11.5 PROTOTYPE AND HIGH-LEVEL DESIGN DETERMINE FEASIBILITY

11.5.1 Feasibility Prototype

A feasibility prototype should always be considered since it is really the only way that the vision and today's reality can be reconciled. The prototype should directly address conceptual concerns and improve familiarity with technologies available. A feasibility prototype is not another word for pilot, since it is not intended to be a complete solution. The objective is to make the decisionmakers in the respective organizations involved comfortable that the ideas are sound and that their concerns have been considered. Specific distributed-related concepts that usually need to be tested are:

- User interfaces (considering existing and new)
- Response time or applications that require access to resources elsewhere
- Program transparency (applicability of existing application inventory)
- New programming techniques
- Connectivity options
- Approaches to central and delegated control
- Data distribution
- Backup/archive approaches
- Software distribution
- Remote problem resolution support
- Openness to growth

11.5.2 High-Level Design

The high-level design maps to the workload characterization and priorities and includes lessons learned in the prototype. High-level designs that were completed before prototype tend to constrain the prototype flexibility, and as such the prototype may hide some significant considerations that may impact the schedule or the budget down the line.

In most instances high-level designs that occur after a prototype tend to be more comprehensive because the learning process derived from the prototype has been incorporated into the design. The key management question here is, *are we stretching our understanding of the problem and the solution or is this project an integration of known elements?* The *known* answer might suggest that the prototype is not required prior to the high-level design step.

High-level design considerations for distributed S/390 solutions include:

- Prototype considerations (both planned and discoveries)
- Sample distribution model of where services are provided

- Connectivity options that the solution must support
- Existing applications interconnection flows
- New application interconnection flows
- Design points of what is acceptable
- Timetable of when specific capabilities are required

Sometimes using an expert system tool to map out the considerations and consequences will provide invaluable insights as to which options are really important and which are only perceived to be important. In many cases the designers are surprised by the outcomes and either change their weighing of importance for trade-off criteria or recognize that some key considerations have been omitted.

I am not suggesting that the designers were less than topnotch or that some super-expert system for designing distributed existed. However, I am suggesting that as the number of considerations increases it becomes more difficult to use traditional two-dimensional matrix approaches and documentation techniques. By the use of expert systems techniques, which are required to input decision criteria into expert systems, many exposures are identified and closed. Additionally, these inputs can then be applied as changes are introduced.

USE WHAT YOU KNOW

- Leverage the architected interfaces
- Your system is comprised of much more than technology
- Bridge from or extend what you are comfortable with
- Don't try installing futures
- Prototype and high-level designs are required

Chapter *12*

Sponsorship and Implementation Approach Make the Difference

Having discussed why companies are installing distributed systems, it is now appropriate to discuss how companies approach *planning and installation* of these solutions.

The first step in this planning is identify the user(s) and sponsor(s), as this will, in all probability, determine the duration of the implementation and the perceived success of the solution.

12.1 USER-DRIVEN SYSTEMS ARE EASIER TO INSTALL AND SUPPORT

As was suggested by the characterization of the three major incentives for pursuing a distributed solution, a prerequisite for a successful implementation is the involvement of the organization that most benefits from the implementation. In fact, it is very important that the organization that receives the most benefit sees itself as a key driver.

If it does, business and technical trade-offs can easily be resolved and extensive contracts specifying what the solution will entail can be substantially reduced. It is also appropriate to recognize that there are more users of information processing equipment than there are IS personnel. Because of this, it is much easier to support the users' desires than trying to drive the user; solutions should be consistent with the needs. Solutions that are for the general good of the company should also provide some value added to the users.

**USER-DRIVEN SYSTEMS ARE EASIER TO INSTALL
AND SUPPORT**

- Easier to pull rope than push
- User motivation and desire are fundamental to success
- Be sure you know who the real user is

12.2 SPONSOR AND USER IDENTIFICATION ARE PREREQUISITES

As discussed earlier, distributed solutions can be sponsored by single end users, departments, geographically distributed organizations, IS, and corporate. However, identifying the "real" user is not always as straightforward as might be expected. Frequently, your customer is not your end user. I have encountered multiple projects that didn't meet the user's expectations even though the IS organization or the vendor thought that they were working with the user.

Sometimes the users are represented by intermediary organizations of the users' selection and sometimes even by service providers who resale their service to the users. Sometimes the user is represented by the driving executive. In these situations it is very possible to meet all of the requirements of the "user" and yet not gain user acceptance.

12.3 THE APPROACH AND SPONSORSHIP DETERMINE THE IMPLEMENTATION CYCLE

Over the past 20 years three approaches to introducing new application systems have surfaced. These have become more obvious in distributed system implementations because of their visibility. The three basic approaches that companies appear to be pursuing (either intentionally or by chance) are *strategic, evolutionary, and reactive*. Each approach is characterized by different sponsors and *install timeframes*. The strategic approach focuses on long-range implications, the evolutionary approach takes small controlled steps, and the reactive approach responds to immediate problems.

Ideally, most companies philosophically prefer the strategic approach. This approach is planning- and control-oriented. It is pursued in order to minimize rework, false starts, and conversions. Unfortunately, this approach is currently characterized with an extended planning and pilot cycle, which takes more time than end users have to spend.

Frequently, this extended process does not meet individual department's needs and has resulted in the growth of departmental systems that are out of the informa-

TABLE 12.1   Implementation Approach Characterization

	Strategic	Evolutionary	Reactive
Sponsored by	Corp/Div	MIS	Department
Method	Studies/pilots	Analyze specific problem	Respond with support negotiations
Justified by	Concept = Corp, Individual = MIS	MIS	Department
Prerequisite knowledge required	Business, technology, vendor, industry, directions	Specific problem alternatives	Containable, can be integrated, how to assume leadership
Time to rollout	1–2 year pilots then gradual rollout	6–12 months from go ahead	Length of time to order and install
Where time is spent	Big picture planning	Logistics	Support flexibility
Stages of implementation	Directions analysis	Savings	Connectivity
	Model solution	Technical solution	System selection
	Pilot planning	Install planning	Install
	Technical planning	Install	Support
	Pilot	Support	
	Begin rollout		

tion system's control or influence. As a result, the company is often forced into a react approach. Table 12.1 highlights some of the key differences in the approaches companies take to implement distributed systems.

The point of the table is to show that the sponsoring organization typically determines the duration of an implementation via the approach they traditionally have used to plan, justify, and fund commitment and rollout. I suggest that identification of the sponsoring organization within the company will help in predicting the pace of the introduction of distributed solutions. I also suggest that upon recognizing these differences and the respective implementation times, each organization can determine which approach (or role) they would like to embrace on a project-by-project basis to meet their specific business needs.

12.4 PLANNING FOCUS (METHOD) IS DETERMINISTIC

Each of the characterized three organizational sponsors has a different orientation and measurement of success.

The corporate staff is driven to view things in a *conceptual* manner and to have their planning orientation focus on the big *picture*. Their measurement is durable solutions that will survive over the investment period and provide a nondisruptive basis for the next generation of solutions. They also focus on the economics of scale in terms of the applicability of a technology to other applications and how it relates to existing and future skills.

The IS organization is driven to focus on specific *problems* that are measured on a day-to-day basis. Their planning orientation and focus tend to be on the *technical* and *financial* benefits of the solution and how they will be able to deliver the service in a timely manner. The IS organization, whether fairly or unfairly, is measured on its day-to-day service, its cost to the business, and its responsiveness to changes in the business. These organizations tend to be more comfortable with familiar technologies and technology-oriented requirements. While they may update their user base regarding technology changes and applications, the users are the real source of business application requirements and justifications.

End user departments are *business-solutions oriented*. Their primary focus is on near-in solutions that address the present year's problems. They are less concerned about the big picture issues that IS and corporate are addressing. They are exposed to a multitude of technologies to address their business problems at trade shows, by vendors, and by consultants. They have a very crisp mission, a budget, and a time frame. The solutions they embrace by themselves address the mission and time frame within their budget. End user departments generally prefer to negotiate for support rather than develop their own expertise. This support should also fit within their three parameters.

12.5 JUSTIFICATION AND FUNDING ARE DETERMINISTIC

The funding for the development and ongoing expenses can dramatically influence the acceptance and duration of implementation.

For example, *corporate* organizations, as a staff function, rarely have the funding to pay for a production rollout. The exception is when the corporation must change its fundamental technology to survive; in this case, corporation pays and recovers from allocations (also referred to as apportionments). In most instances, however, corporate organizations tend to justify the *seed money* from a strategic perspective to demonstrate feasibility and appropriateness. Once this has been justified and accepted as a strategic direction, IS usually has to justify the distributed systems from a budgetary standpoint and establish a way for expense recovery. This can substantially elongate the implementation due to resistance to the recovery schemes, staffing implications, or even end user acceptance.

IS-sponsored projects tend to be driven by corporate direction, service-level requirements, resource restrictions, and expense reductions. The primary source of funding is from existing charge-out and service fees or from redirection of some of the proceeds of those fees by finding techniques for *savings,* or from containment of expenses, or staff growth. IS is usually ill-prepared to justify a strategic system unless the budgetary impacts are supported by its customers both financially and in standing up as a sponsor (e.s., an end user group). Many organizations usually have to stand up in support. This tends to elongate the business cycle prior to the allocation of resources and commitment to an implementation plan.

Departmental projects tend to be the easiest to justify in very crisp business terms associated with the line of *business* they are addressing. The approval generally must come from the business unit that is implementing the solution. If the business unit's budget can support the expense, the process is very straightforward. This justification shows schedule, profitability, return on investment, and is directly associated with a profit and loss statement. The primary potential roadblock to a quick implementation is the business unit's capital plan. This drives the business unit to incremental solutions that fit within its allocated annual budget or to leasing.

12.6 CONFIDENCE REQUIRED BEFORE COMMITMENT

Before any of the sponsoring organizations are willing to commit to the implementation, each requires some fundamental level of *confidence* that they are making a sound decision.

The *corporate* sponsors need to know their company's business directions, the technology trends, where the vendors are going, and where the industry is going. This focus on directions is important because the corporate decision is committing the corporation to a *long-range* plan with substantial *investment* along the way.

The *IS*-sponsored implementations are substantially less directions-oriented since the *payback* period is usually within the first or second year and the size of the investment is not anywhere as far reaching as the typical corporate plans require. The IS organization needs to be convinced that the implementation addresses the specific problem being focused on and that the implementation will not introduce new larger problems.

Efforts sponsored by the *end user department* typically require assurance that the implementation will assist in establishing the desired *line of business leadership* at an affordable cost. If end user departments make the implementation commitment, they have assured themselves that there are additional solutions available that will help contain any technical problems that might surface, and that interfaces with the central information system are possible.

12.7 ROLLOUT TIME IS PREDICTABLE

In corporate-sponsored projects, the largest part of the time is spent in positioning, evaluating, and planning. The rollout time frame is typically very lengthy in the first stages of the corporate-sponsored projects. A pilot of two or more years is common for corporate-sponsored projects. However, the pilots dramatically accelerate after corporate is comfortable with the technologies and solutions, assuming that the funding is in place due to well-planned-out physical install cycles and multiple systems are involved.

For IS-sponsored projects the largest portion of the elapsed time is associated with the logistics of introducing the new solution into the existing support and operational structure. IS-sponsored projects tend to take *6 to 12 months* to see fruition, typically because of the budget cycle and the rigor used to provide a solution transparent to the end user.

For user (department)-sponsored projects the largest portion of the implementation time is spent on convincing themselves that they can get the necessary support to meet their business needs and that the solution they select will provide sufficient flexibility to accommodate change. The end user/department-sponsored project is usually extremely rapid from decision to install time. The departmental solution is typically chosen because of *close-in availability* of a solution. In department-driven solutions the ability of the system's vendor to deliver the required hardware and the application install time may well be the gating *factors*. The majority of these systems tend to be new applications or to have a very simple conversion, so little transition time is required.

12.8 USE ALL THREE APPROACHES

Each of the three approaches has its strengths and its exposures. It is also important to note that all three approaches need not be *mutually exclusive,* and in larger companies they rarely are. The three approaches can be very complementary if the corporate information systems organization maps a parallel pilot recognizing and leveraging the distributed systems solutions and the lessons learned by IS. IS can provide some very constructive guidelines for the departmental solutions and structures itself to support departmental systems independent of who made the purchase decision.

By separating systems into control systems and user systems and focusing on the overlaps, it is possible to use a different approach for each application implementation. For example, control systems typically require a strategic approach, user systems by their very nature and required user drive tend to be reactionary, and the overlap between the user and control systems tends to be evolutionary.

This type of focus separation allows companies to spend a different amount of time on each project and retain the necessary control while improving responsiveness.

SPONSORSHIP AND IMPLEMENTATION APPROACHES ARE KEY

- User sponsorship helps implementation
- Strategic (rollouts begin in two-plus years)
- Evolutionary (solution appears in six-plus months)
- Reactive (already installed or within three months)
- Approaches can be complementary with solid architecture

Chapter 13

A Vision and Comprehensive Project Plan Is Required

13.1 DON'T TAKE YOUR EYE OFF THE VISION

The *approach* to implementing the distributed application will have a dramatic effect on its *success and acceptance*. The successful approach will continually balance the key trade-offs between the strategic requirements (corporate influence), the more-tactical requirements (IS influence), and a specific organization's day-to-day business requirements (departmental influence).

As was discussed earlier, a mix of these approaches appears the most practical given the business pressures and high expertise required to single out and project the system of the 1990s in technical detail. Any or all of the decision approaches could be appropriate for a project, but an overall approach should be *declared* in order that the technical and business issues can be addressed in the context of the project assumptions.

In situations where technical and business issues are not declared and understood, the decisions may not reflect the desired objective, especially with passing time and staff turnovers. When decisions don't follow a theme the implementers become confused, and this surfaces in the technical solutions. If the objective changes—and it can—then this change should also be declared.

An example scenario of changes to the decision approach is:

Event 1: A vision for the system of the 1990s is presented by corporate. This vision typically incorporates the technology currently beyond our economic reach, but clearly on the horizon.

Event 2: A platform is selected based on the application characteristics of the 1990s solution.

Event 3: A prototype plan is outlined and hardware and software are selected to test its feasibility.

Event 4: Some of the current systems or business applications require a new solution. Perhaps the vision base can be employed for these applications.

Event 5: The application is *ported.* The focus changes from feasibility to practical considerations associated with incompatibilities with the prototype platform.

Event 6: The people working on the prototype begin feeling pressure, because incompatibilities with their prototype start to surface.

Event 7: Having lashed together a platform that minimizes end user and application change, the focus moves to performance.

Event 8: Costs become a focus item.

Event 9: Project is terminated on this platform due to costs. The platform is abandoned.

In the previous scenario, the management and decision approach changed at Event 5. The options were to: 1) go on with the feasibility prototype; 2) provide an immediate base for the application at hand; or 3) a combination of the two.

If the first option were selected, anything learned during the effort could have been factored into the prototype and a separate business solution that did not diverge too far from the end target could have been pursued by the team assigned to address this tactical problem.

If the second decision option were selected, the prototype should have been formally stopped and the application specifically addressed. This might have included reassessing the platform since the time frame and workload mix did not match the vision. The application may be much more transaction-oriented today and the vision may be much more interactive-oriented.

If the third option were selected, the parameters associated with the application should have been changed to accommodate the vision. This accommodation includes increasing the capacity and absorbing the delta expenses as part of the prototype effort, even after the system is in production. This requires altering some of the systems management techniques to more closely reflect the systems of the 1990s, which will trade-off compute and storage capacity instead of highly skilled operations and support personnel.

If no management decision is made (or reaffirmed) at Event 5 time frame, then the vision may well be in danger and the credibility of the decisionmakers at risk. Obviously, this situation is not exclusive to a distributed systems environment. However, distributed systems tend to involve more organizations in terms of participation and support. Distributed solutions also tend to have more hardware and software on the users' premises, and the changes or problems are more evident than those contained in the glasshouse; therefore more organizations and people are involved.

For example, consider a performance problem that requires a system upgrade. In the glasshouse this would be scheduled for some off-shift time and the problem resolved. In the distributed environment the user may have to come into the office to let the installer onto the premises or the user organization may be asked to replace the system hardware. Now to make this a little more complex, consider that this has to happen at multiple locations.

The best advice to minimize these situations is to clearly identify pilots as pilots with the users' understanding that they may be asked to participate in several types of support activity and that the configurations aren't finalized until the pilots have met the users' expectations. The pilots should also be flexible enough so that their specifications can be changed as the user learns more about the application. In many pilots that I have reviewed, some of the rigid end-user interface specifications were substantially more rigid in the IS organization's mind than in the users'. Straightforward solutions were not being implemented until the user was consulted directly.

13.2 A GOOD HIGH-LEVEL CHECKLIST IS REQUIRED

Table 13.1 represents a distributed systems implementation checklist that can be used as a planning tool. These checklist items summarize some of the key considerations that have surfaced during the implementation of distributed S/390 systems. While most of the considerations are equally relevant for planning any large systems effort, the implication of having multiples physically outside the glasshouse introduces some additional need for user department participation and the selection of a timely yet robust platform that can be grown and managed economically from a remote location.

13.2.1 A Plan with Crisp Measurables Is Key

A high-level project plan with crisp measurables is key to any successful project. However, if the project is associated with some elements of discomfort or concerns,

TABLE 13.1   Distributed S/390 Implementation Checklist

- Application identification
- Approach decision
- Management approach selected
- Software and hardware platform selection
- Feasibility
- High-level design
- Project plan measurables
- Sponsors identified
- Planning considerations and process
- Installation approach
- Operations interfaces and services

these concerns should be translated into testable measurements that should be performed at appropriate stages in the project. It has been proven repeatedly that concerns are usually well-founded. Although many of the concerns cannot be addressed to everyone's satisfaction, it is important to make sure that they are covered in the plan and not just covered verbally. It is also important to continually review the measurables, not only for progress but also for continued applicability.

Sometimes, especially in longer projects, some of the objectives change. It is appropriate to make sure that success measurables continue to map to what the principals expect, especially if they have reprioritized or rethought the objectives. The changing of priorities is usually not a significant exposure in specific single-application projects with well-defined business goals since the changes can be readily communicated. Frequently, however, distributed solutions tend to address multiple applications and various degrees of central and decentral control and budgeting. As such, the objectives and other measurables are much more sensitive to changes.

13.2.2 A Staged Attack Plan Helps

Having done the initial characterizations, established the measurables, completed the prototypes, selected the platform, and acquired committed sponsors, the next step is planning. This involves establishing crisply detailed plans for:

- Application(s) definition and sizings
- System configuration specifications
- Installation approach
- Installation tools and facilities
- Automation levels, roles, and rules
- Management process
- Installation
- Operation

13.2.2.1 Application(s) Definition and Sizings. This entails establishing workload scenarios and design point ranges including system costs per unit, total solutions costs, as well as gaining agreement from the sponsors. It is important to determine whether the specific application is justified on its own or requires other applications dependencies or savings.

The application workload scenarios should include expected transactions, interactions, growth, storage capacity, workload characterization—in terms of potential bottlenecks such as heavy I/O to a specific data base—intersystems communication, etc. Much of this information can be gained from the existing applications running at central and by extrapolating to those items that are affected by remoteness. This characterization will be very important as it will be used at regular intervals to make sure that the assumptions are materializing, and if they are not, to make certain the appropriate focus is placed on achieving them or formally altering them and predicting any changes in the end solution.

13.2.2.2 System Configuration(s) Specifications.

System configurations should be brought forward based on the projected workload ranges and the various affordable design points. It is important to remember that multiple systems in geographically remote locations are more inconvenient to alter (from a hardware standpoint) than are systems in the local computer room. The inconvenience manifests itself in labor hours and overall time elapsed to effect a change (responsiveness), remember the actual hardware change will take substantially less time to effect than will the travel time to the location and back. As a result, the systems configuration should be designed to require minimal hardware changes, most of which can be effected from a remote location.

As a counterbalance to this, the value of the solution and the minimum cost must be assessed, and a satisfactory solution found. Beware of quick judgments. For example, it may appear that a substantial dollar savings would be achievable if the storage capacity were reduced by x MB. Unless it would substantially alter the acceptance of the solution, the dollars may be best spent on hardware initially, versus at a later time. It is also important to recognize that small multiples, large multiples, and very large multiples have different economic factors and these should be acknowledged when trying to apply simple rules.

Be sure to include the capacities required for remote and unattended management. This includes items such as alternate system for backup, backup data, alternate IPLable packs, etc. (Consider local cartridges for emergency situations.)

13.2.2.3 Installation Approach.

The method of initial and subsequent rollout needs to be considered. The installation of initial pilots may well require much attention and onsite presence in order to assure that the system is installed correctly and that the impression of a quality install is left with the user. The method of overstaffing the install may be planned for the first several systems and used as a learning vehicle as the final install is developed. Avoid making the pilot a *learn under fire* experience for the end user department.

An installation plan my opt to go through three stages of rollout: pilot, singletons, and multiples. The pilot approach may be different (enhanced for each install), the singletons may still require special attention. The ideal is that after this progression the multiples are business as usual.

13.2.2.4 Installation Tools and Facilities.

It is important to assess how each system will be built early since, as the number of systems increases, the change management and physical resources become prohibitive if an inappropriate technique is used. Some information systems organizations opt to build each system at a time because the system programmer believes that it is his or her mission to optimize the program libraries and disk space per system.

This could become a problem as the number of systems increases. Other approaches include a basic systems configuration and selected libraries being distributed based on the application set. In both these instances change-control mechanisms must be employed, but the packaged approach reduces the complexity and install time while positioning for more effective maintenance.

For example, IBM provided a software preload service with ES/9370 that allows the IBM customer to ship the base and or selected packages to the manufacturing location and have the software *applied* on the disks so when the system arrives it is IPLable without the need for a local systems programmer or trained administrator. If this approach is opted, the information systems organization must develop a technique to apply newer software upgrades once the preloaded system becomes operational. A technique for upgrading to a new operating system release is also important. The significance of an operating system versus application is the sheer volume of programs that might have to be sent electronically (line or tape) to accomplish the upgrade.

13.2.2.5 *Automation Levels, Roles, Rules.* Another aspect of planning is to address the automation levels associated with unattended operations, automated operations, and remote operations. The scenarios must be developed to deal with *all situations* such that the role of the local user (or administrator) can be crisply defined and so that the skill levels required locally are consistent with expectations.

It may sound as if *all* these *situations* will require a major piece of work, but planning may not have to be as exhaustive as it sounds. For example, the inclusion of a simple rule that causes all unexpected (not programmed for) messages to be routed to a special operator at a geographical support center addresses *all situations*. It is also important to watch out for switching roles between what is done locally and remotely. The unattended mode, automated mode, and remote operations mode may end up with conflicting rules if an overall system analysis and walk-throughs are not done.

13.2.2.6 *Management Process.* The management process considerations are as important as all the technical considerations. Checkpoint and milestone meetings with the sponsors are very important to keep all the participants involved and comfortable with the progress. Each such meeting should include a revalidation of the initial objectives and the measurables that reflect that these objectives are being or will be realized. It may be appropriate to have an outside assessment of the high-level design, the plan, and the pilot for comfort level and to minimize surprises.

13.2.2.7 *Installation.* The installation process is the execution of the plan. An installation list (bill of materials) and process should be prepared which addresses:

- Hardware/software order/delivery dates
- Software loads both initial and subsequent (these are often very different)
- Initial setup (system, services, network, terminals, services, user identifiers, accounting codes, space, access authorization, responsibilities)
- Installation tracking

During the install process, be sensitive to any surprises. Surprises that are problems should obviously be fixed, but the nature of the surprise should be considered in light of the plan and how this helps or could affect rollout, service, cost, etc.

13.2.2.8   Operation. From an operational standpoint, make sure that the important operator interfaces are well-understood and have been factored in. A demo is always appropriate. Everyone learns from them. Consider the following areas in the assessments and plan in a distributed environment that supports a mixture of personal, user, and control systems:

- *Central System Operator Interfaces:* This includes programmed operators[1] such as those used by NetView, operator interfaces to the hardware, operating system and subsystems (e.g., CICS).
- *Backup/Archive Considerations:* These include local/remote backup, automated backup, user-invoked recovery, system-invoked recovery, local/remote archive, and user-invoked retrieval.
- *Performance Management Considerations:* These include data collection, data reduction, real-time analysis, alerts, programmed actions.
- *Availability Management Considerations:* Alerts (automated or from hotline), automated response/actions, diagnostic information, logs, skill (availability of support tools).
- *Change Management Considerations:* Change control (scheduling), change preparation (testing and packaging), change distribution, change application, change backout, and logging.
- *Problem Management Considerations:* Alerts, problem entry (where), problem tracking, relationship to change process, network tools, host tools, skills (availability of support tools).

In addition to the more traditional list of considerations just cited, application and network support are two more areas that deserve special attention. The term "application support" here is meant to address remote problem determination and administration of the application. Most systems provide operating system and subsystem mechanisms and tools to support problem determination. What mechanisms are provided to support application problem determination?

For example, how effective can problem determination be if the user must try to remember what went wrong and try to reconstruct the situation? Transaction manager systems, for example, go to great lengths to provide diagnostic and status information to minimize such exposures. They also restrict the number of things that can go wrong. For this reason, some companies are using CICS/VS on VSE and MVS for supporting decision-support applications, rather than the open environment provided by VM/CMS and TSO.

The term "network support" here is meant to address attachment to a private or

---

[1]*Programmed operators* are programs usually provided by the vendor or developed by the systems programmers to respond to system messages.

public backbone network and the considerations involved. The key considerations are associated with the reliability of the tail circuits, the backbone WAN, the LANs, and the systems and software connected across these. The developers of SNA have spent substantial investment to provide end-to-end controls for communications sessions.

Other implementations have used different philosophies of connectivity management. When merging these philosophies, it is important to verify that the service expectations are aligned with the technology and philosophy being used. Just because some portion of the session is on SNA, doesn't imply that the same level of network management and control is available to the entire path. This is a two-edged sword. Sometimes the solution doesn't require all the controls, and the traditional approach may be overkill. At other times the service level expectations are set based on the use of full SNA support.

A VISION AND PROJECT PLAN ARE REQUIRED

- Don't lose sight of the vision
- The objectives must be understood by the team
- There is no substitute for a high-level checklist

Chapter *14*

The Application and Five Factors Determine the Platform(s)

14.1 APPLICATION IDENTIFICATION COMES FIRST

It is important to have a crisp *characterization of the applications* up front. Once the applications have been characterized, they can be analyzed for their applicability to distribution. Initially, this analysis can be (and probably should be) done without considering hardware and software requirements. These requirements will surface from the analysis. The software, hardware, management approach, and plans can then be generated from this characterized outline.

The *initial analysis should examine the driver (motivator)* for the application. Is this a technology-driven, organization-driven, or department-driven application? Is it sponsored by corporate, information systems, or the end user department? Consideration of these questions will assist in calibrating the technical scope, life of application, and installation window.

For example, technology-driven applications will tend to align with existing internal systems in terms of the accounting, controls, response time, turnaround time, function, and serviceability. Since applications and operating systems may handle each of these differently, it is important to identify those elements that are essential before doing extensive product analysis.

Each of these elements can probably be associated with critical considerations such as value—dollarized—in user terms and information systems terms; constraints in terms of resources, skills, time frames; and technology in terms of the architectural implications of existing solutions or corporate strategy. The urgency and priorities are driven by the sponsoring organization, as discussed earlier.

A TECHNOLOGY-DRIVEN EXAMPLE

A warehouse inventory control application is currently implemented on a central host system. It has been there for the past 15 years and has evolved from a batch-only job to an online and batch job. In order to be more responsive, the inventory has been bar-coded and scanning devices have been provided for the pickers to use as they pick the load for each shipment. A small data-collection system has been distributed to each location to update the inventory as reported by the scanners both for incoming and outgoing shipments. "Bill of Lading," "Ship To," and other required forms are printed via a printer remotely connected to the host. The data-collection processor keeps local inventory and also sends the outgoing shipment data to the host to reflect any order discrepancies, e.g., out-of-stock or short quantities.

For out-of-stock and short orders, a central program searches to see if the remaining portion of the order can be fulfilled from another location. The focus is on minimizing additional costs while providing good service. Another key incentive is to avoid loss of revenue.

Recently a central site outage due to a natural disaster caused line outages, which interfered with this company's ability to fulfill its orders. The subsequent analysis brought to light several other concerns as well. Shrinkage (loss of inventory, breakage, etc.) had been increasing the frequency of out-of-stock conditions and the partial order practices were impacting margins. There were discussions of distributing the central system and the responsibility for out-of-stock resolution. The distribution of the system would substantially reduce the impact of a single failure. The distribution of the inventory control to each warehouse manager put the focus on the source of the problem. The headquarters executives had mixed emotions: Would the distributed systems cost more? Would the distributed systems replace the central system? Was resystemization required? Can inventory control be given to the warehouses?

Solutions to address all these concerns exist. The executives' challenge is to pick one that matches their emotional, budgetary, and control needs. A technology-driven solution would be the least disruptive solution for this company based on the current infrastructure. In other words, this company should extend its central implementation outward rather than delegate based on how they feel. Did you notice that the warehouse was not requesting the local solutions?

The *actual number of distributed nodes* expected is also a significant factor, as is the rollout timing until the changes might be required. The number of nodes changes the weight of some of the considerations. For instance, if the information systems group were evaluating a single remote printer and concentrator node, the primary considerations would focus on the function, skills, and time to implement. Compatibility with existing systems would not be as key as would the skills on-hand to design and implement.

On the other extreme, if multiple (more than 10) distributed nodes or a new application that would add to the existing nodes were planned, then operations and relationships with existing solutions would become an important factor due to fundamental numeric considerations. Consider that a single problem takes 1 minute to resolve on a host. Now consider that the same problem could occur on multiple hosts (distributed nodes) at the same time.

For example, if the 1-minute-to-fix problem occurred on 10 systems within a 5-minute window, the average perceived fix time would increase to 2 minutes. Twice the number of fixers must be called into play. Even if these problems occurred over the entire day, 10 minutes would be expended rather than 1. In short, as the number of nodes increases some changes to the way they are supported must also occur in order to provide quality service with existing staffing. This is why there is such an intense focus on systems and network management automation and newer technologies for distributed solutions.

Examine whether *information from multiple locations* is involved in the application. The considerations should be based on the basic differences that distributing data introduces: longer elapsed time between local and remote data requests, availability of all desired elements at each data request, the bandwidth available for remote data requests, currency of the local or remote data. There are limited tools available to assist this data-placement analysis.

Consider seeking out such tools as you determine the strategies associated with data replication, currency, placement, synchronization, current and future transport, and availability technologies. These tools must be related in the software and application as the implementations frequently alter the conceptual analysis results. While these may sound like ominous considerations, there are many systems implemented today that address user requirements with existing hardware, software, and communications systems solutions. However, each system is architected to its own application and was arrived at by addressing the above considerations. In short, some major application-related questions must be addressed before one worries about platforms. These include:

- Motivation
- Number of nodes
- Ownership (application and data; they could be different)
- Interdependencies with other application systems
- User usage scenarios (planned and ad hoc). Central provides logic and user-supplied logic
- Benefits analysis (positioning, savings, responsiveness)
- Clear statement of objectives of the solution (measurables)
- Time frames (prototype, pilot, rollouts)

- Users' expectations and new responsibilities
- Service levels (existing, new, value, cost)
- Milestones (measurables, technology check)

14.2 PRELIMINARY PLATFORM SELECTION

The platform selection process can be very simple or very complex, again depending on the management approach being pursued (strategic, evolutionary, or reactionary). Some key considerations which assist in the selection are:

- Application availability
- Workload characteristics
- Control styles
- Architecture
- Experience

I will explore these considerations using four IBM operating systems (DPPX, MVS, VM, and VSE) that are currently used in distributed implementations with the ES/9000 air-cooled models as a basis for comparison. For discussion purposes, these operating systems tend to be representative of the various IBM- and non-IBM-based operating systems, fundamental implementations, and design points.

14.2.1 Application Availability

The first and probably most important step is assessing whether the application can or should be bought or built. Many departments select the platform based on application availability. It is desirable to have the IS organization assist in the platform selection to assure growth and integration compatibility.

For department-driven applications considerations might include using MUMPS/VM and PICK/VM platform (see appendices), which provide the ability to leverage specific application solutions on the S/390 systems management base, but exploit more flexible end-user-oriented solutions. Although these use VM as the underlying platform, VM can be transparent to the MUMPS or PICK application users and developers. The VM platform adds:

- Systems and network management
- System-specific reliability and service support
- Testing, development, and backup environment capabilities

in the distributed implementations which want the flexibility of user systems but would like the underlying rigors that IS typically provides for control systems.

The overall considerations for application availability are represented in Table 14.1.

TABLE 14.1 Application Availability

Application Acquisition Options	Motivations	Platform Drivers
Buy	Application commercially available and meets both immediate and longer range requirements.	Platform(s) determined by existing applications. Selection of platform then based on existing skills, hardware/software investments, and application operating costs.
Contract	Application not available and software integrators provide such solutions.	Platform usually determined by integrator's experience and existing hardware/software investments.
Port	Applications exist on different platform and lend themselves to porting.	Prerequisites and corequisites usually determined by the from environment. A primary consideration is to assure that porting makes sense from the application design standpoint.
Build	Unique application or unique performance requirements that must be developed by internal people because of experience, sensitivity, etc.	Provides decision flexibility and is often the least desired option due to the investment, time, prerequisite research, and systems analysis, usually determined by the from environment. A primary consideration is to assure that porting makes sense from the application design standpoint.

14.2.2 Workload Characteristics

From the centralized information systems organization's viewpoint, MVS is usually the operating system of preference when distribution of services from central—with retainment of control—is the objective. MVS provides familiar controls to the large IS organization and accommodates the various workload environments. Unfortunately, the MVS solution is not always viable for small systems because of systems price (hardware, software, environmental requirements) and systems staff productivity when considering multiples. Table 14.2 suggests small S/390 operating platforms based on the current centralized environment or an existing distributed en-

TABLE 14.2 Workload Characteristics

New Workload Characterization	New Workload Description	Current Environment		Air-cooled S/390 Target Platform
Transaction	The majority of the workload is heavily oriented to preplanned interactions. The high focus is on the consistency in response time and cost of each interaction.	MVS	CICS	VSE/CICS MVS/CICS
		MVS	8100 DPPX	DPPX VSE/CICS
		VSE	CICS	VSE/CICS
Interactive	The majority of the workload supports unstructured interactions as is characterized by office, decision support, research, development activity. The focus is on value to support the users' assignment rather than the specific interaction. Combinations of graphics, image, text, computation, and data query are typical.	MVS	TSO	VM/CMS
		VSE	ICCF	VM/CMS
		MVS	8100 DPPX	VSE/CICS
		VM/VSE	CMS	VM/CMS
		VM/CMS		VM/CMS
		VAX/VMS		VM/CMS (FlexLINK or Interlink)
		SUN		VM/CMS (FlexLINK)
		UNIX		VM/CMS (TCP/IP)
Batch	The majority of work is associated with work packages submitted to the system. The focus here is on turn around time and cost.	MVS		VSE
		VSE		VSE
		VM/VSE		VSE or VM/VSE VSE or VSE & PR/SM
MIX	A combination of the above is required. The key will be the percentage of each of the above as part of the overall workload for a given time period, peak hour for example.	MVS		VM/VSE MVS
		VM/VSE		VM/VSE

vironment and the target environment's expected workload characteristics. (Yes, batch is still very necessary in many operational environments, even in *LANs!*) The key considerations appear to be the mix of the target workload and the current environment.

The mixed VM environment can be either VM/CMS or VM/VSE. A key discriminator is the workload mix itself. For example, a 30 percent transaction level intermixed with 40 to 50 percent interactive level is certainly a VM/CMS and VM/CICS candidate. On the other hand, if the work level is transaction oriented for more than 40 percent of the workload, then VSE is the best implementation candidate. An alternative that could provide the functional benefits of both CMS and VSE platforms is VM/VSE. SQL/DS data bases can be shared between the environments.

14.2.3 Control Styles

The type of management control that the organization uses or desires to pursue will also weigh heavily in determining the platform operating system. Much has been done to minimize the difference in systems management considerations (for DPPX, VM, VSE, and MVS) to make them less important than workload considerations. In other words, the mechanisms for managing multiple remote VM systems and VSE systems from central are approaching those of DPPX (DPPX was expressly designed for distributed operation). However, the application management techniques require scrutiny. Interactive systems platforms such as VM allow for degrees of application management control delegation ranging from total delegation, shared central and delegated, and central control.

VSE, together with SQL/DS and QMF, is also very appealing to some installations because of the control at the system and service level and the openness for queries at the user application level. (See Table 14.3 for example guidelines.)

The primary consideration is the degree to which the user department or the IS

TABLE 14.3 Control Styles

Type of Control	Description	Platform Operating Systems
Centralized Tight	Tight central control appears very much like the existing central operation today with regards to systems management disciplines.	DPPX, VSE and MVS
Centralized Loose	Loose central control uses many of the existing central management technologies but delegates certain responsibilities to the user community. This delegation may occur with new tools, new approaches or education. New approaches that do not impact existing solutions and require little user education appear the most attractive.	VSE or VM
Delegated Support	The departmental system owner delegates some or all of the systems management disciplines to a service (could be the information systems organization) but retains the authority to establish the department's own standards and schedules. The service does not influence the standards in terms other than providing cost trade-offs considerations.	VM or VSE

organization controls the environment and the application. A mixture appears to provide the greatest leverage for flexible user-oriented applications. Office applications might be a good candidate for mixed control (centralized loose or delegated support).

14.2.4 Architecture

The degree that a strategic decision affects the platform selection should be weighed in light of schedules, current function, rework, and conversion. Table 14.4 reflects some of the major considerations. In some cases, air-cooled systems that can accommodate MVS workload may still be the best solution (e.g., an ES/9000).

Conversions are becoming more and more costly to both businesses and vendors. As a result, coexistence technologies continue to surface to enable exploitation of new price performance and function, with minimal impact on existing applications. This trend allows for more flexibility than does choosing a single base. SAA provides a directional statement of where IBM investments are going.

The primary consideration is the use of architected interfaces that will allow porting the application to new platforms. CICS, for example, provides the CICS

TABLE 14.4   Architectures Considerations

Approach	Description	Air-Cooled S/390 Systems Environment
Current Architectures	Can the solution be built on current architectures (hardware, software, and subsystems) levering existing experience and tools? Is it economically or technically feasible to use the existing architecture considering the systems cost? Can some portion of the architecture be leverated (e.g., the hardware, the operating system, the subsystem, the applicaiton)?	VSE, CICS, SQL/DS, DLI, VSM, SQL/DS, VM/MUMPS, PICK on VM, DPPX, MVS, CICS
Architected Interfaces	Can the solution be built on architecture that has well documented interfaces (e.g., SAA) such that the state-of-the-art technologies are leveraged and the investment protected?	VSE, CICS, SQL/DS, DLI, VM, DPPX (DPPX/CICS[a])
Strategic Architectures	Should the solution be built on the selected strategic architecture(s), e.g., SAA?	VM or MVS
Coexistence	Does the architecture accommodate existing investments and demonstrate flexibility to accommodate new technologies?	VM or MVS

[a]DPPX CICS Application Interface statement of direction

TABLE 14.5   Experience Considerations

Type	Description	Possible Air-cooled S/390 Paths
On hand	Will the solution be enabled using the current experience base?	DPPX → DPPX/370 PICK → PICK on ES/9000 MVS → MVS VM → VM VM/VSE → VSE or VM/VSE VSE→ VSE
Minor investment	Will the solution leverage existing skills and experience building on them?	DPPX & MVS & CICS → VSE & CICS MVS → VSE MVS → VM MVS → VM/VSE MVS → MVS
Major investment	Will the solution require substantial retraining or hiring investment?	DPPX & MVS →VSE & CICS MVS → VSE MVS → VSE MVS → VM VSE → MVS VSE → VM
High invention	Does the solution require high creativity skills and experience in areas that have known scarce sources?	Prototype concepts with VM then apply above.

applications the ability to be ported between MVS and CICS. The greater the application's reliance on special platform features that are either implicit or explicit in the application, the less portable it is.

14.2.5 Experience

Sometimes available experience becomes a significant factor as a function of the creativity and time frame required to implement a solution. A decision to use a certain product because of existing experience may be best. Sometimes, taking a little risk is suggested, but in either case a prototype is recommended in order to minimize surprises. Table 14.5 offers some criteria and possible platforms. The primary objective is to minimize risk and leverage existing skills. *Outsourcing* (contracting the IS service) is currently being used by some companies to reduce the skill factor from the decision process. The focus is then primarily on risk associated with the implementation and second sourcing flexibility.

14.3 SUMMARY

If the organization weighs the abovementioned considerations, it will more easily make a preliminary platform selection that can be prototyped if agreed to by the sponsors. The decision pivots more on the availability of the application, the workload, etc.

PLATFORM SELECTION

- Identify the application drivers
- Buy, contract, port, or build
- Transaction, interactive, or mixed
- Tight, loose, or delegated control
- Existing or strategic interfaces
- Existing or new skills

Chapter 15

Connectivity Provides Far Less Function and Requires Far More Expertise Than Expected

This ominous chapter title is intended to sensitize the uninitiated to the fact that when they hear or read that some product connects to some system, very little has been said. Even the most experienced managers fall into the trap of thinking they have all the necessary information. The normal assumptions come into play when one reads the product specifications. In many cases what you don't see will impact you, especially when multiple protocols, physical media, and software are involved. I am not suggesting that vendors are failing to state the necessary information for their products (in fact, most provide excellent product data), however, most products in the connectivity arena are merely specific elements associated with connecting two or more applications. There are many special considerations that are assumed by the potential buyer but not necessarily implemented as expected.

The best safety mechanism that I have found is not to assume. If the connectivity for your application isn't specifically documented, ask. This chapter discusses some of the considerations.

15.1 CONNECTIVITY GOES FAR BEYOND PHYSICAL CONNECTION—PROTOTYPE

When planning for system interconnection, most technical staffs begin with the physical network (e.g., channel-to-channel, line, LAN) and then focus on the sharing of the transmission media. This effort introduces discussions of communication protocols at multiple layers and management of the network. The underlying assumption is that this is the most complex aspect of the connection. While transmission media, protocol selection, and network management are very important to response time, availability, and expense, the application connection support is equally important.

It is very important to explore application-to-application support in terms of the protocols it supports, and on which media. At the current time, this must typically be done on a product-by-product basis.

Ideally, in homogeneous environments such as SNA-based networks, the subtleties are substantially reduced. However, even in this type of environment, the operating system specifics, native attachment specifics, and release level sensitivities are all as important as the media, protocol, and network management level. Additionally, when mixing operating system environments and application platforms, the interapplication capabilities become important. SAA has established a blueprint, but until all the products have implemented the common intersystem protocols, the designers must be very sensitive.

For heterogeneous environments, three approaches are being used to address the interfacing needs: protocol gateways (e.g., conversion to SNA LU6.2 or LU2 using IBM 3270 protocols), common protocols (e.g., TCP/IP and OSI), and special adapters, e.g., FlexLINK and Interlink). Again, each of these approaches must be mapped specifically to the application requirements. For example, if the gateway is interfacing to an application that expects an IBM 3270 interface, does the gateway emulate all the features that the application expects? Similarly, if LU6.2 is used by the gateway that you are considering, does the application at the requesting end use the application-specific protocols that your application expects?

An example of this application-specific protocol is a phone call to a person in a hotel room in foreign country. You are familiar with the phone protocols on your end. You are greeted by the hotel operator who quickly converts to your language and connects you to the room of the person you called. He responds with "Hello, how are you?" Then the problem begins—those are the only English words he knows!

CONNECTIVITY GOES FAR BEYOND PHYSICAL CONNECTION—PROTOTYPE

- Physical connections are only the beginning
- Do your applications support the protocols?
- Only way to find subtleties is to demo and prototype
- If it can't be demonstrated or easily prototyped, reconsider

Checklists provide very high-level filter and highlight items and attributes that should be considered, but they rarely cover mismatches with your expectations. With this understanding, it is very important to develop a functional demo and prototype before full commitment. There are very few endeavors that cannot be exercised in this manner before one has to make substantial investments. If a heavy investment is required for the demo or prototype, you might want to reconsider what it is that you are testing and why it is so complex to demonstrate the relevant considerations.

15.2 MULTIPLE CONNECTION SOLUTIONS ARE INEVITABLE

Most large companies are currently experiencing a dramatic increase in the use of information systems. Many of the installed solutions are the result of individual implementations such as personal computer solutions, minis, and *LANs* implemented by departments and individuals without the involvement of the information systems organization. Implementers and end users of these solutions are rapidly recognizing the need to access data on central and other organizations' systems.

In many instances these independent systems or *LANs* do not have the necessary prerequisites or the flexibility to access the host or other *LANs*. Access to hosts usually requires IS involvement. IS assists as well as ensures that security and integrity are protected.

User systems (*LANs*) access to other user systems (*LANs*) usually begins with direct LAN-to-LAN connections. Typical connection solutions include bridges,[1] routers,[2] gateways,[3] protocol converters, and program-to-program interface software. As the need for telecommunications management increases the number of lines begin straining the budget and the need for line coordination among *LANs* becomes apparent. At this point ways of using the enterprise WAN often become appealing. Solutions to this growing requirement include SNA gateways, SNA protocol converters, and TCP/IP X.25, as well as specialized proprietary protocol converter solutions. In these instances these conversions or packaging is done solely to provide transport and the data is often restored to original protocol at the other end. Most large companies will utilize multiple such solutions in any distributed implementation.

---

[1]*Bridges* are comprised of hardware adapters and logic that allow a workstation or server on one LAN to address a workstation or server on an adjacent LAN using the same protocols. They operate within the OSI model datalink layer.

[2]*Routers* are adapters and logic which introduce more sophistication over bridges with functions such as new addressing, frame formatting, and isolation (subnetworks) for inter-LAN communications. They are usually used for interconnecting LANs using different protocols (e.g., Ethernet and Token Ring). They connect networks at the OSI network layer. They offer more function and overhead than bridges.

[3]*Gateways* are adapters and logic that provide more complex functions for linking dissimilar computer and networks. They are used to encompass network addressing, network isolation, protocol conversion, device emulation, etc. They operate at all levels of the OSI model stack (layers).

A key consideration is that making a connection interface look like a supported device or control unit, does not mean that the same level of services are available from the required configuration of hardware and software. For example, one *LAN* installation that wanted to use the company's SNA WAN periodically encountered some communications difficulties. The *LAN* users had *plugged in* as a 3270 using the same communication hardware as with the 3270. They called the IS network operations to provide problem diagnosis as they normally do for their network attached control units. The network group was unable to use their normal software tools because the appropriate modems were not being used. Very specialized line tracing equipment had to be employed. It took several days of problem determination to identify an incorrect modem setting. These types of situations are not uncommon across the entire range of hardware and software associated with connectivity. Similar problems have been encountered in determining the source of a failure when device emulation doesn't quite match up. Since the multiple solutions tend to be inevitable, the supporting organizations should be prepared to deal with the challenge using viable solutions and tools.

MULTIPLE CONNECTION SOLUTIONS ARE INEVITABLE

- Lots of connectivity options are available
- Many are well-suited to their environment
- Interconnection will be inevitable

15.3 HETEROGENEOUS ENVIRONMENTS SHOULD CONSIDER LU6.2 INTERFACES

The most exercised approach to connecting geographically distributed application on IBM S/390 systems from non-IBM systems is via SNA connections. Most OEM vendors provide SNA device and LU6.2 emulation. There are essentially three standard emulation interfaces used to access the SNA host: emulate a remote job entry device for batch file transfer, emulate an IBM 3270 (LU2) for host transaction or interactive access, and use LU6.2 protocols to communicate with an application or service on the host written to the LU6.2 interface (e.g., an application interfacing with APPC). LU6.2 provides a well-architected and resilient application-to-application programming interface.

The use of an SNA protocol interface leverages existing network management experience and provides a comprehensive set of system management tools to manage performance and availability. A primary objective is to accomplish the same level of manageability and controls afforded by the SNA tools.

CONNECTIVITY

- Prototype connections with target environment
- Prototype application end-to-end flows
- Multiple protocols and implementations are inevitable in an enterprise
- Most S/390 connectivity is via LU2 or use LU6.2
- Application-to-application connections should consider LU6.2 using APPC

Chapter *16*

Interoperability and Multiple Standards Are in the Cards

16.1 MIXED ENVIRONMENTS HERE TODAY

It seems no matter how hard we try to avoid it, mixed hardware and software continue to be with us. In 1964, the introduction of the S/360, together with emulators, allowed many enterprises to make a strategic decision to consolidate and centralize their data processing equipment with the IBM S/360 family of products. This was meant to achieve certain economies of scale, effectively utilize scarce resources and skills, and establish appropriate data controls. Now, more than 25 years later, a typical information systems environment (from an enterprise view-point) is frequently reminiscent of the pre-1964 computing era (see Figure 16.1).

Business requirements have driven solutions to include a myriad of system environments, some standalone, some interfaced via emulators, some interfaced with special facilities, and some integrated built upon mixed IBM and non-IBM hardware and software. The picture gets even more complex when one considers the variations of operating systems, transaction managers, and data systems. Even the single hardware architecture didn't preclude the need for multiple operating systems, subsystems, and interconnection, because of cost and support trade-offs.

Technology has come a long way over the past 25 years, and from an overall information systems management standpoint, the ideal solution model continues to be built on a single hardware and software architectural base ranging across the entire system spectrum, at least for control systems. That is, a single-user system, a distributed multi-user system, and the mainframes would be able to run the same application and be perceived as a component of a global single system.[1]

---

[1]The label *single image* is often used to describe this.

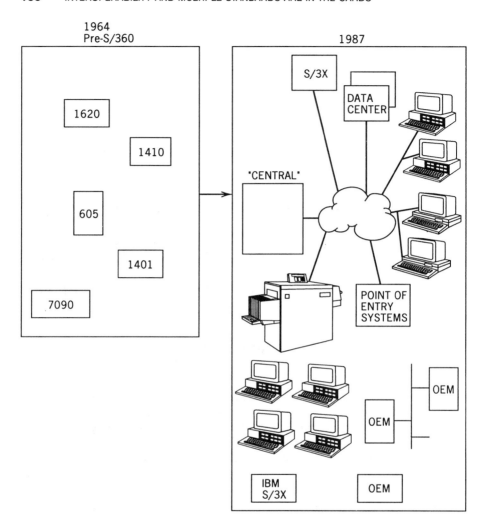

Figure 16.1   A typical 1987 environment.

This model is preferred by the IS organization because of the very large investment and experience base in the training, documentation, applications, data processing professionals, skills, and experience that surround the existing mainframe(s)
applications. The challenge is to achieve the same level of function, performance,
and controls on the smaller configurations as the larger systems supply, within a
consistent price-per-user range[2] and without adding additional staff.

[2]The *price per user* is usually calculated by adding up the cost associated with the hardware, software,
connections, support, and any special environment charges and dividing the sum by the number of users
served. For departmental systems, it is sometimes very difficult to establish support and administrative
costs because these may be provided informally.

16.2 MIXED ENVIRONMENTS HERE TOMORROW

Today CIOs are facing increasing pressures to make far-reaching architectural platform decisions while responding to very tactical requirements necessitated by organizational, business, and technological changes. These decisions are even more complex than those made in the 1960s, because the number of systems owned by a company is in the hundreds and many are data and procedurally interrelated. This makes a total replacement strategy extremely difficult. On the other hand, attempts to maintain the status quo have typically not met the business needs.

The primary considerations are the investment (protection and new), responsiveness, and service level. Some companies are focusing on the application base as the primary investment to be preserved. Others, in order to be responsive, are replacing the older applications with packages, and still others are converging to common hardware and software bases in order to provide the necessary service level and controls.

In general, many companies have evolved a strategy that preserves and grows their applications while methodically converging and growing the underlying system elements to create a cross-system platform. Three distinct strategies are being used to obtain this convergence:

- Support existing diversity with coexistence and integration strategy demanding interfaces among the various software platforms.
- Solve immediate application needs on a responsive and expandable tactical platform that is consistent with the software platform base.
- Make new major investments on strategic platforms usually involving a focus on a consistent software platform and convergence to a common hardware architectures for all control systems.

All three strategies are being employed by various enterprises, usually as a conscious decision on a project-by-project basis. The resulting enterprisewide business solutions are combinations of many configurations with very large pipes[3] connecting them, independent of where the systems are physically located. As the speed of these pipes increases, the distinctions between mainframes, minis and micros blur in terms of capacity, and focus tends to be on how the configuration and its applications are managed—e.g., standalone, autonomously interconnected, cooperative coordinated, distributed systems managed centrally, distributed servers managed locally or centrally, etc.

These configurations defy an oversimplified label such as personal computer (micro), LAN, mini, mainframe, etc., and the terms "distributed processing" and interoperability tend to surface. As a result, vendors must provide a variety of solutions. For example, IBM provides multiple-system families and products such as the IBM Personal System/2, IBM Application System/400, IBM Enterprise

---

[3]*Pipes* in this context refers to interconnection media. Examples include buses, channels, LANs, phone lines, etc.

Systems/390 family, and specialized systems (hardware and/or software) to address these needs.

MIXED ENVIRONMENT

- Multiple software and hardware architectures
- Various design points
- Coexistence, integration, new platforms strategies
- Specific strategy per business problem
- Departments addressing their own strategies

16.3 SINGLE HARDWARE BASE WANTED

The number of different configurations currently being installed in volume and the different approaches being used to manage these solutions within an enterprise, or even within an office, shows that the requirements and trade-offs are very diverse. An important consideration that cannot be overlooked, however, is that there is frequently an assumption that the underlying hardware supporting the configurations is becoming less important than the application for the business area that it serves.

The ideal successful solution provides the flexibility, responsiveness, necessary services, and controls at a price that matches the need. Unfortunately, this is where the ideal and the realities clash. The old saying that a chain is as strong as its weakest link applies here. Reliability, control, integrity, support, flexibility, and price are not currently hardware-platform insensitive and trade-offs have to be made, often on an application-by-application basis. The CIO's challenge in this regard is to make these trade-offs consciously so that controls can be put in place or at a minimum be easily added.

As an example, a division president was told that his most popular product was stalling and that daily sales were dropping sporadically. This was contrary to his expectations and he sent an auditor to look at how the data was being collected. A significant discrepancy was found; the high-order digits were being truncated. Upon further investigation, it was found that one of the programs that had been ported in a change a year before responded differently than it had on the source machine. It had been programmed to hardware-specific implementation; now in the new environment it truncated the high-order numbers without any notification.

One way to reduce the frequency of these occurrences is to use a common hardware architecture.

In response to customer requests for a common hardware architecture base, vendors continue to expand their system bases. In the S/390 context, IBM has continued to focus on expanding its mainframe base on both the low end and high end,[4] from single user S/370s to S/390s that support thousands of users with different workloads and requirements.

As of this writing there are four distinctive hardware implementations whose use depends on where the systems are housed:

- On, under, or beside the end user's desk—the S/370 is on a card
- In office space shared by several users—the S/370 is on a card or is a S/390 rack drawer
- In a small computer room (glasshouse)—the S/390 is in a rack drawer or frame
- In a large computer room (glasshouse) with environmental conditioning—the S/390 is housed in a computer complex of several frames

The differences include environmental considerations in terms of space required for the entire system, often referred to as "footprint"; the human factors such as noise generated and esthetics—the system's appearance in the workplace—ability to operate the hardware; do problem diagnosis; provide fixes from a remote location; and the ease of upgrade.

16.4 EXTENDING MAINFRAME ARCHITECTURES

Until the late 1980s the S/370 implied a controlled environment and an IS staff. The introduction of the ES/9370, a super-minicomputer[5] system moved the mainframe software and hardware architecture implementations to the end users' office environment. The ES/9370 was the first S/370 system that was designed for shared usage in the office environment. It provided a broad range of rack-mounted input/output and storage-device adapters with the CPU (see Figure 16.2).

This S/370 provided a way to extend the IBM S/370 investments, experience, and skills to remote locations. Additionally, multiple non-S/370 operating systems and applications were ported to use the S/370 strengths and economies without requiring conversions. Both IBM environments, such as DPPX, and non-IBM environments, such as MUMPS and PICK, were ported in their entirety. To many, this appeared to be the long-awaited platform solution for those who wanted a single architecture for mainframe and distributed systems. The initial orders and expectations were very high. The expected volume of installs, however, did not materialize

---

[4]*Low end* and *high end* refer to ends of the processor spectrum, usually based on capacity and price.
[5]*Super-minicomputer* refers to a new class of minicomputers that are capable of doing the work that was once only in the domain of large general-purpose computers. This class of computer differs from its larger siblings in that it does not require the environmental conditioning of the larger systems. It is typically self-contained, that is, the peripherals are mounted within the rack rather than externally attached. It is also usually substantially less expensive than the larger systems. It differs from the minicomputer in its capabilities and capacity. Super-minicomputers should not be confused with mini-supercomputers, which are highly specialized for extended precision and high-volume calculation-oriented applications.

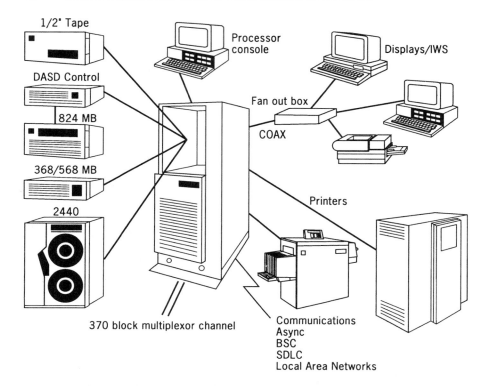

Figure 16.2 *An outside-the-glasshouse ES/9370.*

in the first years of availability. The focus had been on the hardware and the operating systems. The necessary distributed systems management software was to rollout over the next several years, dampening the rapid installation of large multiples. Identifying applications that could easily be distributed without replicating substantial software products and applications was equally challenging since this replication could become very expensive in terms of software licenses and support costs.

During the same period, competing alternative distributed implementations such as remote personal computers with mainframes and *LANs* were becoming extremely popular. Additionally, the IBM AS/400 system was introduced as an application solution-oriented system with hundreds of applications that departments could install and manage. These solutions had no history and could be implemented much more rapidly for specific requirements, assuming that there wasn't a need for a tight relationship with existing applications.

For some IS organizations the introduction of distributed small S/370s were very challenging, especially as they discovered that extending the mainframe was not as easy as installing some new standalone applications managed by the requesting department. This was especially true if the applications had not been designed with unattended or remote operations in mind.

Many companies quickly learned that there were some significant differences between systems designed for departmental management and systems built upon the mainframe and central management infrastructure. Some discovered that the most responsive action was to allow departments to install specialized solutions. Others found that robust solutions for multiples required the rigors and capabilities currently only available to S/370 systems, but also learned that these often had long implementation cycles.

By year-end 1989, many information systems organizations had altered the way they responded to their users' information needs and the way they approached systems implementation and management. In many cases they had become much more pragmatic. During this time, IBM had enhanced the S/370 VM/SP and VSE platforms to provide high-function distributed capabilities from a service and systems management standpoint, taking advantage of some of the lessons learned by their previous distributed implementation experiences with packaging, connectivity, and operations.

Systems could be ordered and shipped directly from the plant with the software already preloaded, which reduced the physical installation time and the need for local technical skills. IBM had also made some very significant changes in the way it priced S/370 software. By then, the ES/9370 systems had quietly but effectively found their place as a distributed system solution. These S/370s and now S/390s are being applied to business and technology management problems—many in uses that no one had even expected—such as to complement the mainframe systems, LANs, AS/400s, and other vendors' systems. But the hardware and the mainframe software didn't turn out to be the complete answer that everyone had wanted.

For the enterprise, this experience confirmed that multiple hardware and software architectures with common interfaces for interoperability, portability, and systems management exploiting the S/370 base are more appropriate than a single hardware or software architecture base. CIOs are closely watching such industry buzzwords as interoperability, client-server, distributed data, unattended operations, SAA, OSI, and *LANs* as they evolve in the information systems in the 1990s. At the same time, they are becoming much more active in standards organizations, and discussions on proprietary versus public interfaces have become commonplace for almost all levels of information systems.

The focus for system selection and implementation has traditionally been from the bottom up, starting with physical protocols and then moving up the stack to the application layers. While these efforts have proved worthwhile, they have not kept pace with day-to-day requirements. For many, because of urgency, the focus is now on the application investments, new application productivity, and on utilizing the departmental efforts rather than system architectural focus.

The ultimate beneficiary of this change in platform[6] selection approach appears to have been the end user, since the changes continue to improve his or her ability to conduct business at a competitive price and provide a responsive technical base to expand upon. This dramatic evolution to "application-driven" solutions has also

---

[6]*Platform* is a term currently being used to describe the "supporting" elements of a system. For example, a foundation is a platform of a house. This term will be used many times in this book.

provided a basis for end users to establish a more cooperative working relationship with their information services organization.

16.5 PLANNED SYSTEMS CONVERGENCE, COEXISTENCE, AND SAA

In response to the desire for common software platforms, extensive vendor driven and user driven standards (e.g., IBM's Systems Application Architecture [SAA][7] and open systems standards such as those being surfaced as part of the Open Systems Interconnect [OSI] efforts) are emerging.

Independent of the increasing emphasis on strategic directions, many CIOs also recognize that some tactical solutions must be implemented even with the promise of the emergence of such standards which have the potential to someday insulate the existing nonhardware investment from hardware change. The hope is that these tactical solutions do not necessarily preclude a merger of the tactical solutions with more strategic standards based solutions in the future. All of these approaches to commonality are being put to the test.

16.5.1 SAA

In 1987 IBM announced SAA, an evolving set of selected architected software interfaces, conventions, and protocols that will be preserved and enhanced to protect their customers' programming investment across IBM's systems. Based on a three-pronged approach, SAA addresses application portability, interoperability, and newer end user presentation technologies.[8]

SAA specifically addresses S/390 (via MVS and VM), AS/400 (via OS/400), and personal computers (via OS/2 EE) environments. Figure 16.3 portrays a model of how the three-pronged approach can be conceptualized. These interfaces can also be viewed as providing consistency for programmers (via common programming interfaces—CPIs[9]), consistent user views, and consistency in communications.

16.5.2 Other IBM Strategic Environments

At the same time, IBM continues to enhance non-SAA-compliant systems to provide their customers with continued growth flexibility. There has been a lot of confusion associated with the implications of SAA with regard to IBM's strategic products—especially non-SAA products. In the S/390 environment, two operating system platform environments have been identified as the strategic target environ-

[7]*Systems Application Architecture: An Overview,* IBM Order No. GC26-4341.

[8]"Writing Applications: A Design Guide," *Systems Application Architecture Series,* IBM Order No. SC26-4362.

[9]Common Programming Interfaces (CPIs) are documented for the SAA interfaces, e.g., C, COBOL, database, dialogs, FORTRAN, presentation, procedures language, query, and communications, etc.

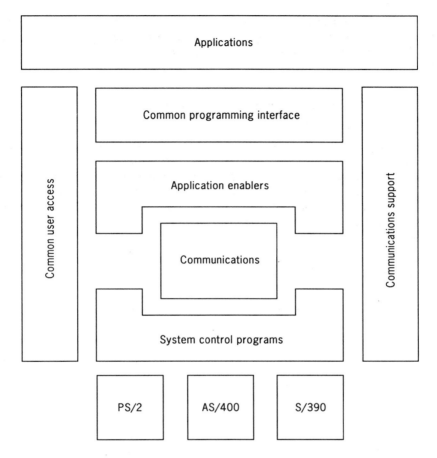

Figure 16.3 The SAA model.

ments for those customers who have a strong business need or desire to provide program portability of their application investment across IBM's hardware and software bases.

There are numerous IBM system platforms that continue to be enhanced with an eye toward SAA-compliant interfaces. Examples are DPPX and TPF. VSE increased its SAA support with VSE/ESA. This approach recognizes that existing customers' investments must be preserved and that different design points demand different platforms. The ground rules for being designated as an SAA platform are rather stiff; the platform must support *all* SAA interfaces and facilities. As a result, business judgment indicates that in many instances, subsets are the most effective mechanisms for the other IBM platforms to participate with SAA. These subsets focus on specific interfaces and are viewed as having an *affinity* to SAA.

Another very interesting attribute of the SAA approach to the consistent user access interface is that it includes the notion that programmable workstations are often between the user and the application on the host. As such, an SAA interface provides an architected model that can be mapped to by a non-SAA-compliant platform.

16.5.3 Applications, Integration, Installation

In 1988, IBM expanded its focus on solutions to encompass those that included non-IBM-developed applications and systems as well as non-IBM system solutions that can include IBM products. Software houses,[10] solution houses,[11] and systems integrators[12] were enlisted as business partners to assist the growth of IBM solutions in order to address the application requirements of the customer's enterprise. Announcements included interconnection to non-IBM systems and the expansion of relationships with non-IBM software and hardware vendors whose products complement IBM's S/370 solutions.

16.5.4 Standards and Open Systems

WHAT'S NEW?

- SAA provides blueprint of interfaces and platforms that IBM has designated for maximum portability, systems data interchange, and systems management
- Open systems connectivity via SAA and non-SAA interfaces
- IBM business partners have been identified to assist in addressing customers' application and installation needs
- Non-SAA operating systems continuing enhancements and positioning for convergence of key interfaces, e.g., DPPX with CICS interface
- A S/390 UNIX platform, AIX/370, a member of the IBM AIX family
- Interfaces among OS/2, S/400, MVS, VM, VSE, DPPX, and AIX enable interoperability
- Interfaces to and from OEM systems to IBM
- Interfaces to OSI being provided

---

[10]*Software houses* is a term used to refer to software vendors.

[11]*Solution houses* is a term used to refer to companies that offer software packages providing total solutions rather than components and tools.

[12]*Systems integrators* is the most recent term for a project management and systems engineering organization that designs and installs solutions.

In addition to IBM's continued expansion of SAA, the 1980s also marked significant changes in open systems standards, for both connectivity and systems platforms for the S/370 and now the S/390.

In 1977, the International Standards Organization (ISO) began to establish a set of standards that would make system components from different vendors more compatible. ISO identified requirements for connectivity, transfer of data, and interoperability of networks that contain processors and components built by different manufacturers, and developed a set of international standards referred to as Open Systems Interconnect (OSI). These standards include a seven-layer reference model, protocols, and service commands for open communications. Systems that adhere to these standards are referred to as open systems.

Following are descriptions of the OSI seven reference-model layers. OSI layer 1 (physical), layer 2 (data link), and layer 3 (network) are concerned with connectivity. Layer 4 (transport) provides end-to-end data integrity to connected end-user systems. Layer 5 (session) manages dialogue between communicating applications. Layer 6 (presentation) selects the syntax the application requires in order to transfer information. Layer 7 (application) provides access between user applications.

As a reference model, various communication interfaces can be mapped to the reference-model layers. Which interfaces are being exposed typically depends on which vendor is involved and the product(s) being sold. For example, most vendors typically expose only those interfaces that they need to provide flexibility or portability. This allows them to optimize and differentiate their functions and services in order to compete, and to protect their internal protocols from exposure. From an application owner's (developer's) standpoint, to protect the investment, the primary focus must be on the application interfaces to layer 7 interfaces.

From a systems builder's standpoint, to allow for flexibility, the focus tends to be on the hardware interfaces that are supported by the software. The following list provides some examples of implementations that might be found at each layer of the reference model (not all examples are perfect fits, but they should convey the concept):

- Application(7):   —enterprise-specific protocols
   —application management protocols[13]
   —system protocols, e.g., file transfer[14]
   —industry-specific protocols, e.g., MMS[15]
   —document-transfer protocols, e.g., X.400[16]

---

[13]*Application management* refers to such capabilities as Virtual Terminal (VT) and Job Transfer and Manipulation (JTM).

[14]File Transfer, Access and Management (FTAM) is a standard to allow applications to transfer files or access records of a file among other systems using a connection-oriented protocol.

[15]*MMS* refers to Manufacturing Message Specification.

[16]*X.400 Message Handling Systems* is a CCITT specification for E-mail. It resides at layers 6 and 7 and is independent of the underlying communications layers.

          —systems or network management (NM) protocols[17]
          —directory services, e.g., X.500

- Presentation(6):   —data transformation
                —data formatting, e.g., ASCII, EBCDIC
- Session (5):   —session connection (dialogs)
- Transport (4):   —class of service connections
               —end-to-end transparent data flows, e.g., TCP/IP, DECnet
- Network (3):   —native, e.g., X.25
- Data link (2):   —S/S, BSC, HDLC, SDLC, ADCCP, CSMA, token
- Physical (1):   —RS232C, V.24, X.21, V.35

OSI/ISO APPLICATION LAYER STANDARDS EXAMPLES*

- Office Document Architecture (ODA)—ISO 8613
- File Transfer, Access and Management (FTAM)—ISO 8571
- Virtual Terminal—ISO 9040
- Network Management—ISO 9595/96
- Manufacturing Message Specification—ISO 9506
- Distributed Transaction Processing—ISO 10026
- Remote Database Access Protocol—ISO 9576
- Job Transfer and Manipulation—ISO 8832/33
- The Directory (CCITT X.500)—ISO 9594
- X.400 Message Handling—ISO 10020/21
- Common Service Elements—ASCE, ISO 8649/50
                           RTSE, ISO 9066
                           ROSE, ISO 9072

*These are in various states of completion by ISO.

The reference-model seven reference layers are in many ways analogous to IBM's seven SNA layers, and many of the services currently being defined are analogous to those architected in SNA and SAA, e.g., SNA Distribution Services (SNADS), Document Interconnect Architecture (DIA), Document Content Archi-

---

[17]There are management components associated with each layer, however, the overall management is in application layer.

tecture (DCA), Distributed Data Management (DDM), and SNA Management Services (SNA/MS).

Perhaps not visible in the United States until recently, IBM has been participating in the development of international standards since 1977, and working with individual standards bodies[18] as well as being an executive member of Corporation for Open Systems (COS). IBM has implemented approximately 30 X.25 products since 1979. In 1983, when the ISO Reference Model became a standard, IBM delivered Open Systems Network Services (OSNS), its first OSI product.

With the increasing trend towards heterogeneous networks, governmental procurement policies, and the influence of several standards and user groups,[19] IBM has continued to focus on solutions using mixed-vendor equipment. In 1986, independent of the OSI activities, IBM announced the Open Communication Architectures (OCA), declaring its intention to extend interconnection of networks and communications products via SNA. It intends to integrate SNA and OSI support wherever appropriate to make applications transparent to underlying protocols. IBM has also established interoperability testing and verification centers for vendors to test their implementation of OSI with IBM, using IBM's General Teleprocessing Monitor for OSI (GTMOSI), Open Systems Transport and Session Support (OTSS),[20] Open Systems Network Support (OSNS),[21] and SNA Network Packet Switching Interface software for X.25 (NPSI).

In 1988, IBM announced a number of new products supporting international standards for Open Systems Interconnection (OSI). The products were presented in the X.400 and FTAM applications (layer 7) context. There are currently two implementations for X.400 support—one implementation for the U.S. and one for the rest of the world.[22] X.400 DISOSS and PROFS use the underlying X.400 support. In the FTAM application context, the OSI/Communication Subsystem[23] and OSI/File Services were introduced worldwide.

They stack up as depicted in Figure 16.4. Note that the intent is to move all OSI applications to a single base supporting layers 1 through 6.[24]

---

[18]Standards bodies that IBM is active in include: American National Standards Institute (ANSI), European Computer Manufacturers' Association (ECMA), OSI Network in the United States (OSINET), OSI interest group in Italy (OSIRIDE), Interoperability Technology Activity for Information Processing in Japan (INTAP), and Standards Promotion and Application Group (SPAG).

[19]This includes standards and user groups such as ISO, ANSI, ECMA, COS, SPAG, Promoting Conference for OSI (POSI), and Manufacturing Automation Protocol/Technical and Office Products (MAP/TOP).

[20]You could think of OTSS as providing the OSI session (5) and transport (4) layers. This is a non-U.S. product.

[21]You could think of OSNS as providing the OSI network layer (3). This is a non-U.S. product.

[22]Giorgio Emo Capodilista and Ron Bostick, "IBM X.400 Programs," *Interface: Technology at Research Triangle Park,* Jan. 1989, pp. 12–14.

[23]Initial support for OSI protocols in SAA is provided by the OSI/Communication Subsystem and OSI/File Services Licensed Programs. These are not available in all countries.

[24]Ron Bostick, "Overview of New IBM OSI Products," *Interface: Technology at Research Triangle Park.* January 1989. pp. 1–3.

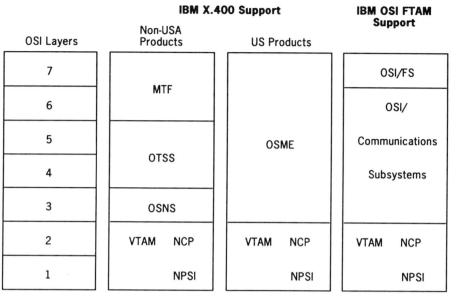

MTF: Message Transfer Facility
NPSI: Network Packet Switching Interface
OSME: Open Systems Message Exchange
OSNS: Open Systems Network Support
OSI/FS: OSI/File Services

Figure 16.4   IBM implementations mapped to OSI reference model.

X.400 support allows messages to be exchanged among dissimilar computing systems using a common OSI protocol via the IBM X.400 Message Transfer Facility (MTF), which is an application of Open Systems Transport and Session Support (OTSS), which in turn uses Open Systems Network Support (OSNS), which uses VTAM in non-U.S. countries. IBM's Open Systems Message Exchange (OSME) is a VTAM application that essentially replaces the MTF, OTSS, and OSNS combination in the U.S. It supports European Profiles.

The IBM X.400 DISOSS Connection and X.400 PROFS Connection program offerings provide for the exchanging of messages to and from DISOSS and PROFS using X.400 protocols as depicted in Figure 16.5. The X.400 connection software prepares the message (transforms text to and from the appropriate international standard or IBM Document Content Architecture) to flow to and from the IBM subsystem.

The DISOSS implementation provides for the addresses to be mapped from a directory while the user provides the address in the PROFS implementation. This figure also depicts that DISOSS can communicate with other DISOSS interfaces such as Personal Services/CICS, Personal Services/TSO, etc., across the SNA network (using LU6.2) and that PROFS can exchange mail with other PROFS

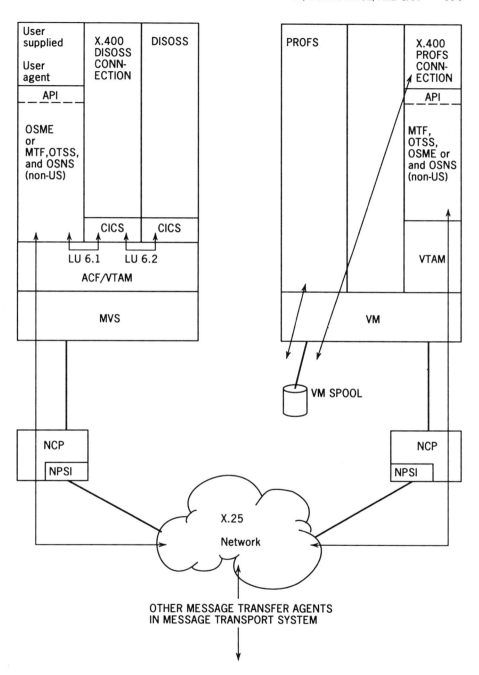

Figure 16.5 X.400 connections.

systems via its remote spooling capability. In this instance, the remote spooling is also connected via an SNA backbone.

IBM's OSI/File Services is an application of OSI/Communication Subsystem that runs in layer 7 of the OSI reference model and is an IBM S/370 implementation of the OSI File Transfer and Management (FTAM) standard for VM and MVS. It provides transfer and management of electronic files between IBM and non-IBM systems using comparable OSI protocols. It supports National Bureau of Standards (T1 and M1) and European Profiles. It supports a subset of MAP 3.0 FTAM[25] specifications for Computer Integrated Manufacturing (CIM).

OSI/Communications Subsystem is a VTAM application which supports US GOSIP,[26] UK GOSIP,[27] CEN/CENELEC, and CEPT[28] Profiles. This is a subset implementation of several management services draft proposals and provides: a base for ISO applications such as message and file transfer; the ability for users to write their own customized applications through an IBM-supplied interface; some network management capability in the form of status alerts to NetView; and the ability to connect to networks via X.25 connection through VTAM or by using the Internet protocol over X.25. The interface to the X.25 connection is via NPSI or VTAM together with the ICA (Integrated Communication Adapter), e.g., ES/9000 rack model ICA with the VTAM.

This implementation provides a subset of OSI Common Management Information Services (CMIS) and OSI Common Management Information Protocols (CMIP). OSI/Communication Subsystem sends OSI management protocols to NetView as generic alerts and the NetView Command Facility is used to communicate between the NetView operator and the OSI/Communication Subsystem command processor. IBM's OSI/Communication Subsystem is an IBM S/390 implementation of OSI layers 3, 4, 5, 6, and 7 executing in VM and MVS, which allows a NewView operator to manage SNA and OSI objects.

16.5.5 Open Systems and SAA

IBM has expanded SAA to include some key OSI protocols[29] in the SAA Common Communication Support (CCS) as part of its objective to provide various levels of coexistence and integration as the OSI standard continues to emerge. OSI/Commu-

---

[25]MAP (Manufacturing Automation Protocol) is an OSI based LAN specification (802.4) which allows the interconnection of devices residing in a plant operational environment.

[26]GOSIP stands for Government OSI Profiles. It is a Federal Information Processing Specification (FIPS) which is to become binding for the various governmental departments in August 1990. US GOSIP allows for grandfathered TCP/IP networks.

[27]UK GOSIP is the UK's OSI Profile. One of its differences from the US GOSIP is that it supports the connection-oriented mode of transmission (the US supports the connectionless).

[28]CEPT is the Geneva-based European Conference of Postal and Telephone Administrations.

[29]The protocols include File Transfer Access and Management (FTAM) ISO 8571; X.400 Message Handling System, Association Control Service Element (ACSE) (ISO 8650); Presentation Layer, Kernal and ASN.1 (ISO 8823 and ISO 8825); Session Layer (ISO 8327); Transport Layer, Classes 0, 2, and 4 (ISO 8073); and Network Layer using Internet (ISO 8473) and Subnet interface to X.25 (ISO 8878).

nication Subsystem and OSI/File Services support user programs written in two SAA high-level languages: COBOL and C programming languages.

In the same open systems vein, IBM and S/390 is also very active in UNIX systems as the interest by many customers, universities, and governments grows. IBM is a key member of the Open Systems Foundation (OSF). It also introduced AIX/370, which will conform to the POSIX standard (IEEE 1003) when the standard is completed. Now AIX is provided for the PS/2, RISC/6000, and the S/390. AIX makes extensive use of TCP/IP.

The key message is that open systems and SAA are evolving standards.

16.5.6 SAA, Convergence, and Coexistence

The long and the short of it is that all of the various approaches that IBM's customers are pursuing to address the problem of bringing their information systems together are being supported, sometimes to the confusion of the executive who wants one clear direction. The basic commercial approach is to use SAA as the roadmap even while using some IBM non-SAA solutions to solve business problems that cannot be directly addressed by the SAA model. This allows an executive to establish a direction while protecting his current investments and retaining the necessary flexibility demanded by today's rapidly changing needs.

An important aspect to note is the prevalence of distributed considerations to all these directions. This reenforces the notion that if the ability to distribute is designed into solutions, you have the option to centralize or distribute solutions based on organizational, technology, or economic needs.

INTEROPERABILITY AND MULTIPLE STANDARDS

- Drivers: increased complexity from multiple systems architectures
- Challenges: protect investments, build on investments, interconnect
- Solutions: documented interfaces, interfacing OEM to IBM systems, interfacing, porting total environments, IBM business partners, standards, open systems standards
- Status: documentation available, application focus, distributed interfaces focus on existing applications, standards still evolving, products available

---

Chapter 17

Multiples Require a Fundamental Change in How Details Are Managed

Probably the most important guideline that I have come across is that associated with managing details. The bottom line is that unless some fundamental breakthroughs are implemented, one can't continue focusing on details at the same level while increasing the number of systems being implemented and managed. A comparison can be made with the process of keeping track of automobile makes, models, and features. Back in the 1950s and 1960s, one could be reasonably knowledgeable in this area. Most people interested in cars could tell a lot about a vehicle by initially identifying some distinguishable attribute, such as the fins, headlights, grill, or emblem. Many people could then go on to tell you what was under the hood, e.g., a V-8 with 350 cubic inches and 305 horsepower. As the number of cars, models, and years increased it became harder to keep track unless you picked a very specific subset or attribute to follow. The same phenomenon is true for systems; how many specialists do you need in the room to make a technical decision about systems today?

Historically, central sites have focused on tuning, optimizing, and tailoring each of their mainframes to best meet the business and financial requirements. This calls for substantial skill, experience, and staff time, because the central site processors typically support a large variety of applications, users, and products. When these organizations distribute processors, these approaches to control are stressed because they have the potential to increase the staff and complexity, while reducing the responsiveness.

Just think of the numerics associated with tuning 100 systems versus the few at central today, especially if they are full clones of the central systems in terms of services. Use of reasonability tests reveals this problem very quickly. If it takes 15 minutes to scrutinize a highly summarized system performance report for each week, it would take 25 hours for 100 systems just to read the analysis. Similarly, if it takes an hour to analyze the system log for messages, the same phenomenon should be expected from each of the systems, assuming they run the same software and are managed similarly.

Two management models which have not stressed the IS organization as much with regards to managing multiple distributed systems have emerged to date. For discussion, let's refer to them as special purpose distributed and loosely controlled distributed solutions.

IS in the insurance industry, retail industry, and banking industry has successfully implemented special purpose distributed solutions for many years. It has implemented point-of-sale systems and agency systems, which provide finite and well-defined functions in a tightly controlled environment.

It has also developed very specific remote management rules, mechanics, and automation. The rules include items such as capacity thresholds. If the threshold is crossed, capacity is added and there is no time to address each system. There is, however, significant focus on selection of the threshold and the approach to writing optimal code. Similarly, all messages regarding the problems are not reported or even saved until some threshold is reached.

In many cases the diagnostic data and diagnosis might create a bigger problem than the original problem if handled in anything other than exception mode. Even alerts are considered extraneous if no meaningful action can be taken. For example, an alert indicating that a remote system is not working during the business day is noticed by the central operator. The operator begins calling the office to diagnose the problem, but is unable to reach the supervisor because the supervisor's phone is busy. It is busy because the supervisor knows the system is down, has cut over to the backup procedures until the system is repaired, and is reporting the problem. This procedure was redundant. On the other hand, if the problem was discovered during off hours and some remote diagnosis could be done, it might have been appropriate to send an alert to dispatch a person to repair the system before the morning, or at least to have the repair person there first thing in the morning. In short, in successful implementations all data and actions are scrutinized in terms of value.

Similarly, manufacturing firms and universities have implemented many loosely controlled distributed solutions. In these solutions the main control is the network across and the selection of some common application-to-application protocols, which, at universities, are mostly batch-, message-oriented, and file-server-oriented. Loosely controlled distributed solutions allow each distributed system owner to manage their own destiny, plus progress and grow the system and services at their own rate. They are independent of changes in other systems. Security is one exception.

The current distributed solutions thrust includes both the special purpose and the loosely controlled solutions, because of breakthroughs in the price, physical size, and environmental requirements. The benefits of the special purpose are specific function, performance, and availability. The benefit of loosely controlled solutions is their responsiveness to the specific user groups' needs.

In the early 1990s, the user population and business requirements are pushing to get both benefits from a single solution. This means that the special purpose solution model must become more flexible by delegation of some level of freedom to the user for ad hoc activities. The loosely controlled solution model will have to become more rigorous with regard to data access, security, and chargeout.

A key consideration that is not always obvious is that there is a cost associated with controls. This cost is associated with tools, storage, alternate access ports, etc. An oversimplified test to demonstrate the choice (risk) associated with controls being made in many departmental systems is to determine how many PC users with hard disks use or even have access to a tape backup. Are they spending hours every week backing up their assets to floppy diskettes? Are they storing selected copies of the diskettes off site in case of a local loss or disaster? In many cases the answer is that the tape drive is too expensive and the operational media is relatively reliable. In other words, a risk assessment has been made. I use the PC example, but I have seen multiple business *LANs* and departmental systems that are taking similar risks with even larger stakes.

The point is that commercial-strength solutions that cover multiple departments and locations will typically be more expensive than singleton solutions where owners make their own decisions (either consciously or unconsciously). The challenge is not to impose unnecessary rigor while providing the appropriate rigor. Appropriateness is a trade-off between what the user really needs and is willing to pay for and the amount of flexibility that the IS organization can afford to provide from a resource and expense standpoint. Solutions include *self-managing systems* with selective user controls.

Some example steps to providing selective control include: providing read access to corporate data for authorized users from extract relational data base copies; delegating the administration to each user or department administrator and providing the backup capacity; similarly using outside help-desk services charging on a per call basis rather than staffing, with the IS or user organization; and allowing the IS organization to negotiate the licenses and support, but letting each department work directly with the vendor or supplier.

MULTIPLES REQUIRE A FUNDAMENTAL CHANGE IN DETAIL

- Central procedures are detail- and element-oriented
- Same levels of details for multiples with same approach is unmanageable
- Options include additional investments or changes to approach
- Approaches should map to the requirements of the specific user base
- Security and data integrity must be maintained
- Approaches to delegation and excess capacity being exercised
- User systems are a form of delegation
- User and control systems must become self-managing

Chapter *18*

CIO Summary

This section has provided some pragmatic considerations and guidelines regarding the implementation of distributed solutions. The experiences of several large S/390 installations provided the basis for the input, and their experiences both positive and negative has provided a very good basis for understanding the requirements for implementing distributed solutions from a management and implementation standpoint. Both hardware and software platforms considerations were included.

- Distributed and decentralized implementations differ
- User-, departmental- and IS-owned systems can be strategic
- Understand your implicit design points
- Unattended and remote operations must be designed in
- Use what you know and have; push from there
- Sponsorship and implementation approach make the difference
- A vision and comprehensive project plan are required
- The application and five factors determine the platform(s)
- Connectivity is far less and requires far more
- Interoperability and multiple standards are in the cards
- Multiples require a fundamental change in how details are managed

The overriding themes in these guidelines and experiences are that of predicting where technology and various solutions tend to go, peaceful coexistence between user systems and control systems, and the need to have the user's (departmental) sponsorship for solutions that require the user to change. In many enterprises, IS has learned that distributed solutions managed by the glasshouse require a new kind of end user partnership that emphasizes the end users' creativity and desires to do certain tasks that are best done by them (*user systems*), while IS focuses on control systems. IS has also learned that distributed solutions require a different level of detailed attention than do mainframe systems—less time must be spent on tuning and maintenance.

An underlying theme is that S/390 architecture provides the basis for examining and implementing a comprehensive collection of hardware, operating systems, and systems management capabilities supported by a multitude of application platforms. All the platforms have placed various degrees of focus on providing remote operations, unattended operations, and distributed functional capabilities. DPPX, VM, and VSE have placed a major emphasis on providing a remote unattended operational environment together with the hardware features of rack-mounted S/390s and card-mounted S/370s.

The rack- and card-mounted S/370s (ES/9370) expanded the S/390's reach downward on the price and environmental requirements. They and their successors are well-suited for an office environment. These systems provide many integrated adapters to address interconnectivity with IBM and non-IBM terminals, workstations, and systems. The price, size, and adapters have increased the uses of the S/390 to include applications that previously required specialized hardware or were not possible because of price and environmental constraints.

In general, the specific platform implementations have provided multiple attachment options and interoperability capabilities to provide flexibility while protecting the enterprise's application and hardware investments. The platforms also continue to provide the necessary tools required to support multiple distributed IBM and non-IBM systems. A key focus continues to be on skills to develop, operate, use, and evolve solutions. The focus on development guidelines and architectures such as IBM's Systems Application Architecture together with a common focus on systems management has substantially increased the flexibility to select the application platform based on the application's requirements, where in the past the systems management criteria predetermined the solution. These considerations make a very good checklist when selecting platforms to invest in.

What Every Systems Architect Should Know about Distributed

This section is intended to provide some more detailed aspects of using an S/390 as part of your distributed solution from an interoperability standpoint. The objective is to provide sufficient detail to help you develop an initial model of your options. Additional sources will be cited to help you pursue more precision or detail.

The focus for this section is primarily the application-to-application considerations; the underlying platforms are discussed later in the Connectivity section. The discussion will consider:

- Distributed application interfaces
- Distributed data base and file implementations
- Complementary (coexistence) services and capabilities
- Distributed office implementations

Chapter *19*

IBM Distributed Application Interfaces

This chapter introduces the fundamental approaches being used to accomplish various degrees of interoperability among IBM and non-IBM to IBM systems.

19.1 THREE INTERFACES

From a connectivity and interoperability standpoint, there are essentially three distributed solutions application platform interfaces:

- Terminal emulation or pass-through
- Batch interfaces
- Task-to-task interfaces (various degrees, including program-to-program and application-to-application[1])

These three interfaces are used by applications, application platforms, and systems services to exchange data, initiate execution of some task, or provide access and delivery of some service. They provide the basis for additional services.

---

[1]The distinctions between the task, program, and application peer communications are relative to the requesting entities. For example, operating systems communicating with one another would use a task-to-task interface, application programs would use a program-to-program interface, and applications using a subsystem would use a application-to-application interface where the subsystem may use either a program-to-program or task-to-task interface.

19.2 TERMINAL EMULATION OR TERMINAL PASS-THROUGH

Terminal emulation or terminal pass-through is relatively well-established, with multiple solutions being marketed. The connectivity of some currently available implementations will be discussed later. The primary considerations are the direction of the pass-through or emulation from an OEM system to an IBM system (typically via a 3270 interface) or from an IBM system to an OEM (typically via an ASCII terminal interface). Key checklist items are features such as screen size expected by application, color, full screen, etc. SNA implementations allow for logons to various systems as part of their networking implementation.

19.3 BATCH INTERFACES

Batch interfaces such as provided by RJE, NJE, RSCS, PNET, and VSE/POWER are probably the oldest implementation used to communicate among similar and different systems.

These batch job subsystems typically emulate Remote Job Entry (RJE) devices such as the IBM 2780 (which uses the BSC protocol, an IBM-defined synchronous pre-SNA protocol), or IBM 3770 (which uses SDLC) and transmits data in 80 column (card) or printline-oriented protocols. The specific implementations are RJE, Network Job Entry (NJE), RSCS for VM, and PNET for VSE/POWER. The SNA implementation provides the necessary communications platform to mask the network. The BSC implementations require point-to-point lines or intermediary spooling and forwarding.

19.4 TASK-TO-TASK

The most interesting areas, and probably those that currently require the most attention, are the task-to-task implementations provided by the system, subsystems, special services, or applications using some combination of the implementations. LU6.2 is beginning to become the common industry task-to-task interface for distributed solutions, when connecting to an IBM system via a network. Probably the most important question not asked soon enough in distributed projects is: What application platforms connect, and how?

The primary focus is usually on the physical and operating environment software connectivity, rather than the actual protocols and capabilities between (among) the target applications. The underlying assumption is that the higher level application-to-application support is already in place. Unfortunately, the quest for such solutions is reminiscent of my college calculus professor's lecture, which usually began with some very fundamental setup steps and left off with, "For the rest you just turn the crank." Based on the number of hours I spent turning the crank, I think I assumed too much. Beware of turning the crank and expecting applications to readily or effectively work together.

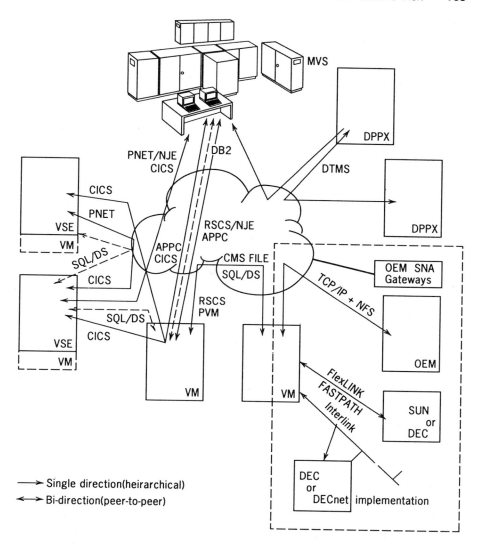

Figure 19.1 *Applications platform interconnectivity example.*

This section covers the application-to-application considerations; the underlying platforms are discussed later in the Connectivity section.

For now, consider the application-to-application options depicted in Figure 19.1. Note that while they all appear to be interconnected, they are implemented with very specific targets and one must be sensitive to the direction of flow. These will be discussed in much more detail in the following chapters of this section.

Figure 19.1 depicts several of the more common application platform interconnect implementations for IBM systems, and recognizes some non-IBM interconnect in the area in the dotted box. A short snapshot of each follows:

19.5 PEER-TO-PEER SERVICES

I will use the term "peer-to-peer" to refer to the communication among multiple systems, subsystems, or programs. Peer-to-peer communications requires an agreed-to protocol and interfaces. The systems, subsystems, or programs do not have to be common.

19.5.1 Program-to-Program SNA Interface

IBM has developed an architected SNA protocol, LU6.2, that provides program-to-program communications by application programs via the SNA network and VTAM. Operating systems provide this capability via an APPC (Application Program-to Program Communication) interface. This interface allows application programs to communicate via the interface rather than focus on the actual communication protocols.

Although APPC and LU6.2 are often used interchangeably, one might think of APPC as the program interface to the services provided by the LU6.2 SNA communications interface in order to communicate peer-to-peer. Currently, there are multiple APPCs implemented, each provided by the specific operating system (e.g., APPC/VM, APPC/PC, etc.). Each provides essentially the same types of services, but they do not necessarily have the same program interfaces. Additionally, not all systems have the same services. This means that the programmer must map the services and requests to make sure that both sides are balanced.

APPC CPI-C is IBM's SAA application-to-application interface built on LU6.2 and accessible via high-level programming languages. Via the architecture work done for SAA in this area, from a programming interface standpoint, APPC CPI-C provides a consistent interface across operating systems. It will still require that the programmer map the available services on the participating systems.

Mapping efforts aside, APPC using LU6.2 has provided a standard SNA-based interface for programmers and vendors to provide peer-to-peer program communications. Multiple OEMs provide an APPC (LU6.2) interface in order to provide IBM interconnection. The most prevalent implementation is used for SNADS, however, several vendors to provide an LU6.2 programming interface so programs from their environment can communicate with programs in the IBM environment.

19.5.2 Application-to-Application Interfaces

Just as APPC CPI-C provides a programmer the ability to write programs that communicate peer-to-peer, several systems and subsystems provide these services on behalf of the using applications. These services can be provided by transaction managers, data base managers, and file subsystems. A variety of techniques, interfaces, and protocols are used to accomplish the connection and communication. Some of these techniques include: transaction routing, function shipping, and remote file access, and remote data base access.

19.5.2.1   Transaction Routing.

IBM provides four transaction managers with the ability to request that transactions be routed to peer transaction managers. IBM's IMS[2], CICS[3], DPPX, and TPF provide the ability to route transactions (in IMS and TPF they are referred to as messages) among themselves (e.g., IMS to IMS, CICS to CICS, DPPX to DPPX, etc.).

In addition, provisions have been made to accommodate intertransaction manager transaction routing (e.g., CICS to IMS, DPPX to IMS, DPPX to CICS, etc.). This is extremely important when dealing with multiple operating systems and various sized systems. For example, a CICS[4] on a PS/2 workstation can route transactions to other CICSs on MVS and VSE or vice versa. CICS can also send transactions to IMS via an intersystem coupling capability (ISC) that implemented an early version of what is now LU6.2.

Transaction routing among different transaction managers is accomplished by sending a specific predetermined data stream to a predetermined transaction on the target system. No program logic is included in the transmission. The programmer also has to be able to write programs to the specific transaction manager's programming interfaces and must map services provided. For example, DPPX/370 provides access to CICS or IMS via a defined interface (the Host Transaction Facility, HTF) to access centrally managed data.

By using a single transaction platform that spans the various operations systems, the programmer efforts to map services and know multiple interfaces is virtually eliminated. The closest such platform today is CICS. The CICS transaction manager in one location provides the ability to initiate and control a transaction at another location. This is referred to as a transaction routing. (The flows will be discussed shortly).

Similarly, using a common application generator—such as IBM's CSP or a high-level language that provides a common interface to system services across multiple operating systems, transaction managers, and data base managers—provides a high level of portability and reduces the need for the programmer to be aware of the differences.

19.5.2.2   Function Shipping.

Just as some transaction managers provide the capability to route transactions (or messages) among themselves and between them and selected other transaction managers, some transaction managers and subsystems provide the ability to ship functional requests to peer transaction managers or subsystems without the need for having an application program on the target system.

[2]IMS is used as the generic acronym for IMS/VS and IMS/ESA.
[3]CICS is used as the generic acronym for CICS/VS, CICS/ESA, VSE CICS/VS, CICS/MVS, and CICS/VM.
[4]CICS OS/2 can also operate on DOS 3.3 or 4.0.

For example, CICS provides the ability to access remote services and distributed (remote) data bases and files via function shipping among CICSs, on MVS, VM, VSE, and other OS/2 CICS systems. A sample scenario includes a VM/CMS user accessing a DL/I data base and VSAM file via the CICS application program interface. The CICS/VM control services on VM provide the ability to initiate requests on its behalf in another CICS (e.g., a data request). This provides for managed access to remote data in the form of DL/I data bases and CICS controlled VSAM data residing on MVS and VSE systems. CICS-controlled VSAM files and remote SQL/DS data bases can be accessed remotely from other VM systems. (The remote SQL/DS request is serviced by SQL/DS and transparent to CICS/VM in this scenario.)

19.5.2.3 *Remote File Access.* Similarly, VM provides for remote VM file access via the VM file system (also know as the shared file system, SFS). The VM file system provides a location with insensitive file-sharing capability via its directory services and uses APPC as its mechanism to communicate among SNA and non-SNA connected VM systems.

19.5.2.4 *Remote Relational Data Base.* As was mentioned in the function shipping scenario, remote relational data base access is supported among VM systems via SQL/DS. SQL/DS uses APPC to access peer SQL/DS systems. Remote SQL/DS is also supported for VSE. If VSE runs as a VM guest, VSE SQL/DS users can access SQL/DS data bases residing on native VM local or remote VM. Using this mechanism, multiple distributed VSE systems running as guest systems on VM and multiple VM systems can access each other's data.

19.5.2.5 *NFS Access via TCP/IP.* VM also provides an NFS file server service accessible from systems that use TCP/IP with NFS (e.g., NFS clients on UNIX-based systems, and OEM systems such as HP, DEC, etc.) via TCP/IP VM. (There is also an MVS version of TCP/IP that supports the NFS feature). TCP/IP, together with NFS, provides a remote user with the ability to share files via the Network File System, transfer files using TCP/IP file transfer capabilities (FTP), and use the NFS support for remote procedure call (RPC, a SUN protocol) to write socket interface programs for program-to-program access.

19.5.3 Intersystem Services

Numerous interfaces and services accessible from non-IBM systems in addition to the TCP/IP capabilities are available on VM. Such solutions include transparent interfaces to the user application or require the user to code to the interface. The actual cross-system access is typically via private and proprietary protocols provided by the vendors. Examples include Interlink and Intel's 9770 Fastpath connection and FlexLINK's software. They both provide bi-directional access to VM and VAX/VMS system services. Intel's Fastpath also provides bi-directional access to SUN. The other OEM-to-IBM interconnect implementations will be discussed in later sections.

Chapter 20

Distributed Data Base/File Capabilities

20.1 INTRODUCTION

This chapter provides a snapshot of the distributed data base and distributed file capabilities available among IBM systems.

In the distributed context there are two ways distributed data base or distributed files are discussed: remote access and data transfer (files, data bases, or portions of data bases). Probably the simplest approach is to transfer the data to the place where it is needed. This could be much easier than transmitting a program to the data, especially if the environments are not all the same. The transmission of the data could provide the best or worst performance depending on the amount of data and the demand for the data by other users at different locations.

To improve upon the response time risks and demand overheads associated with transmitting batches of data, multiple variations of splitting data bases have and are being implemented. These include partitioning the data (e.g., by state), subsetting the data and distributing it to the various locations, and variations of these mixed with access to central data bases. The primary considerations are not only the time to extract and distribute the data, but also the ease with which data can be updated while assuring timeliness and data integrity. Various approaches have been implemented, but no simple general algorithm has surfaced to date.

The chapter will focus on remote access (on an individual record, segment, or multiples) implementations, some of which can be applied to the various approaches to distributing data. File transfer will be discussed in the connectivity sections.

Just as distributed data can be accessed via remote access or data transmission techniques, there are also two very different approaches to managing distributed

189

data base or distributed file system accesses. Some implementations use a transaction manager, while others use only a data base manager. The differences can be significant with regard to control and performance based on current implementations. Each approach, as can be expected, has its own strengths and focus areas.

The transaction manager approach provides the best controls, but requires that transaction manager versions or comparable services with common interfaces and rules be present on all the participating systems. The CICS family currently provides the most comprehensive solution if one is selecting a solution that provides the controls, security, accounting, and administrative rigors across IBM systems. Transaction manager interfaces tend to be proprietary. They are difficult to map to because of the significant number of controls that are expected to be exchanged in order to operate as a peer control system. Because of this complexity, there are very few transaction manager implementations across vendors.

The distributed (remote) file or data base system approach is also frequently used. It is probably much more frequently used than transaction manager implementations when one considers the number of *LANs* and departmental systems that use this approach. These interfaces tend to be less complex, and as a result lend themselves to more ready access from other operating system environments. The application program interfaces tend to be published (e.g., SQL) or relatively easy to intercept and handle on behalf of the requesting program. There are a multitude of such implementations on the market today. The foremost consideration to date is the need to allow multiple updates to various distributed data bases while assuring data integrity.

20.2 A TRANSACTION MANAGER EXAMPLE—CICS

CICS is frequently used for implementing distributed data bases. Many installations are running various types of distributed CICS implementations. For example, CICS can run geographically dispersed, locally dispersed, and on the same processor using the Multiple Regional Operation (MRO) capabilities. Using both the transaction routing and the function shipping capabilities, the CICS platform can provide for both remote access and the ability to send the transaction to the data. CICS uses an APPC service to communicate and provides for multiple location update. Using these capabilities, partitioned data bases, subset data bases and central data bases can be configured to meet the response and currency needs. Alternate paths implemented via the network reduces risks of communication outage impacts.

20.2.1 Function Shipping

The function shipping capability allows a CICS application program to request data either through a DL/I or File Control[1] (VSAM) interface, as well as providing

---

[1]File Control is a CICS-provided file interface to VSAM services. It is used for applications that do need the additional functionality and controls that relational data base services such as DB2 and SQL/DS provide or the controls that DL/I provides.

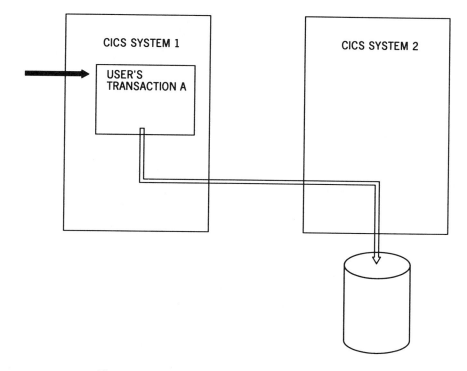

Figure 20.1 *CICS function shipping (e.g., data request).*

temporary storage and transient data capabilities (which are beyond the scope of this publication); see Figure 20.1. Figure 20.2 illustrates CICS flows among various S/390 operating systems. In the configuration depicted, an application on the VM system using the CICS application program interface can assess CICS accessible data from another VM, VSE, or MVS. Similarly, applications (transactions) on the VSE or MVS systems can access CICS accessible data on the other system.

CICS assumes the data integrity and overall management responsibility. In adverse conditions, such as a communications failure or component failure associated with the request, CICS rules of recovery are applied. CICS on OS/2,[2,3] VM, VSE, and MVS can use CICS on VM, VSE, and MVS as a server using the function shipping capabilities (see Figure 20.3).

CICS/VM and CICS OS/2 (and the announced DPPX interface) are special implementations since, rather than providing a CICS environment, these are imple-

---

[2]CICS OS/2 operates on both IBM DOS 3.3/4.0 and OS/2 EE. Function-shipping to CICS/MVS, CICS/OS/VS, or CICS/VSE is supported via LU2 or LU6.2. Function-shipping to VM is supported via LU6.2 only.

[3]The host-based CICS provides a data-conversion capability to map and convert personal computer ASCII data to EBCDIC.

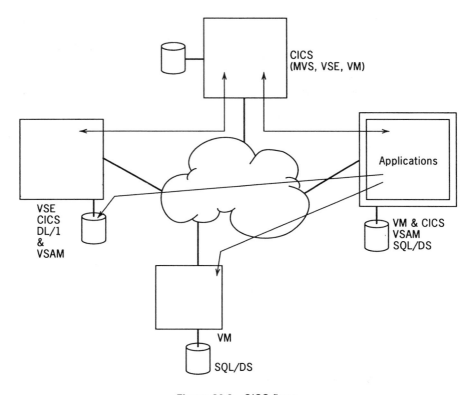

Figure 20.2 *CICS flows.*

mented with CICS application program interfaces and use the native operating environment to provide the underlying services. This implementation allows the integration of some environment-unique services with the standard CICS applications.[4]

For example, CICS/VM provides an application program interface that allows the application programmer to integrate VM services and CICS services into end user services. This lends itself to providing seamless access to these services. For example, a PROFS user could issue a single command with some data, which could cause access to local and remote CMS files, VSAM files and SQL/DS data, CICS-controlled data on VSAM or DL/I (on VSE or MVS), and then come right back to the user's PROFS screen. Data that a CMS user application can access is mapped out in the following VM application data table. A relatively new capability, SQL/DS Application Interface for VSAM (SAIV), is an optional SQL/DS feature that provides users of CICS/VM with a VSAM interface to SQL/DS.[5] This interface allows:

[4]The integration of environment-unique capabilities may limit the portability.
[5]SQL/DS provides its own distributed support.

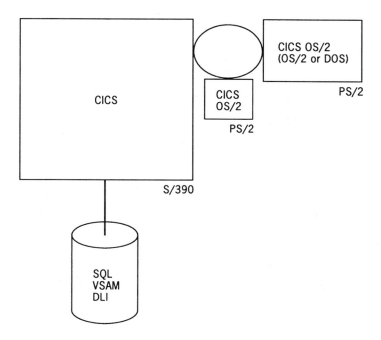

Figure 20.3   CICS OS/2.

- One application program to own a SQL/DS data base in a VM-connected machine
- CICS transactions written or VSAM access to SQL/DS data (migrated from VSAM) without changing them. Access is provided by an emulation function that processes VSAM requests.

A key benefit of this implementation is that the interactive user has direct access to local and remote production data. Consider the two scenarios in Figure 20.4.

20.2.2   Transaction Routing

Similarly a whole CICS transaction can be routed to another CICS system, enabling the application to use the data bases of the target system. Figure 20.5 illustrates how two CICS systems can process transactions asynchronously. In this situation, transaction A is not dependent on the status of transaction B. (Not available on CICS/VM.)

Besides asynchronous processing, CICS can also process distributed transactions synchronously (see Figure 20.6). Programs must be coded to explicitly support this. In this case, there is a very close relationship between transaction A and B.

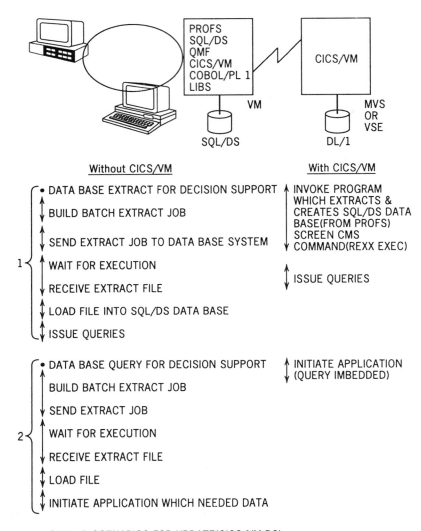

Figure 20.4   *CICS/VM distribute DL/I extract and SQL/DS query scenario.*

20.3   A TRANSACTION MANAGER EXAMPLE—DPPX/370

DPPX/370's Distributed Resource Manager allows application programs to transparently access data bases on peer systems with full recovery support, and allows transaction processing users to transparently access transactions on peer systems. (See Figure 20.7.) DPPX was designed with this in mind.

DPPX/370 Router provides full screen access to applications on peer and host

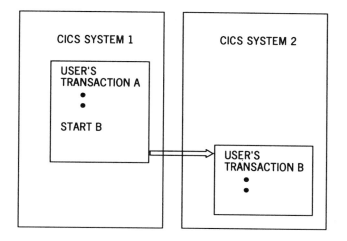

Figure 20.5 *Distributing asynchronous transactions across CICS systems.*

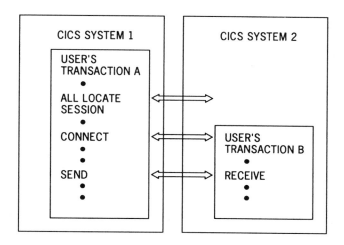

Figure 20.6 *Distributing synchronous transactions across CICS systems.*

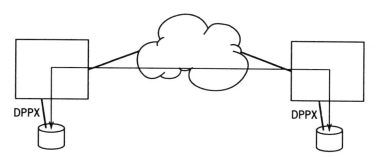

Figure 20.7 *DPPX/370 flows.*

systems. Using the Host Transaction Facility, a DPPX application can interface with CICS and IMS DC (the IMS data communications component), and cause a transaction to be initiated on that host to provide the requested data.

20.4 A DATA MANAGER EXAMPLE—SQL/DS

SQL/DS is a relational data base manager that provides *distributed* relational data base access for VM and VSE when VSE is running as a VM guest system. (See Figure 20.8.) SQL/DS also interfaces with DB2.

SQL/DS on VM provides the ability for an application program to access a remote VM SQL/DS data base transparently. With VSE/SP, SQL/DS will be able to communicate with other SQL/DS subsystems on remote VSE systems via the support provided by VM.

Each participating VSE SQL/DS will be able to communicate with the other VSE SQL/DSs or provide access to a VM-based SQL/DS data base. The obvious prerequisite is that each participating VSE must be a guest on a VM system (Figure 20.9).

While the application program may access remote data transparently, it must be aware which data is remote when updates are involved. Two phase commit is provided to support multiple *distributed* relational data base updates using the *remote unit of work* level of implementation. This allows a system to commit or roll back on entire group of updates.

20.5 A FILE MANAGER EXAMPLE—VM FILE SYSTEM

VM supports distributed files that can be transparently accessed by CMS applications. The VM shared file system uses the VM APPC services to ship the requests among the participating processors. The files can be shared among multiple users with one user having update authority and the others using only read mode. Data integrity for read-only users is provided by the system during update. (see Figure 20.10)

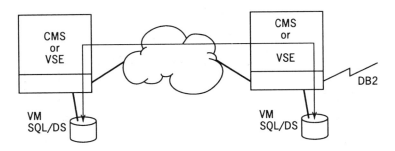

Figure 20.8 *SQL/DS flows.*

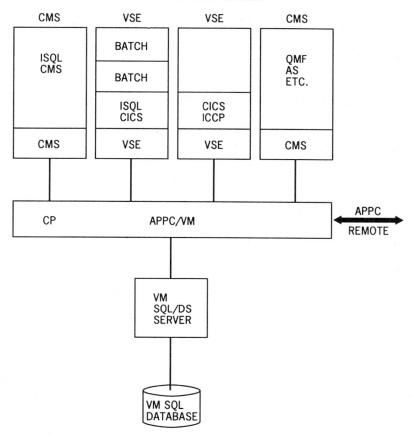

Figure 20.9 *SQL/DS VSE Guest implementation.*

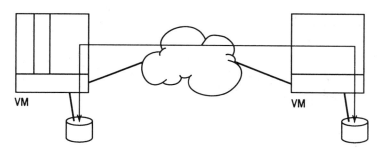

PROVIDES:
* TRANSPARENT ACCESS TO CMS FILES

* SHARED FILE ACCESS LOCAL AND REMOTE
  (SINGLE UPDATE, MULTIPLE READ)

Figure 20.10 *VM distributed files.*

20.6   A CLIENT-SERVER EXAMPLE—NETWORK FILE SYSTEM

Network File System (NFS) is a protocol developed by Sun Microsystems that uses the IP functions of TCP/IP to allow a set of cooperating systems to access each other's file systems as if they were local.

NFS provides file server support for NFS 3.2 protocols developed by SUN Microsystems Inc.

VM (and MVS) have implemented the file server functions only (see Figure 20.11). IBM's AIX and many OEM vendors have client and server implementations. (Clients can be thought of as requestors.) A user on a client system can access data from the server(s) transparently. NFS does not employ locking, but ensures write integrity. The user's application is responsible for logical data relationship integrity. NFS uses Remote Procedural Call (RPC) as the basis for communication between client and server. For example, in a VM server environment, the remote execution server protocol (*daemon*) is used to invoke a CMS EXEC and receives the results back at the requesting system. This means that code must be present in the target system to initiate the request in that system.

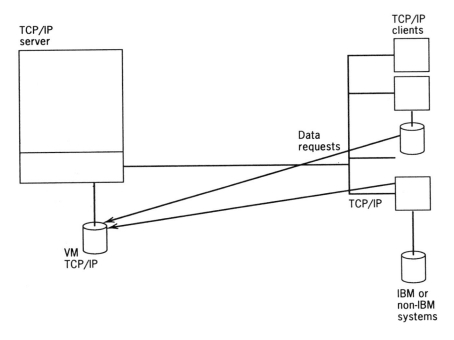

Figure 20.11   *TCP/IP server flows.*

20.7 DISTRIBUTED DB AND FILE SUMMARY

When distributed data based implementations are being assessed, the key considerations are typically the level of function and context of management control desired. Currently, CICS appears to provide the most rigorous management control for transaction oriented systems. It provides cross-system data access to MVS, VSE, VM, and PS/2 systems. The designer must be sensitive to the intersystem considerations.

For distributed relational data bases, the interface of preference is SQL, which is supported on MVS, VM, and VSE/VM by IBM as well as several other vendors.

There are also multiple non-IBM products that provide heterogeneous and homogeneous distributed access. Some of these implementations use proprietary data bases while others provide a layer above other vendors' data bases and files. When making a decision in this area, a key consideration is urgency and retaining compatibility with strategic interfaces. The objective would be to minimize the impact of the trade-off while responding to the need.

Chapter *21*

Complementary Services Capabilities

In this chapter, the term "Complementary Services" is used to discuss the application of S/390s (specifically the rack-mounted models to enhance existing IBM and non-IBM systems' capabilities and services. The discussion focuses on IBM host and intelligent workstation extensions with such approaches as using Micro Channel S/370s and S/390s as intelligent control units, IBM workstation servers, and various LAN servers managed from the host.

21.1 INTELLIGENT CONTROL UNIT

An intelligent control unit is a technology management oriented solution driven by the information systems organization. This type of solution incorporates the capabilities of a general-purpose processor to augment the traditional control unit functions in order to provide more connectivity flexibility, improve the manageability and service level, and potentially reduce communications costs or limitations.

Figure 21.1 depicts an ES/9000 as an intelligent control unit supporting network connectivity (line concentration), local printers, and disk storage.

Example applications of an intelligent control unit are: remote printers, remote tape, and remote image workstations.

The benefits of an intelligent control unit are:

- Ability to store significant amounts of data local to the peripherals
- Reduction in the dependency on line availability
- Ability to mix peripherals attached

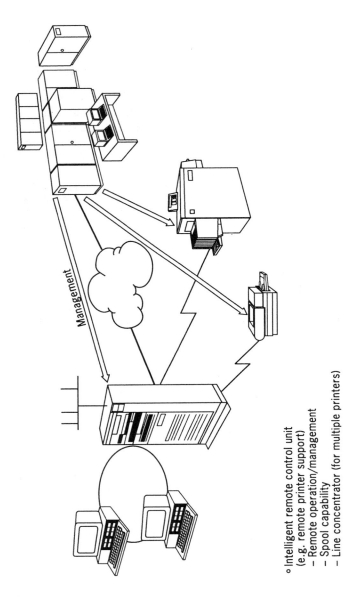

o Intelligent remote control unit
  (e.g. remote printer support)
  − Remote operation/management
  − Spool capability
  − Line concentrator (for multiple printers)

Management

Figure 21.1 *Intelligent control unit.*

- Ability to monitor and control peripherals from central
- Ability to distribute devices that are typically only channel attached (e.g., IBM 3800 and IBM 3820 printer or 3840 tape drives)
- Ability to support bandwidth-sensitive workstations (e.g., graphics applications) by doing the image capture and storage local to the workstation rather than immediately shipping the bulk data to the host and shipping it over the wire later or via tape.

Traditional control units are specialized computers, typically optimized for interfacing with very specific peripheral interfaces and connected to a channel or line.

An intelligent control unit is essentially a general-purpose processor that provides the flexibility to attach multiple peripherals, as well as to provide general-purpose functions to the control unit. These general-purpose functions include: disk storage, the ability to tailor services via standard programming approaches, and the ability to utilize existing systems management tools and expertise.

While an intelligent control unit has the functions of a general-purpose system, there are some key prerequisites that must be met for the unit to be viable. The intelligent control unit should look like and behave like a control unit from a department's viewpoint; that is, it should be a "black box." Additionally, it should have a strong host affinity, provide high reliability, availability, and serviceability, and be available at a price that is consistent with the value or savings.

21.1.1 S/390 as a Control Unit

The ES/9000 was designed with remote service in mind. The ability to remotely access the hardware and software from a central location is fundamental to the design of the hardware and supportive software. From a physical standpoint, the rack fits into the commercial office environment in much the same way as the traditional control unit does. All the required adapters and most of the peripherals can be economically placed within the rack (e.g., DASD, tape, communications adapters, terminal control units). This hardware and systems design, together with preload delivery options, make it a very attractive consideration when placing peripherals remote of the glasshouse, and when concentrating terminal/workstation connections to a host.

21.1.2 Host Affinity

The ES/9000 can run DPPX, VM, and VSE, the communications, and the disk storage hardware within the rack. The information systems organization can take advantage of its existing investment and experience with network and systems management as well as systems services in order to provide the desired services remotely with the required systems controls. The operating system and environment, for the most part, is transparent to the general user and give it the "control unit" appearance both physically and from a local operational standpoint while being managed as a S/390 from central.

21.1.3 Reliability, Availability, Serviceability (RAS)

A remotely managed system must be designed with RAS and remote service in mind. High reliability and maintenance support functions must be built in. The ability to access both the hardware and software from a location remote from the system is fundamental to the design of the hardware and supportive software.

21.1.4 Price

The low end models' (especially the Micro Channel 370) price and capabilities, together with preload delivery options, make it very attractive financially, when contrasted with the cost of the reliable sneaker net,[1] manually initiated local backup, local storage, and mailing off-site alternative currently being used by many departments for backing up or restoring backup data for their *LAN* or PC users.

21.2 S/390 WORKSTATION SERVER

The S/390 workstation server is a technology-management-oriented solution driven by the information systems organization in order to provide its end users with local S/390-managed data, services, and resources (see Figure 21.2). For example, the information systems organization may determine that it could substantially improve the service to its end users whose workload is mixed between the PC[2] and the S/390 services, or who currently use only 3270-type terminals.

By utilizing the PC and the S/390 workstation server, better response time and availability to end users in some rural locations can be provided. The S/390 workstation server allows for reductions in line costs if the terminal connections, the printer connections, etc. were consolidated. Placing the required data bases, files, and print services locally and still providing normal 3270 access to the host achieves substantial response time improvements due to local data access.

Additionally, the PC users can augment their disk storage, archival, and backup needs without relying on line availability. A good example application that provides this function is CAD (computer automated design) which can download images and operate on them locally a multiple number of times. This substantially reduces line capacity requirements and improves response time.

By using a configuration that includes the S/390, VM, and ECF[3] functions such as file transfer (including ASCII to EBCDIC conversion), SQL/DS access, print, etc., the PC user can access the S/390 services provided on the local S/390 or on another remote host, as well as store PC files on the S/390 in S/390 formats. This allows the sharing of files among the CMS and PC users. Similarly, using CICS

---

[1]*Sneaker net* is a network where part-time employees deliver output or support distributed peripherals.
[2]PC will be used as a generic for IBM PCs and IBM PS/2s.
[3]ECF is the label for the IBM Enhanced Connectivity Facilities which support personal computer access to S/390 resources via a documented interface (Server-Requestor Programming Interface, SRPI) and server facilities on both VM and MVS systems.

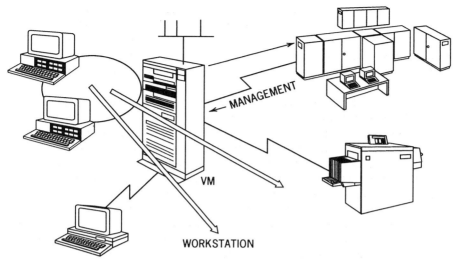

o S/390 WORKSTATION SERVER(ECF, VM NetView)
 – LOCAL HIGH-SPEED CONNECTION FOR
  * SHARED FILES
  * LARGE FILES
  * SQL/DS DATA BASES
  * SHARED & HIGH QUALITY PRINTERS
  * LINE CONCENTRATOR(FOR MULTIPLE
    TERMINALS & SESSIONS)
  * REMOTE OPERATIONS/MANAGEMENT

Figure 21.2 S/390 workstation server.

OS/2 with VM or VSE users can share S/390 services and data from their intelligent workstations or from their 3270 terminals.

This S/390, 3270, and PC configuration provides improved response time by providing some local S/390 transaction capabilities, line concentration, and network off-load, and extends central systems and network management.

The key distinction between the intelligent control unit and the IBM workstation scenario is the introduction of services that support the PC on the S/390; other than this, the benefits are the same. The combination of intelligent control unit and IBM workstation servers occurs frequently.

21.3 *LAN* SERVER APPLICATION

The key distinctions between the intelligent control unit, the IBM workstation server, and the *LAN* server application scenarios are that the intelligent control unit and IBM workstation scenarios are driven by the information systems organization for technology management, while the *LAN* server application is typically driven by the end user for local LAN support and connectivity to host data.

The key impetus for such a *LAN* server application is to share high-priced resources, gain access to storage capacities beyond those available to a micro, and provide a common approach to connecting to the various hosts (and other *LANS*). A major obstacle to using the glasshouse capacity as a server for response-time-sensitive applications is the line speed and the overheads associated with transmitting data across a wide area network.

As a result, multiple approaches to moving some of the glasshouse-managed data to a S/390 closer to the LAN with appropriate measures to reduce the overheads between the user system and the server application are being implemented. Often, trade-offs between control, currency, and response time must be made. As the price of the hardware and associated software decreases, the viability of this increases. In the *LAN* server context, generalized operating systems and processors are used for control, consolidating various device and workstation types, and handling complex network requirements. They are rarely used for high-speed disk services.

The S/390, using VM with such facilities as ECF, TCP/IP; NetWare for VM[4] and CICS OS/2; and VSE with CICS OS/2 provide tested bases for such implementations using remote management and access to S/390 capacity and RAS.

ECF provides a good example of the types of services that can be provided on a S/390: data base services, virtual disk, virtual file, virtual print, file copy, and the ability to run host commands from the personal computer. Figure 21.3 is a representative ECF with VM configuration.

By using data base services, the PC user can access data through a SQL query and update the local data base. The virtual disk makes S/390 storage capacity available as if it were PC storage. Using ECF the data is stored in PC format and can be shared by multiple users concurrently in read-only mode. ECF virtual file also gives the appearance of a personal computer file. However, it is stored in S/390 format and the files can be shared[5] among S/390 applications and services as well as by multiple PCs. Virtual print support provides support to convert character data streams from such printers as the IBM Proprinter to an IBM 1403 or IBM 3800 printer format.

By using services such as provided by ECF in combination with such systems management facilities such as provided by VM Backup/Archive and NetView, the LAN server user can delegate the data management and network management to a central service.

TCP/IP also provides a base for disk capacity and file sharing using the NFS feature of VM TCP/IP (see Figure 21.4). Additionally, TCP/IP can act as a gateway function among TCP/IP networks, or TCP/IP and SNA networks. Again, by using VM Backup/Archive and VTAM, the LAN server user can delegate the data management and network management to a central service.

Similarly users of Novell's NetWare can also provide local S/390 capability to

[4]NetWare for VM is a S/390 and Novell NetWare *LAN*-based product sold by Phaser Systems that allows NetWare LAN users to access files and services on the S/390 as though they were physically on the *LAN*.
[5]So that VFILEs can be shared, ECF must provide data transformation serves. Transforms for formats include data from the Personal Decision Series, BASIC, dBASE III, DIF (Data Interchange Format), and Lotus 1-2-3).

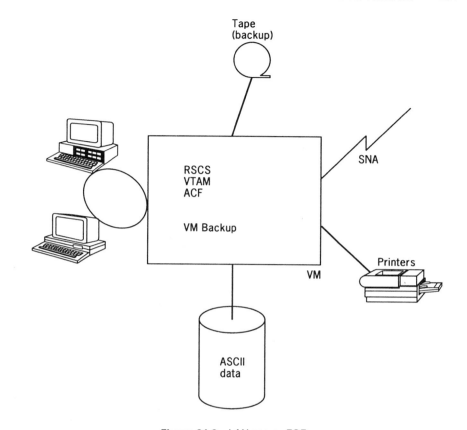

Figure 21.3 *LAN server ECF.*

their *LAN* server using Phaser Systems' NetWare for VM (see Figure 21.5). Through use of this product, a Novell NetWare *LAN* user has the ability to connect to a local or remote S/390 as well as remote NetWare *LANS* via the SNA backbone. NetWare for VM and its MVS counterpart product, NetWare for MVS, provide: NetWare-based file services on the S/390, batch services, and routing services to other S/390 or other NetWare *LANs*.

This, in combination with Novell NetWare-provided SNA interfaces,[6] allows for NetWare LAN servers or users to use or share S/390 capacity and resource management, copy files between environments (bi-directionally to and from the S/390 operating environment to PC format in the S/390 or to the LAN server or personal computer providing the necessary data transforms[7]), copy files from the S/390

---

[6]Novell provides IBM 3270 and LU6.2 emulators.
[7]Formats transformed include: Data Interchange Format (DIF) files, Lotus 1-2-3 (WKS) files, and ASCII (ASC) files.

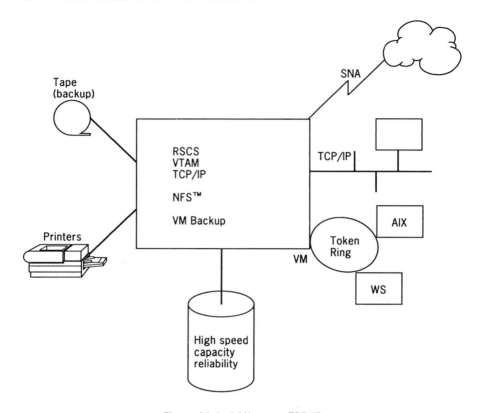

Figure 21.4 *LAN server TCP/IP.*

virtual disk to the LAN, submit work for batch processing (e.g., printing), access 3270 applications, and use the centrally managed wide area network for LAN-to-LAN sharing.

The file services provide NetWare file storage on the S/390 in VSAM relative-record data sets. The implementation provides read/write access locking at the byte level.

CICS OS/2, as described earlier, provides a client capability for both DOS and OS/2-based workstations, which allows the MVS,VSE, or VM systems either local or remote to provide data server capabilities.[8] This type of implementation fits in where there is a mix of IBM 3270 terminals and PC workstations, since both can be readily accommodated and the PC can be exploited as more than an emulation vehicle improving performance. Similarly, PASF[9] can be implemented on the workstations and on the VM server to provide office support via PROFS.

[8]CICS OS/2 can also cause transactions to be executed in the VSE CICS system.
[9]*PASF* refers to PROFS Application Support product, which provides menus and cooperative processing support for PC workstations. OfficeVision Direct Connect succeeds this product in the OfficeVision family.

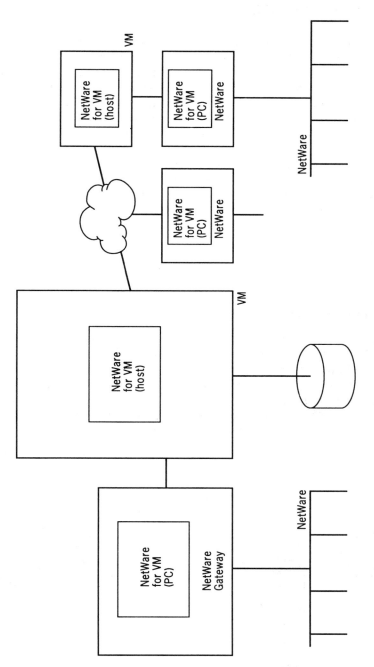

Figure 21.5 S/390 services for NetWare users.

21.4 SHARED RESOURCE AND SERVICES

In addition to intelligent control units, IBM workstation servers, and LAN servers to complement either the S/390 or intelligent workstations, there is an increased focus on integrating systems to capitalize on existing investments while exploiting some key IBM and S/390 strengths. Several products have recently emerged to address physical device extensions, such as using IBM peripherals from an OEM system, or IBM services from an OEM system, or even to manage an OEM system via IBM services. Such solutions include Interlink, FlexLINK with Intel's Fastpath, and VM TCP/IP.

Each of these solutions tends to address a specific set of problems, but sometimes the features tend to overlap and the distributions are blurred. To provide some insight on this, three interoperability categories will be discussed. These are based on the connectivity via:

- DECnet
- System coupling
- TCP/IP

21.4.1 Interoperability via DECnet

Interoperability with VAX/VMS is the ability to execute tasks on either the S/390 or VAX/VMS systems. An example might be to access a file on the ES/9000 using a standard VMS program (see Figure 21.6).

Interlink provides for interoperability via its SNS/SNA Gateway family of products. Variations of product combinations provide for numerous features, including bi-directional data transfer, transparent access to IBM or DEC resources, and functions from either environment, electronic mail bridging, program-to-program com-

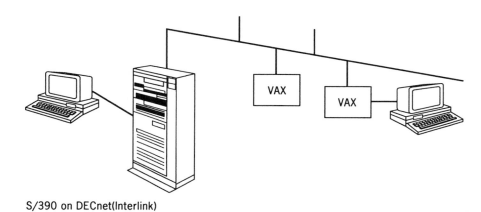

S/390 on DECnet(Interlink)

Figure 21.6 Interlink interoperability.

munications or/and VT and 327X terminal emulation. (The SNS/327X solution has a DECnet SNA 3270 Terminal Emulator prerequisite.)

The foundations for the interoperability services are SNS/Link. There are two significant differences from the other solutions discussed. The implementation uses native IBM and DEC interfaces (no special interface is required) and the solution only requires software on the ES/9000, introducing no changes to the existing VAX systems software and hardware. ES/9000 attachments are via standard Ethernet attachments that are either directly to the ES/9000 adapter or via the IBM 8232 (see Figure 21.7).

SNS/Link provides connectivity between a 9000 and a system on a DECnet network. This software solution on the 9000 provides for transparent file transfer, sending messages, sharing hardware resources, and accessing applications between DECnet attached systems and 9000 systems. It also supports mail bridging and RSCS/NJE gateway features. It provides high-speed disk-to-disk through-put to 500 Kbps.

SNS/Link also supports connectivity via the IBM 8232 LAN Channel Station or IBM's 3172. This provides up to 1 Mbps disk-to-disk through-put. Standard functions include both IBM- and DEC-initiated file transfer, a data dictionary, DEC-initiated record level access, data translation between DEC and IBM data types, and security interfaces (e.g., VM/RACF). A 256 simultaneous logical sessions capability is provided. Other products of the SNS/SNA Gateway Family also permit interoperability between DECnet networks through an IBM host.

Two program-to-program interfaces are supported: LU6.2 and native DECnet in SNS/LU6.2 and SNS/Program, respectively. The LU6.2 interface, which has some DEC software prerequisites, allows a programmer to write a DEC program to access LU6.2 interfaced programs in the ES/9000. The SNS/Program allows the program to transparently access the ES/9000 and has Interlink's software map to the ES/9000 service.

21.4.2 Interoperability via Systems Coupling

OEM coupling solutions allow other systems to include ES/9000 hardware or software capability as part of (or an extension to) the existing system. Coupling is used to connote interconnection bandwidth, with the objective being to approach channel rates for the integration.

Intel's FASTPATH 9770, together with FlexLINK or FlexLINK and VM TCP/IP combinations, provide for applications that need very high bandwidths. They provide the following functions:

- Multiplexer: high-speed, high-reliability session manager, supporting up to 512 concurrent users
- Tape archive: one-step backup of VAX disk to IBM tape gives VAX users access to highly reliable IBM tape drives and tape library management systems
- File exchange: high-speed, bi-directional file transfer and remote file utilities (file server)

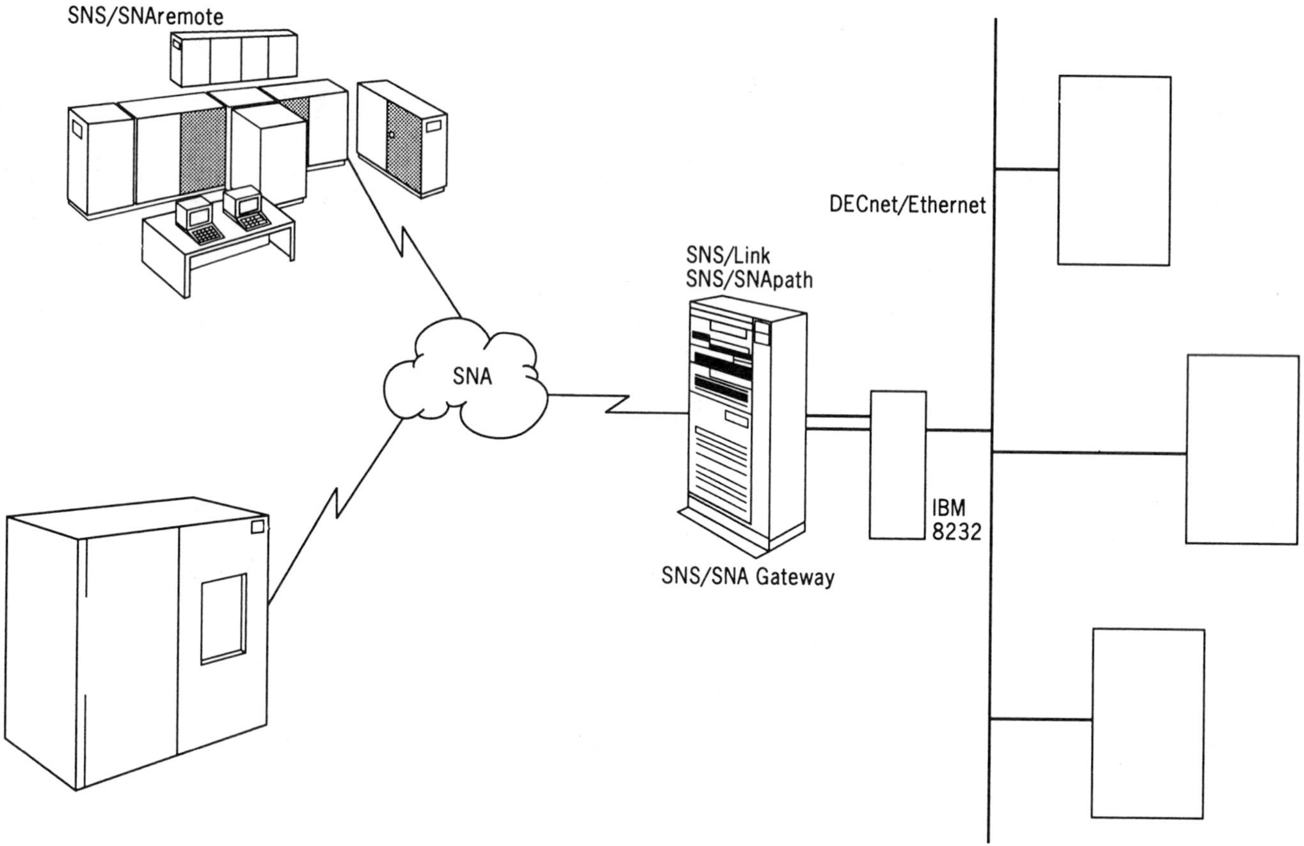

Figure 21.7 Interoperability among DECnet and SNA connected nodes.

DECnet/Ethernet

IBM
8232

SNS/Link
SNS/SNApath

SNS/SNA Gateway

SNA

SNS/SNAremote

- Remote task activation: interactive and batch ability to activate processing on a remote system (RJE)
- Terminal emulation (FullView): allows IBM and VAX users to access either IBM or VAX full-screen applications and allows the functions of the terminal keyboards to be dynamically changed.
- MailBridge: allows transparent VM and VMS mail exchange

The effective data transfer speeds are a function of the software interconnect. The Intel 9770 operates at channel speeds. FlexLINK's memory-to-memory (from one system to the other) transfer rates are between 1.2 and 2.5 Mbytes.

Figure 21.8 illustrates Intel's FASTPATH 9770 being used to provide multiple connectivity options. A complex array of multivendor equipment can be networked together over a TCP/IP network. Additionally—by using FlexLINK—VAX disk data could be archived directly to the IBM system's tape drives. In this network, users have access to the IBM mainframe from any node. Users on the VAX could take advantage of IBM's tape technology, the VM tape and backup management systems. Standard VMS commands could be used to write VAX disk data directly to the IBM tape without intermediate disk storage. Backups may be initiated by VAX users, IBM users, or either system's time-of-day clock.

Intel's FASTPATH control unit with Ethernet application adapter supports IBM VM TCP/IP for communications between TCP/IP coupled VAX environment. Flexlink provides a specific interface to provide the Flexlink services. An example of an integrated application solution using FlexLINK software follows.

A major West Coast bank depends on IBM systems for security and cash transaction processing and loan servicing, while an extensive DECnet environment sup-

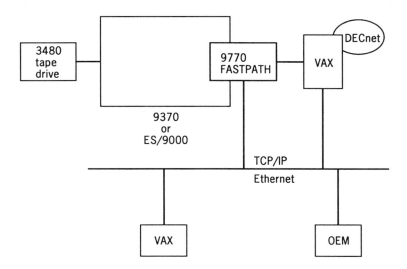

Figure 21.8 *Intel 9770 TCP/IP and FlexLINK configuration.*

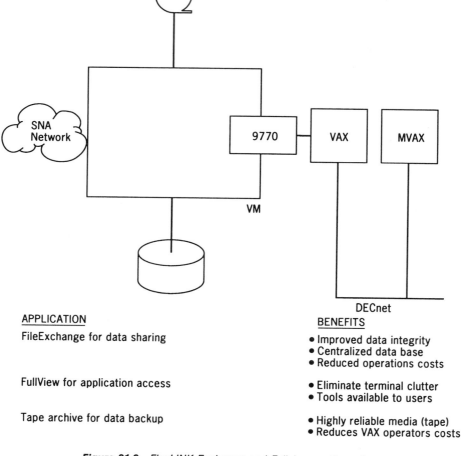

APPLICATION

FileExchange for data sharing

FullView for application access

Tape archive for data backup

BENEFITS

• Improved data integrity
• Centralized data base
• Reduced operations costs

• Eliminate terminal clutter
• Tools available to users

• Highly reliable media (tape)
• Reduces VAX operators costs

Figure 21.9 *FlexLINK Exchange and Fullview configuration.*

ports financial analysis and reporting. FileExchange is used by the bank's operations and analysis staffs to share large volumes of data and the terminal emulation products allow users to log on to applications in both the IBM and DEC environments from a single terminal (see Figure 21.9).

In the previous scenario, FileExchange eliminates the need to maintain duplicate data on both IBM and DEC systems, thus improving data integrity and lowering operations costs. The FullView products allow authorized employees to access a wider range of corporate applications.

21.4.3 Interoperability with TCP/IP

Transmission Control Protocol/Internet Protocol is a set of protocols or programs that provide communication and file transfer capabilities between systems from

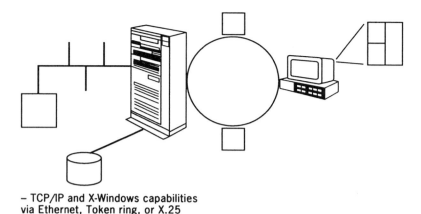

– TCP/IP and X-Windows capabilities
via Ethernet, Token ring, or X.25

Figure 21.10 *TCP/IP and X-windows interoperability.*

over 150 different vendors. Some of the functions provided by VM TCP/IP include
the following (see also Figure 21.10):

- File transfer across mixed vendor environments, providing data sharing and
  resource utilization.
- Network File System (NFS) server
- Remote Procedure Call (RPC)
- Remote execution
- C and Pascal subroutine interface to TCP and UDP (which provides applica-
  tion-to-application programming interfaces)
- X-window clients[10]
- Connection and access to existing TCP/IP networks from IBM systems includ-
  ing MVS, VM, AIX family and PC DOS.
- Gateway into SNA (SMTP/FTP/TELNET)
- Use SNA backbone

Together, these allow for resource capacity and expense sharing in a very heterogeneous environment.

[10]X-window clients are required to allow a CMS application to use or be a window on a bit-mapped high-
resolution display on a workstation which has an X-window server (e.g., an AIX RT, RISC/6000, or
AIX PS/2 workstation).

Chapter 22

Distributed Office Capabilities

This chapter describes how enterprises can interconnect multi-architecture systems with various operating systems to share electronic mail using an S/390 system as a central exchange. The focus is on the awareness of IBM's and other vendors' various solutions. It should be recognized that the products and support will change but the direction appears consistent.

22.1 INTRODUCTION

The Office is one of the most popular distributed application areas, since it crosses most industries. Many users are directly affected by electronic office support. IBM Professional Office System, more commonly referred to as PROFS, and Personal Services, and the recently introduced OfficeVision provide a broad range of facilities for S/390 office applications.

The installation of any electronic office system can be extremely simple or a significant challenge, depending on the approach taken. A primary consideration is the function or services that one is trying to include in an office solution (e.g., notes, documents, calendars, directories, administrative services, etc.). The most universally important capability is electronic mail, often referred to an E-mail.

The term E-mail itself may be evolving to mean much more than it was initially meant to encompass. There is a trend to expand the term to encompass electronic transport of objects in a store-and-forward manner. Services associated with the expanded label include: electronic document exchange (EDI), editable document exchange, electronic report distribution, object library and archive services, con-

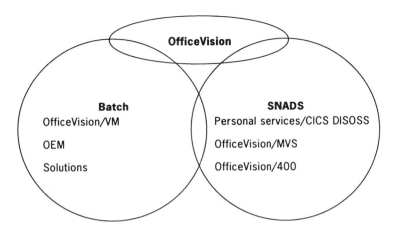

Figure 22.1 *Batch, SNADS and OfficeVision intersection.*

ferencing, and forms routing.[1] The focus in this chapter will be more specifically oriented towards sending electronic letters, or electronic messaging.

Because electronic mail is such an important function for many end users, it is desirable to introduce new solutions or to augment old solutions in a single step. Unfortunately, it is usually neither practical nor feasible to cut everyone over to a new system in one quick step. The enterprise's distributed office solution may require multiple integrated solutions based on the equipment and operating systems installed to support the line of business applications.

In order to discuss the various distribution implementation options used to support the office E-mail, I've arbitrarily divided the implementations into two general areas: batch distribution and SNADS. The two implementation areas converge when the usage requires interconnection.

In my arbitrary lumping of E-mail implementations into the two major categories, the recently announced OfficeVision implementations also converge with both (see Figure 22.1). This is appropriate, since OfficeVision is an SAA application that uses the programmable workstation (PWS) as a point of integration to S/390 implementations as well as the AS/400 and OS/2 LANs using a consistent user access (CUA) graphics user interface.

OfficeVision is a family of office products that are grouped in series: OfficeVision/2 LAN Series, OfficeVision/VM Series, OfficeVision/MVS Series, and OfficeVision/400 Series.

The IBM OfficeVision/2 Series ties together OS/2-based applications and interfaces to the S/390. It can distribute and receive mail from users on the same Token Ring LAN, a connected Token Ring LAN, VM, MVS, VSE,[2] or OS/400 system. It

---

[1]*Electronic Mail: Technology, Applications, and Infrastructure,* Soft-Switch, Inc., May 1989.
[2]Attachment to MVS and VSE is via DISOSS.

presents a consistent user access graphical interface with office objects represented pictorially. The IBM OfficeVision/2 LAN series consists of OS/2 Office server(s) and combinations of OS/2 and IBM DOS-based OS/2 Office requesters on a Token Ring LAN.

The IBM OfficeVision/VM Series includes a base product OfficeVision/VM and three features: OS/2 Office feature, DOS Office Direct Connect Feature, and OS/2 Office DOS Requester feature. IBM Executive Decisions/VM is an optional product in the OfficeVision/VM Series. It augments the communication-oriented services (mail) with the ability to access[3] and analyze[4] business information via an icon-oriented user interface.

IBM OfficeVision/MVS series is an extension of Personal Services/CICS, Application Support Facility, and the Personal Manager Program Offering. Release 1 uses existing interfaces of CICS, DISOSS, and GDDM and will have the DOS Office Connect feature. Release 2 will add support for the consistent user access from OS/2 EE workstations.

The IBM OfficeVision/400 Series (formerly called AS/400 Office Release 2) introduces SAA office by providing for interconnection to VM,[5] MVS,[6] and LAN environments.

For the following discussion, consider OfficeVision/VM as an extension for PROFS and OfficeVision/MVS as a follow-on for Personal Services/CICS. I will discuss OfficeVision after discussing batch and SNADS.

22.2 BATCH DISTRIBUTION

The primary IBM batch distribution implementation is PROFS, which is based on a VM platform. OfficeVision/VM can be substituted for PROFS in this chapter.

22.2.1 PROFS

For installations with all VM systems, PROFS provides for centralized and distributed options for notes and documents. PROFS also provides cross-systems calendaring for participating PROFS systems. This allows users on different systems to check calendars. Additionally, some administrative tools that identify aged notes and facilitate sorting, reviewing, and purging the logs,[7] as well as automatically aging and purging documents and notes,[8] are also available.

Distributing PROFS systems is relatively straightforward, but naming conven-

---

[3]An interface is provided to Dow Jones News/Retrieval.
[4]Interfaces to IBM's Application System and SQL/DS are provided.
[5]An SNA or BSC RSCS bridge is provided that can be specified at configuration time. The bridge senses the protocol required depending upon the device type sending.
[6]The bridge supports NJE protocols for file transmission.
[7]PROFS Note Maintenance Facility.
[8]*PROFS Retention Management System (RMS) Program Description and Operations Manual*, IBM Order Number SH21-0038.

tions, nickname files, and user service access inventory becomes very important if movement among systems is expected.

PROFS, together with several gateways, provides a solid office base for VM systems, internetworking with multiple PROFS, other IBM office solutions, and OEM E-mail solutions using the batch interface for distribution (see Figure 22.2).

Users can access PROFS directly, via a 3270 network log on, via 3270 pass-

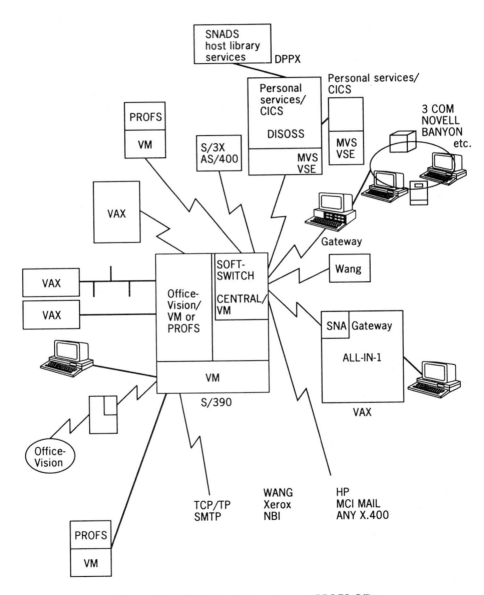

Figure 22.2 *Distributed heterogeneous PROFS Office.*

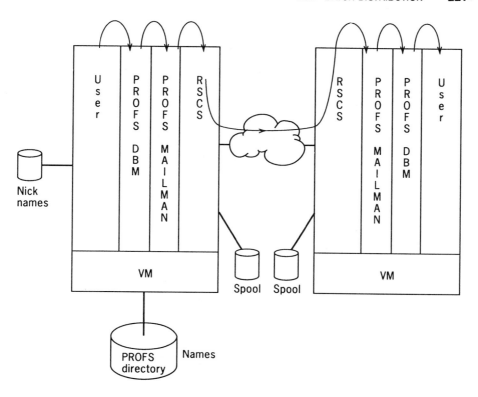

Figure 22.3 *PROFS-to-PROFS flows.*

through emulators, or distribute via batch file transfers to PROFS users on other systems. PROFS uses RSCS as its distribution transport mechanism. Figure 22.3 depicts the flow.

Use of SNA as the network connection mechanism for RSCS provides a point-to-point (or spool-to-spool) solution. Other connection alternatives using RSCS as store-and-forward bases can also be employed, but these can introduce delivery delays and sometimes lost mail.

For IBM systems users who are not all connected to VM PROFS systems, mail can be sent to PROFS users via bridges. These bridges are SNADS Systems Network Architecture Distribution Services SNADS-based. Examples are:

- VSE Personal Services users using DISOSS
- MVS users using DISOSS and/or DOSF
- S/36 users using Personal Services/36

Examples include sending mail between MVS DISOSS users and PROFS users (see Figure 22.4), and S/36s users and PROFS users (see Figure 22.5). SNADS implementations will be discussed later in this section.

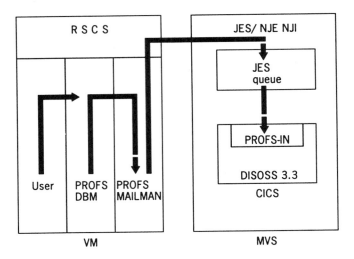

Figure 22.4 PROFS to DISSOS flows.

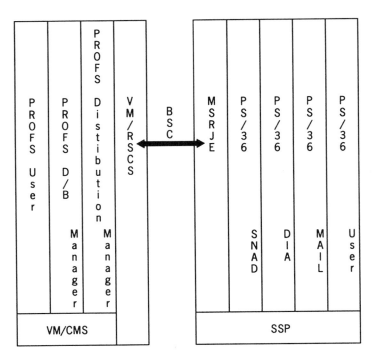

Figure 22.5 PS/36—PROFS connection flow.

From an expedience standpoint, if E-mail is the only objective, the batch transfer provides the most effective and transparent mechanism to introduce E-mail across a heterogeneous software and/or hardware base. PROFS uses VM's RSCS as its batch interface for notes distribution.

IBM batch interfaces to PROFS exist for note exchanges among:

- PROFS users on other VM systems
- CMS users and PROFS
- All SNADS implementations
- TCP/IP users and PROFS users

Non-IBM system attached users can also send notes to PROFS via software gateways and software/hardware gateways that use the RSCS interface.

22.2.2 PROFS and TCP/IP Users

PROFS and TCP/IP users can exchange mail either directly or via the PROFS Extended Mail product.[9] Users on TCP/IP systems send mail to other TCP/IP systems. The VM TCP/IP system may forward the mail to RSCS, where it would be picked up by the PROFS user (see Figure 22.6).

PROFS Extended Mail program provides some ease-of-use features to facilitate sending mail across TCP/IP interfacing to TCP/IP SMTP services. The program provides the ability to use TCP/IP user names in the note or in the PROFS names files. The appropriate TCP/IP and RSCS instructions will be added so that the user will not have to add any additional information for messages or replies.

22.2.3 PROFS and DEC VMS Users

There are six major solutions available today to address mail exchange among PROFS and VMS users, not including TCP/IP. They use:

- FlexLINK
- Interlink
- Jnet
- DECnet/SNA PROFS/MR
- Soft-Switch

Soft-switch will be discussed in more detail in the SNADS implementation portion of this section.

22.2.3.1 Intel Fastpath and FlexLINK. FlexLINK software, which works together with Intel's 9770 (an ES/9000 rack-mounted option), provides a function

---

[9]*PROFS Extended Mail User's Guide and Installation Manual,* IBM Order Number SH21-0044.

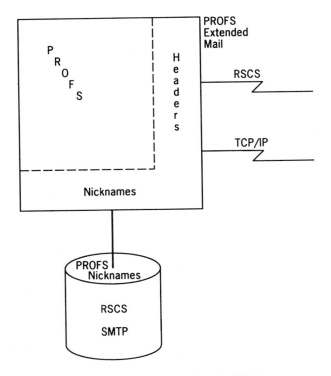

Figure 22.6   *PROFS Extended Mail*

called MailBridge on both the VM and VMS systems. MailBridge is a transparent bridge between major IBM and VAX electronic mail systems at direct connect speed. In VM-VMS environments, it connects VM PROFS and VM NOTE to ALL-IN-1 and VMSmail (see Figure 22.7). In MVS-VMS environments, it connects ADR eMail and ALL-IN-1 and VMSmail. All features of ALL-IN-1, PROFS and electronic mail are supported, except for acknowledgement/return requested features.

22.2.3.2   *Interlink.* Interlink provides SNS/Mail for exchanging messages and notes (not documents) among PROFS, ALL-IN-1, and VAXmail. The Interlink solution allows for Ethernet attached VAX/VMS users to participate in a PROFS office system for electronic mail without any changes to the VAX/VMS hardware or software (see Figure 22.8). The ES/9000 requires the Ethernet adapter or an IBM 8232 or an IBM 3172 Interconnect Controller and the Interlink SNS/Link or SNS/Connect and SNS/Mail software (VM).

22.2.3.3   *Jnet.* Another approach that uses a standard batch interface is Jnet, from Joiner Associates, Inc., which requires no new software on the IBM side. Jnet offers a simple coexistence solution; within the IBM network, Jnet appears to be

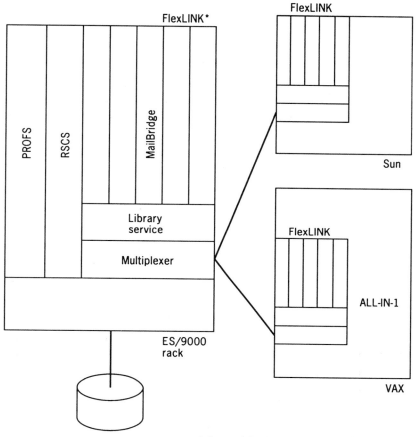

* Corequisite Intel's 9770 on ES/9000

Figure 22.7 *FlexLINK MailBridge.*

another node (see Figure 22.9). It emulates IBM protocols in a VAX-like way so both IBM and VAX users continue to operate in a familiar environment. Jnet implements a secure, store-and-forward, multivendor, peer-to-peer network. Users can send messages and notes (not documents) bi-directionally between PROFS and ALL-IN-1 via VMS mail.

There are essentially two user interfaces: ALL-IN-1 interface and VMSmail interface. The ALL-IN-1 interface accepts electronic mail from ALL-IN-1 electronic messaging for porting to the NJE network. Addressing is transparent to the sender if the intended recipient has been registered in the User Profile Master by the ALL-IN-1 system manager, and users can be registered as either CMS NOTE or PROFS NOTE users. User names and nodes can also be explicitly addressed.

The VMSmail interface accepts electronic mail from VMSmail for posting to the

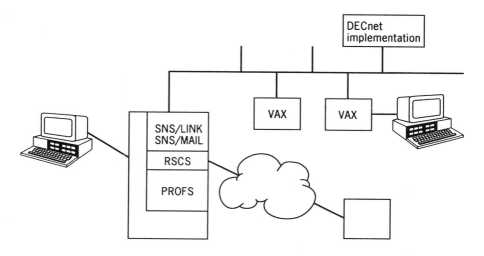

Figure 22.8 *Interlink SNS/Mail (MailBridge).*

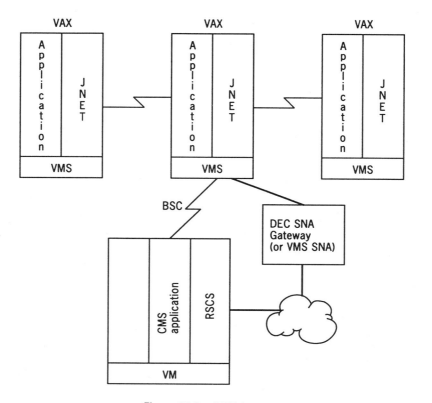

Figure 22.9 *JNET (mail).*

NJE network. Jnet delivers all mail from NJE via VMSmail. ALL-IN-1 users can import unread VMSmail into the ALL-IN-1 mailbox either automatically or manually. (This is comparable to CMS reading PROFS mail or directly from PROFS.)

Jnet uses standard IBM communications devices, has no new commands for IBM users or system managers, and supports PROFS and CMS notes. The Jnet software runs fully integrated on Digital's VAX/VMS, including VMS Version 5. It is simple to install and uses standard Digital communications devices. Jnet can connect directly with NJE via the VAX BSC support or can access NJE SNA with co-requisites Jnet NJE SNA Access and DEC's SNA/Gateway product.

22.2.3.4 *DECnet/SNA Message Router/PROFS.* Digital Equipment Corp.'s approach to interfacing with PROFS is via one of three SNA gateways and a software component (MR/PROFS) that prepares and accepts PROFS mail from and to ALL-IN-1 (see Figure 22.10). This software interfaces with RSCS.

22.2.4 PROFS and Other OEM Systems Users

WANG is addressed with the IBM OEM PROFS Interchange as well as Soft-Switch. Soft-Switch provides a substantial set of OEM support.

Soft-Switch, which will be discussed in the SNADS Distribution section, provides a bridge capability to PROFS for numerous OEM office systems.

22.2.5 OfficeVision/VM

The latest IBM office introduction that fits into the batch implementation mail category is OfficeVision/VM. It, together with OS/2 Office Feature, OS/2 Office

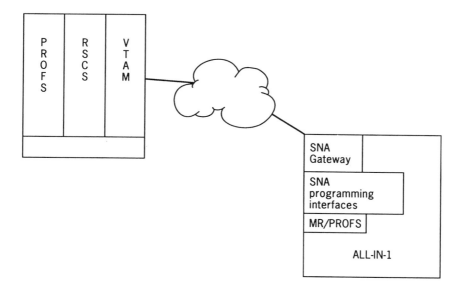

Figure 22.10 *DECnet/SNA MR PROFS.*

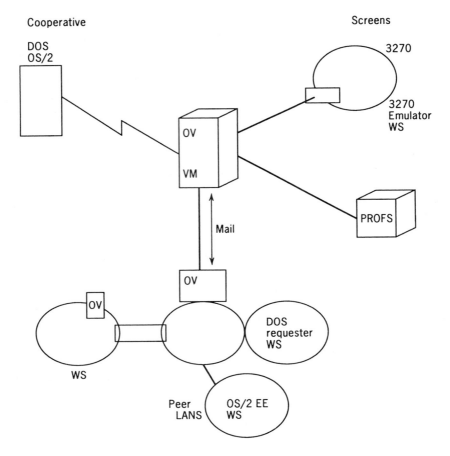

Figure 22.11   *PROFS and OfficeVision/VM.*

Requester Feature, DOS Office Direct Connect Feature, IBM Executive Decisions/VM, and OfficeVision/2, provides mail support such as: send/reply/forward notes and documents, carbon copy, and acknowledgements to and from a VM host with either OfficeVision/VM or PROFS—and to any other systems that are connected or bridged via that host (see Figure 22.11).

OfficeVision/VM is built on existing IBM VM office products—PROFS (for electronic mail and calendar services), PROFS Application Support Feature (PASF,[10] for application navigation), and DisplayWrite/370 (for document processing)—and utilizes the capabilities of PC and PS/2 workstations[11] and *LANs*.

---

[10]PASF provides an integrated interface for PC end users that allows them to access both host and PC services from full-screen menu. Services include office, text, decision support, and data base access functions.
[11]DOS Office Direct Connect Feature includes functions of PASF. However, PASF Version 2 Release 2.2 and the PROFS Personal Computer Support feature are not compatible with OfficeVision/VM.

With the introduction of the OfficeVision series, users of PCs, PS/2s, and IBM 3270s can either directly access PROFS, cooperatively access workstation and host offices services, and distribute mail to PROFS via OfficeVision/2 servers as depicted in Figure 22.11. In this depiction, PC workstations can access OfficeVision VM directly using OfficeVision Direct and PASF, IBM 3270 and 3270 emulations can access the system directly, and other PROFS systems can exchange mail. OfficeVision LAN OS/2 workstations with OfficeVision clients can access the OV/LAN server to exchange mail among other clients on the LAN or other LANs. Similarly, OV/LAN mail can be sent to OV/VM and can be accepted from OV/VM. DOS workstations can use the DOS Requester capability to access the OV/LAN server.

22.3 SNADS DISTRIBUTION

22.3.1 SNADS Implementation

Another mail distribution implementation uses the IBM Systems Network Architecture Delivery System (SNADS) interface. Many hardware vendors provide a SNADS software interface. IBM provides SNADS via Distribution Office Support System/3770 (DISOSS/370) or DISOSS. DISOSS also implements the Document Interconnect Architecture (DIA), which provides architected commands for such services as accessing a file, searching, retrieving, printing, and distributing documents.

DISOSS is an application service that runs as a CICS application in VSE and MVS environments and provides an electronic information exchange capability by providing a safe-store-and-forward distribution service and library service for text, image, and files. Unlike the batch approach, which uses system and user spool space, DISOSS is a library. In addition to electronic mail interchange, DISOSS supports library sharing by multiple office products, printing documents using Advanced Function Printers (this Advanced Function Printers support includes fonts, images, graphics, and text), storage of notes, documents, and binary files. An X.400 DISOSS Connection program is also available.

DISOSS runs on MVS or VSE and provides a broad spectrum of distribution and library services for many IBM products. These include:

- IBM Personal Services/CICS
- IBM Personal Services/TSO
- IBM Personal Services/36
- IBM Personal Services/PC
- AS/400 Office
- IBM PROFS
- DPPX/370 and DPPX/8100
- Other DISOSS host
- Workstations attached to DISOSS

The DISOSS Library Services' Extended is an associated product which, in addition to providing search tools, allows OfficeVision/VM Series users, IBM PROFS users, OfficeVision/2 Series users, and IBM PS/38 users to access DISOSS libraries at different DISOSS nodes.

Users wishing to use the safe-store-and-forward capabilities and document exchange capabilities on VM can consider Soft-Switch's Central/VM.

22.3.2 Personal Services/CICS

Personal Services is a group of IBM products providing electronic mail functions in different environments (MVS, VSE, S/36, PC). Personal Services/CICS is the product of this family running on MVS or VSE in a CICS environment. Personal Services/CICS users can send E-mail (messages, notes, documents) directly to any

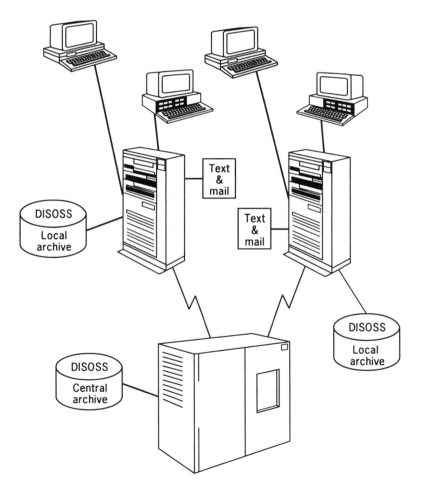

Figure 22.12 *VSE Personal Services/CICS.*

users who work in the same Personal Services/CICS environment. Mail distribution to users who are outside the same Personal Services/CICS environment has to be handled by DISOSS.

VSE systems use Personal Services/CICS to provide E-mail capability (see Figure 22.12). PS/CICS provides for the creation of notes and messages and distributes mail locally or ships it to remote systems via DISOSS. PC documents can be shipped to PS/CICS via DCA documents prepared by Display Write Release 4 Text Editor. Once in PS/CICS, they can be distributed locally or given to DISOSS for distribution.

22.3.3 DPPX/370 Office Support

DPPX/370 provides electronic mail support within a system or across a network. SNADS is used for communications between systems and for mail exchange with any other IBM system supporting SNADS. More recently, DPPX has announced office support that resembles Personal Services.

DPPX/370 via DISOSS provides access to centralized office support applications such as PS/CICS and PROFS. DPPX/370 users can simply log on to PROFS or Personal Services/CICS via the Routing Facility. DPPX/370 also allows users to access DISOSS libraries on the host, thus providing archival storage and the ability to share documents.

22.3.4 Soft-Switch

Soft-Switch provides software that allows users to distribute notes, documents, and messages across various systems. The document or note is translated to the receiving system's format. Soft-Switch Central provides translation, routing, logging, access control, and directory functions. Soft-Switch provides access to the backbone from X.400, SNADS, and SMTP (see Figure 22.13).

With a combination of Soft-Switch's Central VM, PROFS Gateway/VM, and MAILWAY Gateway/VM in conjunction with MAILbridge servers,[12] and Soft-Switch SNADS gateways for LANs,[13] customers can integrate multivendor electronic mail networks on a SNADS backbone. Vendors such as Dialcom and Western Union have licensed the protocol used with MAILbridge in order to interface to Soft-Switch.

Soft-Switch supports access from and to the enterprise backbone for:

IBM PROFS	Novell MHS	IBM PS/36,	MCI Mail
DEC	Dialcom	PS/38	TRT(Telex)
VMSmail	IBM AS/400	HP	DEC ALL-
cc:Mail	Office	DeskManager	IN-1[14]

[12]DEC networks, HP networks, Wang Networks, and Novell MHS access the backbone with Soft-Switch MAILbridge, which resides on a single node in the reference network and transparently interfaces to that mail system. Communications with Soft-Switch Central is via a Soft-Switch defined protocol.
[13]Support for 3+Mail, Banyan Mail, Higgins, and Network Courier is provided this way.
[14]Digital's MAILbus provides access protocol support for X.400, DISOSS, PROFS, and TCP/IP.

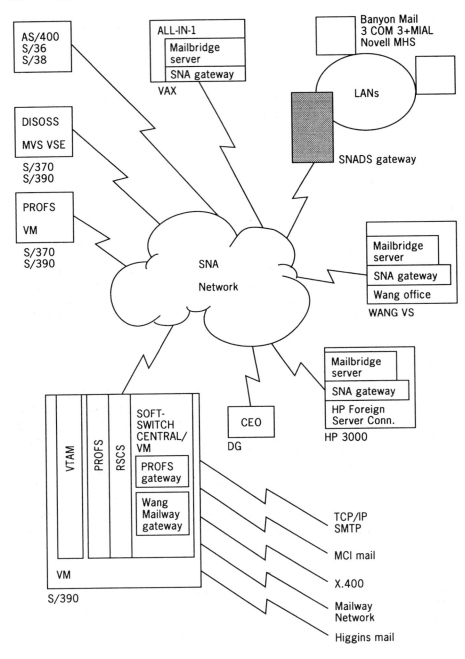

Figure 22.13 *Soft-Switch connectivity.*

MEMO	Wang	The Coordinator	3Com 3+Mail
CCI (Telex)	MAILWAY	CompuServe	Framework III
IBM DISOSS	Higgins	OfficePower	MaxCom
Wang	Telemail	IBM 5520	X.400
OFFICE	ALIS	Data General CEO	connections
Banyan Mail	Western Union	The Network Courier	over X.25
			links

22.3.5 DECnet/SNA MR SNADS

Just as with interfacing with PROFS, Digital Equipment Corp. employs the three SNA gateways and a software component (MR SNADS), which sends and accepts mail from ALL-IN-1 to DISOSS or Soft-Switch (see Figure 22.14).

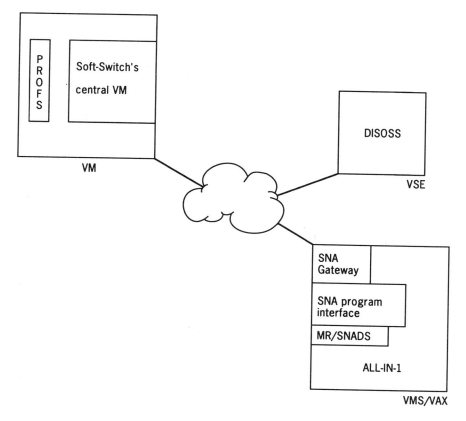

Figure 22.14 *DECnet/SNA-MR SNADS.*

22.3.6   OfficeVision/MVS

Just as the OfficeVision series extended the batch distribution implementation, it also extends the SNADS implementation to enhanced workstation and *LAN* support using DISOSS/370 to provide shared library and remote distribution.

OfficeVision/MVS is built on existing IBM office products: Personal Services/CICS (for electronic mail), Application Support Facility (ASF) for MVS (for application navigation), and DisplayWrite/370 (for document processing). With the introduction of OfficeVision/MVS Release 2, users will be able to access PS/CICS services directly or through an OS/2 Extended Edition LAN. Additionally, by using OfficeVision/MVS together with NetView Access Services, the Application Connectivity and TSO Application Access features—CICS, IMS, and TSO—environments can be accessed in a more integrated manner.

DISOSS is the primary interchange vehicle for OfficeVision/MVS, PS/CICS (MVS and VSE), and PS/TSO. OS/2 Office Feature LAN server interchanges mail with VSE via DISOSS.

22.4   DISTRIBUTED OFFICE SUMMARY

There are numerous approaches to providing E-mail to an enterprise and across enterprises. The most prominent S/390 products that support E-mail distribution among multiple systems and workstations are PROFS (OfficeVision/VM)-Personal Services/CICS with DISOSS. The OfficeVision Family provides a LAN-based integration of mail services across the SAA environments and uses OfficeVision/VM and PROFS, OfficeVision/MVS and Personal Services, and DISOSS to provide mail-exchange with host-based users and services. OfficeVision also extends the cooperative processing access to the host-based services so that both direct and store-and-forward approaches are available to the user.

Multiple solutions exist to provide physical and logical connection with mailboxes from multiple IBM and non-IBM systems. Some of these mail boxes use batch mechanisms building upon the system's batch input/output capabilities such as RSCS and NJE for file transfer, and others use a SNADS-based implementation taking advantage of the architected interface (SNADS), the architected document interchange capabilities (DIA), and even the architected document content capabilities (DCA).

Both batch and SNADS distribution approaches are extensively used for exchanging mail among IBM and non-IBM systems. Batch interfaces support both SNA and non-SNA S/390 attachments. Implementations using the batch interface can provide the necessary transforms at the originating system or workstation by some intermediate service between the sender and the target mailbox, or by a service at the target mailbox. The SNADS implementation requires an SNA (LU 6.2) or OSI[15] connectivity to the participating systems or workstations and it.

PROFS (OfficeVision/VM) provides support for notes and documents for VM-

---

[15]IBM implementation and availability of OSI services may be country-dependent.

based systems and has the ability to support mail input from TCP/IP[16] and to accommodate X.400[17] mail.

SNADS on the S/390 is implemented via DISOSS. It supports E-mail library and distribution services across MVS, VSE, VM, OS/400, and OS/2 environments using the DIA interfaces as well as accommodating OSI-based implementations via X.400.[18]

Notes are the easiest mail to exchange, which is why E-mail systems are used most often for notes. *Stapling* other types of data to the note is also becoming very popular—e.g., sending a copy of a spreadsheet associated with a note or even a FAX.[19] However, considerably more care must be taken to find a common standard when exchanging documents that are to be operated on electronically, especially formatted documents.

When evaluating the various implementations, be sensitive to the terminology: messages, notes, or documents. Mail transfer lets notes and messages be sent to other uses on any remote system. Notes go into the receiver's incoming mail basket. Messages typically only appear on the receiver's screen if the destination user is active, and do not go into incoming mail. Documents require format standards and considerations and must be specifically explored even if all the appropriate software is in place. For example, frequently, organizational or site-specific standards for fonts, style services, and printer settings are implicitly implemented as defaults. Therefore, this information does not necessarily flow with the transmitted document. This may well result in a document that has the same content, but which is very different-looking, arriving at the destination.

When evaluating solutions for coexistence, consider how flexible the addressing is. Addressing resolution is a major consideration. If address resolution is different between systems, then user involvement in the resolution is important (though usually undesirable). Other considerations include whether notes can be sent to more than one user. If so, determine whether the users can be on different systems and if confirmation notices will be received when the note is sent. If the note is not sent, determine what type of notification can be sent to the user, indicating that there was a problem in mail transfer. Also, give attention to how the edit code translations are handled, since not all vendors distinguish between notes and documents.

Usually, when office systems are being distributed or interconnected, naming conventions become very important. A solid base allows for movement of a person among systems without the users that send mail to the person ever noticing. This can be addressed with directories and some consistent rules.

---

[16]PROFS Extended Mail.

[17]X.400 PROFS Connection.

[18]DISOSS X.400 Connection.

[19]The abilities to scan and both send and receive a FAX document are provided via the IBM Office Facsimile Application (OFA). A programmable workstation can create or scan in a document and then attach a transmittal sheet. The document is then sent to a FAX gateway server that dials the destination FAX (either a Group III FAX machine or another OFA server). The FAX can also be rerouted and/or printed. OfficeVision/VM Series and OfficeVision/MVS Series (Release 2) can route these FAX documents as incoming mail.

WHAT EVERY SYSTEMS ARCHITECT SHOULD KNOW

- Three general distributed interfaces: terminal emulation, batch device emulation, task to task program interface (also called program to program)
- Full function distributed heterogeneous databases across multiple platforms is still pushing the state of the art
- IBM's CICS provides a good model for a distributed transaction manager
- Multiple IBM and other vendor products provide ways to use S/390s to support or interoperate with other systems
- Many solutions to provide enterprise wide E-mail among heterogeneous platforms using a S/390 as the E-mail server are available

Section 4

What Every Systems Manager Should Know about Operations

A comprehensive systems management approach is required to effectively introduce and economically operate distributed systems that have a strong dependence on or relationship with a host system. This section discusses the comprehensive set of distributed systems and network management tools currently being used with and from the IBM S/390. The theme revolves around the NetView family of products and the convergence of tools and services for nodes, networks, and systems management. This convergence has evolved into IBM's systems management strategy—SystemView.[1]

This section will focus on the capabilities that are relevant for a distributed S/390 with an emphasis on the ES/9000 rack models consideration since they represent the current state-of-the-art in the distributed S/390 arena for distributed S/390 hardware. An underlying assumption of the following discussion is that the current data centers and network operations have well-established system management disciplines at various states of automation.

---

[1]SystemView is the label given to IBM's systems management strategy focused on assisting in the planning, coordinating, and operating of enterprise-wide systems. It is based on open standards such as OSI, SAA, and SNA and includes new components. The direction is toward self-managed systems and focuses on end-users' access to applications, application and systems management, and data and systems management.

Chapter *23*

Distributed Environment Management

23.1 DISTRIBUTED SYSTEMS MANAGEMENT FACILITIES

In Chapter 10, the discussion focused on the management approaches and pre- or corequisite requirements associated with distributed systems management. In this chapter the focus is on how IBM's systems and network management software work together to provide an effective distributed systems management basis for managing an enterprise's ever-increasing number of components with the need for 24-hour, seven-days-a-week operational availability.

Systems and network management include a multitude of disciplines:

- Operations management
- Problem management
- Change management
- Configuration management
- Performance management
- Security
- Accounting

It is immediately obvious that the disciplines must be heavily intertwined if they are to produce the high availability, quality performance, and economic efficiencies demanded by today's business environment. In the spring of 1986, IBM announced NetView and identified it as the basis for an extensive set of tools and facilities to manage the network and distributed nodes (communications network management and systems management).

The NetView product is the combination of several discreet network management products that emerged in the late 1970s and early 1980s. Subsequently, the NetView name has also come to be used to refer to a family of communications management products that extend beyond the management of communications lines and nodes to include enhanced log on services, performance monitoring, software distribution, file transfer, voice network administration, and distributed node[1] and LAN[2] management.

From an evolutionary standpoint, NetView is most advanced in network management associated with SNA networks, voice and data networks, and WANs in general. IBM's operating systems are converging on NetView as the basis for distributed management from S/390 operated networks. *LAN*[3] management beyond the physical transport aspects is still in its infancy, since *LANs* are still evolving. In all cases, NetView appears to provide a solid foundation. I see a very close evolution between remote system management and unattended operations implementations and what LAN management will evolve into. For this reason, much of this section will focus on how distributed S/390s, and especially rack-mounted ES/9000s, are being managed.

The NetView family now contains:

- NetView
- NetView/PC (for non-SNA, non-S/390, and non-IBM)
- NetView Performance Monitor (NPM)
- NetView Distribution Manager (NetView DM)
- NetView File Transfer Program (for MVS)
- NetView Access Services (for MVS)
- NetView Graphics Monitor Facility and NETCENTER
- Interfaces to IBM LAN Network Manager
- Interfaces to OSI CMIP/CMIS (OSI/CS) and the TCP/IP based SNMP (VM TCP/IP)

This NetView family is augmented by additional network and systems management capabilities:

- Operating specific programmable interfaces and operators (e.g., OCCF for VSE, PROP for VM, and DHCF for DPPX and AS/400)[4]
- Change distribution tools such as DSX and DSNX

[1]*Node* in this context refers to a distributed system. This could be a nearby host or a geographically remote system.
[2]LAN is this context typically means Token Ring and does not include servers.
[3]*LAN* in this context refers to the composite of connections, servers, clients, and their administration and management.
[4]Logon to an AS/400 via Netview requires Host Command Facility (HCF) and TAF on the S/390 host and Distributed Host Command Facility (DHCF) on the AS/400.

- NetView operator access to 3270 interfaces via Terminal Access Facility (TAF) to such environments as CICS/VS, IMS/VS, and HCF
- Remote hardware console access from NetView via Target System Control Facilities (TSCF)[5]
- Collection of various system logs and accounting data via the Service Level Reporter (SLR)[6]
- SAA Delivery Manager customizes, controls, and delivers software to OS/2 workstations from the S/370 or S/390
- SAA Asset Manager/MVS supports business administration and inventory of hardware and software
- Operations Planning and Control/ESA automates and controls workloads by scheduling and running remote and local production jobs according preset rules.

Together, these provide a comprehensive utility and service base for operating in a distributed environment, which includes a mix of networks, systems, and operating systems.

Additionally, the Information/Systems family of products provides an operational and administrative base for change, problem, and configuration management (information management). These products also provide access to relevant IBM support data (Information/MVS, Information/VM-VSE, Information Access, Information Data, and Information Library).[7]

DISTRIBUTED SYSTEMS MANAGEMENT FACILITIES

- S/390-based family of system and network management facilities
- Single product for operating a network
- Evolving base for remote and automated operations
- Platform to manage distributed S/390s
- Platform to manage non-S/390s, non-SNA networks, and non-IBM systems

---

23.2 A CENTRALIZED OPERATIONS FACILITY—NETVIEW

NetView has evolved from the consolidation of several major network functions into one product (a command facility, a hardware monitor, a session monitor, and a

---

[5]*Target System Control Facility General Information,* IBM Order Number GC28-1063.
[6]*Service Level Reporter (SLR): General Information Manual,* IBM Order Number GH19-6529.
[7]*Introducing the Information Family, VM/SP, and MVS,* IBM Order Number GG34-4045.

status monitor). It provides automation services for the SystemView concept. It includes major automated operations features to handle system and network commands and messages, remove the need for operator intervention, and provide greater operator productivity in dealing with the more complex aspects of running a distributed network. NetView includes enhanced operator productivity and automation capabilities. Some specific capabilities are:[8]

- SAA high-level procedural language (REXX[9,10]), which enables programmers to intermix REXX instructions and NetView commands in programs
- High-level language support for C and PL/I allows systems programmers to write more easily and command processors and exits (defined interfaces into specific program modules) when necessary
- Support of Knowledge Tool for developing knowledge-based systems
- High-level language application program interfaces for user exit routines and command processors. (HLL API[11])
- Some network asset management automation, such as the ability to collect data from 3725/NCP, 3174 controllers, IBM 586X, or 7868 modems (e.g., serial number, machine type, model number, engineering level, port number, power on indicator, etc.), which is very important for problem management
- Alert routing and centralized alert logging and display, allowing operators to monitor alerts occurring in many different domains with a single monitor panel
- LU6.2 communication enabling customers and vendors to write network management applications that communicate with NetView
- NetView Bridge provides an interface for accessing and updating external data bases by customer NetView applications. IBM's Info/Management product uses this.
- NetView Graphics Monitor Facility provides integrated graphics for monitoring SNA resources. This is OS/2 based allowing the integration of operator access to other network and systems management interfaces (both 3270 and OS/2 based interfaces).
- NETCENTER provides for monitoring and controlling SNA and non-SNA resources ranging from displaying graphical locations on a map down to physical and logical elements.

NetView management capabilities are implemented around a hierarchical control concept. A copy of Netview is designated as a central point of control (referred to as

[8]Leif Hjetting, "NetView Release 3 Primer," *IBM International Technical Support Center Bulletin,* IBM Order Number GG24-3368.
[9]REXX is the acronym for Restructured Extended Executor Language.
[10]M. F. Cowlishaw, *The REXX Language: A Practical Approach to Programming,* Prentice-Hall, 1985.
[11]HLL API is the acronym for High Level Language Application Program Interface, which supports direct call to routines via a PL/I or a C macro.

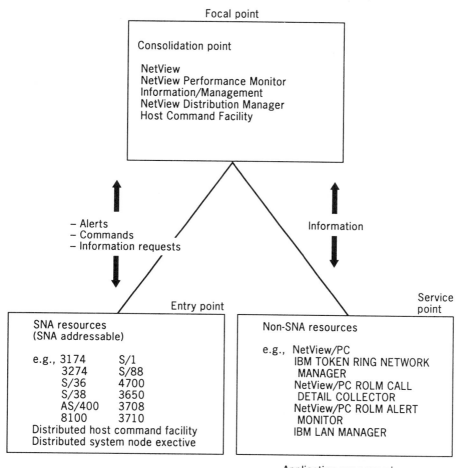

Figure 23.1 NetView Control hierarchy (focal point, entry point, service point).

a focal point), and the other SNA network attached SNA-addressable components are designated as entry points (see Figure 23.1).

Entry point products include IBM communication components such as IBM 3174, IBM 3274, IBM 3710, IBM 3708, IBM 3725, and IBM systems such as S/1, S/38, S/36, AS/400, and S/390s with NetView or equivalent components (e.g., those provided within DPPX/370). The primary role of the entry point from a communication management standpoint is to collect, log, and forward the appropriate data to the focal point.

To accommodate addressing devices and services that are not directly addressable by SNA, an interface—NetView/PC, which acts as a service point—has been provided. This software interface facilitates the forwarding of non-SNA-based data to the focal point for analysis (this forwarding is often via alerts). IBM uses the NetView/PC interface to support IBM Token Ring LANs.

Vendor- or customer-written programs can interface with NetView/PC to collect and exchange data (which could be commands to the non-SNA addressable device). More than 30 vendors have indicated that they plan to use the NetView/PC interface.[12] Some are already delivering.[13] Some vendors have also implemented some network management functions via bypass programs. These are implemented with software that resides both on the gateway and on the focal point host. These programs typically use an SNA device emulators interface to communicate with host resident applications, which in turn interface to NetView. The LU6.2 communication capability provides a more straightforward interface.

The primary distinction between entry point and service point is the level of integration from a network and systems management standpoint; entry points are managed from the focal point while service points have to initiate alerts to cause action. Programs can and are being written by vendors and the IS organization to coreside with the focal point NetView to solicit status.

NetView is becoming an industry standard for managing non-IBM systems and services from central. For example, Interlink provides a NetView port into DEC systems (SNS/NETconnect), and the Bytex Corporation has software that allows control of its newest matrix switches by NetView.[14]

The significance of the various vendor implementations using NetView is that centralized operational support via NetView is recognized as a required, viable, and pervasive solution to address distributed systems and components independent of the hardware or software vendor. The objective is clear: provide as much remote control and unattended capabilities as possible.

NetView is evolving in function and capability, as well as in areas of operator interfaces, automation and operator support, and openness to other standards. For example, IBM has introduced the NetView Graphics Monitor Facility running on a PS/2 to show geographical and logical representations of the network and demonstrated how different colors could be used to designate trouble alerts.[15] IBM has shown an internal PC-based expert system referred to as the Virtual Route Analyzer, which is being used as an engineering tool to pinpoint evasive network performance problems.[16] NetView is also evolving to operate with OSI protocols through devel-

---

[12]Morris Edwards, "OSI and IBM: Challenge for Lead in Integrated Network Management," *Communications News,* Oct. 1988, pp. 35–41.

[13]Marc E. Cecere, "Easing the Burden of Network Management," *LAN Technology,* June 1989, pp. 25–31.

[14]George Briggs, "BYTEX Posts 20% Sales Hike," *Management Information Systems Week,* Feb. 13, 1989, p. 28.

[15]Barton Crockett, "Net Control Meet Draws Int'l Experts," *Network World,* May 22, 1989, pp. 1, 46.

[16]Wayne Eckerson, "IBM Offers Peek at SNA Expert System," *Network World,* June 26, 1989, pp. 1, 66.

opment work on the National Science Foundation's backbone network, NSFnet. Currently, the network is based on TCP/IP, but it will eventually migrate to OSI protocols.[17]

NETVIEW

- A focal point for operations
- Programmable interfaces
- Accommodates automation for mixed environments
- Interfaced by multiple vendors
- Sophisticated graphical interfaces emerging
- Expert system based tools emerging

23.3 NON-SNA ADDRESSABLE COMPONENTS

NetView network management has been extended beyond the SNA environment to provide an integrated management of SNA and non-SNA network components via NetView/PC. NetView/PC is a PC-based management tool that provides for monitoring and problem determination of various technologies such as LANs, multiplexors, voice/data integration, and intelligent switches from IBM and non-IBM vendors. It can work in conjunction with NetView at remote locations or as a standalone facility. For remote management, it provides two communication paths—one to NetView for alerts and one to CICS/VS Distributed Data Management via LU6.2 for file transfers.[18]

NetView/PC is a set of software and hardware components that provides for local management services such as monitoring forwarding alerts, performing problem determination, reporting test results, and collecting performance data, as well as providing a host data transfer facility to interface with CICS/VS.

NetView/PC uses a coprocessor referred to as the ARTIC card (A Real-Time Interface Coprocessor), which off-loads the PC by handling the communications functions for the SNA-related protocols such as LU6.2, PU 2.0, and SDLC. The board includes a microprocessor memory and software.[19] A remote console facility that allows console control from remote NetView/PC is also part of the base software.

---

[17]Morris Edwards, "OSI and IBM Challenge for Lead in Integrated Network Management," *Communications News,* Oct. 1988.

[18]Heinz Kolmer, "NetView/PC Primer," *IBM International Technical Support Centers Bulletin,* IBM Order Number GG24-3115.

[19]Lee Manttelman, NetView and NetView/PC: IBM's Dynamic Duo, Part II, *Data Communications,* April 1987, pp. 191–207.

NetView/PC provides an application interface used by the IBM LAN Manager and ROLM exchange applications, as well as vendor- or customer-written services.

23.4 MANAGING LANs FROM CENTRAL

As stated earlier, *LAN* centralized management is still in its embryonic stage. Most of the support is at the physical LAN level, and related to devices on that LAN. Interfaces with servers are still ahead of us. The merger of the two networks is occurring via the workstation (e.g., IBM's Distributed Console Access Facility—DCAF allows remote access to DOS and OS/2 workstations and servers) which allows the windowing of multiple interfaces.

Many *LAN* vendors are exploring approaches to providing interfaces so that the *LANs* can be supported from remote (centralized) locations via NetView. This is becoming more of a requirement as the functions and services increase with the associated complexity and skill requirements.

NetView interfaces from LANs are currently supported in a variety of ways and via a combination of products and interfaces. IBM's LAN management products have centered around Token Ring networks (Ethernet products are evolving to protect the customer's investments). In this environment, if the LAN is primarily used for connectivity to host sessions (3270 sessions), then host NetView should provide the necessary network management. These network management capabilities can be augmented by the 3174 Token Ring Gateway or the IBM PC Emulation Local Area Network Management Program, which forward alerts to NetView. If interactive control capabilities are desired, NetView/PC—in conjunction with the IBM LAN Manager—is used. (IBM LAN Manager is not to be confused with Microsoft's OS/2 LAN Manager.) When the IBM LAN Manager is used in conjunction with IBM's Token Ring Bridge Program, the LAN Manager can collect management information on bridged LANs.[20] (See Figure 23.2)

IBM's LAN Network Manager can operate in conjunction with NetView directly. NetView operators can use more than 80 commands to support remote Token Ring network LAN users in addition to handling alerts.

Similarly, the AS/400 can be configured to collect and report event information from Token Ring network and forward this information to another AS/400 or up to NetView.

Most *LAN* vendors—including Novell, Banyan, 3COM, and Microsoft—have stated their intent to support NetView and to provide NetView interfaces through the NetView/PC application program interface[21] and/or other ways. In addition, some of these implementations will provide for bi-directional controls. (Some vendors see an operator at the LAN using NetView services via screens.)

---

[20]Lex Molenroek and Guillermo Diaz, "IBM LAN Manager and NetView/PC Planning and Installation for Token Ring Networks," *IBM International Technical Support Centers Bulletin*, IBM Order Number GG24-3128.

[21]Marc E. Cecere, "Easing the Burden of Network Management," *LAN Technology*, June 1989, pp. 25–31.

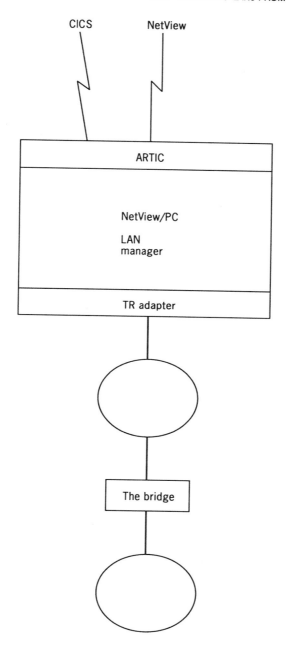

Figure 23.2 *Netview/PC and LAN management.*

Implementations include using IBM 3270 emulators for NetView access, IBM 3770 emulators for data transfer to NetView applications, bypass programs built using various underlying emulators, as well as NetView/PC.[22],[23],[24]

It is important, however, to recognize that NetView support stops at the *physical unit* (PU), not the *logical unit* (LU); therefore, for *LANs* that emulate 3270 control units as gateways, the management visibility stops at PU, the gateway.

23.5   USER SERVICE ACCESS

When dealing with remotely located users, it is important to provide a rigorous method for access control, providing application status, and informing the users of application events.

NetView/Access is a network-based application that controls SNA logon access, assists authorized users in connecting applications across systems, and provides a single logon procedure for accessing all application programs in your network (single access control). It can be set up to automatically log users on to application programs they are authorized to use. It provides a mechanism that the central administrator can use to control which applications a user is authorized to access, and only exposes those applications the user is authorized to access on the screen.

NetView/Access also allows users to work with a single application program (pass mode) or several application programs simultaneously (relay mode), all from a single terminal. It lets the user transfer data from screen to screen. It also allows users to secure terminals while keeping several sessions active.

To provide a vehicle to communicate with the SNA users, IBM offers a product that uses NetView/Access to inform users about the status of all applications in SNA network and supplies further information about individual applications. This includes such operational information as why the application is not active and when it will be active again, as well as when a new release will be installed, or news about the entire network. This product is the SNA Application Monitor (SAMON).[25]

23.6   FILE-TO-FILE TRANSFER

Probably one of the most frequently used services by distributed systems is the transfer of files to other distributed locations or to the central location.

NetView File Transfer Program for MVS (NetView FTP)[26] provides a system-to-system file transfer capability across an SNA network. It can exchange files with

[22]Patricia Keefe, "One-Stop 3Com, SNA Control," *Computerworld,* May 8, 1989, pp. 66–67.

[23]Elisabeth Horwitt, "3Com Outs Netview Link on OS/2," *Computerworld,* Feb. 13, 1989, p. 6.

[24]Paul Desmond, "Software Links NetView, NEC's Net Mgmt. System," *Network World,* May 22, 1989, p. 46.

[25]*NetView Access Services (NetView/Access) SNA Application Monitor* (SAMON). IBM Order Number G511-1013.

[26]*NetView File Transfer Program for MVS.* IBM Order Number G511-1059.

systems that have NetView FTP for MVS installed, or to systems that have the IBM File Transfer Program V2 installed (MVS, VSE, VM). This program transfers VSAM entry sequential and keyed data sets, sequential files on tape or disk, and single members of partitioned data sets.

The program's highlights are its focus on operational considerations, effective use of communications resources, and security. NetView FTP provides the ability to send unlimited file sizes with very large blocks (32 Kbytes). The transmission is direct file-to-file using SNA compression and compaction and two parallel transfers. It supports RACF and VSAM password protection for security and checkpointing, with automatic or manual restart for error recovery.

File transfers can be executed under end user control via interactive and batch user interfaces. The files are dynamically allocated and created at sending and receiving nodes.

Chapter 24

Managing Distributed S/390s

Having reviewed NetView and its capabilities, let's look at the systems management aspects of running a distributed system. S/390-based operating systems probably have the most comprehensive systems management rigors, since they have a solid 25-year base of experience and continually expanding rigor. As has been shown in the CIO section, from a software standpoint, the S/390 is no stranger to working in a distributed environment. Now the focus is on how to operate the hardware and software remotely and how to deal with the geometry of volumes (the number of systems and elements to manage.)

Figure 24.1 provides a high-level snapshot of the typical software configurations for VM, VSE, and DPPX/370. An effort was made to map comparable functions at each node. VM and VSE operating systems have evolved as basic operating systems and separately ordered system service and utility products. These have been packaged for those that prefer to receive a prepackaged set of products. These packages are referred to as VM/IS and VSE/SP. DPPX, on the other hand, was designed and built as a single operational environment product. DPPX/370 retains this structure by continuing to provide all its components in an integrated system. Communication and remote operator functions, such as those provided by VTAM and NetView functions, are part of DPPX/370 and are not identified as separate components.

24.1 REMOTE OPERATIONS

As mentioned earlier, two ports are required to effect remote operations: the port to the operating system and subsystems, and a port to the hardware system (the service processor provides the physical hardware management and diagnostic interface).

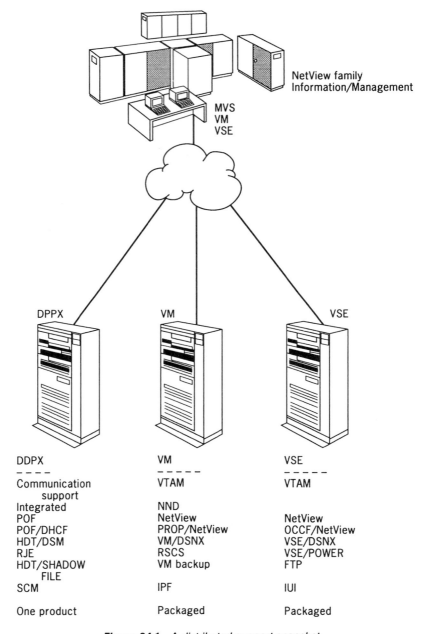

Figure 24.1 *A distributed support snapshot.*

The operating system's port is provided via the combination of the communications adapters (or communication processors, e.g., IBM 37×5) and the appropriate telecommunications access method or networking software. Many implementers prefer leveraging their experience base with SNA. They install VTAM on the node and provide host access to the system services via a program interface (e.g., NetView at the host to NetView-PROP for VM, and NetView to NetView-OCCF for VSE, HCF-DPPX).

Other software console connection options are available. For example, some distributed VM implementers use PROP-to-PROP sessions to manage remote consoles as an interim step to the more comprehensive functions provided by NetView.

24.2 UNATTENDED OPERATIONS

The following discussion will focus on software as it relates to unattended operations. Several of the hardware capabilities, like remote power on and microcode distribution, have already been discussed.

DPPX, VSE, and VM provide the capability to test for conditions and to filter and act on software messages. Each environment, however, displays a variation in the functions currently available and announced. Each system has a different design point. But the key point to note is that VM and VSE have moved a long way toward providing the necessary distributed systems management function, including unattended operations. DPPX, because of its fundamental design point for distributed, has the most sophisticated capability. DPPX essentially manages itself.

24.3 CHANGE CONTROL AND DISTRIBUTION

Using the NetView distribution capabilities (see Figure 24.2), the software is sent to each node using specially designed distribution software. Files transmitted are called objects. In order to differentiate between software functions required at the host and software functions required at the node, I will refer to the host functions as the pitcher function, since it pitches the software to the remote nodes. Similarly, I refer to the node software, which receives the distributed objects, as the catcher function. Files transmitted are called objects.

Here are the key points regarding change distribution and control:

- NetView Distribution Manager (NetView DM) is the primary distribution pitcher
- DSNX and native DPPX/370 functions provide the catcher function
- From an applier standpoint, DPPX/370 has the highest level of control
- VM provides the greatest number of subsystem sensitive appliers[1]

[1]Applier refers to the software necessary to take the software received and install it with the appropriate parameters and controls.

o NetView DM "pitches" files
  to "catcher"
  – MVS, VM, VSE, DPPX
    central site
o Post processors
  – Apply
  – Libraries
  – Network tables
  – Files

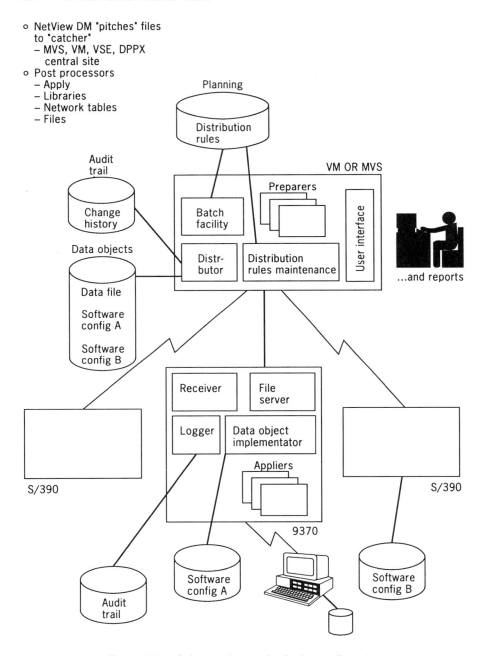

Figure 24.2   *Software change distribution configuration.*

- From a maintenance application standpoint, DPPX/370 again provides for the easiest way to manage rigor. DPPX/370 also has a substantially smaller set of program product components
- VSE leverages the MSHP tool. DSX sends the tested file to VSE DSNX, which in turn will initiate an MSHP job at the node, which will apply the PTF[2]
- SAA Delivery Manager customizes, controls, and delivers software from the S/390 (or S/370) computer to OS/2 workstations.

VM products do not typically employ a commonly used maintenance tool. However, this may not be as problematic as it might appear. In the distributed context, maintenance is expected to be applied and controlled on a business-as-usual basis to the centrally managed copy (or copies), and then the files (or complete minidisks can be distributed). This may be a more effective method of operation because of the VM system software delivery techniques and software promotion techniques.

During pilot implementations, it has also been noted that in some environments many of the above features are too rigorous for systems programmers' needs, especially in the area of change distribution. During the pilots and discussions with distributed systems planners, it was discovered that they would prefer to transmit volume copies (in dump/restore format) rather than specific objects. The emphasis here is to reinforce the message that vendors will provide the required functions, but implementers will decide what best suits their requirements.

24.4 DPPX/370

DPPX/370[3] provides the most sophisticated implementation for operating unattended nodes. It was designed to operate in a hierarchical distributed data processing environment and its entire structure is designed around that concept. The design point for DPPX/370 was 24-hour operations, and therefore the fundamental systems' actions and reactions were built with the idea that the system would be unattended and that central should deal with significant problems.

Unlike VM and VSE, which provide platforms for a myriad of IBM and other software vendor products, DPPX/370 is a single integrated product and has a single service stream. Installation and replication is easy and quick. All aspects of the system are controlled by the programmed operator. A complete set of predefined actions is supplied with the system. The system automatically recovers from most hardware, software, communications, and system software errors without human intervention. DPPX/370 is managed from an MVS (and VSE) host with NetView access to DPPX/370 through HCF. (See Figure 24.3.)

DPPX/370 provides high system availability through self-tuning capabilities, shadow files with online resynchronization, data bases reorganized while in use,

---

[2]PTF refers to problem temporary fix, which is code that provides a problem fix or bypass until the fix is incorporated into the next release of the product.
[3]*DPPX/370 General Information Manual,* IBM Order Number GC23-0640.

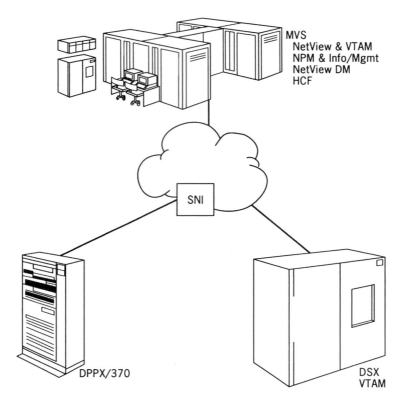

Figure 24.3 *DPPX distributed environment.*

online configuration/reconfiguration, and automatic error recovery with automatic logging of failure data and fast re-IPL.

DPPX/370 uses NetView Distribution Manager (or DSX) from MVS hosts or DSX from VSE/SP hosts as its pitcher. NetView DM provides a central object control repository that provides for defining, storing, planning, distribution, tracking, distribution and data integrity, and security. These services can be accessed via a batch or interactive interface. There is also an optional operation interface that allows the operator to control transmission operations and handle abnormal transmission situations. This can optionally use the Terminal Access Facility (TAF) in the MVS, which provides a terminal session with NetView.

DPPX/370 has system software that catches the transmitted objects. They are applied in a dynamic manner that accommodates the changes to be readily backed out, should they cause a problem.

24.5 VM

VM was designed with distributed users in mind, thereby minimizing the need for operator interventions from the outset. Each user is essentially given their own virtual system. Each VM user has their own logical console and VM provides them with the ability to run in unattended (or disconnected) mode. For those situations that require an operator action (typically, system failure or network actions), VM provides the most flexible unattended operations, using the programmed operator capability of PROP and EXECs.

The major difference between DPPX/370 and VM systems management approach is that VM is peer- rather than hierarchy-oriented. Each system can be a fully standalone system or be managed from a central system. The significant difference between the DPPX/370 implementation and VM is that VM provides the option to implement various degrees of autonomy, while DPPX/370 was designed with unattended but host dependency in mind.

VM unattended operations is accomplished with such tools as PROP (the VM programmable operator), PVM (used to access a console from other VM systems), and NetView. Many distributed users begin by using PROP as the entry vehicle. This provides the staging for introduction of change to their operations and support staffs.

VM also provides an alternate nucleus capability, a standalone serious abnormal termination recovery capability, filtering of messages (up to 99% interception), some executable procedures (REXX execs) that check the health of services, servers, or specific users, as well as a heartbeat function that causes an auto re-IPL. Additionally, VM Backup provides an automated backup, archive, and recovery capability that essentially requires no manual intervention.

VM operations and unattended operations can be managed from other VM or MVS systems using NetView (see Figure 24.4). VM also introduced an enhanced file system that reduces the space management administration tasks, substantially decreasing the need for administrator involvement. Additionally, VM/IPF provides some enhanced user administrative dialogs, which reduce the need to log on to the remote node to set up users.

VM uses NetView Distribution Manager from MVS and VM and a pitcher. Currently, VM can also use the VM/DSNX product as a pitcher.

VM uses VM/DSNX as the catcher that receives the transmitted objects and files them. VM/DSNX also provides applier function, which applies the designated software at specific times.

Appliers deal with the different types of data. The VM appliers are synchronous events and therefore an optional completion acknowledgement exec is provided to assure the central location that the object has been applied. Should a backout be required, an operator is required to log on to the remote node and switch to the earlier copy.

The VM Performance Planning Facility (VMPPF) is an analytic systems planning tool to address performance and capacity objectives. It uses actual collected performance data as a basis to recommend a VM configuration to meet the requested performance objectives.[4]

All of these system management software components have been packaged (e.g., VM/IS) with appropriate how-to-use documentation.

---

[4]*VM Performance Planning Facility General Information*, IBM Order Number GG34-2126.

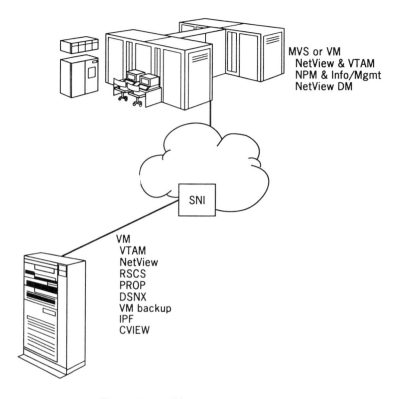

MVS or VM
NetView & VTAM
NPM & Info/Mgmt
NetView DM

SNI

VM
VTAM
NetView
RSCS
PROP
DSNX
VM backup
IPF
CVIEW

Figure 24.4 *VM distributed environment.*

24.6 VSE

VSE has provided a level of unattended operations via OCCF dialogs and OCCF interfaces for several years. The necessary components were provided and the more sophisticated implementers built the necessary flows and dialogs.

VSE, unlike DPPX/370 and VM, is transaction and batch oriented. VSE, in the distributed context, has historically provided an intermediate data center production environment that was operated locally and connected to the corporate network for CICS/VS terminal or intersystem access and batch data interchange. VSE also has been a hierarchically managed system with software and systems support provided from central and local operations to handle tape operations, set up, and batch the workload. With the workload shifting to more online access (via CICS/VS), the notion of unattended has become very important for this online and batch system.

VSE provides unattended operations capabilities (see Figure 24.5) by providing the necessary components and dialogs to accomplish the automation. These include: centralized unattended node support with OCCF R1.3, time-dependent batch job dispatching, NetView on each node to work with OCCF, node customizing (auto-

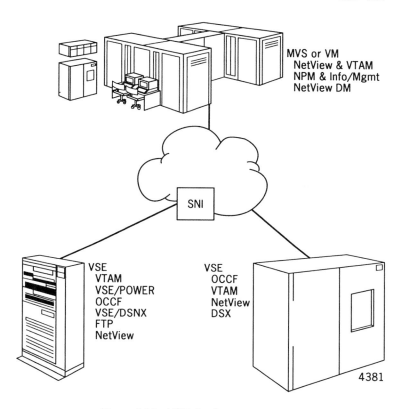

Figure 24.5   *VSE distributed environment.*

matic), automatic startup, automatic message handling, message routing, automatic restart, and automatic shutdown.

Extensive logic is included to provide heartbeat monitoring[5] and recovery capability. Additionally, significant enhancements have been made in the unattended aspects of batch jobs. Very comprehensive scheduling capabilities have been included in Release 4.1.1 and its follow-on VSE/ESA releases.

VSE uses NetView DM on MVS (or DSX on MVS and VSE) as its pitcher and VSE/DSNX as the catcher. VSE/DSNX provides the following functions:

- Send/receive data objects
- Retrieve data objects
- Delete data objects

---

[5]*Heartbeat monitoring* is a term used to describe a "health checking" mechanism. The system or component is being regularly monitored. If the "heart is beating," the system or component is okay; if not, appropriate action is taken. The use of the term *heart* as part of the description indicates the importance of the process.

- Initiate a batch job
- Write a message to the operator console

VSE/DSNX will handle the following data objects:

- VSAM data (fixed record length), KDS, ESDS, and SAM[6] files in VSAM-managed space
- VSE library data

VSE continues to have a dependency on tape distribution for applying new releases of the operating system.

---

[6]KSDS, ESDS, and SAM are acronyms that refer to keyed and sequential access method approaches that VSAM provides to store and access data.

Chapter 25

Managing Mixed Operations

Having reviewed the various capabilities of node operating systems, it is important to recognize that while a single node operating system or hardware architecture may be desirable from a systems management standpoint, in practice, this is typically only a goal. This is due to economics, application requirements, technology changes, and organizational changes which invariably introduce a base system mix.

NetView provides the common denominator for retaining and evolving the required operational controls across a broad diversity of IBM and non-IBM distributed nodes and equipment. The NetView family of products addresses the need for inclusion of host, network, node, and terminal as important elements to provide end users with satisfactory service levels.

In my coverage of systems management, very little attention has been or will be spent on the systems management administrative tools. This topic is worthy of a book in itself, and is very important when one considers the responsiveness and productivity of the IS administrative personnel. Such capabilities are provided by a combination of NetView and tools such as IBM's Information System/Information Management and installation-developed tools. The distribution of geographically distributed S/390s is essentially a logical extension of the solutions typically already installed as part of the ES/9000 systems management and network management strategy.

An addition to the mixed operations management is provided by Interlink via the SNS/SNA Gateway Family, specifically with the SNS/NETconnect and SNS/Link product.

Figures 25.1 and 25.2 depict operating and controlling software distribution across mixed environments and systems.

Figure 25.1 depicts mixed operations. This includes the capabilities to process

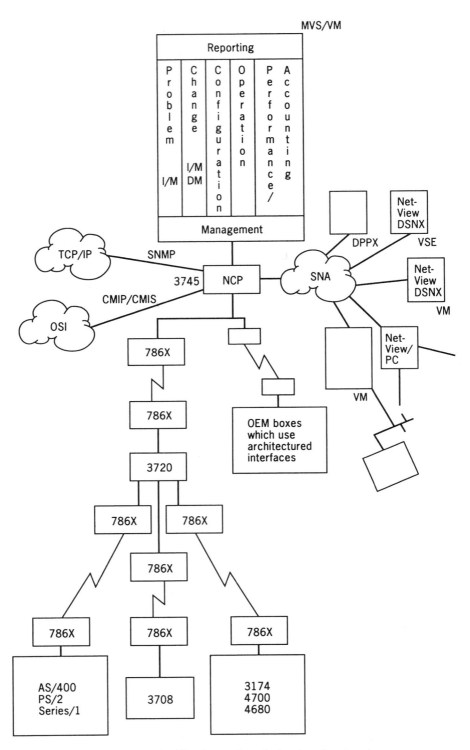

Figure 25.1 *Mixed operations (network and systems).*

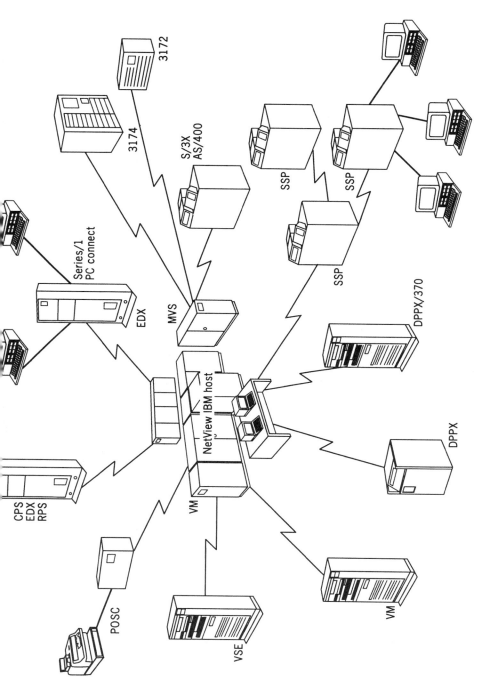

Figure 25.2 Mixed network and distributed support.

3172

3174

S/3X
AS/400

SSP

SSP

SSP

DPPX/370

DPPX

Series/1
PC connect

EDX

MVS

NetView IBM host

VM

CPS
EDX
RPS

POSC

VSE

VM

263

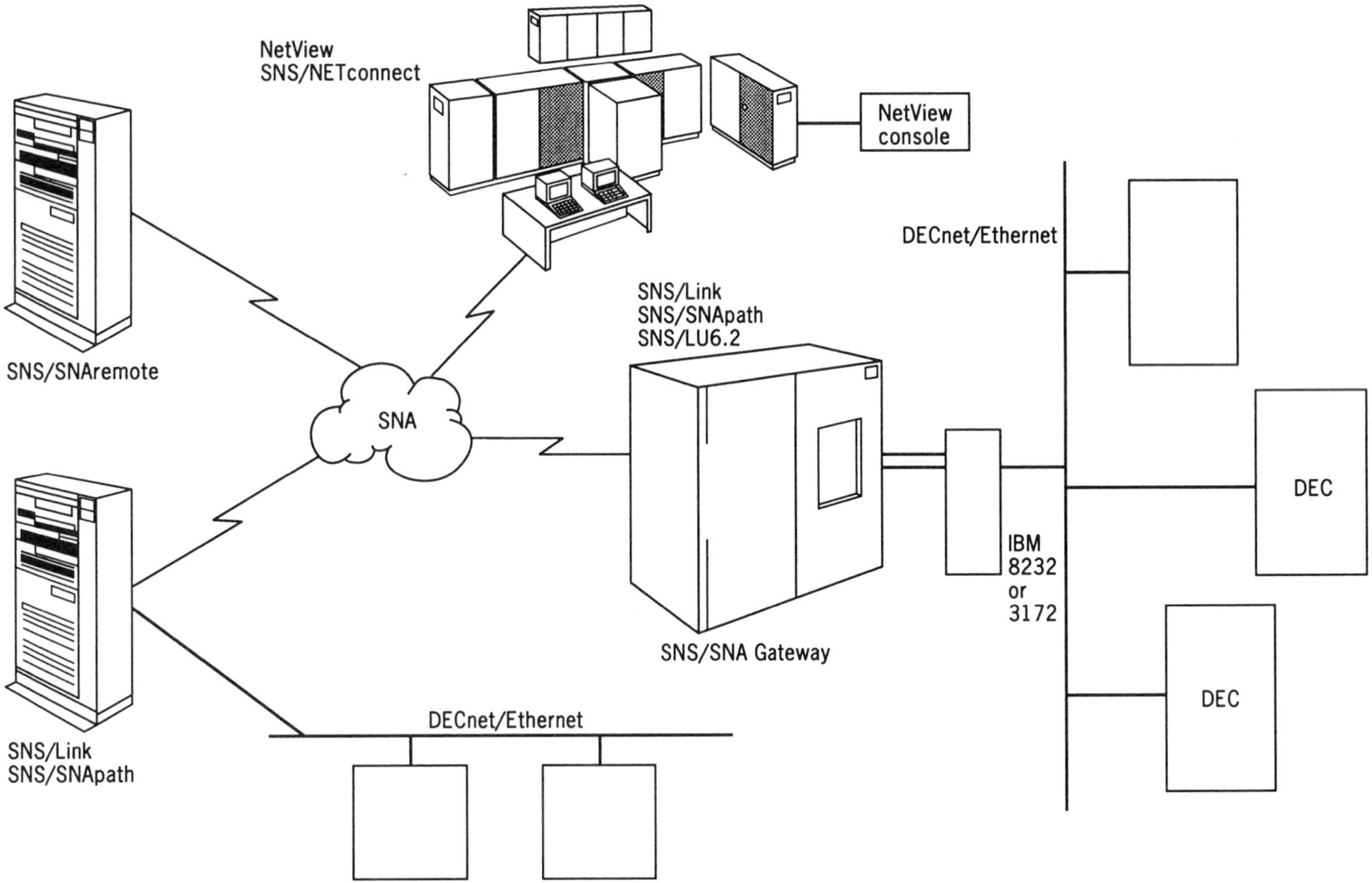

Figure 25.3 NetView SNS/NETconnect.

Labels within figure:

DEC

DEC

DECnet/Ethernet

IBM
8232
or
3172

NetView
console

SNS/Link
SNS/SNApath
SNS/LU6.2

SNS/SNA Gateway

NetView
SNS/NETconnect

SNA

DECnet/Ethernet

SNS/Link
SNS/SNApath

SNS/SNAremote

normal operational commands across the network as well as accepting and processing of alerts, capturing diagnostic information and statistics, and providing access to execute problem determination and to cause the appropriate actions to be taken. This operational management can accomplished from a central location using NetView and its associated systems management products. In this case three different networks (an SNA-based network, a TCP/IP network and an OSI network) are used. The TCP/IP network uses the Simple Network Management Protocol (SNMP) to which NetView interfaces. Similarly, OSI standards have defined the Common Management Information Protocol (CMIP) and Common Management Information Services to which NetView interfaces. A key observation that should be made is that all of IBM's communications equipment is implemented with systems and network management in mind as exemplified by the systems and devices in the figure. Another point is that other manufactures' equipment is frequently also managed from NetView using SNA and NetView defined interfaces.

Figure 25.2 depicts a sampling of the variety of nodes that can have software distribution from central using NetView Distribiution Manager and its associated products. The figure depicts PCs, SSP nodes (System Support Program) which are representative IBM S/36 and IBM AS/400 nodes, DPPX/370 nodes which are representative of IBM 8100, ES/9370, Micro Channel 370 and rack-mounted ES/9000 nodes using DPPX, IBM Series/1 nodes using such operating systems as CPS (Control Program Support), EDX (Event Driven Executive), and RPS (Realtime Programming System), point of sale controller nodes (POSC) such as IBM 4700 systems, IBM 3174 and IBM 3172 controller nodes, as well as other S/370 and S/390 systems nodes using VM and VSE operating systems. IBM's new SAA Delivery Manager enables the customization, control and delivery of software to OS/2 workstations.

SNS/NETconnect provides the ability of monitoring, managing, and controlling DECnet Phase IV networks via NetView. SNA networks, S/370 and S/390 nodes, and DECnet can be managed with a single console (see Figure 25.3).

SNS/NET connect uses NetView (NPDA) to report DECnet events with familiar IBM alert formats and screens. It provides realtime accessibility to standard DECnet management tools (NCP) for monitoring, controlling, testing, and configuring DECnet networks. (NCP is the standard Digital command language, a part of DECnet which is used to monitor and control the DECnet.)

Chapter 26

Distributed Systems Management Summary

In summary, all of the three systems (DPPX, VM, and VSE) provide necessary unattended operations and automation in order to effectively manage distributed S/370 and S/390 systems, which in turn can be used as a platform to manage complementary solutions and intelligent workstations.

Each operating system environment has a unique approach to the rigors, but functionally they are quickly converging. However, the fundamental design points and characteristics of each system will not go away over the next few years. This means that for solutions that are pivotal on the fundamental design of a specific operating environment, the decision should be straightforward. Further, the convergence allows the implementer who does not have a unique distributed support requirement to focus more on the applications available, the function and the timeframes that meet his requirements rather than having to make an operating system decision because of a small technical feature's availability.

WHAT EVERY SYSTEMS MANAGER SHOULD KNOW

- Remote unattended operations requires software and hardware
- Automated operations goes beyond simple message response
- Managing multiples requires rigorous control platforms
- A distributed management platform must support mixed environments
- S/390 along with NetView provide state-of-the-art platforms
- The same technologies apply to managing the data center as dark rooms

TABLE 26.1 Distributed Systems Management Capabilities

DISCIPLINES	FUNCTIONS	NODES		
		VM	VSE	DPPX
Installation	Packaged	yes	yes	yes
Unattended Operations	Health check	yes	yes	n/a
	Auto bringup	yes	yes	yes
	Spool purge	yes	yes	n/a
	Self tuning	no	no	yes
	Backup/archive	yes	no	yes
	Mirror data	no	no	yes
	Alternate system	yes	yes	yes
	Auto dial out (to host)	yes	yes	no
Operations Management	Remote bringup	yes	yes	yes
	Message routing	yes	yes	yes
	Remote commands	yes	yes	yes
	Programmed automation	yes	yes	yes
	User screen access	yes	no	no
Problem Management	Send alerts	yes	yes	yes
	Problem source identification	yes	yes	yes
	Action recommendations	no	no	yes
	Problem logging at host	yes	yes	yes
Unattended Change Management	Self-configuring	no	yes	yes
	Pre-load (initial install)	yes	yes	yes
	Remote install	yes	yes	yes
Change Management	Receive software changes	yes	yes	yes
	Apply changes	yes	yes	yes
	Change scheduling	yes	yes	yes
	Change notification	yes	yes	yes
	Change tracking	yes	yes	yes
	Change backout/recovery	manual	manual	yes
Configuration Management	Inventory data base (host)	yes	yes	yes
	Device connectivity	manual	yes	yes
	Network & terminals	manual	manual	yes
	Topology (administration)	yes	yes	yes
Network Performance Management	Response time monitoring	yes	yes	yes
	Node utilization	yes	yes	yes
	Network utilization	yes	yes	yes
	Online tuning	yes	yes	yes
Account Management	Connect time	yes	yes	yes
	Network usage	yes	yes	yes
Remote Administration	User enrollments	yes	yes	yes
	Disk storage management	yes	yes	yes

Table 26.1 provides a summarized snapshot (early 1989) of the functional capabilities required to manage distributed systems, using the ES/9370 and the operating systems that run on it as a basis. The view is from both the distributed node and central site capabilities.

What Every Systems Implementer Should Know about Connectivity

This section provides an outline of some of the major connectivity, interconnect, and network attach considerations, using the ES/9000 rack-mounted system as a frame of reference. The need for connectivity flexibility is demonstrated herein. The topics covered are:

- Physical connectivity: attachment to ES/9000 rack-mounted
- OEM SNA Gateways: OEM connection to ES/9000 services
- Application Interconnect Platforms: basis for application connectivity
- ES/9000-to-SNA Network attach

Very specific products and implementations are described in this section. They are subject to change with new releases and new features. It is recommended that you work directly with the vendor or your specialist when you need very specific and current details. In general, it is important to be aware of the various approaches offered and the types of interfaces they support.

Chapter *27*

S/390 Connectivity

27.1 S/390 PHYSICAL CONNECTIVITY

In the context of discussing distributed systems from a hardware and communications flexibility standpoint, it is important to consider the physical configurations that one typically associates with systems, but often overlooks. To bring this into perspective, I suggest that you take a quick look at the combination of equipment tied together on your *LAN,* in a department's computer area, or in the IS computer room. Note the number of boxes—servers, gateways, and control units—in addition to the communications adapters and wiring equipment.

The traditional S/370 typically used the outboard device also. The newer rack-mounted models (S/370 and S/390) configurations use channels and integrated bus attachment for connecting peripherals to the CPU and its mainstorage.

The non-rack models use the channels and control units to attach peripherals (some products have separate control units, while others have the control unit integrated with the peripheral itself). An IBM 37XX communications controller (e.g., IBM 3745, 3725, or 3720) interfaces with the channel and provides a communication front-end to manage the communications interfaces. The combination of the communications controller hardware, communications controller resident software (ACF/Network Control Program, ACF/NCP), and CPU-based software (e.g., ACF/VTAM and ACF/TCAM) provide a communication subsystem that manages the connections and provides a transparency of the network to the application programs.

The IBM 4331, 4341, and 4361 provide an integrated communications adapter option in addition to the channel attachment options. These tend to be referred to generically as ICAs. This ICA has the appearance of a channel and communication controller. Software executing on the CPU (e.g., VTAM and operating specific communications software) and microcode in the adapter provide the communications subsystem services.

The ES/9370 and its follow on ES/9000 models were designed specifically for a distributed environment making extensive use of the rack as the housing for its peripherals, associated controllers, and control units.[1] All of its peripherals, e.g., DASD, tape, communication controllers, and control units can be placed in the rack with the CPU. The configurations were intended to provide both communications and other peripheral device flexibility both with in-rack placement and in-board and out-board attachments via the channel.

In the communications arena, the rack-mounted systems support both integrated optional adapters and the ability to use traditional channel attached communication processors. They also provide substantially more flexibility than do the IBM 4331, 4341, and 4361 ICA. They provide four types of integrated communications subsystems controllers as well as an integrated control unit in the form of a workstation controller, which allows the attachment of 3270-type devices and OEM devices. Multiples of these communications controllers can coexist. The Intel 9770 is also available as an in-the-rack channel attached controller, which supports a variety of OEM device attachments. (See Figure 27.1.)

The four integrated communications subsystem controllers are the telecommunications subsystem controller, the ASCII subsystem controller, the IBM Token Ring subsystem controller, and the IEEE 802.3 Local Area Network (LAN) subsystem controller.

The telecommunications subsystem controller consists of a communications processor component and line adapter cards that support access to switched telephone networks or nonswitched voice grade and telegraph lines. Protocols supported include: U.S. Telegraph Control Type 2 (TTC2), Binary Synchronous Communication (BSC), Synchronous Data Link Control (SDLC), and High-Level Data Link Control (HDLC).

The ASCII subsystem controller provides for the attachment of a variety of asynchronous devices such as display stations, printers, plotters, graphic equipment, and personal computers. This controller supports ASCII devices and converts them to 3270s; allows transparent transmission of data; and supports ASCII mode.

In addition to the integrated adapters that were introduced for the ES/9370, several more communications-oriented rack-mounted channel-attached communications controllers have emerged. Specifically, the 3174 Establishment Controller and the 3172 Interconnect Controller as depicted in Figure 27.1. These provide similar capabilities to the integrated adapters; however, they tend to provide a richer set of options and more capacity. The 3172 Interconnect Controller is extremely interesting in that it can provide a LAN gateway, a Fiber Distributed Data Interface (FDDI) gateway, or a remote VTAM channel-to-channel connection. As a LAN gateway it

---

[1]The IBM 4331, 4341, and 4361 have integrated adapters, but the peripherals themselves typically attach outside of the frame.

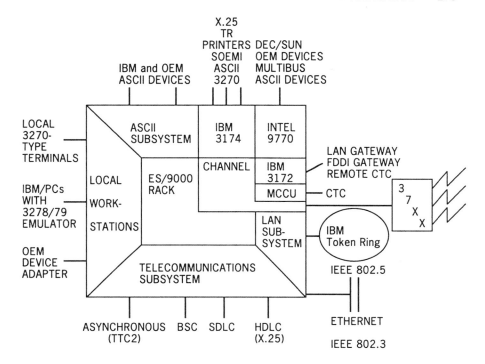

Figure 27.1 *ES/9000 rack-mounted models physical connectivity.*

supports SNA, TCP/IP, OSI/Manufacturing Messaging System (OSI/MMS), and AIX. It supports all major IBM and non-IBM LAN environments including Token Ring, Ethernet V2, IEEE 802.3, MAP 3.0 broadband and carrierband, IBM/PC Network broadband and baseband, and DECnet via SNS/SNAgateway from Interlink. The Remote Channel-to-Channel feature allows the 3172 to be connected with up to 4 T1 links and connected to the S/390 via one or two channels. When used as a FDDI gateway (it conforms to ISO 9314 standard) it allows SNA or TCP/IP networks to use a high-speed LAN backbone.

A Multi-system Channel Communication Unit (MCCU) feature was introduced with the ES/9000 rack models to allow parallel channel-to-channel attachment among three other ES/9000 systems.

27.2 S/390 SOFTWARE CONNECTIVITY

Together with the appropriate communications software platforms, the ES/9000 rack provides a very comprehensive and diverse connectivity base. (See Figure 27.2 and Table 27.1 for a 1989 snap shot using the ES/9370.)

TABLE 27.1 Summary of Communications Lines and Protocols

Telecommunications	VM	VSE	DPPX/370
	Yes	Yes	Yes (2)
TTC2 Protocol:			
V.24/V.28 (RS-232-C) Interface (75-19,200 bps)			
Point-to-Point Switched Line	VM	BTAM	No
Point-to-Point Nonswitched Line	VM	BTAM	Yes
V.11 (RS-422-A)(75-19,200 bps)			
Directly attached System-to-System	VM	BTAM	No
Directly attached System-to-Work Station	VM	BTAM	No
BSC Protocol (1)			
V.24/V.28 (RS-232-C) Interface (600-19,200 bps)			
Point-to-Point Switched Line	VM	BTAM	
Point-to-Point Nonswitched Line	VM,VTAM	BTAM,VTAM	
Multipoint Nonswitched Line	VM	BTAM	
V.35 Interface (2,400-64,000 bps)			
Point-to-Point Nonswitched Line	VM,VTAM	BTAM,VTAM	
V.11 (RS-422-A) (2,400-64,000 bps)			
Directly Attached System-to-System	VM,VTAM	BTAM,VTAM	
SDLC Protocol:			
V.24/V.28 (RS-232-C) Interface (600-19,200 bps)			
Point-to-Point Switched Line	VTAM	VTAM	Yes (3)
Point-to-Point Nonswitched Line	VTAM	VTAM	Yes
Multipoint Nonswitched Line	VTAM	VTAM	Yes
V.35 Interface (2,400-64,000 bps)			
Point-to-Point Nonswitched Line	VTAM	VTAM	Yes
X.21 Interface (600-64,000 bps)			
Point-to-Point Switched Line	No	VTAM	–
Point-to-Point Nonswitched Line	VTAM	VTAM	Yes
V.11 (RS-422-A)(2,400-64,000 bps)			

...HDLC LAP-B protocol.

Interface / Protocol			
V.24/V.28 (RS-232-C) Interface (600-19,200 bps)	VTAM	VTAM	Yes
X.25 Packet-Switching Network			
X.21 Interface (600-19,200 bps)	VTAM	VTAM	Yes
X.25 Packet-Switching Network			
X.25 Communications	Yes	No	No
X.25 Protocol:			
V.24/V.28 (RS-232-C) Interface (2,400-19,200 bps)	TCP/IP		
X.25 Packet Switching Network			
X.21 Nonswitched Interface (2,400-64,000 bps)	TCP/IP		
X.25 Packet-Switching Network			
V.35 (2,400-64,000 bps)	TCP/IP		
X.25 Packet-Switching Network	TCP/IP		
IBM Token-Ring (IEEE 802.5)	VM,TCP/IP,VTAM	VTAM	Yes
IEE 802.3 LAN (Ethernet)	VM,TCP/IP	No	
S/370 Block Multiplexer Channel	Yes	Yes	Yes

Notes:

1. For BSC transmission, VTAM supports 3270-type devices only.

2. DPPX/370 support for the Telecommunications Subsystem Controller is limited to the protocols TTC2, SDLC, and HDLC LAP-B.

3. Auto Answer from PU 2.0 & PU 5.

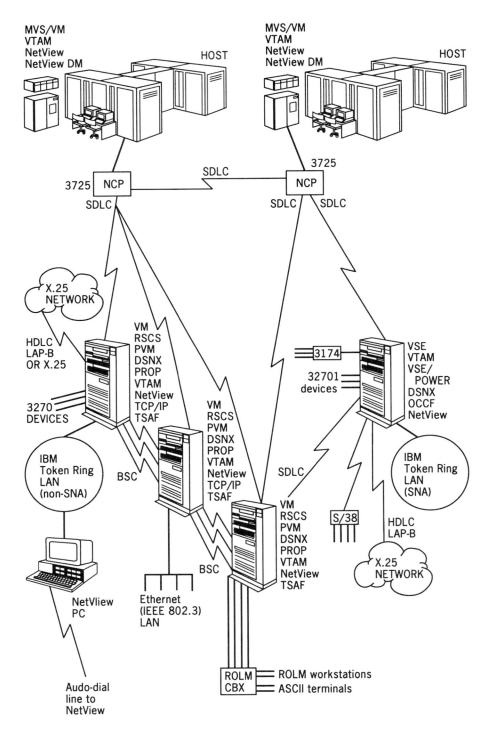

Figure 27.2 Communications support.

27.3   S/390 NETWORK CONNECTIVITY

When connecting S/390 nodes to a network there are five definitive configuration options that should be reviewed. It is likely that each organization will have a combination of these:

- Backbone integration (see Figure 27.3)
- Single node (see Figure 27.4)
- Multiple node (see Figure 27.5)
- Peer cluster (see Figure 27.6)
- Multi-enterprise or independent networks (see Figure 27.7)

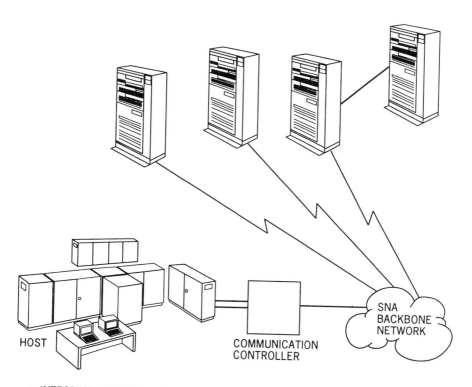

HOST

COMMUNICATION
CONTROLLER

SNA
BACKBONE
NETWORK

o INTEGRATE NODES INTO EXISTING NETWORK
o ANY TO ANY CONNECTIVITY
o CONNECTS UP TO 255 PROCESSORS IN A
  SINGLE NETWORK

Figure 27.3   *Backbone integration connectivity.*

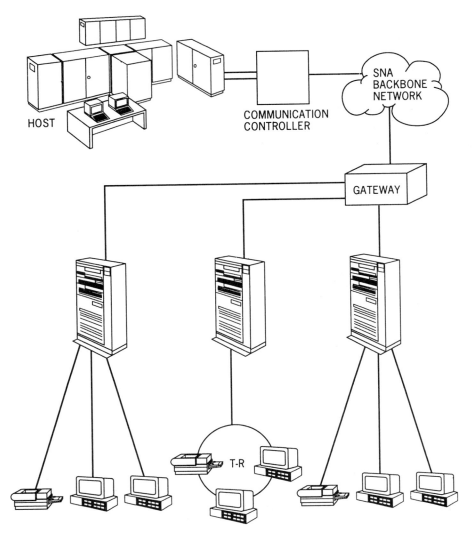

o EACH NODE IS A SEPARATE NETWORK
o ANY TO ANY CONNECTIVITY
o EASY REPLICATION OF 9370 INSTALLATION
o MINIMIZES THE IMPACT OF CHANGE

Figure 27.4 *Single node connectivity.*

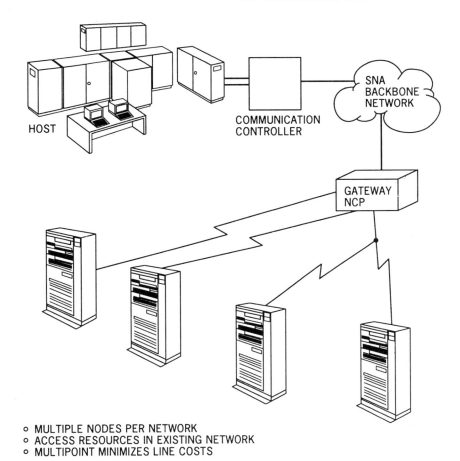

HOST

COMMUNICATION
CONTROLLER

SNA
BACKBONE
NETWORK

GATEWAY
NCP

o MULTIPLE NODES PER NETWORK
o ACCESS RESOURCES IN EXISTING NETWORK
o MULTIPOINT MINIMIZES LINE COSTS

Figure 27.5   *Multiple node connectivity.*

The primary differences between these options are a function of access scope and the flexibility of adding nodes, network size, and line optimization[2] (as noted in the following charts). The last consideration (Figure 27.7) has to do with managing or connecting to autonomous networks that are interconnected. The SNI[3] gateway provides a mechanism to isolate each network from a management standpoint, while providing the required connectivity. In multi-enterprise situations, this SNI

[2]*Planning for a 9370 SNA Distributed Network,* IBM Order Number GC30-3475, pp. 25–36.
[3]SNI refers to SNA Network Interconnect. This provides a level of addressing structure and naming convention independence while providing the ability to communicate across SNA networks to predefined destinations. It provides a gateway between two or more SNA networks.

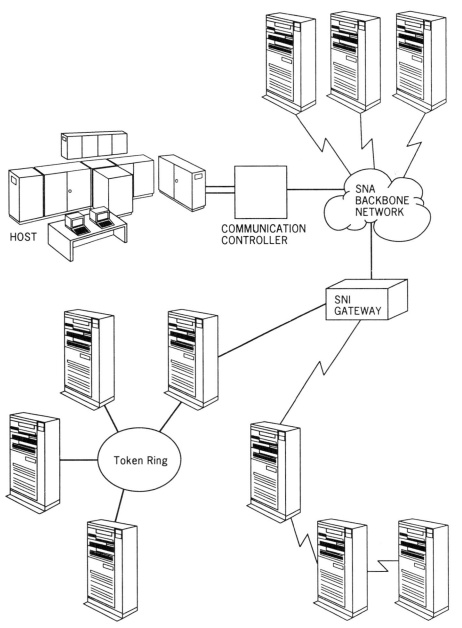

○ MULIPLE CLUSTERED NODES PER NETWORK
○ ANY TO ANY CONNECTIVITY
○ MINIMIZES LINKS BETWEEN NETWORKS
○ LOCALIZES THE IMPACT OF CHANGE

Figure 27.6 *Peer cluster connectivity.*

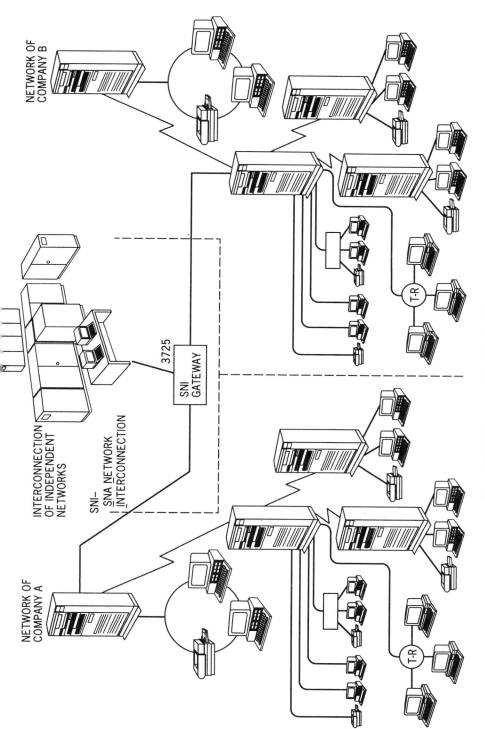

Figure 27.7 Interconnection of independent networks.

283

gateway and network backbone might be provided by a service to act as a connection for multiple enterprises and assure the security, intersystem communication integrity, and flexibility. For example, the IBM Information Network provides the ability to connect its customers' hosts and networks to communicate with its services or use its communication backbone via SNI gateways.

Chapter *28*

OEM SNA Gateways

To this point, we have reviewed interconnect solutions that require software on the S/390. Other interconnect approaches include solutions that interface to architected interfaces on the S/390 system.

Because of the investment protection associated with interfacing to an architected and documented interface and the pervasive use of SNA in IBM solutions, many vendors have developed their protocol converters based on the SNA-defined interfaces. Some vendors offer other levels of interfacing to provide those users who have special requirements with an interoperability solution. Many of these solutions also leverage the SNA capabilities.

Several products are referred to as network processors or servers. For discussion purposes, I characterize these protocol converters as gateways that essentially provide protocol conversion for access to the S/390 via SNA. These products also provide for line concentration and frequently supply some end user enhancements and services.

Mitek's OpenConnect, Forest Processor, some of Interlink's SNA/Gateway family, Intel and FlexLINK or TCP/IP, and DECnet/SNA Gateway tend to be representative of this type of gateway.

In general, these OEM-to-SNA gateways provide basic protocol conversion and line connection (concentration) to IBM SNA interfaces. Additionally, they may provide bi-directional support and, frequently, some user productivity features (such as hot key) for additional value added and product differentiation.

28.1 MITEK OPENCONNECT SERVER

Mitek Systems provides high-speed channel attach (1.8 Mb) or remote access (19.2 Kb or 256 Kb) hardware/software connectivity between IBM SNA and Ethernet TCP/IP environments.

These connection options are provided by Mitek's OpenConnect server models M2030 and M2130, which are referred to collectively as M2X30. The M2030 connects to the ES/9000 via direct channel attachment and the M2130 connects through an SDLC line. This connection is augmented by software products on either the TCP/IP system or the IBM system or both.

The Mitek OpenConnect server is augmented by several software products and offerings. They reside on the TCP/IP systems, the Mitek server itself, or on the IBM host. These offerings include the Presentation Services family, TELNET/FTP Clients, and TELNET Server.

Presentation Services (PS) is a family of software products designed to allow workstations on Ethernet TCP/IP Networks to communicate with IBM SNA. These software products reside on devices manufactured by Sun, Apollo, Hewlett-Packard, AT&T, Tektronix, Convex, MIPS, Unisys, NCR, CDC, DEC, and IBM.

Capabilities provided by the Presentation Services product line include:

- PC File Transfer between TCP/IP hosts and IBM SNA systems
- 3770 Remote Job Entry (RJE)
- 3270/3770 Terminal Emulation

Also featured is an Application Program Interface (API) that allows Ethernet host programs to access IBM SNA hosts. Use of these products does not require special software, nor does it require software changes in the IBM SNA operating system.

Mitek's TELNET/FTP Clients are IBM host program offerings. These products allow you to access Ethernet TCP/IP host applications from your 3270 terminal and perform file transfers to or from any processor on the TCP/IP network.

Mitek's TELNET Client application allows a 3270 terminal to emulate a terminal on the TCP/IP network. In this mode, the 3270 has access to applications on any of the TCP/IP network processor or other gateways that support TELNET terminals. The TELNET Client application is accessible from any terminal on the SNA network.

With Mitek's FTP Client application, both binary and ASCII files can be transferred to or from any processor on the TCP/IP network. Any 3270 on the SNA network, any terminal using Mitek's PS 3270 emulation on the TCP/IP network, or any terminal using Mitek's TELNET SERVER can initiate the FTP File Transfer.

TELNET Server is an optional feature available on Mitek's OpenConnect Server Models M2030 and M2130. This application permits terminals and systems on an Ethernet TCP/IP network that support a TELNET Client to connect to the Open-Connect Server and use the fullscreen 3270 emulation in the server to access IBM systems on an SNA network. Besides providing fullscreen 3270 emulation, this application also allows high-speed graphics pass-through from IBM mainframes to asynchronous terminals and workstations on TCP/IP networks.

Most major systems and terminal server vendors provide TCP/IP (which is supported by over 150 vendors) and TELNET to allow basic interactive terminal communication with all systems on the network. With this application added to the OpenConnect server, terminals on system workstations that support TCP/IP and

TELNET have access to the 3270 applications available on IBM hosts. The product emulates an IBM 3278 Model 2, and requires no special or additional software on the TCP/IP network. TELNET Server also supports TN3270.

The TELNET Server allows a single logon to the mainframe while in fullscreen 3270 mode, and invokes the desired graphics application.

Mitek's SNA gateway provides access from CAD applications in IBM (list available from Mitek) to Apollo, Sun, DEC, and other workstations. Figure 28.1

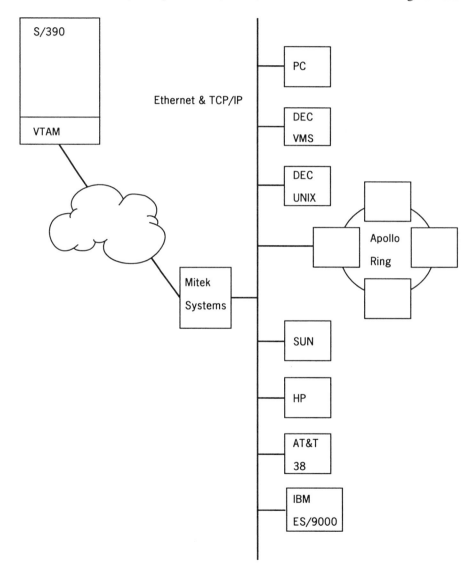

Figure 28.1   *Mitek OpenConnect server.*

illustrates two large Ethernet networks, one channel attached and one attached via a communications line. Users on the TCP/IP network can access the S/390 as terminal users, large files can be transferred, 3270 users can access TCP/IP systems, and data can be shared among the TCP/IP systems. Line costs for RJE can be reduced by consolidating RJE activity across TCP/IP broad band.

28.2   FOREST NETWORK PROCESSOR

The Forest Network Processor (FNP) is a gateway that provides connectivity between IBM systems and various non-IBM networks, including DEC, Hewlett Packard, Burroughs, and Unisys. The product provides any-to-any services for the systems connected to it without any gateway software at either system. Within the FNP, this solution provides:

- Network Virtual Terminal: a user's native terminal connected to their native computer is made to appear to a foreign computer as one of its own directly connected fullscreen terminals (VSE bi-directional and to VM)
- Network Virtual Printer: printers are made to appear local to the FNP connected processors
- File Transfer: exchange of files between computers of different types[1]
- Remote Job Entry: submission of batch jobs to a foreign computer type from the user's native computer
- Program-to-Program Communication: programs running on different computer types can exchange data through a pragmatic setup
- "Hot Key" Support: the user may have multiple virtual terminals active and "jump" between active terminal sessions (from FNP to IBM system)

The FNP uses a virtual terminal interface to allow the initiation of file transfers and setups.

The FNP is connected to the other computers via either serial lines or LANs depending on the computer type, configuration, and network topology. Terminals normally remain cabled to their native computer, so FNP services can be provided to all users with no need to make any changes to their existing network. A single FNP can provide links into multiple hosts.

For example, the FNP permits a manufacturer with many similar plants to have its DEC and HP computers on the shop floor communicate with the mainframe at headquarters or distributed S/390. Figure 28.2 illustrates an IBM-based solution that uses communication to exiting computers. The gateway allows the SNA-based access to a locally or geographically distributed ES/9000 or a mainframe via a shared local line and SNA backbone, saving money and further establishing SNA as the customer's standard network.

[1]This support exists and there is a statement of direction for VM at the time of this writing.

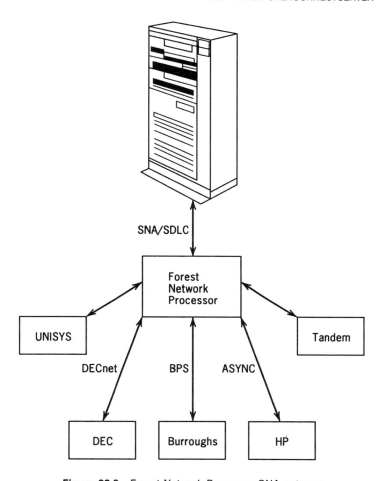

Figure 28.2   *Forest Network Processor SNA gateway.*

28.3   INTEL'S FASTPATH MULTIBUS AND TCP/IP

Intel's 9770 FASTPATH is a channel attached, high-performance control unit for making multiple connections between an S/390 and non-IBM hardware. It is available as a freestanding unit or may be mounted directly in an IBM 9309 rack as an integrated part of an ES/9370 or ES/9000 (Figure 28.3). In either case, it is channel attached. The Intel 9770 provides the ES/370 with an open connectivity architecture allowing custom connections. Intel also provides turnkey hardware and software solutions for an S/390 to communicate with up to:

- 4 DEC/VAX networks, and/or SUN workstations
- 256 ASCII devices

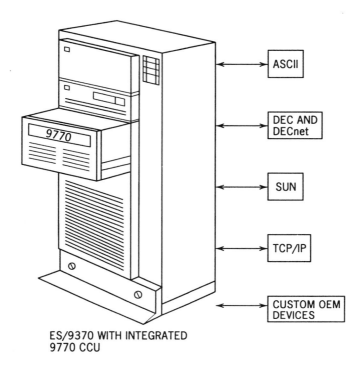

ES/9370 WITH INTEGRATED
9770 CCU

Figure 28.3 *Intel 9770.*

- 6 Ethernet networks running TCP/IP
- 4 OSI networks, either 802.3 or 802.4

Multiple connections can be intermixed across the same control unit, with data transfer rates of 2.5 Mbits per second and higher. As an open connectivity platform, the 9770 provides a standard IEEE 796 MULTIBUS interface to the S/370. Since there are over 2000 MULTIBUS boards available, virtually any type of connection can be supported, including special peripherals, process control equipment, high-speed data collection, specialized communications, networks, etc.

28.4 INTERLINK SNS/SNA GATEWAY

As was mentioned earlier, the SNS/Gateway Family (Figure 28.4) provides a set of solutions for office and interoperability among ES/9370 VM systems and systems using DECnet implementation. Several vendors have implemented a DECnet inter-face. Implementations are available for such systems as IBM PCs, Apple's MacIn-tosh, SUN, Alliant, and others. Connectivity to these systems is also supported using Interlink. SNS/SNA Gateway also provides a network gateway capability and

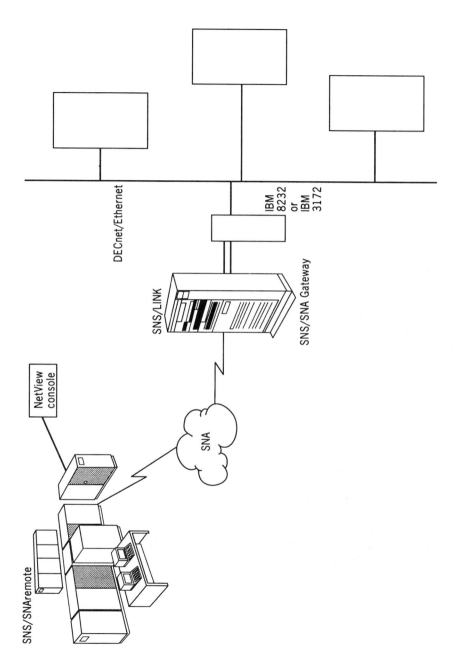

DECnet/Ethernet

IBM 8232 or IBM 3172

SNS/LINK

SNS/SNA Gateway

SNA

NetView console

SNS/SNAremote

Figure 28.4 SNS/SNAgateway family.

provides an SNS/LU6.2 tool to develop LU6.2 applications. From a connectivity standpoint SNS provides end node or full DECnet Phase IV routing (Level 1 and Level 2) over an SNA backbone or link.

SNS/LU6.2 allows a company to write programs enabling applications in a DECnet node in one city to communicate with an application on an IBM host in another city. Prerequisites include DECnet/SNA APPC/LU6.2 Programming Interface V2 or later, on each DECnet node, to be accessed using SNS/LU6.2.

28.5   DIGITAL EQUIPMENT CORP./IBM INTERCONNECTIONS

Digital Equipment Corp. provides several gateway solutions (Figure 28.5): VMS/SNA, DECnet/SNA Gateway-ST, and DECnet/SNA Gateway-CT.

VMS/SNA V1.3 provides a low-end protocol conversion capability. It provides a single system interconnect, allowing up to 16 concurrent sessions, and runs on VMS V4.7 and VMS V5.0 compatible systems.

DECnet/SNA Gateway for Synchronous Transport (ST) V1.0 provides an upward extension of DECnet/SNA Gateway and allows for network-to-network interconnect with the following support:

- One line at 256 Kbps
- Two lines at 128 Kbps
- Four lines at 64 Kbps
- Up to 128 concurrent sessions.

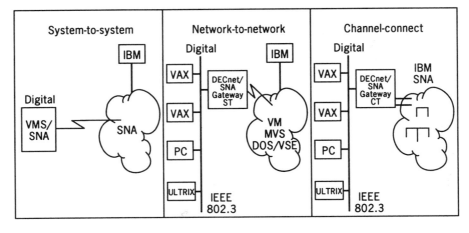

Figure 28.5   *DECnet/SNA implementation.*

DECnet/SNA Gateway for Channel Transport (CT) V1.0 offers channel attachment to S/390s. It is based on DEC Channel Server hardware and is a functional peer to DECnet/SNA Gateway-ST. It supports up to 255 concurrent sessions.

These gateway connection options provide a platform for DEC, such as 3270 Terminal Emulator; an LU6.2 application development interface; and an RJE emulator.

Chapter 29

Application Interconnect Platform

To this point, we have touched on all the fundamental building blocks associated with application interconnect platforms. Now we can quickly review the options in the context of:

- Program-to-program (task-to-task)
- Terminal pass-through
- Batch interfaces
- Interoperability services (e.g., mixed environments)
- Application-to-application (e.g., PROFS to Personal Services/CICS).

However, in order to analyze the various interconnection and interoperability approaches, it is important to note how each implementation is configured as well as the interface(s) they present. I will use the label "gateway" to represent the service that each configuration provides. These gateway implementation categories are relevant from the standpoints of configuration flexibility, systems transparency, performance, and control.

29.1 GATEWAY CONFIGURATIONS

The representative gateway configuration categories are:

- Standalone gateway: neither IBM nor OEM system is affected by gateway, e.g., Forest Network Processor (see Figure 29.1)

Standalone gateway
  – Local or remote connect
  – Device/protocol and/or function conversion
  – Transparent to both systems: each sees native interfaces

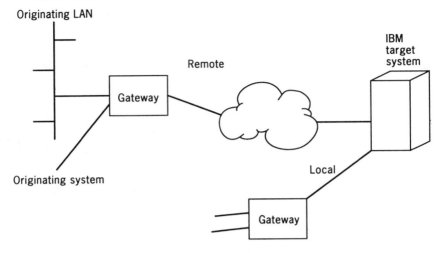

Figure 29.1 *Standalone gateway.*

- Gateway on OEM system: the OEM system has software/hardware to convert to IBM protocol (see Figure 29.2)
- Gateway on IBM system: the IBM system has the software and/or hardware to accommodate the OEM, e.g., Interlink (see Figure 29.3)
- Gateway on both: both systems have software/hardware to interface (see Figure 29.4)
- Gateways among IBM systems: IBM subsystem interconnections (see Figure 29.5)

In practice, an application gateway provides an application interface that masks the underlying gateways. It is the implementer's challenge to provide the most appropriate mix to meet the operational, performance, functional, and interface needs. The selection may be very different based on the priorities of the requirements.

We can now expand the analysis to the application interconnect platforms.

29.2 PROGRAM-TO-PROGRAM PLATFORMS

When reviewing program-to-program protocols that are used with S/390, one notices that there are really only a small set of protocols, which are usually driven

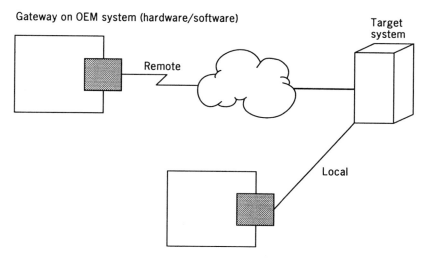

o Fully compatible protocol appearance to
  – Network
  – Target system communication software
  – Target application software

o Device-oriented gateways initiate sessions

o LU6.2-oriented session initiation implementation specific

o Transparent to target system

Figure 29.2   *Gateway on OEM.*

by the systems being interconnected and by the underlying physical connection. Once one gets past LU2 work arounds, the primary protocols are: APPC (LU6.2), TCP/IP, and private (Interlink and FlexLINK). Note that APPC is treated as a service interface and LU6.2 is the VTAM protocol that applications can use without the service interface. For example, CICS and VM/CMS APPC provide APPC services to their applications.

Both ends of the connection must be able to interface with one another and the application you have in mind must be able to interface to the protocol or service. For example, an office uses LU6.2 for DISOSS. Most OEM attach solutions have gravitated to the LU6.2 standard, but not all have provided an open application program interface or mapped their support to deal with an application on the S/390. DEC, FlexLINK, and Interlink have. Consider the following program-to-program connectivity configuration. (See Figure 29.6 and Table 29.1.)

Once the ES/9000 has been connected to an SNA service, the software can establish a session across other SNA nodes. In fact, Interlink exploits this feature and allows DECnet-to-DECnet task-to-task activity over the SNA network using the

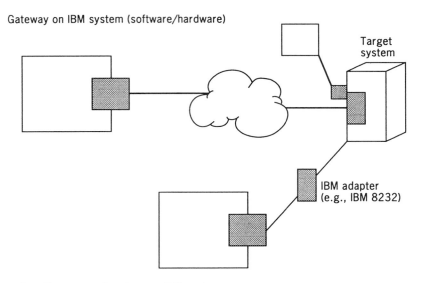

Gateway on IBM system (software/hardware)

Target system

IBM adapter (e.g., IBM 8232)

o Function conversion done on IBM system

o Communication protocol adapters provided on either side

o Can be transparent to OEM systems, dependent on where protocol adapters placed

Figure 29.3 *Gateway on IBM system.*

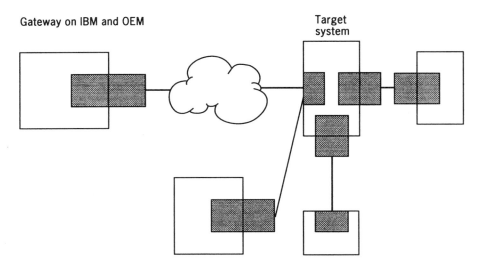

Gateway on IBM and OEM

Target system

Hardware adapters on either/or both ends

Software function handlers on both ends

Local or remote attachment

Both systems require additional software/hardware

Figure 29.4 *Gateway on both systems.*

Gateways among IBM systems

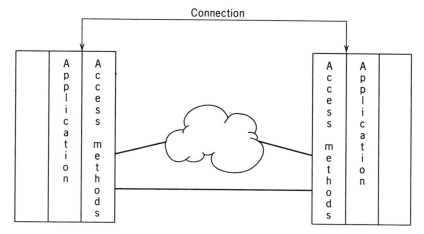

Same or different IBM hardware systems and software

Access methods and interfaces for user-written applications

Subsystems provided application-to-application services
(e.g., CICS, SQL/DS to SQL/DS)

Systems and network management integrated

Connectivity can be transparent from application code
and system software

Figure 29.5 *Gateway among IBM systems.*

ES/9000 as a gateway. From the diagram, one can see that more information is required when making an assessment. Consider the OEM/IBM platform summary table at the end of this chapter (Table 29.6). This should make your considerations more specific. (Again, this is not meant to be an exhaustive list.)

29.3 TERMINAL PASS-THROUGH

Although pass-through appears to be a terminal connection to the destination, it is in fact a specialized program-to-program protocol and service. There are two directions that users may want to pass-through: to the S/390 and from the S/390. Many solutions address access to IBM from OEM systems and vice versa. These can be seen on the OEM/IBM Interconnect Platform Matrix (see Table 29.6) at the end of this section and many other solutions are depicted at end of this chapter.

In this chapter, the primary focus is on access to S/390 services from non-S/390 systems as well as distributed S/390 attached terminals and workstations.[1] S/390

---

[1] The term *distributed S/390 attached terminals and workstations* is meant to distinguish the local host direct connection from those terminals and workstations that are attached to the network.

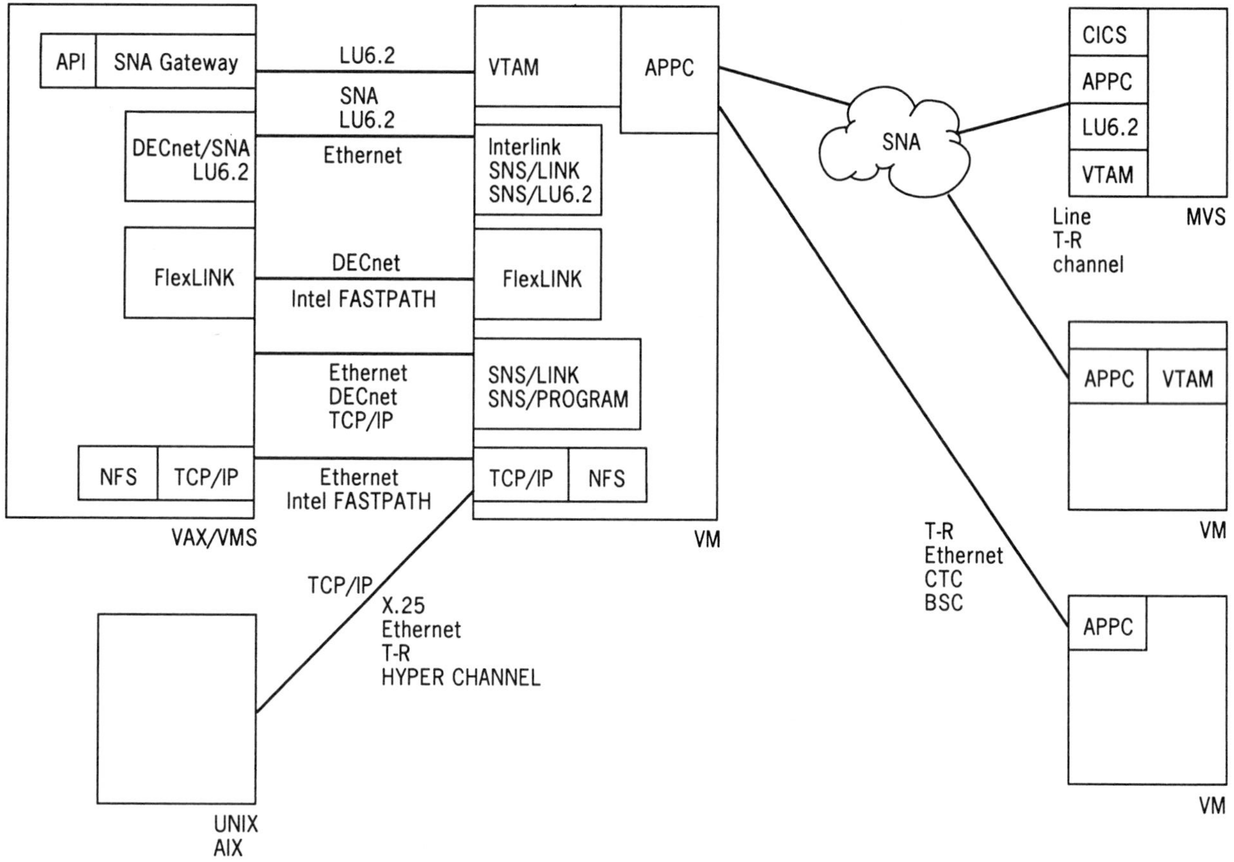

Figure 29.6 Program-to-program.

300

host access for interactive and online services is accomplished by emulating an IBM 3270 to attach to an SNA frontend or backbone network or to attach via channel connection. This emulation provides a managed access to the application program at the host. 3270 emulation techniques have been employed for over 15 years; however, the recent growth of LANs and the desire of *LAN* workstation users to access host applications and services without a terminal adapter card per workstation has caused an increase in the number of terminal pass-through implementations. In other words, the IBM 3270 interface has become a de facto non-S/390-to-S/390 programming interface.

The level of 3270 support (e.g., lines per screen and the colors) provided for is an important consideration. Keyboard mapping for program function keys and special control keys also requires scrutiny. From a user standpoint, the less visibility of the other system's characteristics, the better. Obviously, as the functionality of the IBM 3270 terminal that is being emulated increases, so do the interface and hardware considerations associated with the non-3270 terminals. As a result, the IBM 3270 terminal most widely emulated is the 3X78 (a monochrome display), followed by the 3X79—both of which have color displays—and then by the 3X79-G terminals that support mainframe graphics.[2]

Many of these 3270 gateway (emulation) programs do much more than provide terminal emulation; they use the 3270 interface attributes to provide a way into the S/390, not only for screen interfaces, but also for file transfer and other program-to-program communications. In other words, many of today's 3270 emulators are designed to fool the SNA network or to fool the network and the destination application interface. Consider some of the representative approaches to the 3270 gateway services (see Figure 29.7).

The most traditional approach is the use of a hardware box that provides protocol conversion. (More than communication protocol is actually accomplished, since the non-3270 device attributes must be mapped to the IBM 3270 attributes).

Protocol converters can connect to 3270 control units (CUs) or connect directly to a network or channel.

Frequently, hardware adapters and software combinations are used to connect individual workstations (e.g., PCs) to the network. This is accomplished via adapters that provide the appearance of a 327X terminal and interconnect to a 3X74 control unit, or via adapters that provide the appearance of a control and associated terminals.

There are essentially two types of 3270 modes emulated. They are referred to as CUT (Control Unit Terminal) and DFT (Distributed Function Terminal) mode, which describe the capabilities of the terminal interface. CUT mode assumes that the terminal is dumb and that the controller is provided for displaying data. DFT mode assumes that many of the cluster controller functions have been distributed to the display station. For DFT mode, the controller assumes intelligence at the terminal (workstation) and allows multiple concurrent mainframe sessions per terminal.

---

[2]Patricia Schnaidt, "In with the Big Boys: Letting LAN Users Access the IBM Mainframes," *LAN Magazine*, April 1989, pp. 66–74.

TABLE 29.1 Program-to-Program Implementations

	Op System			SNA Attach Support					TCP/IP Attach Support						Private						
	VM	VSE	DPPX	SDLC Line	Channel	Token-Ring	X.25	BSC Line	Ethernet	X.25	Token-Ring	PCnet	PROnet	Hyper-channel	Ethernet	X.25	Token-Ring	PCnet	BSC Line	Channel	Intel 9770
Standalone Gateway (an intermediary among participating systems)																					
Gateway on OEM System (software/hardware on OEM system provide IBM interface)																					
DECnet, SNA Gateway — VMS APPC – > LU6.2	•	•		•	•																
Gateway on IBM and OEM (software/hardware on all participating systems provide interface)																					
Intel 9770 — VMS < – > FlexLINK Library Services < – > VM	•																			•	•
TCP/IP — All TCP/IP < – > TCP/IP NFS RPC (VM)	•			•	•				•	•	•	•	•	•							
Gateway on IBM System (software/hardware on IBM system provides interface – OEM uses native)																					
Interlink — DECnet – >	•								•						•						

IBM systems provide interface)

IBM VTAM	LU6.2 <-> LU6.2	•							•	•			•	•			•
IBM VTAM	LUO <-> LUO	•		•				•	•	•			•	•			•
IBM APPC services (includes TSAF)	APPC <-> APPC	•				•		•	•	•		•	•	•		•	•
IBM APPC Services (includes TSAF)	APPC <-> LU6.2	•				•		•	•	•		•	•	•		•	•
IBM APPC Services (includes TSAF)	APPC/VM <-> APPC/VM											•	•	•		•	•
IBM PVM	PVM <-> PVM	•				•		•	•	•			•	•		•	•
DPPX	DPPX/370 <-> DPPX/370		•	•		•		•	•	•							
DPPX	DPPX/370 <-> DPPX/8100		•	•		•		•									
DPPX	DPPX -> CICS/VSE	•	•	•		•		•		•							
DPPX	DPPX -> CICS/MVS		•	•		•		•		•							
DPPX	DPPX -> IMS DC		•	•		•		•		•							
CICS	CICS/VSE <-> CICS/VSE	•		•		•		•	•	•							
CICS	CICS/MVS <-> CICS/VSE	•		•		•		•	•	•							
CICS	CICS/VM -> CICS/MVS	•				•		•	•	•							
CICS	CICS/VM -> CICS/VSE	•		•		•		•		•							

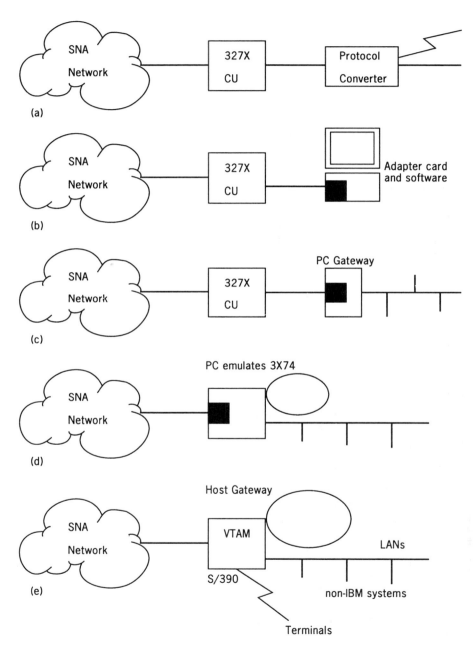

Figure 29.7 *3270 pass-through approaches.*

Therefore, the richer program-to-program functions are based on DFT implementations. For example, DFT mode allows the workstation to determine the LU type being used (e.g., it allows PCs to communicate via advanced protocols such as LU6.2). It also expects that the workstation has complete control over datastream between host application and the workstation.

The viability of these approaches to emulating 3270 workstations was enhanced with the introduction of the IBM 3270 PC when IBM introduced a Low Level Language Application Program Interface (LLLAPI), which consists of numerous (more than 100) functions that provide for session establishment, control, and communications.[3] The 3270 protocols are then extensively used to communicate with software at the S/390.

The S/390 host software being interfaced may be standard IBM-provided interfaces for 3270 screen-oriented applications, or the software may be included in programs that are invoked to allow the transfer of data in either direction.[4]

In order to reduce the number of adapter cards and mainstorage per workstation, workstations and terminals are frequently connected to a host (local, mini, or mainframe) or a LAN gateway server, which connects to the network with the appearance of a 3X74 control unit. In these instances, each workstation has software that provides the user terminal interface and communicates with the gateway server.[5] Usually, substantial main storage savings associated with SNA networking per personal computer can be realized, but this depends on the level of services being used at the workstation. Many *LAN* packages provide proprietary interfaces to enable programs to be written to access S/390 applications via the 3270-based protocols from the workstation. They frequently use NETBIOS[6] interfaces between the workstations and the gateway server. Several vendors also provide their own proprietary protocols.

A key point when considering gateways is the understanding that NetView supports SSCP to PU end-to-end. If the implementation does not include a PU per LU, the network management capability is limited to the control unit (PU), not the emulated LU. A similar network management consideration concerns security. Some gateways and emulators allow both static and dynamic sessions. Dynamic sessions may represent a security exposure, depending on their implementation. IBM supports the static sessions only in order to minimize security exposures.[7]

Using the 3X74 cluster controller, IBM 3725, 3745 FEP (front end processor), or workstation adapter and IBM's Token Ring Interface Card (TIC) for physical con-

[3]Subsequently, additional interfaces have been provided to assist in increasing application development driven by PC-to-mainframe communication requirements (e.g., Entry-Level Emulation High-Level Language Application Program Interface (EEHLLAPI) and Emulator High-Level Language Application Program Interface (EHLLAPI).

[4]3270 implementations require that the 3270 end initiate the action and the S/390 applications respond to the request.

[5]In SNA terminology, this communication capability is called the *protocol boundary*.

[6]*NETBIOS* refers to IBM's Network Basic Input Output System interface, which is a software interface that allows computers to communicate over a LAN. It provides both session and message (datagram) interchange.

[7]Zak Kong, "Tracking IBM's Gateways," *Computerland*, Jan. 23, 1989, pp. 81–85.

nection allows each workstation to retain its PU2 status. Each workstation uses IBM's PC 3270 emulation software to achieve 3270 communications functionality. OS/2 Release 1.2 Extended Edition appears to provide PU support per workstation by requiring a full SNA protocol stack[8] in each workstation.[9]

One pass-through mechanism that is often forgotten or taken for granted because it employs real IBM 3270s is VTAM and a communication adapter. In the distributed context, this solution employs distributed S/390s, which have inexpensive terminals and workstations, as well as LANs attached. These S/390s, with the use of standard SNA capabilities, provide session establishment of IBM 3270s through the local processor to the destination application.

Another S/390-based 3270 pass-through mechanism that now also uses SNA as an underlying communication mechanism is IBM's VM/Pass-Through[10] (referred to as PVM). PVM has provided host-to-host 3270 pass-through across channels and BSC lines for many years and added Ethernet in 1987. As of late 1988 it could operate on an SNA-managed network.

The non-IBM-to-IBM interfaces work on the same fundamentals as were just discussed. However, they come from a somewhat different base, in that unlike PCs, which tend to have much the same terminal geometry of IBM 3270s, these systems in many cases come from an almost entirely different fundamental base. Since most of these non-IBM systems have established environments and interfaces, the challenge of providing a terminal gateway is frequetly complex, due to the mapping of one environment to the other. The solutions in Figure 29.8 have taken on this challenge. Table 29.2 describes these by illustrating a gateway-type operating system and communication mechanism.

29.4   BATCH INTERFACES

Similar to pass-through, most systems allow for the transmission of files between (among) the various systems. We expect a batch interface to provide this capability. S/390 traditionally uses MVS/JES2, VSE/POWER, and VM/RSCS to support these interfaces and uses NJE, VSE POWER, RSCS, and Remote Job Entry (RJE) software/hardware for intersystem transmissions and services. These interfaces have become the intersystem standard for remote job submission, file transfer, and output distribution and services. Note that the batch interface is asynchronous from a work movement standpoint. ("Asychronous" is synonymous with "store-and-forward" in this context.) The input and output for these implementations typically use the geometry of 80 column cards and 133 column lines as their logical unit of transfer.

[8]*Protocol stack* refers to the architectural layers defined for communications protocol.
[9]Joseph Mohen, "IBM's OS/2 EE Gateway Extends SNA into LANs," *Network World*, June 26, 1989, pp. 1, 39, 62.
[10]Noah Mendelsohn, Mark H. Linehan, and Bill Anzick, "Reflections on VM/Pass-Through: A facility for Interactive Networking," *IBM Systems Journal*, Vol. 22, Nos. 1 and 2, 1983, pp. 63–79.

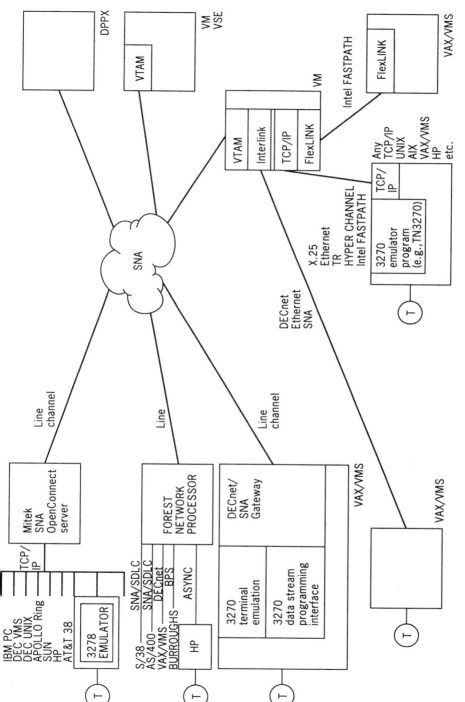

Figure 29.8 3270 terminal pass-through.

TABLE 29.2 Terminal Pass-Through Matrix

		IBM Interface																				
		Op System			SNA Attach Support					TCP/IP Attach Support						Private						
		VM	VSE	DPPX	SDLC Line	Channel	Token-Ring	X.25	BSC Line	Ethernet	X.25	Token-Ring	PCnet	PROnet	Hyper-channel	Ethernet	X.25	Token-Ring	PCnet	BSC Line	Channel	Intel 9770
Standalone Gateway (an intermediary among participating systems)																						
Forest Computer Inc. (FNP)	DECnet Burroughs HP TANDEM Unisys -> 3270	•	•	•	•																	
Gateway on OEM System (software/hardware on OEM system provide IBM interface)																						
MITEK Systems Corp.	SUN APOLLO AT&T Tektronix KORBIX IBM DEC TCP/IP -> 3270	•			•	•																
DECnet/SNA Gateway	VMS 3270TE Ultrix 3270TE MS-DOS 3270TE	•	•	•	•																	

...ticipating systems provide interface)

Intel 9770	SUN/OS - > FlexLINK UTS - > Fullview VMS - > Fullview Fullview - > 3270	•
TCP/IP	ASCII emulator - > 3270	•
Gateway on IBM System (software/hardware on IBM system provides interface - OEM uses native)		
Interlink	DECnet - > Interlink - > 3270	•
Gateways among IBM Systems (software/hardware on IBM systems provide interface)		
IBM VTAM	logon network	•
IBM PVM	PVM < - > PVM PVM < - > 3270	•
IBM DPPX	DPPX < - > 3270	•

The IBM 2780 BSC[11] and 3780 BSC protocols are the most frequently used non-SNA communication protocols, since these are supported by the IBM remote batch subsystems. Similarly, the IBM 3770 is the most frequently emulated SNA remote job entry protocol.

Once the communication session is accomplished, the data will be treated as a punched card input stream. The batch gateways must support the job control language conventions of the receiving S/390 system. These conventions include the documented interfaces in IBM publications as well as the installation-unique parameters related to security, accounting, job priorities, output routing, etc.

In addition to these conventions, the gateway provider will frequently offer appropriate S/390 programs that will be invoked by the batch job in order to supply the requested services (e.g., create a file or read a file and transfer its contents to the remote workstation or system. Figure 29.9 depicts representative implementations and Table 29.3 reflects a matrix of these.

For applications requiring more execution controls, interoperability services or an implementation built on synchronous program-to-program protocols are required.

29.5 INTEROPERABILITY SERVICES

While the necessary prerequisite tools to provide intersystem access are provided by program-to-program protocols, terminal pass-through, and batch interfaces, some solutions have provided an additional layer of services, which ease the application-to-application communication and management. Example services include file-to-file transfer (synchronous), record level extract and transfer, character code translation (ASCII to EBCDIC), and command remapping.

In these cases, software on the non-IBM system, within the IBM system, or on some intermediary component change the syntax, semantics, character representation (ASCII and EBCDIC),[12] and values to align with the target systems rules. There are essentially two approaches: transparent and intermediary service interface.

Transparent implementations include hooks[13] somewhere in the path between the source request and the target destination. These hooks understand the application level protocols and transform the requests and data into the appropriate commands, formats, and values.

Intermediary implementations provide a new programming interface and services that the programs must adhere to in order to effect the desired requests across the

[11]BSC refers to IBM's Binary Synchronous Communications protocol—a half-duplex, character-oriented protocol used for remote batch devices and some terminals. There are numerous versions of BSC, but 2780, 3780, and 3270 represent the majority. The 3780 version provides space compression.

[12]EBCDIC (Extended Binary Coded Decimal Interchange Code) is an 8-bit code to represent characters used on S/390 systems.

[13]*Hooks* is jargon that refers to a program exit or a spoofing interface, which allow another program or service to examine the data or requests.

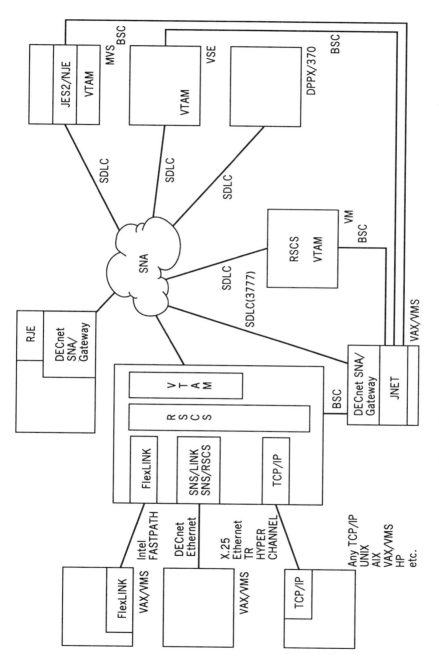

Figure 29.9 *Batch interface (file-to-file batch transfer).*

TABLE 29.3 Batch Interface Matrix

	Op System			SNA Attach Support					TCP/IP Attach Support						Private						
	VM	VSE	DPPX	SDLC Line	Channel	Token-Ring	X.25	BSC Line	Ethernet	X.25	Token-Ring	PCnet	PROnet	Hyper-channel	Ethernet	X.25	Token-Ring	PCnet	BSC Line	Channel	Intel 9770
Standalone Gateway (an intermediary among participating systems)																					
Forest Computer Inc (FNP) DECnet– > Burroughs– > HP– > 3270 RJE	•	•																			
Gateway on OEM System (software/hardware on OEM system provide IBM interface)																					
MITEK Systems Corp. SUN APOLLO AT&T Tektronix KORBIX IBM DEC TCP/IP – > 3270	•			•																	
DECnet/SNA Gateway VMS RJE (37XX)	•	•		•																	
Other OEM/SNA sol-				•																	

312

Gateway on IBM and OEM (software/hardware on all participating systems provide interface)

Intel 9770	VMS - > FileExchange VM	•
TCP/IP	TCP/IP NFS < - > TCP/IP NFS	•

Gateway on IBM System (software/hardware on IBM system provides interface - OEM uses native)

Interlink	DECnet- > Interlink- > file	•

Gateways among IBM Systems (software/hardware on IBM systems provide interface)

IBM RSCS & VSE/Power	RSCS < - > RSCS	•
IBM RSCS & VSE/Power	RSCS < - > Power	•
IBM RSCS & VSE/Power	Power < - > Power	•
IBM RSCS & VSE/Power	RSCS < - > NJE	•
IBM RSCS & VSE/Power	Power < - > NJE	
IBM DPPX	DPPX < - > DPPX	
IBM FTP	MVS < - > VSE	
IBM FTP	VSE < - > VSE	
IBM FTP	VSE < - > VM	•
IBM FTP	VM < - > VM	•

Application Gateway (provides an interface built upon connection gateways)

Joiner Associates Inc. (JNET)	VMS < - > RSCS	•

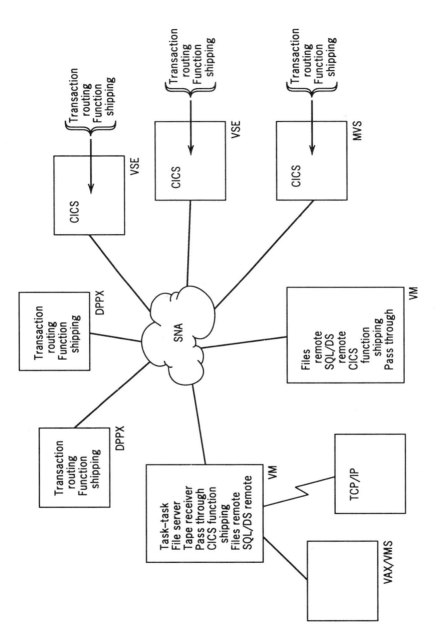

Figure 29.10 Interoperability services.

TABLE 29.4 Interoperability Matrix

		IBM Interfaces																				
		Op System			SNA Attach Support					TCP/IP Attach Support						Private						
Gateway		VM	VSE	DPPX	SDLC Line	Channel	Token-Ring	X.25	BSC Line	Ethernet	X.25	Token-Ring	PCnet	PROnet	Hyper-channel	Ethernet	X.25	Token-Ring	PCnet	BSC Line	Channel	Intel 9770
Gateway on IBM and OEM (software/hardware on all participating systems provide interface)																						
Intel 9770	VMS/FlexLINK <-> FlexLINK VM	•																				•
TCP/IP	All TCP/IP <-> TCP/IP	•								•	•	•	•	•	•							
Gateway on IBM System (software/hardware on IBM system provides interface - OEM uses native)																						
Interlink	VMS-> Interlink-> VM Netview	•														•						
Gateways among IBM Systems (software/hardware on IBM systems provide interface)																						
IBM DPPX	DPPX <-> DPPX			•	•	•	•	•														
CICS	CICS/VSE <-> CICS/VSE		•		•	•	•	•														
CICS	CICS/MVS <-> CICS/VSE		•		•	•	•	•														
CICS	CICS/VM-> CICS/MVS	•			•	•	•	•														
CICS	CICS/VM-> CICS/VSE	•	•		•	•	•	•														
CICS	CICS/VSE <-> IMS/DC		•		•	•	•	•														
IBM SQL/DS	SQL/DS <-> SQL/DS (VM coreq.)	•			•	•	•	•													•	
IBM VM File	file <-> file	•			•	•	•	•													•	

315

TABLE 29.5 Application-to-Application Matrix

		IBM Interfaces																				
		Op System			SNA Attach Support					TCP/IP Attach Support						Private						
		VM	VSE	DPPX	SDLC Line	Channel	Token-Ring	X.25	BSC Line	Ethernet	X.25	Token-Ring	PCnet	PROnet	Hyper-channel	Ethernet	X.25	Token-Ring	PCnet	BSC Line	Channel	Intel 9770
Gateway on OEM System (software/hardware on OEM system provide IBM interface)																						
DECnet/SNA Gateway	MR PROFS	•			•	•																
DECnet/SNA Gateway	MR SNADS	•	•		•	•																
Gateway on IBM and OEM (software/hardware on all participating systems provide interface)																						
Intel 9770	ALL-IN-1 < - > PROFS	•																				•
TCP/IP	SMTP	•								•	•	•	•	•	•							•
Gateway on IBM System (software/hardware on IBM system provides interface - OEM uses native)																						
Interlink	ALL-IN-1 < - > PROFS	•														•						

316

Company	Connection																							
Joiner Associates Inc. (JNET)	VMS -> PROFS																		•				•	
Soft-Switch Inc.	ALL-IN-1 < – > Higgins Mail < – > Banyan Mail < – > 3COM < – > TCP/IP(SMTP) < – > Novell < – > X.400 < – > WANG Mailway < – > HP < – > PROFS																		•				•	
Soft-Switch Inc.	All above < – > DISOSS																		•					
IBM PROFS Extended	TCP/IP(SMTP) < – > PROFS•						•		•		•	•							•					
IBM Office Interconnect Facility	VMS < – > WANG OIS < – > WANG VS Mail < – > WANG VS Off < – > PROFS DISOSS.																	•	•					
IBM DISOSS	DISOSS < – > DISOSS															•	•		•					
IBM PROFS/DISOSS	DISOSS < – > PROFS															•	•		•					
IBM PROFS	PROFS < – > PROFS															•	•		•					•

317

TABLE 29.6 OEM/IBM Interconnect Platform Summary

(Specific ES/9370 DPPX, VM, VSE Focus - These Solutions May Support Other IBM Hardware/Software)

Feature/Function	FlexLINK	Forest	Intel	Interlink	Mitek	Jnet	IBM TCP/IP	Digital
Protocol	Proprietary, SOD-1, OSI, SOD-1, DECnet	SNA/SDLC, DECnet (pt.-pt.), Pole Select (Burroughs)	FlexLINK, ASCII, MULTIBUS, TCP/IP, OSI, SOD-1, DECnet	SNA, DECnet, Ethernet	SNA, TCP/IP (Ethernet)	SNA, BSC, NJE	Ethernet, Token-Ring, SNA, PC Net, ProNet, X.25	SNA
ES/9370 Hardware Connection	7170, DACU, 9770, Fastpath	FNP	9770, Fastpath	8232 or 9370 Ethernet Card	SNA Host M2030 or M2130	ICA, 37XX	37XX (X.25) adapter, 8232, S/1, 9370, Hyper Channel	37xx Channel
Maximum Connection Distance	4 Kilometers	SNA Remote	4 Kilometers	Local or Remote (SNS/PATH)	SNA (remote or channel)	Remote	Local or Remote	SNA (remote or channel)
IBM Hardware Requirements	Channel	SNA	Channel	8323 Channel or Ethernet Transceiver	M2030 (Channel), M2130 (37XX)	Channel ICA	See Hardware Connection	DECnet/SNA to 37XX, DECnet/SNA 8S to 37XX, DECnet/SNA CT to Channel
Operating System (IBM)	VM	VSE, VM	VM, MUMPS/VM	VM	VM, VSE	VM	VM, PC-DOS, AIX	VM, VSE
Operating System (OEM)	VMS, SUN/OS	Ultrix, VMS, MPE (HP), MCP (Unisys), Tandem	VMS, SUN/OS	VMS, Ultrix, RSX, Tops (10/20), any DECnet implement	Any that supports TCP/IP	VMS	Any that supports TCP/IP	VMS

ments	...products	...RSCS, VSE/POWER, DPPX/370-6	...TCP/IP	...Gateway products	...VTAM, Mitek Telenet/FTP clients, DPPX/370	...	...TCP/IP	...RSCS, VSE/POWER, DPPX/370
OEM Software Requirements	FlexLINK products	Native	FlexLINK, TCP/IP	DECnet	Mitek Presentation Services	Jnet	TCP/IP	DECnet, SNA
Terminal Emulation								
3270 Full Screen	Yes	Yes	Yes	Yes-5	Yes	No	Note 2	Yes
ASCII Full Screen	Yes	Yes-4	Yes	Yes	Yes	No	Note 2	–
Graphics	No	No	Yes-ASCII	No	Yes-ASCII	No	No	–
Remote Job Entry	No	Yes	Yes	Yes	Yes	Yes	No	Yes
Task-Task Communication	Yes	No	Yes	Yes (LU6.2 in '89)		No	No	Yes via APPC
RSCS Support	Yes	Yes	Yes	Yes	No	Yes	Yes	–
SNA Connection	SOD-1	Yes (LU6.2), SOD-1	SOD-1	LU6.2	Yes	Yes-3	Yes	Yes LU6.2
Remote Program Init.	Yes	No	Yes	Yes	No	Yes	No	No
File Transfer	Yes	Yes	Yes	Yes	3270 File Transfer	Yes	Yes	MVS only
Remote Printing	Yes	Yes	Yes	Yes		Yes	No	Yes
Data Transfer Speed-7 (instantaneous not effective speed)	1.2-2.5 Mb/s	Communication E-net	500-2500 Kb/s	500-1000 Kb/s	1.8 MB - 19.2 Kb/s	2400b/64Kb	30-200+ Kb/s	19.2 Kb

Notes:

1. SOD - Statement of Direction
2. VM to VAX = No; RT to ASCII = Yes; ASCII to VM = Yes (Requires TN3270)
3. SNA support requires DEC's SNA Gateway or VM SNA
4. With VM, 3270 emulation supported INTO VM only. No support for 3270 devices in VM to emulate OEM devices
5. DEC pre-reqs.
6. DPPX supports SNA attachment for LU 0, 1 and 2.
7. Effective data transfer speed is a function of application. (FlexLINK is memory to memory, the others are raw capacity.)

different systems. These implementations provide a common denominator service that all participants must use.

In practice, most implementers would prefer a transparent approach, since it allows the extension of the current program inventory without modifications. The primary considerations associated with transparent implementations have to do with performance (in terms of response time) and the ability to specify addresses of destinations. Ideally, if the program interface were architected with distributed in mind, the parameters for performance and addressing would also be included.

SAA Common Programming Interfaces is an example of this type of consideration. The SAA CPIs are high-level language called (as opposed to macro expansions) interfaces that can be used to communicate within the same system or across a network. The fact that a callable interface is presented to the application program allows for changes to be provided in the underlying services without any modifications being made (the program need not even be recompiled). A traditional concern is that there are usually overheads associated with this type of implementation.

The trade-offs relate more to business than technical considerations. If programs are designed with flexibility in mind, the enterprise can be much more responsive to technology (hardware and software) and data and services placement changes. If the programs are optimized to a very specific interface that is not architected for distributed, or the programmers opt not to write the programs in a manner that exploits that flexibility, the programs may be extremely cost efficient today, but lock the enterprise into a specific technology or configuration.

VM and AIX systems currently provide a multitude of distributed-oriented interfaces. As the SAA rollout continues, all SAA platform environments will provide interoperability among each other at the system service level (e.g., distributed file, distributed database, etc.). MVS and VSE use transaction managers such as CICS and IMS to provide interoperability to their applications. CICS and IMS mask the application program from distribution, since they control the environment and allow the administrator to set tables that provide the placement and address mapping. Figure 29.10 depicts some of the interoperability services that are available. The table in the appendices depicts the interoperability interconnections that support this picture (see also Table 29.4).

29.6   APPLICATION-TO-APPLICATION

From a positioning point, I have separated interoperability from application-to-application by asserting that there is a difference between system services and business applications. Business applications address business problems, such as sending mail from one person to another. Interoperability services or more fundamental services (e.g., terminal pass-through) are used to accomplish the passing of the necessary data.

In other words, PROFS is an application that supports application-to-application exchange, since it provides the business professional with a mechanism to exchange mail with others independent of location and which PROFS system they are on.

Applications gateway

Same or different IBM hardware systems and software
(both IBM and non-IBM)

Application interface masks connectivity and
differences (e.g., office with DISOSS)

Requires software with compatible function and
interfaces

Typically built upon some combination of the
previously described gateways

Figure 29.11 *Application-to-application.*

Similarly, OfficeVision provides a comparable capability among users of the PS/2, S/390, or AS/400. Distributed applications are still in relatively short supply. However, there are numerous applications that support distribution. (See Figure 29.11 and Table 29.5.)

29.7 OEM/IBM INTERCONNECT PLATFORM MATRIX

Table 29.6 is an interconnect platform matrix reflecting a 1989 snapshot of DPPX, VM, and VSE support. An interesting exercise would be to map the entries to the status today, just to get a feel for the trends.

Chapter 30

Connectivity Summary

When considering system-to-system attachment, it is important to focus on the applications, subsystem, and system management tools that support each connection option. It is also important to distinguish between the device connectivity and system-to-system connectivity. The common denominators for analysis are the physical media sharing and the common management tools, but equally important are the interfaces with existing applications. These have been discussed in software and hardware implementations, which can be characterized as: program to program, terminal pass-through, batch interfaces, interoperability services, and application-to-application. The key considerations are highlighted on the next page.

These have been reviewed as program-to-program, 3270 pass-through, batch interfaces, interoperability services, and some applications. The services described in the chapters on IBM Distributed Application Capabilities, Distributed Data Base and File capabilities, Distributed Office, and Complementary Services are all based on some combination of these capabilities.

From a S/390 perspective, the S/390 platforms provide a very comprehensive base for connecting IBM and non-IBM terminals, workstations, and systems. Many IBM and other vendors' products address various aspects of connection and interoperability. Rack-mounted and card-mounted S/370s have expanded the versatility of the S/390 so that it can be moved out into the remote extremities of the enterprise to act as an interconnection mechanism to support an extremely broad set of IBM and non-IBM equipment and software, while providing a platform for remotely managing many aspects of these configurations. There has been minimal discussion of OSI application interfaces since these are in the embryonic stages. This has been a bottom-up rollout focusing more on the underlying layers and not as much time has been spent on the integration into existing applications.

CONNECTIVITY

- Physical system-to-system connectivity
- System-to-system protocols

TERMINAL PASS-THROUGH

- 3270 terminal pass-through
- Asynchronous (often referred to as ASCII devices)

PROGRAM-TO-PROGRAM PROTOCOLS

- Synchronous (program-to-program)
- Asynchronous (program-to-batch-to-program)

APPLICATION-TO-APPLICATION (AND APPLICATION SERVICES)

- These are application specific
- Same or mixed distributed environments

WHAT EVERY SYSTEM IMPLEMENTER SHOULD KNOW ABOUT CONNECTIVITY

- Many layers of protocols and functions must be considered when mixing platforms and vendors
- Considerations range from application specific requirements to physical connection specific support
- Multiple connectivity and interoperability products are available
- Most prevalent IBM S/390 application interface by non-S/390 systems is as an IBM 3270 using SNA followed by LU6.2
- Gateways placed in various portions of the network configuration provide for the application access

Summary

This book is really five books about distributing the glasshouse, with the content presented at various levels of detail hopefully sufficient enough to provide an overview of the management and technical issues being faced and the solutions being used by IS executives and their management staffs today.

The largest portion of the book is targeted at addressing the management issues, technology trends, standards activities, and approaches being used to deal with business needs with timely but resilient solutions. These were presented pragmatically, based on the activity that I have personally been involved in, and the opinions are my own. The other sections are intended to explore some of the underlying mysteries of how distributed systems can interconnect, exchange data, provide interoperability, and be technically managed from central using existing skills and tools.

I have sketched out the evolution of the glasshouse from standalone distributed systems through various stages of centralization and distribution of compute power and data to the present. Now the focus is on providing solutions that harness the end user's energy to apply computer technology to solve immediate business needs with user systems or departmental systems while providing a platform to continue to grow the control systems and provide the necessary services, data, and control among the user, departmental, and control systems.

I have also highlighted the need to use various hardware and software platforms to solve business problems for economic, investment protection, business needs, and skill reasons. In this context, I have touched upon the various approaches that are being pursued to accommodate various hardware and software platforms by using both vendor (e.g., SAA) and public standards (OSI); providing multiple coexistence mechanisms, which include interoperability platforms such as IBM's SNA and SAA distributed implementations as well as using OSI interoperability mechanisms and more tactical solutions such as TCP/IP; porting entire environments to a common hardware base (e.g., AIX/370, DPPX/370, MUMPS/VM, PICK, etc.) and providing a very broad spectrum of compute power on a common hardware architectural base (e.g., the S/390 with the ES/9000).

My hypothesis is that with this historical and capability overview one can predict where the technology and business solutions are leading us and how we'll be able to influence the solutions rather than being driven by them.

Several chapters were focused on management considerations associated with implementing and managing multiples in a distributed environment, as well as with the need to recognize that a fundamental change in the amount of detail and control exerted is necessary in order to be more responsive and influential in providing information systems solutions from the IS.

Using the S/390 as a frame of reference has provided a base for communicating the evolving IS base for the past 25 years. The S/390 systems software, hardware, and peripherals have expanded to meet the IS capacity, connectivity, integrity, security, and management needs and have now extended out of the glasshouse into the office, store, and onto the plant floor.

We have touched on many of the facets of distribution and some of the attributes and history of the S/390, as well as how it fits with different specific user systems and complements non-IBM computing environments. Much can be learned about systems and effective solutions from studying the evolution of S/390. With systems implementations, history *does* tend to repeat itself as has been witnessed by the evolution of minicomputer and PC solutions. The primary lesson that was learned was that problems can be addressed with various solutions and involvement by IS, but recognition of the design point and the degree of flexibility the solution must have is fundamental to a successful system life.

The fundamentals are:

- Availability of applications
- Connectivity and interconnectivity at the software and hardware levels
- Ability to access and share data
- Ability to manage the solution independent of the equipment and software placement
- Ability to economically manage multiples
- Ability to distribute portions of the solutions for organizational and technical reasons without having to rewrite the application

From a hardware technology standpoint, CPU power has and will continue to grow much more rapidly than the I/O storage mechanisms and the links between systems in terms of data access and transfer time. This signals that storage hierarchies, data distribution and caching schemes, and large amounts of in-storage programs and data approaches (e.g., ESA/390) will be the technical focus areas of the integrated system of the 1990s. (In this context, integrated system does not mean integrated on a single hardware processor or platform.) Perhaps the measurement of distributed systems capacity of the 1990s will be by the number of logical I/O requests (messages) serviced from remote systems and logical I/O requests serviced locally rather than by the number of Mips (millions of instructions per second) that a complex of processor can deliver.

In conclusion, the S/390 mainframe, its architecture, its applications, its system management capabilities, and its evolution have provided a very open-ended set of solutions for addressing distribution of compute power both within and outside the glasshouse, and appear to be providing the resilience that will support these business and new requirements for many years to come in conjunction with complementary solutions.

Appendix A

The S/390 Software Platforms

This appendix chapter briefly describes operating systems that run on the S/390. For this systems software platform, the focus is on those operating environments that can operate on an S/390 outside of the glasshouse using the ES/9000 rack models as the hardware base. This provides the largest variety of software platforms on a common hardware base. The discussion includes a thumbnail recap of such IBM operating systems as AIX, MVS, VM, VSE, DPPX, and TPF, as well as some operating environments that run on S/390, such as MUMPS, PICK, and MUSIC. There is no intent to cover these systems comprehensively, as to describe any one of these operating systems, a separate book would have to be written. The intent is to highlight some roots and operational differences for various platforms on the S/390, and to demonstrate the versatility of the hardware as a system platform. The primary purpose is to highlight the variety of platforms and orientations that can be run on and with the S/390 base.

A.1 MVS

MVS is the generic acronym for IBM's Multiple Virtual Storage. The MVS and its predecessor operating systems focus on resource sharing optimization for managing multiprocessors and high-performance/capacity devices[1] for high-transaction, interactive, and batch workloads. It is used extensively on ES/9000 class systems for online transaction processing, batch applications, and interactive development. It is

[1] High-performance and high-capacity devices—for example, an IBM 3990/3390 storage configuration can have up to 120 Gbytes of data with a 256 Mbyte cache.

the successor to IBM's OS/PCP, OS/MFT, OS/MVT,[2] VS1, and SVS,[3] which were all IBM S/360 and S/370 operating systems with increasing levels of functional and hardware sophistication. It comes in several versions, each one providing more levels of sophistication with regard to hardware exploitation.

MVS/SP Version 1 (MVS/370) supports 24-bit addressing, which provided 16 Mbytes addressability shared for common system areas, with the remainder available for each address space. Subsequent versions have extended the addressing to 31-bit. This is referred to as MVS/SP Version 2 (MVS/XA) for extended virtual storage addressing. MVS/XA supports 31-bit addressing, extending the virtual addressing capability of each address space to 2 gigabytes,[4] Additionally, the real addressing was also extended to 31-bit.

MVS/SP Version 3 (MVS/ESA) provides for even larger in-storage addressing and execution. Using the MVS/ESA capabilities, a program written to execute in a 31-bit addressing mode can have direct access to two other 2-gigabyte address spaces concurrently executing directly out of the primary address space. It is therefore possible to address up to a theoretical limit of 16 terabytes.[5] Additionally, MVS/ESA provides high performance data spaces, referred to as hiperspaces, which provide a very efficient temporary workfile capability. A data window service provides a high-level language program (an assembler language program) to scroll over the hiperspaces as portions of their primary address space.[6] (See the storage layouts[7,8] in Figures A.1–A.3.)

These enhancements substantially expand the limits of a program and substantially reduce the disparity of I/O access time and mainstorage access time. They provide sophisticated storage hierarchies (such as expanded store), and reduce overhead by operating on the data as if it were in real storage from the program address space. Hiperbatch and Hipersorting exploited these returning large percentages of elapsed times. In 1990, MVS/ESA increased its capabilities together with the ES/9000 introducing ESCON channel support, cooperative processing (APPC),

---

[2]OS/PCP provided a primary control program for a single application program at a time. OS/MFT and OS/MVT provided multiprogramming with a fixed and variable number of tasks, respectively. The programs were responsible for their storage management tied to the partition- or region-allocated size or real storage. Programs that needed larger sizes implemented various overlay schemes or used system managed temporary space.

[3]VS1 and SVS were the virtual based followon systems to OS/MFT and OS/MVT. SVS was also referred to as VS2, which later grew into MVS. SVS provided a single virtual storage that extended the composite coexisting programs and operating system to 16 Mbytes for systems that had less than 16 Mbytes real main storage.

[4]2 gigabytes = 2,174,484,648 bytes.

[5]The 16-terabyte (16×10^{12} bytes) capacity is arrived at by using multiple gigabyte address spaces that contain data (data spaces). The 16-terabyte capacity is currently a theoretical limit since it is beyond the paging capacity of the operating system at this time.

[6]C. E. Clark, "The Facilities and Evolution of MVS/ESA," *The IBM Systems Journal,* Vol. 28, Nol 1, 1989, p. 134.

[7]Michael Haupt, "ESA Implements Expanded Addressing," *Mainframe Journal,* Feb. 1989, pp. 41–47.

[8]K. G. Rubsam, "MVS Data Services," *IBM Systems Journal,* Vol. 28, No. 1, 1989, pp 151–164.

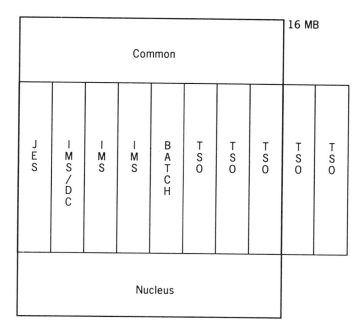

Figure A.1 *MVS/370 storage layout.*

enterprise operations products, the Sysplex capabilities to manage loosely coupled systems, as well as various availability and serviceability enhancements and the newly announced integrated cryptography processor.

MVS/ESA supports hot standby backup for online production systems with Extended Recovery Facility (XRF) for IMS and CICS systems.

MVS was optimized for large systems resource management. As a result, it tends to use a disproportional amount of system resources in the smaller S/370s in terms of mainstorage, disk storage, and system cycles. MVS use on the very small S/370 systems, e.g., the ES/9370, is limited to MVS/370, primarily because the hardware only provides 24-bit addressing. Today, MVS/370's use on ES/9370 tends to be limited to very specific applications[9] or services. In a distributed environment, MVS, in general, has typically been used for large, remotely managed ES/3090 systems, ES/4381 systems, or the very high end of the ES/9370 processor line. The introduction of the ES/9000 rack and air-cooled frame models which have full ESA support and greater capacity has substantially increased the viability of distributing MVS systems.

[9]The Real-Time Plant Management Integrated System is one such application. It supports monitoring, simulation, and control functions in process plants. The system combines an ES/9370, MVS, a rack-mounted S/1, and the appropriate environmental software to provide a total solution.

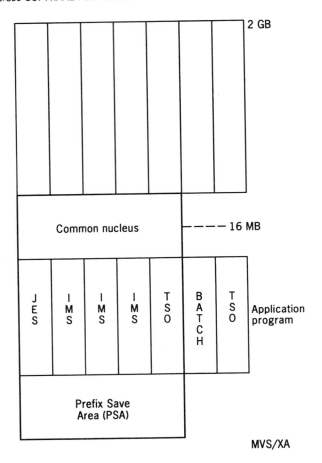

Figure A.2 *MVS/XA storage layout.*

MVS

- Resource management for large user population applications
- Sophisticated performance-management mechanism
- MVS/390: 24-bit addressing
- MVS/XA: 31-bit addressing
- MVS/ESA: hiperspace, Sysplex, cooperative processing, enterprise operations
- Extend Recovery Facilities for CICS and IMS

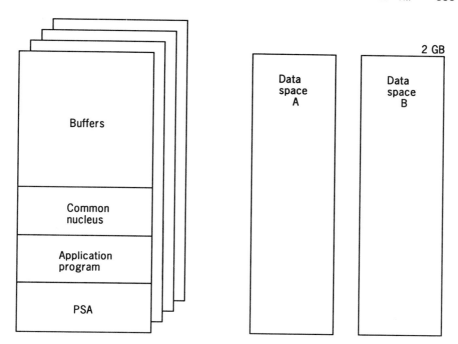

Figure A.3 *MVS/ESA storage layout.*

A.2 VM

VM is the generic acronym for IBM's Virtual Machine system. VM is the label of a S/390 hypervisor,[10] which supports other S/370 and S/390 operating systems,[11] and a conversational monitor referred to as CMS (see Figure A.4). VM is used extensively for interactive applications including office, decision support, as a platform for other systems (e.g., MVS, VSE, AIX, MUMPS, MUSIC, etc.), and application development. Many MVS and VSE applications are built on VM. It comes in various versions, again based on its hardware exploitation. Its strength is its openness and its ability to quickly support new and different interconnection options and facilities. It also allows for porting VSE- and MVS-developed code.

VM/SP supports addressing 16 Mbytes (24-bit addressing) within the system and provides some very sophisticated distributed and networking functions. VM/HPO (High-Performance Option) is an extension of VM/SP, improving performance on the more sophisticated S/370 hardware configurations (e.g., 3090). While it also supports 16-Mbyte addressing by the user systems (24-bit addressing), VM/HPO

---

[10]The term *hypervisor* in the VM context refers to VM's ability to simulate multiple images of S/390 machines with virtual devices at the same time. Other S/390 operating systems can run in a VM virtual machine environment as though they were running on a dedicated real S/390 configuration. These operating systems might even be using devices and storage that are not really present on the base system.
[11]The other operating systems are referred to as *guests* or *guest operating systems*.

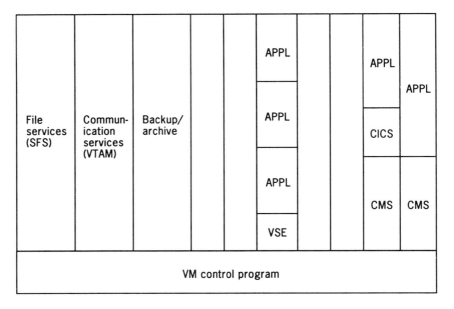

Figure A.4 *VM storage layout.*

allows the system to use greater than 16-Mbyte system storage. VM/XA is the successor to VM/SP HPO, and provides 31-bit addressing by user programs and minidisk caching.

In 1988 VM/SP, together with the ES/9370, focused on distributed functions and enhanced distributed systems management capabilities. It now provides the ability to access distributed files, distributed relational data bases, and access host CICS services. It also distributed systems administrative functions and distributed systems management functions, as well as numerous connectivity options. VM/SP can be ordered as part of VM/IS. VM/Integrated System (VM/IS) is a label given to a packaging of VM/SP together with the most frequently used software products, as well as selected optional products. These products are packaged and integrated together with menus and documentation targeted for the end user and systems administrator. VM/SP functions and packaging were driven by the change in target environments from the glasshouse out to distributed locations where operators and skills would be a scarce commodity.

For the 1990s VM/ESA provides a single VM platform replacement for VM/SP, VM/HPO, and VM/XA including the strengths of each of the three environments including high-end resource exploitation as well as distributed environments with such important services such as 2-gigabyte address spaces, minidisk caching, parallel and ESCON channels, APPC, distributed and shared file services, and a Resource Recovery Interface (RRI supports two-phase commit capability for objects identified to the interface). Additionally as of this writing *LAN* support facilities such as Workstation DataSave Facility/VM for data backup and Personal Workstation Communication Facility/VM access are emerging to provide VM services to workstations and *LAN*s.

VM

- Interactive open system
- S/370 and S/390 hypervisor
- Distributed file and SQL/DS
- Distributed resource support
- Unattended operations capabilities
- Emerging workstation support
- VM/ESA succeeds VM/SP, VM/HPO, VM/XA

A.3   VSE

VSE is an acronym for IBM's Virtual Storage Extended operating system. VSE is used extensively for transaction and batch job environments for S/370 and S/390 uniprocessors. This operating system is essentially a functional subset of MVS used extensively on the air-cooled models and some liquid-cooled models of the S/370 and S/390. VSE supports 24-bit application addressing. CICS Multiple Region Option (MRO) provides a storage-to-storage mechanism of distributing CICS functions within the processor to provide more address space than one address space can provide. Recent enhancements have substantially increased the number of partitions and the amount of addressibility available to the application partitions.

Initially the VSE system storage and partitions were implemented as depicted in Figure A.5. This was followed by VSE with Virtual Addressing Extensions (VAE). With VAE, address spaces can be added (up to nine address spaces), providing up to 128 Mbytes of addressability, as depicted in Figure A.6. VSE/ESA has increased the number of partitions by providing the ability to dynamically allocate and deallocate up to 200 additional partitions (in their own address spaces). VSE/ESA also enabled the placement of VTAM and Power into their own address spaces providing greater virtual addressability for the application partitions. VSE/ESA Power exploits the ESA access registers to support interpartition communications. The VSE/ESA implementation includes support for the ES/9000 parallel and ESCON channels and Dynamic Channel Subsystem with allows I/Os initiated down one path to complete by returning via another path (Dynamic Path Selection and Reconnection).

When the VSE workload expands beyond a uniprocessor the workload can be run on a dyadic or multiprocessor by splitting the workload and using multiple guests on

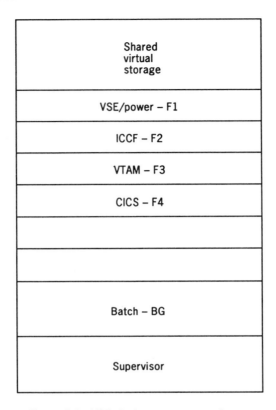

Shared virtual storage
VSE/power – F1
ICCF – F2
VTAM – F3
CICS – F4
Batch – BG
Supervisor

Figure A.5 *VSE single space storage layout.*

VM or using PR/SM, which is a standard ES/9000 feature, or the applications can be ported to MVS. Both the VM and the PR/SM[12] feature provide for exploitation of multiprocessors via CICS intersystem coupling (ISC). In both these cases, the VSE systems make extensive use of VSE's distributed capabilities among VSE systems. VSE and CICS/VS also provide for distributed transaction processing and data base capabilities among multiple VSE systems and MVS systems, as well as supporting CICS/VM and CICS OS/2 CICS services. Because of the investments in training and peopletime often required to convert to MVS, some companies that need immediate increased system capacity use the VM and PR/SM capabilities for running multiple copies of VSE as a transition mechanism to MVS.

The VSE system continues to be enhanced in its distributed capabilities, especially in the areas of automated operations and unattended operations. These are discussed in the Operations section of this book. Additionally, VSE/ESA supports Extended Recovery Facility (XRF), which provides for the monitoring and subse-

---

[12]PR/SM provides up to 14 copies of systems with dedicated resources using the same physical system depending on the model.

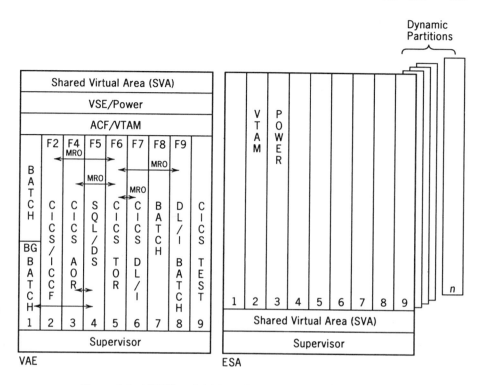

Figure A.6   *VSE Virtual Address Extensions VAE and VSE/ESA.*

quent switch over to another CICS system should a problem occur on the primary system.

VSE can be ordered in a systems package (SP) which includes its most frequently used software products, such as CICS. The package substantially reduced the time to plan and install the system.

VSE

- High-performance transaction and batch applications
- Functional subset of MVS
- Packaged with CICS and VTAM
- Distributed transaction and data base among CICS systems
- Unattended operations capabilities
- Extended Recovery Facility for transaction processing

A.4 DPPX/370

DPPX is the generic acronym for IBM's Distributed Processing Programming Executive. DPPX has been used extensively to address remote branch offices, agencies, shop floors, and warehouse requirements for point-of-entry data collection, inquiry, local invoicing, reporting, etc. These systems are most typically found in the insurance and manufacturing industries.

DPPX/SP runs on the IBM 8100 and DPPX/370 runs on the ES/9370 and the ES/9000 rack models. DPPX/370, as its SP predecessor, is designed to work in partnership with MVS, providing the hierarchical host to the DPPX operating system and applications. Applications are developed at the MVS host and prepared for downloading to the DPPX node. DPPX provides a specialized operating system environment designed to operate in an unattended and distributed mode. The operating system is selftuning and extremely dynamic for handling change control and application updates. Standard features include:

- Dynamic nondisruptive configuration and reconfiguration
- Nondisruptive data base creation, reorganization, and deletion
- Automatic data duplication and resynchronization via shadow file
- Distributed shared base support (commit, backout, etc.)
- Automatic recovery and error conditions recording

DPPX, unlike the MVS, VM, and VSE operating systems developed and shipped as separate components (products), is fully integrated and designed with unattended and remote operations in mind. DPPX is a closed system in that development is done on MVS and only preplanned transactions are executed on it, making it a very effective distributed transaction processor. DPPX/370 was ported from a non-S/390 architectural base intact, and has maintained its application interfaces while exploiting the added performance that the ES/9000 made available. Addi-

---

DPPX/370

- Transaction-oriented distributed operating system
- Designed for unattended operations
- Designed to be managed from an MVS host
- Ported from IBM 8100 System
- Supported on Micro Channel 370 and rack S/370 and S/390 models
- CICS application program interface

tionally, a CICS application program interface was recently announced for DPPX/370,[13] thus providing a closed, unattended, multi-user CICS transaction processor.

The operational attributes of DPPX are discussed in the Operations section of this book.

A.5 AIX

AIX/370 is a member of the AIX (Advanced Interactive Executive) family that spans systems from the Personal System/2, through the RISC System/6000 to the ES/9000. It also exploits unique processor capabilities as the ES/390 Vector Facility. AIX is a multi-user, multitasking virtual memory operating system providing an environment with large files and highend compute capability to satisfy those users who wish to use UNIX[14] on the S/390. It is fundamentally an open distributed systems platform, and as a result is comprised of a multitude of functions that have various sources and philosophies. UNIX-based systems are widely used in the engineering and scientific area, and are starting to be used in some commercial areas that need high computational capabilities and wish to utilize capabilities such as X-Windows to display multiple very-high-resolution screens.

UNIX-based systems have evolved from a number of standards, and many are still evolving. AIX is derived from UNIX System V source from AT&T together with many generally available enhancements, such as features of System V.2 and BSD (Berkeley Software Distribution) 4.2 and 4.3 AIX will conform with POSIX[15] standards when it is completed. AIX also includes some unique IBM extensions. These include: kernel and function extensions; user interfaces and services; commands, utilities, and subroutines; and data and file management extensions.

A number of shells are provided, including DOS (PC DOS) and a windowing environment from Massachusetts Institute of Technology (X-Windows). C and VS Fortran compilers are source-code compatible between the different hardware platforms.

Connectivity with other IBM and non-IBM systems is provided using TCP/IP interprocessor communications function, NFS distributed file capability, X-windows client function, Transparent Computing Facility (TCF),[16] IBM Token Ring, and X.25. ASCII terminals are supported by AIX when they are attached to an AIX workstation. AIX/370 also provides file and system printer support for personal computer on PS/2 DOS users.

---

[13]DPPX/370 CICS Command-Level Interface and COBOL II Facility Release 2 with the CICS Command Language Translator provide closer MVS affinity for application development.

[14]UNIX is a registered trademark of AT&T Bell Laboratories.

[15]POSIX is a trademark of the Institute of Electrical and Electronics Engineers (IEEE) and the standard is IEEE 1003.1. It will become the standard for the Portable Operating Systems for Computing Environments.

[16]Transparent Computing Facility is based on work done at the Locus Computing Corp. This facility allows the distribution of data and processes among processors of TCF cluster (a collection of TCF nodes connected via an IBM Token Ring or Ethernet LAN, or a channel-to-channel adapter).

AIX/370 runs as a guest under VM and coexists with other guest operating systems such as VSE or MVS on the same processor. AIX/370 is supported in 24-bit and 31-bit addressing mode. In VM/370 mode, 8 Mbytes of process size are available per user. In VM/XA mode, 768 Mbytes are available for the user process. AIX/370 is intended to replace IBM Interactive Executive/370 (IX/370), which also ran on VM.

AIX/370 users can access existing CMS (and MVS/TSO) programs by submitting commands via AIX/370's on-host facility. They can also send files to and receive files from other users in a network accessed via the NJE facility of Remote Communication Subsystem (RSCS).

Electronic message sending, communications between systems, file transfers, and full screen text editing are provided by INmail, INnet,[17] FTP, and INed[18] programs developed by INTERACTIVE and ported to AIX/370.

AIX/370

- IBM S/390 family member of AIX
- Architected for distributed systems
- Source from AT&T UNIX System V
- Features from System V.2 and BSD 4.2 and 4.3
- Includes X-windows and NFS
- TCP/IP primary communication protocols
- Hosted on VM

A.6 TPF

TPF (Transaction Processing Facility) was designed and jointly developed by IBM and several major U.S. airlines for airline reservations systems in the late 1950s and 1960s. By the early 1970s, TPF evolved from an airline control program (ACP) and was in use for nonairline applications such as:

- Hotel reservations
- Credit authorization/verification
- Car rental reservations/billing
- Police car dispatching

[17] A trademark of the INTERACTIVE Systems Corp.
[18] A registered trademark of the INTERACTIVE Systems Corp.

- Electronic funds transfer switching
- Online teller memo posting
- Message switching
- Loan payment processing
- Communication transaction routers

TPF currently handles some of the largest financial systems and is used for operating across multiple geographically separate data centers (frequently managed by different companies). This system's hardware and software are designed and configured for reliability. System application availability levels exceed 99.9%, and annual outages are reported in minutes for the entire year.

The programs are typically written in assembler language. IBM C/370 language support has also been implemented. Some installations use SABRETALK,[19] a higher-level development language resembling PL/I.

TPF is a highly tuned, general purpose, message-based, high-capacity transaction processing system. It handles simple messages for query, update, and switching. The system environment is highly optimized to exploit the S/390 hardware to maximize response time, capacity, and availability. Transaction rates exceed 1,600 messages per second. Configurations include tightly and loosely coupled environments. Facilities are also provided to interface with IMS and CICS systems.

As a point of interest, many of the recent PC and minibased servers exploit techniques similar to those used by TPF to accomplish the high-message performance. The S/390 hardware architecture provides TPF with a very reliable and flexible base. As depicted in Figure A.7, the TPF configuration allows multiple processors to be added within the same frame as allowing loosely coupled systems to be added to the disk storage.[20] Similarly, TPF systems are used in distributed applications, using multiple TPFs systems geographically placed as communication switches (rerouting messages) and for processing local data.

TPF

- High-transaction (message) rate processor
- Extensively used in reservation, credit checking, and message routing
- Applications written in assembler, C/370, and specialized languages
- Interfaces with CICS and IMS
- Provides for vertical, horizontal, and geographical growth

---

[19]SABRETALK is a programming tool developed by Eastern Airlines.
[20]*Transaction Processing Facility Version 3 (TPF3) General Information Manual Release 1.0*, IBM Order Number GH20-7521.

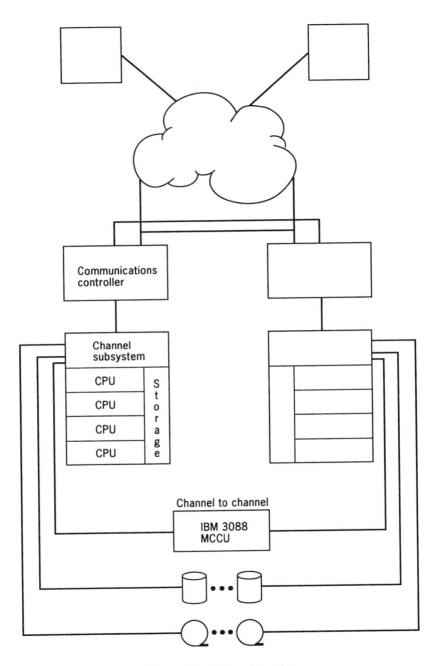

Figure A.7 *TPF configuration.*

A.7 PICK

PICK is an operating system developed by Dick Pick in the late 1960s. By the middle of 1988 it had about 130,000 mainframe and minicomputer installations worldwide and an additional 80,000 installations on personal computers. There are now more than 2,000 established applications that use PICK as their operating-environment base. Typical applications are order entry, transaction processing, invoicing, bill collections, inventory management, wholesale distribution, records management, repetitive manufacturing, and college and university administration for small to intermediate-size businesses.

PICK provides a relatively easy way to implement an applications environment, and presents a very straightforward user interface. It uses an asynchronous terminal interface[21] and ASCII terminals.[22]

Most PICK end user applications are turnkey and installed by dealers; the fact that PICK is the underlying operating system is usually obscured. PICK can be used as the native ES/9370 operating system or it can use VM/SP as its platform. The platform approach allows for activities such as development, test, and backup to be done at the same time. In the standard PICK environment, these are serialized steps. Additionally, all the distributed VM capabilities are available. The Ultimate Company provides the PICK platform for the S/390 as well as several non-IBM systems.[23]

PICK

- Widely used interactive application platform
- Very large install base
- Runs on multiple vendor hardware and software bases
- Runs either native or on VM with S/390
- Uses an ASCII terminal interface
- Applications typically implemented as turnkey
- S/390 provides increased capacity and distributed support

---

[21]IBM mainframe systems have traditionally optimized their performance by using synchronous (or buffered) terminal interfaces to reduce the number of interruptions being handled by the central processing units. Several system implementations are designed to operate on an asynchronous basis. PICK is one such operating system. To accomplish a similar touch and feel, PICK uses the ES/9370's ASCII Subsystem Controller with some specialized algorithms.
[22]ASCII terminals transmit data using an American National Standard Code for Information Interchange (a 7-bit code), one character at a time.
[23]The Ultimate Company also provides PICK-based systems on a multiuser micro system based on the Motorola 68020, minicomputers based on the DEC LSI11, an offering based on Honeywell DPS 6, a series of 32-bit Honeywell-based super-minicomputers, another super-minicomputer offering based on VAX with VMS and a MicroVax II implementation, and a Tandem fault-tolerant implementation.

The running of PICK applications on an IBM S/390 base again demonstrates the flexibility of the architecture and its ability to port entire environments. PICK-based applications can now run on Honeywell, Digital, and IBM hardware.

A.8   MUMPS

MUMPS was developed in 1967 at the Massachusetts General Hospital in Boston, and was named the Massachusetts General Hospital Utility Multi-Programming System. It is a language and associated environment that is in worldwide use in medical, commercial, and industrial applications.

The standard MUMPS programming interface is a general purpose, high-level programming language designed for interactive data management applications. It is an ANSI[24] standard (X11.1-1984).

MUMPS is implemented in interpretive and compiled versions. MUMPS/VM[25] features a precompiling and pseudo code interpreter combination that appears as an interpreter to the user. It is relatively simple to learn and use; many implementers cite that there are substantial productivity advantages over most other programming languages[26] and that the "possible drawback of slow speed—inherent in an interpreted language—is offset by the [productivity] cost savings.[27] MUMPS implementations cross multiple computer architectures, vendors, and operating systems (e.g., UNIX, Xenix, DEC VAX VMS and PDP-11, and HP, just to identify a few). MUMPS/VM is implemented with a 3270, an ASCII terminal interface. For applications that use the asynchronous terminal interface and the nature of the input

---

MUMPS/VM

- A widely used interactive application platform
- Runs on multiple hardware and software bases
- Runs on VM with S/390
- Uses an ASCII terminal interface
- Interpretive high-level programming language
- S/390 provides increased capacity and distributed support

---

[24]ANSI stands for the American National Standards Institute, an organization sponsored by the Computer and Business Equipment Manufactures Association for establishing voluntary standards.

[25]Micronetics Design Corp. provides the MUMPS/VM sold by IBM for the S/370, as well as an IBM PC MS-DOS version.

[26]J. Y. Smith and W. J. Harvey, "MUMPS Is Germinating Business Productivity," *Journal of Systems Management,* April 1988, 26–31.

[27]R.G. Davis, "System Design Implications," *MUMPS Special Edition,* 1988, pp. 28–30.

and subsequent application design, S/390-based applications require an ASCII adapter. IBM's ASCII Subsystem Controller and the Intel 9770 can be integrated into the ES/9000 rack. Intel also provides an outboard channel-connected unit for non-rack models.

A Host File Server (HFS) allows users to access VM/CMS files, should that be required.

A.9 MUSIC/SP

MUSIC/SP (The McGill University System for Interactive Computing/System Product) provides an integrated host/workstation environment especially designed to meet the needs of universities and colleges. It provides an operating environment that supports word processing, electronic mail, teaching programs, statistics, graphics, personal computing (using the Personal Computer Workstation component of MUSIC), batch processing access, and access to other interactive systems such as TSO, CMS, or CICS. It can run either as the primary operating system or as a guest operating system on VM (see Figure A.8). MUSIC/SP is a multi-user, multifunction, interactive system, complete with a collection of application programs, compiler interfaces, and utilities. It coexists on the same system as VSE and MVS, and allows for ASCII terminals or 3270 terminal access to MUSIC, CMS, or guest environments.

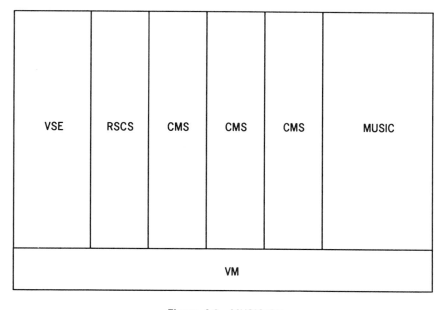

Figure A.8 MUSIC/SP.

MUSIC was developed at the McGill University in Montreal, starting in 1967. It was announced as an IBM product in 1972. Its design philosophy was that it was easy to use without the end user having to become a programmer. It provides realtime control of users, dynamic space allocations, and read/write file sharing with a maximum program size of 1 Mbyte. It also had to provide the necessary administration controls for resource consumption, terminal use, and security. It supports a multitude of language interfaces, such as: APL, assembler language, several variations of BASIC, several variations of COBOL, C, several variations of FORTRAN and PASCAL, PL/I, REXX, and RPG II. Other facilities include a variety of popular third-party statistical packages and computer-aided instruction tools.

MUSIC can cooperatively work with a personal computer. The Personal Computer Workstation (PCWS) provides personal computer cooperative processing with the host MUSIC by providing the appropriate connection logic so that users can work on their personal computers and switch to the MUSIC system when needed.

Appendix B

Operations Checklist

This checklist is provided to recap some of the important operational aspects of any system, which become even more important in a distributed environment and should be considered and factored in any solution. Demos are always appropriate; everyone learns from them. Consider the following areas in the assessments and plan:

B.1 CENTRAL SYSTEM OPERATOR INTERFACES

B.1.1 Programmed Operators

- NetView (VM, MVS, VSE host)
- NetView and/or PROP for VM node
- NetView and/or OCCF for VSE node
- NetView and HCF (at MVS host) and DPPX/370 at the node
- NetView and SSI for MVSs, IMS, and CICS

B.1.2 Operator Interfaces

- CMS for VM
- Console support, ICCF and CICS for VSE
- TAF for access to CICS and IMS consoles
- NetView for NetView console and NetView Graphic Monitor
- NETCENTER
- CVIEW access for shared viewing of 3270 screens

B.2 BACKUP/ARCHIVE

- Local/remote backup
- Automated backup
- User-invoked recovery
- System-invoked recovery
- Local/remote archive
- User-invoked retrieval

B.3 PERFORMANCE MANAGEMENT

- Data collection
- Data reduction
- Realtime analysis
- Alerts
- Programmed actions

B.4 AVAILABILITY MANAGEMENT

- Alerts (automated or from hotline)
- Automated response/actions
- Diagnostic information
- Logs
- Skill (availability of support tools)

B.5 CHANGE MANAGEMENT

- Change control (scheduling)
- Change preparation (testing and packaging)
- Change distribution
- Change application
- Change backout
- Logging

B.6 PROBLEM MANAGEMENT

- Alerts
- Problem entry (where)

- Problem tracking
- Relationship to change process
- NetView tools
- Host tools
- Skills (availability of support tools)

B.7 APPLICATION SUPPORT

Application support addresses remote problem determination and administration. Most systems provide operating system and subsystem mechanisms and tools to support problem determination. But what mechanisms are provided to support application problem determination? For example, how effective can one be if the user must try to remember what went wrong and try to reconstruct the situation? Transaction managers, for example, go to great lengths to provide diagnostic and status information to minimize such exposures. For this reason, some companies are using CICS/VS on VSE and MVS for supporting decision-support applications rather than the open environment provided by VM/CMS and TSO. Functions like CVIEW are surfacing for *LAN*s (e.g., DCAF).

B.8 NETWORK SUPPORT

Network support addresses attachment to a private or public backbone network and the related considerations. The key considerations are associated with the reliability of the tail circuits, the backbone WAN, and the systems and software connected across these. SNA has spent substantial investment to provide end-to-end controls for sessions. Other implementations have used different philosophies of connectivity management. When merging these philosophies, it is important to verify that the service expectations are aligned with the technology and philosophy being used. Just because some portion of the session is on SNA doesn't imply that the same level of network management and control is available to the entire path. This is a two-edged sword; sometimes the solution doesn't require all the controls and the traditional approach may be overkill. At other times, the service level expectations are set based on the use of full SNA. As a result, the major checklist items are:

- SNA
- Non-SNA
- Network management—NetView and its interfaces
- Network attachment—native or gateways

Glossary

A

Advanced Communications Function for the Virtual Telecommunications Access Method (ACF/VTAM): An IBM-licensed program that provides single-domain network capability and, optionally, multiple-domain capability. It controls communication and the flow of data in an SNA network between terminals and application programs running under VSE and OS/VS2. Application programs use either GET and PUT or READ and WRITE macro instructions to request the transfer of data, which is performed by message handlers.

American National Standards Institute (ANSI): An organization whose purpose is establishing voluntary industry standards.

ANSI: American National Standards Institute, an organization sponsored by the Computer and Business Equipment Manufactures Association for establishing voluntary standards.

AP: Attached processor.

APA: All points addressable.

APPC: IBM's Advanced Program-to-Program Communications

Application: (1) A generic term to refer to the usage of technology. (2) A label for a program. (3) A label for a set of programs and procedures to accomplish a business purpose. This term is broadly used in all contexts. Philosophically, an application is the sum of the components between the reference interface or component and reference user. For example, a subsystem is an application to the operating system. A program that uses the subsystem is often referred to as an application of the subsystem, etc.

APPN: IBM's Advanced Peer-to-Peer Networking.

ARCNET: Was developed by Datapoint Corporation. It provides a 2.5-Mbit-per-second token passing network using a distributed star topology over coaxial cable.

ARPANET: Advanced Research Projects Agency Network. A networking project initially sponsored by the Defense Advanced Research Projects Agency (DARPA) to link government research centers and universities. TCP/IP protocols were pioneered on ARPANET.

ASCII: Designation of the American National Standard of Information Interchange ASCII terminals are terminals that transmit data using the ANSII code for Information Interchange (a 7-bit code) a character at a time.

Asynchronous: (1) Without regular time relationship; unexpected or unpredictable with respect to the execution of a program's instructions. (2) Pertaining to transactions that are processed independently of and simultaneously with the continuing work of the requesting user or application. For example, the keyboard of a terminal user who requests an asynchronous transaction remains unlocked while the transaction is being processed. (3) Contrast with Synchronous.

Asynchronous Communication Adapter: Feature 6032 in the 9370 Information System. The Asynchronous Communication Adapter is an I/O controller, supporting half-duplex operation, with up to four asynchronous communication lines to attach ASCII devices to a 9370 processor. Each line can be independently configured for interface and line speed. Synonymous with Asynchronous Four-Line Adapter.

B

Bps: An instantaneous data rate. Could mean bits per second or bytes per second depending on its context. Some people prefer to use bps with a small *b* to refer to bits and a capital *B* to refer to bytes. Therefore, bps might refer to bits per second and Bps might refer to bytes per second.

Baud: A term that is often used interchangeably with bps (bits), and which refers to a unit of signalling speed equal to the number of discrete conditions or signal events per second.

Bridges: Comprised of hardware adapters and logic that allow a workstation or server on one LAN to address a workstation or server on an adjacent LAN using the same protocols. Operates within the OSI model data link layer. A recent extension might be remote bridge, which provides for the connection of the MAC layers of two remote LANs via a telecommunication link transparent to the end users.

BSC: IBM's Binary Synchronous Communication protocol, a half-duplex character-oriented protocol used for remote batch devices and some terminals. There are numerous versions of BSC, but 2780, 3780, and 3270 represent the majority. The 3780 version provides space compression.

C

CAD: Computer Aided Design.

CADAM: Computer-Graphics Augmented Design and Manufacturing (trademark of CADAM, INC.).

CAD/CAM: Computer Aided Design/Computer Aided Manufacturing.

CAEDS: Computer Aided Engineering Design System (TM, Structural Dynamics Research Corp.).

CATIA: Computer-Graphics Aided Three-Dimensional Interactive Application (TM, Dassault Systems).

CCITT: An international standards body, the International Telegraph and Telephone Consultative Committee.

Canned Packages: An expression used to describe a packaged solution that is ready to use as a complete solution versus a set of components that the user has to integrate.

Channel: (1) A path along which signals can be sent—for example, data channel, output channel. (2) A device that connects the processing unit and main storage with the I/O units. (3) A marketing expression that refers to the way products reach the market.

CICS: IBM's Customer Information Control Systems, which is currently implemented in two variations. It is file and data base accessed on IBM's MVS and VSE operating systems. It is also implemented as an integrated service in IBM's VM and OS/2 environment. All environments have the ability to access data among participating CICSs, providing full integrity. Transaction routing (somewhat analogous to the IMS message switching) is only available among VSE and MVS implementations.

CICS/ISC: IBM's CICS/Intersystems Communications, which ties two CICS domains together.

CIO: Chief Information Officer, a title meant to encompass the support and management of an enterprise's information. This may be a staff or line function. In either case, the position is responsible for the effective application of information system technologies to address an enterprise's business challenge.

Closed: The controlled number of parameters, choices, interfaces, and components exposed to the programmer or user.

CMS: IBM Conversational monitor system component associated with IBM's VM operating system.

CNM: See Communications Network Management.

Coaxial Cable: A cable consisting of one conductor, usually a small copper tube or wire, within and insulated from another conductor of larger diameter, usually copper tubing or copper braid.

Common Communications Support: Provides consistent communications architectures across SAA environments for connecting applications, systems, networks, and devices.

Common Programming Interface: Provides languages, commands, and calls that allow the development of applications that are more easily integrated and moved across environments supported by SAA.

Communication: The process of sending or receiving data between two points of a network.

Communication Controller: A type of communication control unit whose operations are controlled by one or more programs stored and executed in the unit. It manages the details of line control and the routing of data through a network.

Communication Link: See Data Link.

Communication Network Management: An ACF/VTAM application program that issues and receives formatted management services request units containing information from physical units.

Communications Controller: A device that directs the transmission of data over the data links of a network. Its operation may be controlled by a program executed in a processor to which the controller is connected or by a program executed within the device. Sometimes called control unit. See also Control Unit.

Communication Link: A link between two service access points that spans one or more data-links over which a session is maintained.

Communications Processor: Feature 6030 in the 9370 Information System. The communications processor is an essential component of the 9370 telecommunications system, which also consists of one or more communication adapters, the telecommunications subsystem microcode, a communication network, and terminals. All 9370 processors support the communications processor; there can be two on the 9373 processor, four on the 9375 processor, and 12 on the 9377 processor. Each communications processor can support up to three adapters— either multiprotocol communication adapters, asynchronous communication adapters, or a combination. The number of adapters is also limited by the aggregate line speed. See also Asychronous Communication Adapter.

Connect: To establish an association between functional units. See also Connection.

Connection: (1) In data communication, an association established between functional units for conveying information. (2) In ACF/VTAM, synonymous with physical connection. See Data Connection, Link Connection.

Control Unit: A device that controls I/O operations at one or more devices. See Controller.

Cooperative processing: Originally used to describe loosely connected processing. It has evolved into more interrelated relationships with hosts. In the emerging SAA context, cooperative processing refers to some well-defined and close relationships among the participating systems and workstations.

CPI: See Common Programming Interface.

CPU: Central Processing Unit.

C&SM: Communications and Systems Management. Encompasses network management together with program updates over networks to provide glasshouse service to network and LAN users.

CTC: Channel-to-channel.

CTCA: Channel-to-channel adapter.

D

DACU: Device Attachment Control Unit. An IBM channel-attached control unit (Block Mux Channel or High-Speed Block Mux channel), which provides four Unibus card slots and two RS232C ports. This product is no longer marketed by IBM.

Darkroom: The label used for a computer room with the lights out. The consoles are controlled from an area physically removed from the computer.

DASD: Direct Access Storage Device.

Data Communication: (1) The transmission and reception of data. (2) The transmission, reception, and validation of data. (3) Data transfer between data source and data link through one or more data links according to appropriate protocols.

DB/DC: A generic label that refers to Data Base/Data Communications used extensively during the 1970s to describe systems such as IBM's IMS, which had two components—a data communications component and a data base component. IBM's CICS also fits into this category.

DB2: IBM DATABASE 2, a relational database management system on MVS.

DCA: Refers to IBM's Document Content Architecture.

DCAF: Distributed Console Access Facility.

DDM: See Distributed Data Management.

DECnet: A Digital Equipment Corp. proprietary network program based on the Ethernet protocol.

Device Control Unit: A hardware device that controls the reading, writing, or displaying of data at one or more I/O devices or terminals.

DIA: IBM's Document Interchange Architecture.

DIF: Display Information Facility or Document Interchange Facility.

DISOSS: See Distributed Office Support System.

Distributed Applications: An application coded in modules so that different routines reside and execute on different systems. Users are unaware of this.

Distributed Data: Data that can be accessed by remote applications or remote users. This data may be distributed in different ways, each providing various degrees of transparency.

Distributed Data Management: The IBM strategic SAA common communications architecture supporting distributed files.

Distributed File: A file that can be accessed by remote applications or remote users. Also, the capability of accessing such a file.

Distributed Function: Splitting an application so that part of its function (logic) is executed on one system, while the remainder of its function is executed on another.

Distributed Office Support System (DISOSS): An IBM program that allows users to file documents in a library of the host system, retrieve documents from the library, distribute documents and messages to other DISOSS users, and keep a log of all documents and messages received.

Distributed Processing: A capability that enables use of applications and data located at remote sites or processors (connected via a communications link) in the same manner as if they were local.

Distributed System: A data processing system in which processing, storage, and control functions, in addition to input and output operations, are distributed among remote locations.

DL/1: IBM's Data Language/1, the IMS/VS data manipulation language—a common high-level interface between a user application and IMS/VS. It is invoked from PL/1, COBOL, or Assembler language programs by means of ordinary subroutine calls. DL/1 also refers to the database system. DL/1 enables a user to define data structures, relate structures to the application, load structures, and reorganize structures.

DNA: Digital Network Architecture. Digital Equipment's architecture—somewhat analogous to IBM's SNA—which was implemented in 1981 to interconnect dissimilar devices over X.25 links.

Document Interchange Architecture (DIA): IBM's DIA provides a set of protocols that define several common office functions performed cooperatively by IBM products. This is documented in Document Interchange Architecture: Technical Reference, SC30-0781.

Document Content Architecture (DCA): IBM's DCA defines the rules for specifying the form and meaning of a text document. It provides for uniform interchange of textual information in the office environment and consists of format elements optimized for document revision. This is documented in Document Content Architecture: Revisable-Form-Text Reference, SC23-0758.

DOS: Disk Operating System. (1) Applies to IBM's S/360 operating system, which was the base for DOS/VS and subsequently DOS/VSE, now frequently referred to as VSE. (2) A generic term applied to Microsoft's MS/DOS and IBM PC/DOS by the PC community.

DOS/VS: IBM's DOS/Virtual Storage.

DOS/VSE: IBM's DOS/Virtual Storage Extended, also referred to as VSE.

DOSF: IBM's Distributed Office Support Facility.

Downsizing: Currently a term used for the organizational size changes as many organizations consolidate, reduce staff management, and put more responsibility in the hands of the line management.

DP: Data processing.

DPPX: IBM's Distributed Processing Program Executive operating system.

DSNX: IBM's Distributed System Node Executive product.

DSX: IBM's Distributed System Executive product.

DXT: IBM's Data Extract product.

E

EBCDIC (Extended Binary Coded Decimal Interchange Code): An 8-bit code to represent characters used on S/390 systems and other IBM systems, terminals, and communications. It is derived from IBM Card code, which explains the way the letter codes are arranged in nonsequential fashion.

ECF: IBM enhanced Connectivity Facilities. A set of products that support a documented interface, which enables personal computer programs to access host resources and services. It is implemented using (Server-Requestor Programming Interface—SRPI) and server facilities on both VM and MVS systems.

EDL: Event-Driven Language.

EDX: Event-Driven Executive.

Environment: A named collection of logical and physical resources used to support the operation of a function.

ESCON: Enterprise Systems Connection Architecture.

ESSL: Engineering and Scientific Subroutine Library.

Ethernet: Was pioneered by Xerox and DEC more than 10 years ago. It operates over a coaxial and fiberoptic cable or twisted pair wire, has a 10 Mbit per second bandwidth, uses a CSMA/CD access (Carrier-Sense Multiple-Access with Collision Detection). Has a strong established base in manufacturing, but has expanded into commercial environments. There are three versions: standard Ethernet, ThinNet, and twisted pair Ethernet. Standard and ThinNet use a coax with a bus topology. Twisted pair Ethernet uses a hierarchical star topology with wiring concentrator hubs. The IEEE 802.3 standard also applies to Ethernet, but is not compatible with the Xerox implementation from a communications standpoint, even though implementers may exist on the same cable. (There are differences between the MAC and LLC layers.)

Extract: The simplest method of accessing distributed data. The user performs two steps: extracting the data into a portable file and loading that file on another system.

F

FDDI (Fiber Distributed Data Interface): A proposed 100 Mbps token-passing ring network ANSI standard.

File Transfer: A degree of distributed file access. A process in which users on one system send files to another, usually via communications software.

File Transfer, Access and Management (FTAM): A standard to allow applications to transfer files or access records of a file defined in a filestore to the open systems network with other systems using a connection-oriented protocol.

FTP: (1) The File Protocol supported by TCP/IP. (2) An acronym used to refer to IBM's File Transfer Programs.

Fullscreen Editing: An editing mode that allows changes to be made in any area of a keyboard-display terminal's screen. Contrast with Line Editing.

Function Shipping: A CICS facility that enables an application to access a resource (such as a file or DL/I database) owned by another CICS system.

G

Gateways: (1) A set of software and/or hardware that allows program interconnection among various systems. (2) Adapters and logic that provide more complex functions for linking dissimilar computers and networks. (3) Used to encompass network addressing, network isolation, protocol conversion, device emulation, etc. Typically operate at the higher levels of the OSI model stack (layers).

GDDM: Graphical Data Display Manager.

Glasshouse: The computer room, data center, or a generalized label for central control and mainframe processing. Its origins stem from the glass walls that encased the computer rooms. Most companies were very proud of their computers. In the mid 1970s, most of the glass walls were replaced with brick to minimize security exposures.

H

Hardware (H/W): (1) Physical equipment as opposed to programs, procedures, rules, and associated documentation. (2) The equipment, as opposed to the programming, of a system. Contrast with Software.

HCF: Host Command Facility is used by DPPX/370 and resides on MVS.

Heartbeat: (1) A term used when monitoring the "health" of a system or component on a regular basis. If the heart is beating, the system or component is okay; if not, appropriate action is taken. The use of the word "heart" indicates the term's importance. (2) Also used to describe the critical cycle of an application, e.g., in a manufacturing application a heartbeat may be one per second to sample all critical variables.

HLL API or HLLAPI: Pronounced "h'loppy," is the acronym for High Level Language Application Program Interface, which supports direct call to routines via a PL/I or a C macro.

Hooks: (1) A jargon term to refer to a program exit or a spoofing interface, which allows another program or service to examine the data or requests.

Host: See Host Processor.

Host Computer: See Host Processor.

Host Processor: (1) A processor that controls all or part of a user application network. (2) The primary or controlling computer in a multiple computer installation. (3) In a network, the processing unit in which the access method for the network resides. (4) In an SNA network, the processing unit that contains a system services control point (SSCP). (5) Synonymous with host computer.

Host System: (1) A data processing system used to prepare programs and the operating environments for use on another computer or controller. (2) The data processing system to which a network is connected and with which the system can communicate.

HPO: IBM VM operating system's High Performance Option.

H/W: Hardware.

Hypervisor: A term used in the VM context that refers to VM's ability to simulate multiple images of S/370 or S/390 machines with virtual devices at the same time. Other S/370 or S/390 operating systems can run in a VM virtual machine environment as though they were running on a dedicated real S/370 or S/390 configuration. These operating systems might even be using devices and storage that are not really present on the base system.

I

IBM Token Ring (compatible with IEEE 802.2 and 802.5 standards): A LAN technology used with the IBM cabling system. It is the fastest growing installed network base. It provides high throughput, up to 16 Mbits per second using a token passing access method, and is highly faulttolerant. It uses token passing via a physical star, logical ring topology.

IBM Token-Ring Network: Token-ring local area network compatible with the IEEE 802.5 standard. It uses IBM Cabling System Type 3 media (telephone twisted pair), which accommodates both cable already in use and low-cost new cable. It is the fastest growing installed network base. It provides high throughput, up to 16 Mbits per second using a token passing access method, and is highly faulttolerant. The devices in the network are cabled to one another in a logical ring. See also Token-Ring Network.

IBM Token-Ring Adapter: Feature 6034 in the 9370 Information System. The IBM Token-Ring Adapter provides a physical link and access control to the IBM Token-Ring Network. It provides IEEE 802.2 function to any protocol stack that supports 802.2 LLC and source routing. It allows communication with all token-ring-connected hosts, controllers, and workstations in IBM and non-IBM environments where matching protocols are available. In transmission speed is 4 or 16 million bits per second. See also IBM Token-Ring Network, Token.

ICCF: IBM's Interactive Computing Control Facility, which runs on IBM's VSE operating system.

IEEE: Institute of Electrical and Electronics Engineers.

IML: Initial microprogram load.

IMS: IBM's Information Management System, which includes a data communications transaction manager and a data management component that can be accessed via the IMS data communications component or batch jobs. IMS runs exclusively on IBMs' highend operating systems, e.g., MVS. IMS systems can interconnect with other IMS systems and CICS systems. The interconnection is at the message level and transactions are switched among the autonomous systems.

IMS/VS: Information Management System/Virtual Storage.

Interface: A shared boundary. An interface may be a hardware component to link two devices or a portion of storage or registers accessed by two or more computer programs.

International Telegraph and Telephone Consultative Committee (CCITT): A committee responsible for worldwide standardization of international telecommunication facilities.

International Standards Organization (ISO): A worldwide committee responsible for promoting standards.

I/O: Input/Output.

IPL: Initial program load.

IS or I/S: (1) Information Systems. A label frequently used to describe the combination of data processing equipment, software, communications, and services provided in order to address an enterprise's informational and data processing needs. (2) An acronym for information systems organization also referred to as the information services organization, the IS (Management Information Systems) organization, DP organization, or even glasshouse organization. It refers to an organization that provides information processing services to end users.

ISC: In the IBM context, refers to Inter-System Communication, a communication between systems that are in different hosts. ISC uses an SNA network to communicate between CICS systems, IMS/DC systems, CICS and IMS/DC systems, and user-written systems that support ISC protocols.

ISCF: IBM's Inter-System Control Facility Guide.

ISDN: Integrated services digital network.

ISO: See International Standards Organization.

IX/370: IBM's Interactive Executive/370, which provided a S/370 VM-based UNIX environment using an outboard processor to handle the UNIX devices (e.g., S/1).

J

JEP: An IBM VSE Job Entry Program.

JES: A generic term to refer to IBM's Job Entry Subsystem(s).

JES2: An IBM MVS subsystem that is a functional extension of the HASP II program that receives jobs into a host system and processes all output data produced by the job.

JES3: An IBM MVS subsystem that is a functional extension of the ASP program that receives jobs into a host system and processes all output data produced by the job.

Job Entry Subsystem (JES): A system facility for spooling, job queuing, and managing I/O. See also JES2, JES3.

L

LAN (italicized): A label currently being used generically to refer to the combination of personal computers and/or minicomputers and services connected by a Local Area Network LAN (not italicized) technology, composite of connections, servers, clients, and their administration and management. Unfortunately, it is not frequently italicized, which causes significant confusion in technical discussions.

LAN (Local Area Network): (1) A data network located on the user's premises in which serial transmission is used for direct data communication among data stations. (2) A network in which communications are limited to a moderate-size geographic area, such as a single office building, warehouse, or campus, and do not generally extend across public rights-of-way, although this appears to be changing. (3) A combination of personal computers, connectivity of these personal computers by such connection technologies as Ethernet and Token Ring, and software control systems that manage the communication and provide sharing services. (4) LAN (in the IBM context), refers to components of the network in the lower two layers of the OSI model as defined by IEEE 802.2 (ISO 8802/2), and the LAN Manager functions, which provide management functions for the lower two layers and data link services to whichever protocol service is provided above. It may or may not include NetBIOS interface and does not include servers. It includes IBM Token Ring and IBM PC Network adapters and drivers.

Line Control: See Link Protocol.

Line Control Discipline: See Link Protocol.

Line Editing: Editing in which data is displayed at a terminal one line at a time and in which the user can access data only through commands. Contrast with Full-screen Editing.

Link: In SNA, the combination of the link connection and the link stations joining network nodes—for example, a System/370 channel and its associated protocols in a serial-by-bit connection under the control of Synchronous Data Link Control (SDLC). A link includes the physical medium of transmission (the link connection—for example, a telephone wire or a microwave beam), the protocol, and associated devices and programming. It is both logical and physical. See also Data Link.

Link-Attached Device: A device that can be attached through a link. The link can be a direct connection attachment to DPPX/370 or a communication attachment using modems.

Link-Attached Terminal: A terminal whose control unit is connected to a computer by a data link. Synonymous with Remote Terminal.

Link Protocol: (1) The set of rules by which a logical data link is established, maintained, and terminated, and by which data is transferred across the link. It includes the format by which control information is passed and the rules by which it is interpreted, in order to transmit data across the link. (2) In SNA, a set of rules used by two nodes on a data link to accomplish an orderly exchange of information. Synonymous with line control. See also Protocol.

LLC: The logical link sublayer of the data link layer of the OSI reference model.

Local Area Network (LAN): See LAN.

Logical Link: A logical connection between two physical units in a network. Synonymous with session.

Logon: The procedure by which a terminal user begins a terminal session.

Loop: In data communication, an electrical path connecting a station and a channel.

LU: A logical unit (LU) can be thought of as a logical part that provides a point of access through which programs and their respective target devices or programs interact across an SNA network. IBM's System Network Architecture defines several logical units types (currently seven major LU types are supported).

LU 0 (LU Type 0 or LU T0): An implementation-defined LU that uses SNA-defined protocols for transmission control and data flow control. LU 0 is used for such applications as IMS/VS communications to an IBM 4700 Finance Communication System, or a Host Command Facility (HCF) communicating with an AS/400-based Distributed Host Command Facility (DHCF), or NetView Distribution Manager to AS/400 Distributed Node Executive (DSNX).

LU 1 (LU type 1 or LU T1): An LU for an application program that communicates with single or multiple device workstations. Examples include: an IMS/VS application communicating with an IBM 8100 Information System, Remote Job Entry with Power/VSE, JES2, and JES3, and IBM 3270 SCS Printer Emulation on the AS/400. The data stream conforms to SNA character string or Document Content Architecture (DCA).

LU 2 (LU Type 2 or LU T2): An LU for an application program that communicates with a single display workstation using the SNA 3270 data stream for interactions or for file transfers.

LU 3 (LU Type 3 or LU T3): An LU for an application that communicates with a single printer using the SNA 3270 data stream. For example, a CICS application that sends output to an IBM 3278 printer attached to an IBM 3274 controller.

LU 4 (LU Type 4 or LU T4): An LU for an application program that communicates with a single or multiple device workstation—for example, CICS/VS communicating with an IBM 6670 Information Distributor.

LU6.0 (LU Type 6.0 or LU T6.0): An LU that is used to communicate with another subsystem, e.g., IMS/VS to IMS/VS via Multiple Systems Coupling (MSC).

LU6.1 (LU Type 6.1 or LU T6.1): An LU that is used to communicate with another application subsystem, e.g., CICS/VS to IMS/VS via Inter-System Coupling (ISC).

LU 6.2 (LU Type 6.2 or LU T6.2): A program-to-program communication protocol. It defines a rich set of interprogram communication services, including a base and optional supplemental services. Support of the base is included in all IBM LU 6.2 products that expose an LU 6.2 application programming interface. This facilitates compatibility of communication functions across systems. LU 6.2 is documented in SNA Format and Protocol Reference Manual: Architecture Logic for LU type 6.2, SC30-3269.

LU 7: LU Type 7 supports sessions between an IBM 5250 display terminal and an application program.

M

Mainframe: Often used to refer to the large systems. It derives from the system configuration that housed the CPU and sometimes the mainstorage in the mainframe and had outboard channels, direct access (e.g., disk drives), and sequential storage (e.g., tape drives).

MAC: The media access control sublayer of the data link layer of the OSI reference model.

MAN: A metropolitan area network that extends the concepts of LANs out of buildings to substantially larger distances than LANs do today. It differs from WAN (wide area network), which refers to telecommunications connections for distances of many miles. The 802.6 MAN standard will accommodate data, digital voice, and compressed video, and is designed to serve as a LAN/WAN gateway. Data rates between 45 to 600 Mbps are expected.

MAP: Manufacturing Automation Protocol, an acronym of the General Motors Corp. for specification of selected OSI protocols over an ISO 88-2/4 token bus LAN for manufacturing environments.

MFT: Multiprogramming with a fixed number of tasks.

MICR: Magnetic ink character recognition.

Minicomputer: A term used to describe a small, general purpose system often defined as a rack-mounted system—but other packaging alternatives are also employed.

MIS: Management Information Systems. An acronym used to describe the umbrella of services provided by the enterprise's information systems group (see also IS). It includes operations, application development, and user support functions, and may or may not include communications.

Modem (Modulator-Demodulator): A device that modulates and demodulates signals transmitted over data communication facilities.

MP: Multiprocessor.

MRJE: Multileaving Remote Job Entry.

MIRO: Multiregion operation.

MSC: Multiple Systems Coupling, an IMS/DC facility that enables two or more IMS systems to be interconnected so that users or applications on one system can invoke an application on another.

MSNF: The IBM's Multisystem Networking Facility feature of ACF/VTAM.

MSRJE: Multiple Session Remote Job Entry.

Multiple Virtual Storage (MVS): An alternative name for OS/VS2, Release 2.

MUMPS: Massachusetts General Hospital utility multiprogramming system.

MUX: Communications multiplexer.

MVS: IBM's Multiple Virtual Storage operating system.

MVS/ESA: IBM's Multiple Virtual Storage/Enterprise Systems Architecture operating system.

MVS/SP: IBM's Multiple Virtual Storage/System Product operating system.

MVS/XA: IBM's Multiple Virtual Storage/Extended Architecture operating system.

MVT: IBM's Multi-programming with a Variable Number of Tasks operating system.

N

NCCF: IBM's Network Communications Control Facility.

NCP: See Advanced Communications Function for the Network Control Program (ACF/NCP).

NetBios: A software interface (Network Basic Input/Output System) originally developed by IBM and Sytek that allows computers to communicate over a local area network. It provides both session and message (datagram) interchange.

NetView: An IBM-licensed program that lets you control, record, and automate certain operator tasks. An operator at the host can use NetView to collect, correlate, and access online data about sessions, routes, and link-attached or channel-attached resources. NetView provides all the functions of Network Communications Control Facility (NCCF), Network Logical Data Manager (NLDM), and Network Problem Determination Application (NPDA), as well as other functions.

NetView Distribution Manager (NetView DM): An IBM-licensed program installed at a host system that provides centrally controlled data distribution and the installation of software changes in SNA networks composed of DPPX/370 and DPPX/SP systems. NetView DM supports installation management services and lets customers centrally schedule and control selected data processing operations throughout their networks. It is a functional extension of Distributed Systems Executive (DSX).

NetView DM: IBM's NetView Distribution Manager.

Network: (1) An interconnected group of nodes. (2) A system consisting of two or more interconnecting computing units. (3) The assembly of equipment through which connections are made among data stations. (4) In data processing, a user-application network.

Network Communications Control Facility (NCCF): A System/370 or 4300 licensed program consisting of a base for command processors that can monitor, control, and improve the operation of a data communication network.

Network Control Program (NCP): See Advanced Communications Function for the Network Control Program (ACF/NCP).

Network Problem Determination Application (NPDA): A System/370 or 4300 licensed program that assists the user in identifying network problems from a central control point using interactive display techniques.

Network File System: NFS.

NFS: Network File System which operates on TCP/IP.

NJE: A term used to refer to IBM's Network Job Entry capabilities, which allow systems to transmit input and output (files) among the participating systems. It is specifically used within the MVS and JES context and generically used when discussing the shipment of the input/out between VM and MVs or VSE and MVS.

NLDM: IBM's Network Logical Data Manager.

NMPF: IBM's Network Management Productivity Facility.

NODE: (1) A junction point in a network, represented by one or more physical units. (2) In SNA, an endpoint of a link or a junction common to two or more links in a network. Nodes can be distributed to host processors, communication controllers, or terminals. Nodes can vary in routing and other functional capabilities.

Nonswitched Connection: A communication line that is permanently connected between two stations (it does not have to be established by dialing). Synonymous with leased connection, leased line, private line, or dedicated line. Contrast with Switched Connection.

Nonswitched Line: See Nonswitched Connection.

NPA: IBM's Network performance Analyzer.

NPDA: IBM's Network Problem Determination Application.

O

OCCF: IBM's Operator Communications Control Facility, which was used on both MVS and VSE operating systems. It is still being used on VSE.

OEM: The term typically refers to Original Equipment Manufacturer. Sometimes it is used as Other Equipment Manufacturer to differentiate from IBM equipment.

Off-the-Shelf-Applications: A term used to describe functionally complete applications that can be purchased. In the PC environment, many off-the-shelf applications, such as spreadsheets, word processors, and desktop publishers, are really tools.

Online: Used to describe computer access via computer terminal to (1) an interactive session or (2) a transaction. In commercial applications, online is often used as a short form for online transactions.

Open: Means that the S/390 exposes multiple-level software interfaces, from the very detailed exits in the operating system to the very high level of application interfaces.

Original Equipment Manufacturer (OEM): A manufacturer of equipment that may be marketed by another manufacturer.

O/S: Operating system.

OS/VS: OS/Virtual Storage.

OSI: Open Systems Interconnect. An ISO standard.

OS/2: IBM Operating Systems/2, the newest IBM operating system for personal computers. It is available in two editions: the Standard Edition and the Extended Edition. The Extended Edition supports a communications manager and database manager.

OS/400: IBM Operating System/400, the IBM operating system for the AS/400 system. Its facilities include an integrated database manager (see SQL/400), SAA Common Communications Support, and data management facilities.

Other Equipment Manufacturer (OEM): Within IBM, a vendor other than itself.

P

PC: (1) A generic term for IBM PCs and IBM PS/2s. (2) Personal Computer.

Peer: In network architecture, any functional unit that is in the same layer as another entity.

PL/1: IBM's Programming Language/One.

Pipes: The interconnection media. Examples include buses, channels, LANs, phone lines, etc.

Platform: The "supporting" elements of a system. For example, a foundation is a platform of a house.

Point-to-Point Connection: (1) A connection established between two data stations for data transmission. The connection may include switching facilities. (2) A data link that connects a single remote station to the computer; it may be either switched or nonswitched.

Point-to-Point-Line: See Point-to-Point Connection.

Port: An access point (for example, a logical unit) for data entry or exit, such as on a 3270 device.

POSIX: A trademark of the Institute of Electrical and Electronics Engineers (IEEE). The standard is IEEE 1003.1. It will become the standard for the Portable Operating Systems for Computing Environments.

POWER: IBM VSE's Priority Output Writers, Execution Processors, and Input Readers.

Processor: (1) In a computer, a functional unit that interprets and executes instructions. (2) A functional unit, part of another unit such as a terminal or a processing unit, that interprets and executes instructions. See also Communications Processor.

PROFS: IBM's Professional Office System.

PROP: IBM VM's Programmable Operator.

Protocol: (1) A specification for the format and relative timing of information exchanged between communicating parties. (2) A set of semantic and syntactic rules that determines the behavior of functional units in achieving communication. (3) In SNA, the meanings of, and the sequencing rules for, requests and responses used for managing the network, transferring data, and synchronizing the states of network components. See also Link Protocol.

Protocol Stack: The architectural layers defined for communications protocol.

PRPQ: An IBM term for Programming Request for Price Quotation.

PR/SM: IBM's Process Resource/Systems Manager is a ES/3090 and ES/9000 feature that provides for the ability to partition the hardware system into multiple independent environments. It provides up to 14 copies of systems with dedicated resources using the same physical system depending on the model.

PS: (1) An acronym for the personal services family of IBM products. (2) Programmed symbols.

PS/PC: Personal Services/PC.

PTF: Program temporary fix, a code that provides fix or bypass until the fix is incorporated into the next release of the product.

PU: Physical unit.

Public Network: A network established and operated by common carriers or telecommunication administrations for the specific purpose of providing circuit-switched, packet-switched, and leased-circuit services to the public. Contrast with User Application Network.

PUT: IBM's acronym for program update tape that contains maintenance.

PVM: IBM's Pass-through Virtual Machine product.

Q

QMF: IBM's Query Management Facility, which accesses IBM relational data bases.

R

RACF: IBM's Resource Access Control Facility security product for MVS and VM operating systems.

RAS: A acronym used to refer to reliability, availability, and serviceability.

Remote Job Entry (RJE): Submission of a job through an input unit that has access to a computer through a data link.

Remote Terminal: A terminal attached to a system through a data link.

Resource: Any facility of the computing system or operating system required by a job or task, including main storage, I/O devices, the processing unit, data sets, control or processing programs, execution time, execution levels, locks, and queues.

REXX: The acronym for Restructured Extended Executor Language, an SAA procedural language.

RISC: Reduced instruction set computer.

RJE: Remote Job Entry.

Routers: Adapters and logic that introduce more sophistication over bridges with functions such as new addressing, frame formatting, and isolation (subnetworks) for inter-LAN communications. Usually used for interconnecting LANs using different protocols (e.g., Ethernet and Token Ring). Connects networks at the OSI network layer. More function and overhead than routers.

ROCF: An IBM hardware capability to access the system console remotely. Remote Operator Console Facility.

RSCS: IBM VM Remote Spooling Communication Subsystem.

RS232C: A standard serial interface.

S

S/S: Start/Stop.

S/36: IBM System/36.

S/38: IBM System/38.

S/370: IBM System/370.

S/390: System/390.

SAA: IBM Systems Applications Architecture.

SAMON: IBM SNA Application Monitor.

SCSI: Small Computer System Interface.

SDLC: Synchronous Data Link Control is a discipline for managing synchronous, code transparent, serial-by-bit information transfer between nodes that are joined by telecommunication links. This is documented in IBM Synchronous Data Link Control Concepts, GA27-3093.

Service Level Reporter: An IBM product that collects and reports service-level-related data such as performance. SLR.

SLR: Service Level Reporter.

SMTP: Simple Mail Transfer Protocol of TCP/IP.

SNA: IBM's Systems Network Architecture.

SNADS: IBM's Systems Network Architecture Distribution Services. SNADS provides an asynchronous distribution capability in an SNA network, thereby avoiding the need for active sessions between the endpoints. SNADS is documented in "SNA Architecture and Protocol Reference Manual: Distribution Services," IBM manual number SC30-3098.

SNA Network Management Architecture: Describes IBM's approach to managing communication networks. The protocols of problem management offer a vehicle for monitoring network operations from a central location. This is documented in "SNA Format and Protocol Reference Manual Management Services," IBM manual number SC30-3346.

Sneaker Net: A network where parttime employees deliver output or support distributed peripherals.

SNI: IBM's SNA Network Interconnect.

SNS/XXXX: Software Network Solution/XXXX, a prefix label for Interlink's SNA Gateway Family.

Software (S/W): Programs, procedures, rules, and possibly associated documentation pertaining to the operation of a system. Contrast with Hardware.

Software Houses: A term used to refer to a software vendor.

Solution Houses: Software packages that provide a total solution, versus components and tools.

Spool: Simultaneous peripheral operations online.

Spooling (Simultaneous Peripheral Operation Online): (1) The use of auxiliary storage as a buffer storage to reduce processing delays when transferring data between peripheral equipment and the processors of a computer. (2) The reading of input data streams and the writing of output data streams on auxiliary storage devices, concurrently with job execution, in a format convenient for later processing or output operations.

SQL: Structured Query Language. Defined by SAA for access to relational data. SQL can be used within applications or interactively to define relational data, access relational data, and control access to relational database resources.

SQL/DS: IBM's SQL/Data System, a relational database management system on VM and VSE.

SQL/400: IBM SQL/400, a relational database product that provides precompiler and interactive support for the AS/400 database manager.

SRPI: Label for the IBM Server-Requester Programming Interface used by ECF.

SSP: IBM's System Support Program.

SSX: IBM's Small Systems Executive.

Starlan: Developed by AT&T. It supports a 1 Mbit per second distributed star topoology with CSMA/CD access. It operates over two unshielded twisted pairs and can be configured using a hub, daisy chain, or both.

Star Network: A network configuration in which there is only one path between a central or controlling node and each endpoint node.

Store-and-Forward Transmission: A manner of transmitting messages through a computer network. Messages are stored before transmission toward the final destination.

Subsystem: A secondary or subordinate system usually capable of operating independently of, or asynchronously with, a controlling system.

Super-Minicomputer: A new class of minicomputers that are capable of doing the work that was once only in the domain of large general purpose computers. This class of computer differs from its larger siblings in that it does not require the environmental conditioning of the larger systems. It is typically self contained, that is, the peripherals are mounted within the rack rather than externally attached. It is also usually substantially less expensive than the larger systems. It differs from the minicomputer in capabilities and capacity. Super-minicomputers should not be confused with mini-supercomputers, which are highly specialized for extended precision and high-volume, calculation-oriented applications.

SVS: Single Virtual Storage.

S/W: Software.

Switched Connection: (1) A mode of operating a data link in which a circuit or channel is established to switching facilities, as, for example, in a public switched network. (2) A connection established by dialing. (3) A telecommunication line in which the connection is established by dialing.

Switched Line: See Switched Connection.

Synchronous: (1) Occurring with a regular or predictable time relationship. (2) Pertaining to requests and/or responses that are processed sequentially. (3) Pertaining to transactions that assume control of a terminal or application, so that the requesting user or application cannot resume work until the transaction is complete and control is returned. For example, the keyboard of a terminal user who requests a synchronous transaction remains locked until the transaction completes. (4) Contrast with Asynchronous.

Synchronous Data Link Control (SDLC): A discipline conforming to subsets of the Advanced Data Communication Control Procedures (ADCCP) of the American National Standards Institute (ANSI) and High-Level Data Link Control (HDLC) of the International Organization for Standardization, for managing synchronous, code-transparent, serial-by-bit information transfer over a link connection. Transmission exchanges may be duplex or half-duplex over switched or nonswitched links. The configuration of the link connection may be point-to-point, multi-point, or loop. In data processing, a collection of people, machines, and methods organized to accomplish a set of specific functions. Systems/370 Block Multiplexer Channel. Feature 6003 in the 9370 Information System. This I/O controller lets you attach one to eight control units for both IBM and non-IBM DASD, tape, display, printer, and other devices. It provides a channel that transmits blocks of data to or from more than one device by interleaving the record blocks. Synonymous with BMPX.

Systems Application Architecture: A collection of IBM software interfaces, conventions, and protocols. It serves as a framework for developing consistent applications across three major IBM computing environments: System/370, AS/400, and PS/2.

Systems Integrators: The most recent term being used for a project management and systems engineering organization that designs and installs solutions.

Systems Network Architecture (SNA): The total description of the logical structure, formats, protocols, and operational sequences for transmitting units through the communication system and controlling the configuration and operation of networks.

T

TAF: Terminal Access Facility.

TCP/IP: Transmission Control Protocol/Internet Protocol.

Telnet: The terminal emulation protocol supported by TCP/IP.

Terminal: (1) A device, usually equipped with a keyboard and a display device, capable of sending and receiving information. See also Remote Terminal, Workstation. (2) A point in a system or communication network at which data can either enter or leave. Terminal Access Facility. A feature of the Network Communications Control Facility licensed program, which lets the NCCF operator control CICS/VS, IMS/VS, TSO, and HCF subsystems from one terminal.

Token-Ring Network: (1) A ring network that allows unidirectional data transmission between data stations by a token passing procedure over one transmission medium so that the transmitted data returns to the transmitting station. (2) A network that uses a ring topology in which tokens are passed in a circuit from node to node. A node that is ready to send can capture the token and insert data for transmission. See also IBM Token-Ring Network, IBM Token-Ring Adapter.

TPF: Transaction Processing Facility.

TSCF: Target System Control Facility.

TSO: Time Sharing Option.

T1/T3: A label for high-speed lines (tariffs) typically associated with high-performance mediums such as fiber optics and microwave (e.g., T1 reflects 1.544 Mbits bandwidth). T3 is also known as DS-3 and supports 45 Mbps (the equivalent of 28 T1 lines.)

U

UNIX: An operating system that has become a de facto standard. Originally developed by Bell Labs, has also undergone modifications at the University of California at Berkeley (BSD).

Upstream: (1) Referring to a machine directly attached to a host processor. (2) In the direction opposite to data flow or toward the source of transmission. (3) Toward the processor from an attached unit or end user. (4) Contrast with Downstream.

User: A person or function requiring the services of a computing system.

User Application Network: A configuration of data processing products, such as processors, controllers, and terminals, established and operated by users for the purpose of data processing or information exchange. The network may use services offered by communication common carriers or telecommunication administrations. Contrast with Public Network.

V

VAX: Virtual Architecture Extended. A family of DEC processors.

Virtual Storage Extended (VSE): An operating system that is an extension of DOS/VS, consisting of VSE advanced functions (the minimum operating system support for a VSE-controlled installation) and other IBM-licensed programs.

Virtual Telecommunications Access Method (VTAM): See Advanced Communications Function for the Virtual Telecommunications Access Method (ACF/VTAM).

VM/370: IBM's Virtual Machine/370 system.

VM (Virtual Machine): In VM/370, a functional equivalent of an IBM System/370 computing system. Each virtual machine is controlled by a suitable operating system. VM/370 controls the concurrent execution of multiple virtual machines on a single System/370.

VM HPO: IBM's Virtual Machine High-Performance Option.

VM/IS: IBM's Virtual Memory/Integrated System.

VM/SP: IBM's Virtual Machine/System Product.

VMPPF: IBM's VM Performance Planning Facility.

VMS: Virtual Memory System. A DEC proprietary operating system.

VM/VSE: IBM's Virtual Machine/Virtual Storage Extended.

VSAM: IBM's Virtual Storage Access Method, which operates on MVS, VSE, and VM.

VSE: IBM's Virtual Storage Extended.

VTAM: See Advanced Communications Function for the Virtual Telecommunications Access Method (ACF/VTAM).

W

WAN: Wide Area Network. When Local Area Network technologies are limited by physical distance in order to connect to another remote LAN or host, a WAN is used. WANs include the traditional network and telecommunication technologies.

Workstation: (1) A terminal or microcomputer, usually one that is connected to a mainframe and/or to a network, at which a user can perform applications. (2) One or more I/O devices from which jobs can be submitted to a host system for processing and/or to which completed jobs can be returned. (3) A configuration of I/O equipment at which an operator works.

Workstation Controller (WSC): Feature 6020 in the 9370 Information System. A Workstation Controller (WSC) allows the attachment of 3270-type devices or original equipment manufacturer (OEM) devices to a 9370 processor either directly or through 3299 Terminal Multiplexors. There can be two WSCs attached to a 9373 processor, six to a 9375 processor, and 12 to a 9377. Each WSC can support up to 32 logical device addresses. Synonymous with Workstation Subsystem Controller.

Workstation Subsystem Controller: See Workstation Controller (WSC).

WSC: Workstation Controller.

X

X.21: A recommendation of the International Telegraph and Telephone Consultative Committee (CCITT) for data transmission over public data networks. It defines a circuit switched protocol for synchronous operation between data terminal equipment and data communication equipment.

X.25: A recommendation of the International Telegraph and Telephone Consultative Committee (CCITT) for public data network packet mode interface between data terminal equipment (DTE) and data circuit equipment (DCE).

X.400: A series of message handling standards recommended by CCITT and endorsed by the International Standards Organization (ISO) and accepted as a standard for the seventh layer of the Open Systems Interconnection (OSI) model. It has been accepted by multiple national standards organizations including the National Bureau of Standards. X.400 is most recognized as an E-mail standard, however, it includes Electronic Document Interchange (EDI), funds transfer, etc. A primary attribute is a store-and-forward nature of the exchange.

X-Windows: A network transparent windowing system that runs on multiple system platforms to support bit-mapped terminals (all points addressable). Uses the notion of a terminal server (X server) and a requesting program client. This gives the programs independence from the physical attributes of the terminal.

303X: 3031, 3032, and 3033 Processors.

308X: 3081, 3083, and 3084 Processors

30XX: 303X, 308X, and 3090 Processors

4300 Processor: Small and moderately sized processors that have evolved from System/370. Series include: 4321, 4331, 4341, 4361, and 4381 Processors.

9370 Information System: A collection of System/370 processors (the 9373 Processor Model 20, the 9375 Processor Models 40 and 60, and the 9377 Processor Model 90) and devices that can be connected together to form a system for distributed processing or for general use. In 1990 the 9371 processor using the IBM micro channel architecture for peripheral attachment was introduced.

Bibliography

Aken, B.R., Jr., "Large Systems and Enterprise Systems Architecture," *IBM Systems Journal*, Vol. 28, No. 1, 1989, pp. 4–14.

Apple Multivendor Network Solutions Guide, Apple Computer, 1989.

Automated Operations Using NetView CLISTS, IBM Order No. SC30-3477.

Barberry, John, Oystein Berg, and Jetty Donders-den Daas, "AS/400 Office Application Programing Interfaces," *IBM International Technical Support Centers Bulletin*, Oct. 1988, IBM Order No. GG24-3306.

Bishop, J.C., T.N. Nguyen, and M.E. Sprague, "Implementing ISCF and ISCF/PC," *IBM Large Systems Technical Support Technical Bulletin*, IBM Order No. GG66-3110, Nov. 1988.

Blandy, G.O., and S.R. Newson, VM/XA Storage Management, *IBM Systems Journal*, Vol. 28, No. 1, 1989, pp. 175–191.

Bordon, T.L., J.P. Hennessy, and J.W. Rymarcyk, "Multiple Operating Systems on One Processor Complex," *IBM Systems Journal*, Vol. 28, No. 1, 1989, pp. 104–123.

Bozman, G.P., "VM/XA SP2 minidisk cache," *IBM Systems Journal*, Vol. 28, No. 1, 1989, pp. 165–174.

Brueggemann, K.H., and Sten Lagersted, "IMS/VS Automated Operations," *IBM International Technical Support Centers Bulletin*, March 1987, IBM Order No. GG24-3149.

Bruns, W. Jr., and F. Warren McFarland, "Information Technology Puts Power in Control Systems," *Harvard Business Review*, No. 5, Sept.–Oct., 1988, pp. 89–94.

Burch, J.G., "CIO: Indian or Chief? Information Strategy," *The Executive's Journal*, Winter 1989, pp. 5–13.

Burtman, Pini, Bernd Saemann, and Paola Zornig Polidoro, "Introduction to Distributed Relational Data," *IBM International Support Centers Bulletin*. Sept. 1988, IBM Order No. GG24-3200.

Cathey, Lenwood, *Managing Multiple 9370's from a Central Focal Point,* IBM Order No. GG22-9115.

Cecere, Marc E., "Easing the Burden of Network Management," *LAN Technology,* June 1989, pp. 25–31.

Chambers, W.C., and R.H. Flores, "IBM Enhanced Connectivity Facilities (ECF) Hints and Tips," *Dallas National Marketing and Technical Support Center,* Jan. 1988, IBM Order No. GG22-9419.

CICS/VM Release 2 General Information, IBM Order No. GC33-0571.

CICS OS/2 System and Application Guide, IBM Order No. SC33-0616.

CICS/MVS Version 2.1 Intercommunication Guide, IBM Order No. SC33-0519.

Clark, C.E., "The Facilities and Evolution of MVS/ESA," *IBM Systems Journal,* Vol. 28, No. 1, 1989, pp. 124–150.

Comer, Douglas, *Internetworking with TCP/IP: Principals, Protocols, and Architecture,* Prentice Hall, 1988.

"Concepts of Distributed Data," *Distributed Data Library,* IBM Order No. SC26-4417.

Console Automation Using NetView: Planning, IBM Order No. SC31-6058.

de la Paisieres, Happy Just, and Bernard Jacquier, "NetView DM Support of S/36 Intermediate Nodes and S/36-Attached PCs and PS/2s," *IBM International Technical Support Centers Bulletin,* IBM Order No. GG24-3208.

de Lorenzo, Mario, and John Stanley-Smith, "Remote Operation of 9370 Systems," *IBM International Technical Support Centers Bulletin,* Oct. 1987, IBM Order No. GG24-3013.

Demers, R.A., "Distributed Files for SAA," *IBM Systems Journal,* Vol. 27, No. 3, 1988, pp. 348–361, IBM Order No. G321-5332.

Distributed Processing Programming Executive DPPX/370, IBM Order No. GC23-0640.

Donovan, John J., "Beyond Chief Information Officer to Network Manager," *Harvard Business Review,* Sept.–Oct. 1988, pp. 134–140.

Electronic Mail: Technology, Applications, and Infrastructure, Soft-Switch, Inc., May 1989.

Enterprise System/9370: Using the Remote Facilities, IBM Order No. SA24-4113.

Espinoza, Jose F., and Barry Stuart, "Personal Service/36—PROFS Bridge," *IBM International Technical Support Centers Bulletin,* June 1987, IBM Order No. GG24-3188.

Gupta, A. (Ed.), *Integration of Information Systems: Bridging the Heterogeneous Databases,* IEEE Press, 1989.

Harper, Bob, et al., "IBM Enhanced Connectivity Facilities Servers/Requesters Product Guide," *IBM International Technical Support Centers Bulletin,* July 1987, IBM Order No. GG24-3190.

Held, Gilbert, *Data Communications Networking Devices,* John Wiley & Sons, 1989.

Herman, Milos, and Stephan Imhof, "Management of AS/400 in SNA Subarea Network Using NetView Products," *IBM International Technical Support Centers Bulletin,* Sept. 1988, IBM Order No. GG24-3289.

Hjetting, Leif. "NetView Release 3 Primer," *IBM International Technical Support Center Bulletin,* IBM Order No. GG24-3368.

IBM ES/9370: The Connectivity Solutions. IBM Order No. G361-0005.

"IBM Enhanced Connectivity Facilities SRPI Guide," *IBM International Technical Support Centers Bulletin*, Dec. 1986, IBM Order No. GG24-3086.

IBM Application System/400 Architecture, IBM Order No. SA21-9978.

Intel's Fastpath: 9770 Connectivity Control Unit Concepts and Facilities, IBM Order No. GA24-4200.

Introducing the Information/Family, VM/SP and MVS, IBM Order No. GG34-4045.

"Introduction to Phaser Systems Application Manager for Local Area Networks—PSAM/LAN." Phaser Company Part No. 001-000001-002, Dec. 1988.

"Introduction to Phaser Application Manager for Networks—PSAM/NET," Phaser Company, June 1988.

Introduction to IBM-S/370-to-IBM-PC Enhanced Connectivity Facilities. IBM Order No. GC23-0957.

Joseph, Gerard, "Introduction to Programming for APPC/PC," IBM International Technical Support Centers Bulletin, Feb. 1986, IBM Order No. GG24-3034.

Kolmer, Heinz, "NetView/PC Primer," *IBM International Technical Support Centers Bulletin*, IBM Order No. GG24-3115.

Lagana, B.P., J.J. Lucas, and R.M. McCutchen, "9370 Integration into an SNA Network," *Large Systems Technical Support Bulletin*, Oct. 1987, IBM Order No. GG66-0277.

Lebrun, Stephane, and Gerald Martinez, "9370 Connctivity—1987," *IBM International Technical Support Centers Bulletin*, IBM Order No. GG24-1592.

Lunn, Stewart, and Choo Hua Chua, "Automated Console Operations for MVS/XA Systems," *IBM International Technical Support Centers Bulletin*, Dec. 1987, IBM Order No. GG24-3142.

Managing Distributed Systems with VM, (video) IBM Order No. GV26-1082.

Martin, James, and Kathleen K. Chapman, "Local Area Networks: Architectures and Implementations," Prentice Hall, 1989.

Martin, James, and Kathleen K. Chapman. *SNA: IBM's Networking Solution*, Prentice Hall, 1987.

Molenbroek, Lex, and Guillermo Diaz, "IBM LAN Manager and NetView/PC Planning and Installation for Token-Ring Networks," *IBM International Technical Support Centers Bulletin*, IBM Order No. GG24-3128.

Moore, R.E., "Utilizing the SNA Alert in the Management of Multivendor Networks," *IBM Systems Journal*, Vol. 27, No. 1, 1988, pp. 15–31.

Mulreany, Michael, J. "IBM Problem Change Management for Voice," *Communications System Bulletin*, Oct. 1988, IBM Order No. GG22-9127.

"NetView/PC Primer," *IBM International Technical Support Centers Bulletin*, Feb. 1988, IBM Order No. GG24-3115.

NetView Distribution Manager, IBM Order No. GH19-6587.

NetView and VM in a Distributed Environment. IBM Order No. GG24-3221.

"9370 Express DASD Pre-load," IBM Order No. GC24-5405.

"9370 Installation Hints and Tips," *IBM International Technical Support Centers Bulletin*, June 1987, IBM Order No. GG24-1544.

Nolan, Richard L., "Restructuring the Data Processing Organization for Data Resource Management," Proceeding of *IFIP'77*, Aug. 1977, pp. 261–265.

"PC Token Ring Network and Netbios Applications," *IBM International Technical Support Centers Bulletin*, Oct. 1985, IBM Order No. GG24-1737.

Pearce, Bruce, and John Smith, "Automated Operations Implementation Guide," *IBM International Technical Support Centers Bulletin*, Jan. 1987, IBM Order No. GG24-3111.

Planning for a 9370 SNA Distributed Network, IBM Order No. GC30-3475.

Prasad, N.S., *IBM Mainframes: Architecture and Design*, McGraw-Hill, 1989.

Reinhold, Alan, "TCP/IP," *Communications Systems Bulletin*, Aug. 1988, IBM Order No. GG22-9125.

Reinsch, R., "Distributed Database for SAA," *IBM Systems Journal*, Vol. 27, No. 3, 1988, pp. 362–369, IBM Order No. G321-5331.

Rose, D.B., and J.E. Munn, "SNA Network Management Directions," *IBM Systems Journal*, Vol. 27, No. 1, 1988, pp. 3–14.

Rubsam, K.G., "MVS data services," *IBM Systems Journal*, Vol. 28, No. 1, 1989, pp. 151–164.

Scalazi, C.A., A.G. Ganek, and R.J. Schmalz, "Enterprise Systems Architecture/370: An Architecture for Multiple Virtual Space Access and Authorization, *IBM Systems Journal*, Vol. 28, No. 1, 1989, pp. 15–38.

Schatt, Stan, *Understanding Local Area Networks*, Howard W. Sams & Co., 1989.

Scherr, A.L., "SAA Distributed Processing," *IBM Systems Journal*, 1988, Vol. 27, No. 3. pp. 370–383, IBM Order No. G321-0091.

SNA/Management Services Alert Implementation Guide. IBM Order No. GC31-6809.

SQL/Data System: Concepts and Facilities for VM/System Product and VM/Extended Architecture Systems Product, IBM Order No.GH09-8044.

Summers, Carmel, and Tony Trace, *Document Distribution Between PROFS and DISOSS Systems*, Sept. 1986, IBM Order No. GG24-3091.

Systems Network Architecture: Technical Overview, IBM Order No. GC30-3073.

Systems Application Architecture—Writing Applications: A Design Guide, IBM Order No. SC26-4362.

Systems Application Architecutre—An Overview, IBM Order No. GC26-4341.

The IBM 9370 Information System Enterprise Solutions by Design, IBM Order No. G580-0888.

"The Staff of Computer Usage Company," *Programming the IBM System/360*, John Wiley & Sons, 1966.

Thoenen, David H., *IBM Network Management: Business Solutions for Telecommunications*, IBM Order No. GG22-9135, Aug. 1988.

Transaction Processing Facility Version 3 (TPF3), IBM Order No. GH20-7521.

Troy, H.Y. (John), and Hjetting, L. *NetView Primer*, IBM Order No. GG24-3047.

VM/SP Trends and Directions, IBM Order No. GG22-9433.

VM/IS: How to Support your Distributed System, IBM Order No. SC24-5355.

VM/DSNX R2 Guide and Reference, IBM Order No. SC24-5381.

VM Distributed Systems and Your Business, IBM Order No. GV26-1019.

VM/IS Setting Up SNA Network, IBM Order No. SC24-5390.

VM Performance Planning Facility General Information, IBM Order No. GG34-2126.

Wheeler, E.F., and A.G. Ganek, "Introduction to Systems Application Architecture," *IBM Systems Journal,* Vol. 27, No. 3., 1988, pp. 250–263.

Willmott, Richard, "Automation of 9370 Systems Using NetView V1R2 for VM," *IBM International Technical Support Centers Bulletin,* May 1988, IBM Order No. GG24-3221.

Wolf, Alfred, et al., "IMS/VS MSC/ISC Implementation," *IBM International Technical Support Centers Bulletin,* IBM Order No. GG24-3282. Oct. 1988.

X.400 PROFS Connection Program Offering: Program Description and Operations Manual, IBM Order No. SB11-8443.

Ziegler, Kurt, J., "Distribution: A New Impetus to Understanding Data," Proceedings of *Jerusalem Conference on Information Technology,* North-Holland Publishing Co., 1978, pp. 311–318.

Ziegler, Kurt, Jr., "Languages in a Distributed Environment," Proceedings of *Guide 48,* 1979, pp. 40–51.

Ziegler, Kurt, Jr., "A Distributed Information System Study," *IBM System Journal,* Vol. 18, No. 3, 1979. IBM Order No. G321-5101.

Index